Praise for The Jedi Handbook

"In this book, Dr. Foldes takes his previous work to a higher level and makes it accessible to a wider audience. The *Handbook* may well prove to be of central importance in solving some of our most corrosive problems. Foldes grounds 'global education' in the philosophical Science (*Wissenschaft*) of Hegel and other idealists and shows its application to bothersome issues in politics, religion, personal relations, health and business. A tour de force."

—JOHN LACHS, Centennial Professor of Philosophy, Vanderbilt University

"Both engaging and erudite, both accessible and challenging, this *Handbook* appeals to scientific and to New Age communities alike in order to make the case that Hegel's philosophical Science is not only relevant but is indeed essential for the genuine healing of our planet."

—MICHAEL BAUR, Associate Professor of Philosophy, Fordham University

"Though professing to be only a 'guide', the principles of *holistic* medicine, healing, and true health brilliantly developed in this book are superior by far to any I have come across in the past thirty years of my practice. There is no area in health and the healing arts and sciences that will remain unaffected … this *Handbook* provides a window into how all body and mind healing will be done in the future."

—KEN YOUNG, M.D., CEO and founder of The Forever Young Clinic

"An eye-opener and wake-up call for this generation. *Absolute Knowledge*, Hegel, the End of History—these are things that everyone should know about. I was very impressed with the ideas in this book and their importance for the healing of our troubled world."

—AGNES LASETCHUK, LCSW, psychotherapist and Interfaith Minister

"'*The Force* permeates all things and binds all things together.' In its essence, *The Jedi Handbook* is nothing but the endeavor to explicate this claim in philosophic/scientific terms, showing how its expansion can be used to change or '*Balance*' our institutions so as to positively affect the health of our planet and realize what is called the 'amazing *Jedi Order.*' The *Handbook* explicates this claim via the esoteric dimensions of all the great world religions, the most recent achievements of the physical sciences and, most importantly, the philosophical achievement of what is here called the 'A-Team,' namely the four idealists—Kant, Fichte, Schelling, and especially Hegel. The key concept that expresses this power of *the Force* is then best summarized in Hegel's famous dictum that 'Substance is Subject' (or Consciousness)—to know and to understand this truth is the mark of a realized or fully enlightened *Jedi*."

—ALEX DELFINI, Professor of Philosophy, Iona College

"A long-overdue comprehensive and scientifically grounded educational program. This is likely to lead to a *revolution* in education at every level … and presented in an engaging *Star Wars* format! A major achievement!"

—RICHARD CURTIS, Educator and Counselor, N.Y.C. Public Education

"*The Jedi Handbook* is an exceptional achievement. It offers us an extraordinary and daring spirituality in which consciousness of self and consciousness of the infinite are one."

—RACHEL RUDANSKY, LMT, Holistic Healer

"*The Jedi Handbook* is an intellectual *tour de force*. As with the Hegelian philosophy which it both teaches and advocates, both its form of explication and philosophical content blend together in a synthesis which, like the *Poetics* of another great philosopher, Aristotle, offers a high minded and therapeutic medicine that is certain to contribute to the purging of our most potent ills. There is an old joke that defines a generalist as one whose knowledge is a mile wide and an inch deep, and a specialist as one whose knowledge is a mile deep, but only an inch wide. Like a true Hegelian, Dr. Foldes masterfully integrates these opposing threads and leads each reader to that secret lair where the pearl of great price, true wisdom, resides."

—GLENN STATILE, Professor of Philosophy, St. John's University

The Jedi Handbook

The Jedi Handbook contains the solution to all of our planet's problems and shows the only way to realize an incredible *JEDI ORDER*—a fully healed and functioning world beyond what we can possibly imagine.

The Jedi Handbook will reveal:

- That human HISTORY is over—How it happened, and What it means.
- That Plato, Hegel, and the *JEDI* philosopher/scientists on our planet have discovered the TRUTH, the *Knowledge of The Force*, and Jedi Absolute Science ... that reveals *what* and *why* the universe is, and *who* we really are.
- That Global Jedi Education alone can heal our planet and permanently eliminate war, terrorism, greed, poverty, inequality, ignorance, nihilism, disease, and death.
- That the real cause of the world's problems is the immersion of the main institutions of society—science, religion, education, politics, etc.—in *the Dark Side* of The Force, which makes healing impossible.
- That what currently passes for "science" is really only a subset of holistic *JEDI Science*. That its *dark* world-view and main assumptions are responsible for the nihilism, depression, and youth alienation that pervades our society and schools.
- That today's mainstream Religions are incapable of healing us due to their erroneous ideas about God and man—and how this can be corrected.
- Why current education on our planet is in fact *mis-education*. And why the introduction of *JEDI Schools* and *JEDI Education* is the fastest way to save our schools and reh   ar the full potential of our children.
- Why our medical doctors and psychiatrists cannot heal us—and what can. What True Healing and Health is and the true cause and cure of all diseases, above all, the dis-ease called "Man."
- Why the New Age Movement is in need of major corrections if it is to realize its true ideals.

All of this and more will be revealed to be the only effective way to heal our world and realize a literal paradise on earth—the glorious *"JEDI ORDER,"* that will finally

"Bring BALANCE to The Force—the
Universe, and Ourselves!"

Global Jedi Education will take everyone on our planet into the amazing Jedi Order by bringing BALANCE to our world's major institutions through Jedi Science, Jedi World Religion (via Jedi Sects), Jedi Education (via Jedi Charter Schools and Universities), Jedi Businesses, a Jedi President/Prime Minister and Third Party, Jedi Doctors and Therapists, and Jedi Artists, Producers, and Media Specialists.

Thirty-five years of research, meditation, and 'channeling' went into *The Jedi Handbook.*

All of its teachings are fully evidence-based and backed by Science, philosophy, reason, quantum physics, transpersonal psychology, systems theory, our religious and spiritual traditions, and the discoveries of Einstein, Schrödinger, Goswami, Laszlo, Wolf, Haisch, Grof, Laing, Watts, Wilber, Reich, Altizer and, especially, Plato and the "A-Team," Jedi Kant-Fichte-Schelling-and-Hegel, who brought the history of philosophy and science on our planet to completion.

THE
JEDI
HANDBOOK
OF GLOBAL EDUCATION

THE
JEDI
HANDBOOK
Of Global Education

A Guide to Healing Your Planet and
Bringing Balance to the Force

Dr. Ken Foldes
Fulbright Scholar

Ω

The Omega Society of World Enlightenment

(past and present members)

Ken Foldes	Alex Delfini	John Lachs	Glenn Statile
Michael Baur*	Ken Young	Alan Watts	Edith Wyschogrod
Zoe Walton	Claudia Bickmann	Fritjof Capra	Richard Curtis
Quentin Lauer	RD Laing	Rachel Rudansky	Janessa Rick
Kate Rose	Peter Breggin	Carol Sosa	Hillary Clinton*
Bernie Sanders	Baba Ram Dass	Elaine White	Nancy Giacalone
Robert Reich	Eckhart Tolle	Stan Grof	Ellen Weiss
Norman O. Brown	Boiragi	Ervin Laszlo	Catherine Pickstock
Stanley Rosen	Les Modell	David Hawkins	Ken Lerner
Henry Harris	Nancy Nadrich	Robert Thurman	Marianne Williamson
Irina Pyatetsky	Elizabeth Gibson	Brian Greene	DG Leahy
Mary Sumbler	Joan Krawchick	Stephen Hawking*	Kenley Dove
Annette Joseph	John McDermott*	Robert McDermott	Tom Altizer*
Wayne Dyer*	Peter Scazzero	John Sallis	Michael Swartz
Amit Goswami	Rob Bell	Otto Pöggeler	Mark Levine
FA Wolf	Darrel Taylor	Robert de Ropp	John of God
			(*Honorary member)

This book was printed in the United States of America.

PREFACE

Congratulations. The millennia-long struggle of *your planet's History is over*. Your scientists and philosophers have found the TRUTH (±), *the Knowledge of the Force*. You are now ready to enter a new phase—*the amazing Jedi Order.* However you must prepare yourselves.

Your world is still battling the Dark Side—war, hate, fear, terrorism, greed, poverty, disease, death, and impending nuclear Armageddon. The Solution is nothing short of a global *Revolution in Education*—a *paradigm shift* from the Dark to the Light Side of the Force!

Your world's Institutions can now teach this higher *Knowledge* and raise planetary consciousness. This will bring *Balance* to the Force in your sector of the Galaxy and usher you into the glorious Jedi Order—your Destiny.

The Knowledge of the Force will reveal to you the true meaning of "Religion," "Education," "Science," "Business," "Health," and "Politics."

Ahead lies the Global Jedi Education solution for your planet and your unique part in the crowning stage of your evolution.

Welcome to the Jedi Order

Obi-Wan Kenobi, Jedi Master
—from a galaxy far, far away

CONTENTS

C O N T E N T S

"You must unlearn what you have learned."

INTRODUCTION

Learn about the Force!
On the Truth

The Solution to Your Planet's Crises

The Jedi Order &
Global Jedi Education

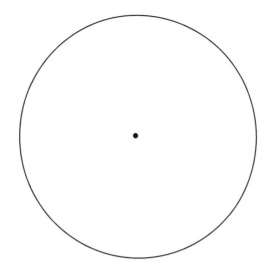

"Learn about the Force.
Unlearn what you have learned."

The Force is the only thing that exists, hence reality is ultimately One, as your science and religion teach. Thus a single Unity underlies everything and everyone on your planet. This unity is the solution to all of your world's problems. The one Force has two sides that are in a unity where the Light Side trumps the Dark Side, such that Consciousness is infinite and all reality. To know and experience this unity is to be a Jedi, the Force itself actualized and individualized.

§1

Noble reader, I, Obi-Wan Kenobi, have the high honor and privilege of introducing you and your people to *The Jedi Handbook* of Global Jedi Education, which gives the fastest way to solve all your world's problems and take your people into the glorious Jedi Order—which already exists but is not experienced by you.

§2

The true cause of all your problems is that your Institutions are keeping your people in ignorance of who they really are and what Reality is. The FACT is there is a single **UNITY** underlying everything but your schools and institutions know nothing about it and are consistently teaching your people the very opposite—the error of the Dark Side of the Force. Steeped as they are in the OUTER material realm of the senses and oblivious of the INNER, your planet's institutions are teaching *dis*-unity, *separateness*, and multiplicity—the cause of all fear, hate, greed, dis-ease, and their effects.

§3

Your only solution is a global *Revolution in Education* ... a change from *mis-education* into error and ignorance, to *the Knowledge of the Force* and *true education*, which is and can only be education into the Truth, into Reality, into What truly IS—The FORCE.

§4

As for the question, "What can I do to help?" the answer is:

> *Be a JEDI ... and help change your planet's dark side institutions. Get involved and participate in the Global Jedi EDUCATION of all your people into the Truth, the Knowledge of the Force, the BALANCE.*

Simply *align* with the Truth—the Force, the Balance, the POINT—that is, realize that you are *already* aligned with the Truth. As you will see,

All you have to do is become POINT-ED.

✺

§5

If your people do *not* implement this *Revolution in Education* the following will continue on your planet unabated:

- *War and terrorism*—which are due to ignorance of Unity and the Truth on the part of your political and religious leaders.
- *Poverty, unemployment, crime, and greed*—which are due to ignorance of who you are and what "politics" truly is—the knowledge of how to realize and maintain the amazing Jedi Order.

- *Financial meltdowns and sputtering economies*—no matter how many regulatory measures or government "bailouts" are enacted.
- *Religious and ethnic hatred* and their consequences—which are due to ignorance of the Unity and Balance underlying the diverse groups and religions on your planet.
- *Education and its problems*—drop-outs, failing students, no direction, etc.,—which will not be helped by pouring money into existing (mis-) education, new buildings, higher salaries, etc.; only the True Education of your people into Jedi will correct and "Balance" the situation.
- *Physical and mental disease, death, and general unhappiness*—which are due to your global culture's ignorance of the Light Side of the Force and what true Health is, and to the "nihilism" and meaninglessness of existence taught by your mainstream sciences and educational institutions.

§6

Thus the only Solution to your planet's problems and the only Way into the Jedi Order is—*Global Jedi Education.* Simply stated: The core of Jedi Education is the *Knowledge of the Force,* and to acquire it one thing and one thing only is required—that you

TRANSCEND YOUR SENSES—And Become Aware of the ONE-POINT or UNITY that alone exists, is your true essence, and the foundation of the amazing Jedi Order.

§7

You need look no further than your own Jedi **PLATO** and his teaching that the senses deceive for the true understanding of what education is. There are three things:

1. **TRANSCENDING YOUR SENSES.**
2. **TRANSCENDING YOUR SENSES. And**
3. **TRANSCENDING YOUR SENSES.**

I, Obi-Wan, will explain.

"The lovers of sights and sounds are far from the Truth." **Plato**

"Do not let your mind follow the call of your Senses." **The Bhagavad Gita**

"You must die to sight and hearing and enter the night of the soul." **Hegel**

§8

> "I will stop my ears and close my eyes and go in ..."
> Descartes

1. PLATO says, and correctly, that there are *two* sides to Reality or "the Force," as we Jedi call it—and not just *one*.

2. However many of your own people believe (especially your scientists) that there is *only one side* [See **Figure 1.**]—the Senses (–), which we shall call "the OUTER," that is, the sense-world of matter/energy in space-time; hence whatever is *not* in space or time *does not exist.*

Figure 1. The OUTER-Sense Domain (–).

3. Your education and media focus mainly on this OUTER dimension, which Plato calls the "CAVE"—forever keeping your people in Dark Side error, illusion, and ignorance.

4. But the truth, the full picture—as revealed by "Polarity"—is rather that an "OUTER" domain cannot exist or be conceived without a *polar opposite* "INNER" domain.

5. And as the *Knowledge of the Force* or Reason teaches, this INNER domain (of Consciousness-Thought) is *alone* true reality—the OUTER domain (of Matter) is *not.*

6. Thus your "educational" problem is simple to state—There is a *second* side or realm of Reality, of the Force—the REAL side (+) or the INNER [See **Figure 2**.]—*and your people are not being taught about it and hence are not living in it.*

7. The INNER, true reality—according to Polarity as you shall soon learn—*is right here and right now* and not in "another world" [See **Figure 3**.]. This INNER realm is what your own philosophers call "A PRIORI" and it exists in all points of the Universe at once. It is ONE and INDIVISIBLE, hence is a single POINT of Consciousness that all your people not only *inhabit* but *are.* Your own "**A-Team**" philosophers (**Kant-Fichte-Schelling-Hegel**) call it the *Transcendental Unity of Self-consciousness (TUA), the Absolute I, and the Concept (der Begriff).* Precisely *here* then, we have the UNITY that is the solution to all of your world's problems.

Figure 2. The TWO Domains: The OUTER -Sense (–) and the INNER-Consciousness (+) Domain.

Figure 3. The Truth: The UNITY of the Two INNER and OUTER Domains (±).

Therefore, according to Plato and to all Jedi true education and the sole purpose of your Universe is simply to become aware of this *second* side of Reality—the INNER, UNITY, the POINT, which *also* contains the OUTER side within itself—by *TRANSCENDING THE SENSES* and all multiplicity and externality, the *first* OUTER side of Reality or the CAVE. This is achieved by REASON (or focus on Universals) and by Jedi POINT-Meditation.

§9

It is important to be mindful that because the Inner contains the Outer within itself, one transcends the Outer *not to remain in the Inner exclusively but to permanently return to the Outer and the World, and thus experience the World in a wholly new and transfigured way.* Only in this way can your Jedi **Nietzsche's** great vision for your planet's future be realized, which can only happen, as he says in *The Will to Power*, when you *"deify* becoming and the apparent world as the only world and call them GOOD."

```
╔══════════════════════════════════════╗
║                                      ║
║            KEY POINT:                ║
║  There is not only one world (the Senses) …  ║
║  but two worlds. And the second world is     ║
║  right here … and now.               ║
║                                      ║
╚══════════════════════════════════════╝
```

§10

The "POINT" will be the primary word I will be using in *The Jedi Handbook* to refer to this *second* true INNER domain of Reality. All Jedi without exception know about this *"sacred Point"* and its powerful significance.

> "The Universe is an Organic Living Whole pervaded by a single intelligence (or *Geist*)."
> Schelling

Hence we will say that true Education— the solution to your world's problems and *the* Way into the Jedi Order—is simply the task of *educating all of your people into the POINT*—that is, into the Jedi Order. It is, as we will say, for everyone to become *POINT-ED*.

§11

Further, as we will see, the Point is both "Concept" (or Thought) and Consciousness (or Intuition), the two forms in which it can be known. However only the *first*, the Concept, gives the complete genuinely *scientific* way of knowing the Point (the Truth or the Force); and it is known only by a few of your philosophers. At the present time your religionists (and mystics) and even your scientists know it, if they know it at all, only in the *second* mode as Consciousness. Hence true education involves nothing but becoming aware of this One Infinite Indivisible Consciousness or CONCEPT, as it is called especially by your Jedi **Hegel** for example, and which is the veritable "DNA," Blueprint, or *Arche* of the TOTALITY of the entire Universe and all it contains.

Your Jedi **Fichte** is another member of the "**A-Team**" of your philosopher-scientists who actually discovered the *Knowledge of the Force* in your planet's history. And he refers to this sacred Point as the "**Absolute I**," which is infinite and all Reality; hence we shall also be making use of the term *"the Absolute I-Point"* in our teaching.

THE TRUTH (±)

§12

To further help you to gain entry into Jedi Teaching, noble Reader, I shall now go a little deeper into the meaning of "the FORCE"—that is, the TRUTH—and especially, Polarity.

THE TRUTH IS THAT THE JEDI ORDER EXISTS NOW, BUT YOU ARE NOT AWARE OF IT. THE FORCE IS THE BASIS OF THE JEDI ORDER. AND NOTHING BUT THE FORCE EXISTS.

Thus there is only ONE REALITY, which we Jedi call "the FORCE." And the Force of necessity transforms itself immediately into the JEDI ORDER. As we have said, the ONE REALITY or the FORCE has *two* polar opposite sides. We call them the Light Side (+) and the Dark Side (–), that is, in the language of your philosopher-scientists, Thought and the Senses, the Invisible and the Visible, Consciousness and Matter, the Inner and Outer, Self and Other, *Subjec*tivity and *Objec*tivity.

> "The FORCE as the Unity-of-Opposites is the absolute TRUTH and ALL TRUTH."
> **Hegel** (*Enc.* §236)
>
> "All opposites are POLAR and thus a unity." **Fritjof Capra**
>
> "That Opposites are complementary gave me the key to the quantum jump."
> **Niels Bohr**

§13

The secret is that these Two sides, represented by your Jedi **Plato's** *Divided Line* [see **Figures 2**. and **3**. above, **[A]** below, and Part I, §56], are in eternal Unity or Balance (±). This is due to the important principle of **POLARITY** or the UNITY-OF-OPPOSITES: "You can't have one without the other" (up/down, inner/outer, north pole/south pole, female/male, freedom/necessity, etc). The one can *never exist apart* from its other or opposite. (Note that the symbol "(±)" will be used to represent the Unity-of-Opposites and the Truth, while the symbol "(+|-)" will stand for the Dis-unity-of-opposites and Error.)

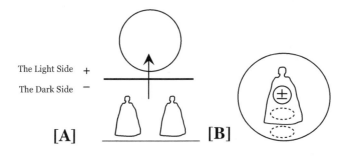

The Light Side +
The Dark Side −

[A]   [B]

§14

> "It is not matter—which is 99% empty space—but *consciousness* that is ultimate reality."
> **Ervin Laszlo**
>
> "In the Self-aware Universe I show how *consciousness* creates the material world."
> **Amit Goswami**

The further secret or truth (known only to Jedi, and to some of your quantum physicists) is that *within* the Force's Unity or Balance, it is the Light Side that "trumps" or predominates over the Dark Side, e.g., *Consciousness* over Matter, the *Inner* over the Outer, *Subjectivity* over Objectivity ... this is because e.g. Consciousness *knows* that it exists, is self-aware, whereas Matter does not and is not. The important result is that Consciousness, the Inner, Subjectivity is **all Reality** (see **[B]**) ... while Matter (Unconsciousness) is **Nothing**—as some of your own scientists have discovered. For example **Sir Arthur Eddington** who states that, "The world we see and experience in everyday life is simply a convenient mirage attuned to our very limited senses, an *illusion* conjured by our perceptions and our mind ... so-called Matter is mostly emptiness... [indeed] the stuff of the world is MIND-stuff"; and **Sir James Jeans** who declares that, "The universe begins to look more like a great THOUGHT than like a great machine. MIND no longer appears as an accidental intruder into the realm of MATTER ... *we ought rather to hail Mind as the creator and governor of the realm of Matter.*"

§15

Moreover and most significantly, Consciousness is **One** and **Indivisible**—this is because Consciousness is the *polar opposite* of Matter or Body, which is Many and Divisible. And note especially that the "trumping" of the Object by the Subject does *not* mean that the Object (the world) is totally done away with ... but rather that the Object has become utterly *subject-ivized* or *saturated* with the Subject (the pure I, consciousness, or the Concept). Hence, in relating to the world you are equally relating to yourSelf.

> "In the Inner (+)—in thought and universality—man cannot hold out; he needs also sensuous existence (-), feeling, the heart and emotion."
> **Hegel.** *Aesthetics,* v. I, 97.

§16

This Unity-of-Opposites, the Balance, is the TRUTH. It is the living core of *the Knowledge of the Force*. It is the absolute proof and certainty that the Jedi Order exists and exists Now, since "Subject" and "Object-ive World" are *inseparable* and in *eternal unity*. Your people merely need to become aware of this FACT through true Jedi education, which again is essentially a movement from the Outer to the Inner and then *back again* to the Outer, and to the *permanent unity* of Inner and Outer, Subject and World. As your Jedi **Hegel** says: "Freedom and Reason consist in this, that I have in *one and the same* consciousness *I* and *the world*, that in the world I find myself again and, conversely, in my consciousness I have what *is*, what has *objectivity* (*Enc.* §424)."

> "You are the Whole, all in all ... *Tat twam asi.*"
> **Schrödinger**
>
> "Nothing exists separately; the separate existence of anything (including myself) is a fiction and impossible."
> **P.D. Ouspensky** (340)
>
> "Only Brahman [The Force] exists, and you yourSelf are Brahman."
> **Ramana Maharshi** 146,60

§17

The Force therefore is *already* and *eternally* "Balanced." This means that the true meaning of our expression *"Bringing Balance to the Force"* is that one simply gain an *awareness* of this present Balance, that the Force's two sides *are* in eternal union.

—It is also well to note my noble Padawan that some of your own philosophers, scientists, and religionists have already found the Truth/*the Knowledge of the Force*, though it is not yet being taught on your planet. For example: **Einstein, Schrödinger, Bohr, Bohm, Wheeler, Laszlo, Bell & Aspect,** qua "non-locality," **F. A. Wolf, Wilber, Goswami, Haisch, McDermott, Altizer, Leahy, Watts,** and **Grof,** qua "transpersonal psychology" and so-called NDE's and OOBE's. As your Jedi **Stan Grof** states:

> The observations from consciousness research dispel the current myth of materialistic science that consciousness is an epiphenomenon of matter, a product of neurophysiological processes in the brain. They show that consciousness is a primary attribute of existence and that it is capable of many activities that the brain could not possibly perform. According to the new findings, *human consciousness is a part of and participates in a larger universal field of cosmic consciousness that permeates all of existence* .... [Furthermore, Grof notes,] *Our true identity is the totality of cosmic creation and the creative principle itself [the Force]."*

And as your Jedi **Erwin Schrödinger,** founder of Quantum Physics observes, "It is not possible that this *unity* of knowledge, feeling and choice which you call *your own* should have sprung into being from nothingness at a given moment not so long ago; rather this knowledge, feeling and choice are essentially *eternal and unchangeable* and numerically *one* in all men ... [Therefore] you—and all other conscious beings as such—*are all in all ... the Whole."*

§18

From all that has preceded many things follow. Among these are:

- The JEDI ORDER, the *unity* of all your people, exists Now and forever. For you all share *the same one indivisible Consciousness.* This absolutely present inviolable *unity* is the solution to all of your world's problems without exception. Therefore your planet's HISTORY is nothing but EDUCATION ... the "time" it takes for your "human" Race to realize the TRUTH ($\pm$).
- Hence your people are already JEDI—one with the FORCE and each other—but not aware of this due to miseducation by your planet's Institutions and your immersion in the Dark Side of the Force (+|-) and the OUTER. This teaches the dis-unity of

opposites and the separateness of your people and nations from each other, and that you are just a Body-EGO or a Part-icular Individual ("P.I.")—this is the root of all fear, hate, greed, sickness, and the true cause of all your problems.

- Therefore as a JEDI you have a Universal Self or are a Universal Individual ("U.I.") and are Immortal because Consciousness is Reality and indestructible ... and your essence is LOVE, which alone exists due to Polarity's eternal unity of Self and Other. Moreover, as a JEDI—who you really are, your true self—not only do you know the TRUTH ... you are the TRUTH. For a Jedi and the Truth, is simply the unity of the opposites, "Universal" and "Individual." Put differently, since there is nothing but the Force, your knowledge of the Force is at one and the same time the Force's knowledge of itself. Your scientists are beginning to understand this and it is the inner teaching of all your religions albeit expressed in coded language.

> "I said you are gods and goddesses (*elohim*)."
> **Judaism**
>
> "*That* which is the finest essence—this whole world has *that* as its Self. *That* is Reality. *That* is the Self. *That* thou art *(Tat twam asi)*."
> **Chandogya Upanishad**
>
> "I live, yet not I, Christ (the Force) lives in me."
> **Christianity**
>
> "Atman is Brahman."
> **Hinduism**
>
> "There is no duality at all (*advaita*), therefore *you yourself* are the non-dual Brahman ... changeless, timeless, without dimensions or parts." **Shankara**

> "Science, *the Knowledge of the Force,* is alone self-knowing TRUTH and the whole of TRUTH." And, "God is your true and essential Self."
> **Hegel**
>
> "The Cosmos is a You-niverse."
> **Fred Alan Wolf**
>
> "We are the Universe now thinking about *itself.*"
> **Teilhard de Chardin**

As your **Albert Einstein**, the founder of relativistic physics, said, "A human being is a part of the Whole, called by us "Universe"—a part limited in time and space. He experiences himself, his thoughts and feelings as something *separated* from the rest—a kind of optical delusion of his consciousness. This delusion is a kind of prison for us, restricting us to our personal desires and to affection for a few persons nearest us. Our task must be *to free* *ourselves from this [Ego] prison* by widening our circles of compassion to embrace all living creatures and the whole of nature in its beauty."— And your astrophysicist **Bernard Haisch** insists that: "It is not matter that creates an illusion of consciousness, but consciousness that creates an illusion of matter. The physical universe and the beings that inhabit it are the conscious creation of a God [The Force] … who is an infinite timeless consciousness … and actualizes his infinite potential through our experience … which is his experience because *ultimately we are him.*" From this it follows, says **Haisch**, that "our lives are the exact opposite of pointless," indeed they are infinitely POINT-FULL (see also sidebars).

"REJOICE FOR THOSE AROUND YOU WHO TRANSFORM INTO THE FORCE." JEDI MASTER YODA

§19

Now although the Jedi Order exists now and you *are* immortal and a Jedi now, you are not *experiencing* this *because of your immersion in the Dark Side of the Force.* You are a victim of the illusion of the self-other *separation* (+|-) of yourself, as a Body-Ego, from everything else. There are TWO ways to experience your True Jedi Self and overcome this separation:

§20

(1) The fastest way to dissolve and overcome this error and become educated into the Truth, is by Laser-Point Meditation-Concentration on the Truth, the Unity of Opposites, or the POINT—*the key to everything* (see below).

§21

(2) The second way is the way of Jedi Science and Reason. It is based on a deeper understanding of the Point's or One Consciousness' essence, which is what your people know of as CONCEPT or THOUGHT, the finest substance in the universe. This way will be discussed later.

§22

The first way can be called INTUITIVE ... and results in the education of an *Intuitive Jedi or Jedi Master*, the second way DISCURSIVE, involving concepts and thought and resulting in a *Discursive Jedi Master* or a *Master Jedi Scientist*. Both ways overlap and involve each other.

Again, it should be noted that the way of Science and Reason has an advantage over the way of Intuition, for only those of the former way have a *complete* and detailed *scientific* Knowledge of the Force and are thus qualified to be "Master Teachers," or Masters of the highest order. However it is nonetheless true that any Intuitive Jedi can become a Jedi Scientist by applying himself in the appropriate manner. So whether you become educated by the Intuitive or Discursive way the goal is the same: *to become POINT-ED*. That is, to unite the *unity* that is yourself with the *Unity* of the Force, rather to attain to the realization that they are already and eternally united.

§23

To sum up: True education is education into the TRUTH or the POINT ... i.e. into a Knowledge of the Force itself, the One Consciousness, the INNER, the Balance, the JEDI ORDER. *The Jedi Handbook* will symbolize this supreme goal of education by a CIRCLE with a POINT at its center (which you can *meditate* on, and which is quite powerful).

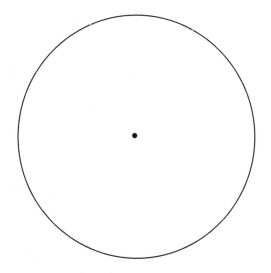

> "To achieve yoga
> (*union, unity*) you
> should constantly
> practice *ONE-
> POINTEDNESS*, free
> from expectations and
> attachment to material
> possessions."
> **The Bhagavad Gita 6:10**

> "To become enlightened
> just bring your mind
> into a POINT, and wait
> for grace."
> **Neem Karoli Baba**

The POINT is *the key to everything* and summarizes all. The "circle" represents the Force, i.e. the Whole, the infinite totality of all that is. The "point" represents both (1) the WAY into the Circle (and into total Health), *and* (2) the Circle itself, whose center is everywhere (as *A priori*), and whose circumference is nowhere.

§24

We use the word "Point" to express the goal of education because (1) in order to TRANSCEND YOUR SENSES and overcome the illusion of the Cave and the Dark Side (+|-) you must develop ONE-POINTEDNESS, the ability to focus on One-Point to the exclusion of everything else (as your Jedi **Jesus** says, "If thine eye be single, thy whole body will be full of light"); and because (2) a "point," in universal geometry, is invisible and indivisible since it is non-extended (without length, width, and height) and the opposite of Matter-Body. Hence focusing on it immediately takes you out of the OUTER sense-realm into True Reality, the INNER realm of Consciousness, Thought, and Universality. Thus, as Apriori it is everywhere and pervades everything and, as noted, contains the OUTER within itself since INNER and OUTER are in eternal *UNITY.*

> "Not only is Science the
> TRUTH aware of itself ... but
> Science also requires that the
> individual (as a *particular* individual)
> *forget about himself* ... and *walk on
> his head* just this once." Hegel

§25

A brief word on SCIENCE in connection with Education.—Notice on the left we have the symbol for Jedi SCIENCE to be used in *The Jedi Handbook*. Science studies the Force, the Whole of what IS (represented by the outer circle) comprised of *Nature, Jedi,* and *Logic.* The lower dotted oval represents Nature, the second dotted oval represents History and the "human" being becoming a Jedi, and the solid-line Figure in the center represents an actualized Jedi *and* the Jedi Order. The "(±)" symbol stands for the Truth, the Absolute I, and the Polarity principle studied in Logic.

Now in *Part I: The Jedi Truth* we will learn about Jedi Science, which was discovered by Jedi **Kant** and **Hegel** and your **A-Team**. We said that "the Point" is both Concept and Consciousness and it is the CONCEPT that is at the center of SCIENCE, which is simply *the recognition of the One Concept in everything.* Science therefore is *the Knowledge of the Force* and simply studies the Force and its process, which involves Three Sciences: LOGIC, the Concept or "seed-Force" *in-itself,* potential and unexpressed; and the Concept or "seed-Force" *for-itself,* actualized and expressed as Jedi/The Jedi Order ... first, as NATURE (*Object*) and second, as JEDI or THE JEDI ORDER (*Subject* or Intelligence) as the Unity of Subject and Object.

> *"Der Begriff ist alles ..."* "The CONCEPT is everything ... it is the *substantiality* of things, the highest *force* and the absolute *force* of Reason ... its sole urge *is to find and know itself* by means of itself *in everything."* **Hegel**

§26

Now the EDUCATION of the individual into a JEDI also involves Three Stages. *Stage One* corresponds with Logic, the Force in-itself, prior to manifestation; *Stages Two* and *Three* together comprise the Force's "education" from "human Ego" to Jedi, that is, from **Stage Two**, Consciousness *of* an Object (or World; "Man" as a separate Body-Ego or "P.I."), to **Stage Three**, Consciousness *of* Consciousness or Self-Consciousness ("Man" as a Jedi or "U.I.," the Force actualized and individualized). The key is that since *Stage Two's* "Object" of

Consciousness *was* Consciousness all along, being educated or "Pointed" simply amounts to overcoming the *illusion* of Consciousness' *separation* from its Object, which really is *itself.* Thus, since true education is education into the POINT, the goal is *to be POINT-ED.*

❧

YOUR PLANET IS **IMBALANCED** BECAUSE YOUR INSTITUTIONS ARE NOT TEACHING **THE TRUTH**

§27

Before we turn to Global Jedi Education itself, let us look at your seven major global institutions, your venues of planetary education, and see what is wrong with them and what has to be done to BALANCE or POINT them.

§28

(1) **SCIENCE**. Your present sciences have succeeded in large measure through technology in bestowing on your people "creature comforts" et al. And it is true that they are currently undergoing a major "paradigm shift"—from *matter* as primary to *consciousness* as primary (M/C to C/M)—which, when completed, will indeed result in an understanding of the consciousness/matter relationship that is closer to the Truth (±). However their fundamental *materialist* worldview— focusing totally on the OUTER (-) and oblivious to the INNER (+) and True Reality—still dominates. Hence your sciences continue to perpetuate the error of the Dark Side (+|-) by disseminating false concepts of yourselves as mortal Body-Ego's and *nihilism,* a universe with no intrinsic value or meaning, where bodily death is the end, with no purpose to human existence; thereby sustaining the problems of your world and keeping you from experiencing Reality (±) and the Jedi Order. Hence, since your sciences are not truly Science—which is the knowledge of the Truth or the Balanced Force, as described above—they must be replaced by and/or incorporated within *True Jedi or Absolute Science*

which, as we will see, your wise ones have already discovered and will be discussed below in *Part I: The Jedi Truth*. Moreover, because of their great authority and influence in education and all areas of your civilization, your sciences in their present condition are perhaps the primary source of error, problems and unhealth on your planet. What you can do is to pass laws demoting them from "Science" to "pre-Science." Most importantly your people and especially your scientists must learn and master Jedi Science and teach it in schools and universities. All of this will be permanently resolved after the Great Science Debate occurs on your planet, as it did on ours eons ago.

§29

(2) **EDUCATION**. In its present state what passes for education in your world is in fact "mis-education," since it is based on your Dark Side materialist sciences which focus students on the OUTER, matter, the many, and not on the INNER, on Unity, Consciousness and True Reality, thus giving a false, dangerous concept of "Woman," of who you are, which promotes nihilism. It lacks the true concept of education (from your Latin, *"e-ducare"*) and is ignorant of the ONE GOAL of all education: for the student to acquire the knowledge of the Truth and Reality (±) and "become" a Jedi, *the Truth, the Whole, the Force aware of Itself*—and above all to learn How to live in the fullness of the Eternal Present. Further, education on your planet is not HOLISTIC since it is not based on Holistic Jedi Science but rather on your fragmented disconnected p-empirical sciences; thus students cannot perceive the *Unity* and relevance of the curriculum, etc. Therefore your planet's form of "mis-education" must be replaced by true Jedi Education based on Jedi Science and the Knowledge of the Force. This can be done immediately by setting up in your nations Jedi Charter Schools, K through 12, and in time Jedi universities, which is discussed below in *Part I: The Jedi Truth* and *Part III: The Jedi Order*. The curriculum will be based on the UNITY-of-Opposites and has two fundamental components, (i) the basic division into Jedi/"human" sciences (+) and natural sciences (-), taught at graduated levels of complexity and sophistication, and (ii) the Jedi CORE, which advances with the two and integrates them

into a Unity (±) and, further, tracks the students' progress towards the supreme GOAL of becoming/being a Jedi, while giving primacy to (+), to Unity, Consciousness, and the INNER, over (-), Multiplicity, Matter, and the OUTER.

§30

(3) **RELIGION**. The religions on your planet today, whatever they may have been in previous ages, are not truly religions insofar as they are not—according to "re-ligare," their concept—accomplishing their ONE purpose of "re-connecting" or bringing into a UNITY (±) the opposites of God and Wo/Man and Heaven and Earth, and taking your people into the Jedi Order, called by them the "Kingdom of God," the "World to Come," the "Just Society," etc., and which in truth exists NOW. They are consequently not HEALING your people but are rather involved in the error of the Dark Side and the *separation* of God and Man, Heaven and the Present, as (+|-). Above all your religions are in perpetual conflict, hate and sometimes war with one another because of their ignorance of the UNITY behind all religions. The quickest, indeed only way to solve this—to overcome their *differences* and realize their Unity—is to create what we will call "Jedi Sects" in all of your religions which include doctrines, supported by their respective scriptures, of the *existing* UNITY (±) of God and Woman as *Jedi*, and Heaven and Earth as *The Jedi Order*.

> "Only by surrendering to pure self-consciousness do you attain the TRUTH."
> **Hegel**
>
> "He who knows himself knows his Lord (Allah)." "When I [God] love my servant I become her Ear through which she hears, her Eye with which she sees, her Hand with which she grasps, and her Foot with which she walks."
> **Islam Hadith.**

§31

(4) **POLITICS**. All the problems in your world today both *within* states and *between* states are due simply to governments and world leaders not being aware of the true concept of "Politics"—not to mention of "Man," "History," "the State" and its true #1 GOOD. This concept, from your Greek "politeia" and "polis," concerns the *knowledge* necessary for realizing and ongoingly maintaining the Jedi Order

and the UNITY of all your citizens and nations, which is based on the FACT of the *One Consciousness, Concept,* and *Absolute I* that all your people share and are. As a result your states, their politics, and politicians are permeated with the Dark Side of the Force (+|-) and hence make bad, unwise *decisions,* laws and allotments of resources—e.g., entanglements in unnecessary costly wars and pouring money into an education that in truth is "mis-education," etc; and further are mired in Ego-centered politics, greed, selfishness, and corruption, with consistently perverted priorities, for example money and things above people. The solution here is to educate leaders, politicians and citizens into the true meaning of politics and the Jedi Order it is meant to sustain. This can be done for example by forming a Third Political Party, a Jedi Party, and electing a Jedi President or Prime Minister, etc.

§32

(5) **BUSINESS**. Due to the mis-education that occurs in your educational systems and general culture the Ego-Dark Side (+|-) method of doing business, based on a fear and lack mind-set, predominates on your planet. Here again money and things have priority over people, their UNITY and their highest well-being, the Jedi Order. The Ego-method must be replaced by the Jedi method of doing business (±) which regards all transactions as "sacred opportunities" for healing and realizing UNITY and the Jedi Order. Jedi corporations and CEO's, furthermore, will make educating their employees and uplifting society and developing nations their top priority, and not profit or themselves—which ironically will result in never before dreamed of profits—which will be used to educate and uplift the entire global society. This can be implemented immediately by individuals, small businesses and corporations, which can also, working in tandem with enlightened governments and the World Bank, permanently solve the problem of worldwide unemployment, homelessness, and poverty.

§33

(6) **HEALTH**: Medicine and Psychiatry. Today's doctors and practitioners in these fields are severely handicapped because, as overly influenced by your Dark Side sciences and world-view, they operate without having the true concepts of "Man" and of "Health" (from your Anglo-Saxon "Hāl") and what it is to

be Healed. The fact is that *true Health*, the goal of medicine and psychiatry, is nothing but becoming ... or rather realizing that one already is ... WHOLE, that is, a JEDI—as one *with* the whole = the Jedi Order, *with* the Doctor and *with* everyone else in society, as sharing with them the same One Consciousness. And "Man" or who you really are, is a Jedi, who is not just a "Body" but a triad of "Absolute I, Mind, and Body"—a Jedi's *Absolute I* being the key, the source, and agency of *all* healing whatsoever, physical, mental-emotional, and spiritual. Today's doctors need to be replaced by or educated into Jedi Master Doctors.

§34

(7) THE ARTS AND MEDIA. On your planet these institutions are for the most part mired in and reflect the (+|-) Dark Side of the Force as disseminated by the major institutions of your global society. The Media are widely controlled by people with base values and unconcerned with the healing of your world, etc., only money and profit count. The Media, television, cable, the internet, satellites, and cell-phones have tremendous potential for realizing UNITY in your world and among your people. Everyone can be Jedi educated and focused at the same time on the Eternal Present, Reality, and the Force, etc. And the Arts, such as movies, novels, and poetry, which must always be kept free and uncensored, are mired mainly in the Dark Side and reflect the dominant p-sciences' world-view that teaches Man is a separate Body-Ego and biological death is final, etc. The solution is to educate Jedi producers, create Jedi shows, and become Jedi Artists.

§35

It is therefore absolutely imperative that all venues of education on your planet immediately STOP teaching Error and the Dark Side, and START teaching the Truth and the Light Side. Otherwise your planet will never be healed, problems will worsen, and possible nuclear Armageddon will overtake you: that is, *you will blow yourselves up* (as happened on your fifth planet, now an asteroid belt).

§36

Also be mindful that the TRUTH and Jedi Education is for everyone: Theists, Atheists, and Agnostics alike; and that Jedi Teaching does harmonize with and does not contradict the essential teachings of your planet's religions.

<h3 style="text-align:center">§37</h3>

So what you must do is simply *UNLEARN WHAT YOU HAVE LEARNED*—and *LEARN ABOUT THE FORCE*. What you have *learned* through the *false- or mis-education* of your global Institutions is the Dark Side of the Force, the *separation* or dis-unity (+|-) of the opposites self and other, us and them, consciousness and matter, divinity and humanity, time and eternity, you and universe, subject and object—an illusion which is the prime cause of your planet's systemic, chronic *dysfunction*: fear, hate, war, ignorance, poverty, inequality, financial meltdowns, unhappiness, alienation, disease, hopelessness, nihilism, and death. You must *unlearn* the error of the Dark Side by *true education* and *learn about the Force*, the Light Side, the Unity of Opposites (±), the Truth, the Balance, and the POINT … which alone will take you into the eternal Present and make you aware of the glorious JEDI ORDER *that exists Now*.

<h3 style="text-align:center">§38</h3>

To do this nothing less than a world-wide *Revolution in Education* is needed, that is, the Global Jedi Education of your entire planet into the POINT.

All you require is to become POINT-ED.

GLOBAL JEDI EDUCATION

<h3 style="text-align:center">§39</h3>

The question then is, How to bring everyone on your planet into the ONE POINT, the JEDI ORDER? How to educate everyone from a Stage Two *EGO* to a Stage Three *JEDI*? How to realize GLOBAL JEDI EDUCATION?

§40

The fastest way to do it is by: BEING A JEDI YOURSELF AND HELPING CHANGE YOUR SEVEN MAJOR PLANETARY INSTITUTIONS.

§41

That is, (1) It is a FACT that your Institutions are your primary agents of education and shapers of planetary consciousness. (2) Therefore you must change them from teaching the Dark Side to teaching the Knowledge of the Force. (3) To do this you need to educate Jedi who will then be equipped to make the necessary changes to your Institutions.

§42

Thus the PLAN of *The Jedi Handbook* of Global Jedi Education is this. The initial need is to educate JEDI who will then serve and work in one or more of your SEVEN major Institutions to effect the needed changes that will educate everyone else into JEDI. So, *The Jedi Handbook* will show **you, the Reader**, first, How to be a JEDI ... that is, who you are and how to live the greatest life imaginable and make every day and every hour of your life count for the healing of yourself and your world. And *second*, it will show you what has to be done in the SEVEN major institutions so you can be in a position to choose which one(s) to best serve in for maximum effect. Readers of the Handbook will be from all walks of life—teachers, congressmen/women, doctors, students, janitors, scientists, businesswomen/men, CEO's, etc—and many will choose to serve in their own fields, circles, and areas.

§43

Special NOTE for Readers: (1) Since this is a "handbook" you can begin anywhere, which is one reason the main points are repeated in each section. But for best results I recommend that you read it, at least the first time, as you would a "book" and in the order in which the sections appear, the Introduction first and so forth. (2) As you begin reading the Handbook, the meaning of certain words may not be fully clear to you at first. Just continue to read and clarity will come. There is a place within yourself that already knows the central TRUTH that the Handbook is designed to communicate, for the

TRUTH in the end is who you really are, your true innermost Self that your Life has thus far prevented you from knowing but can be accessed by simply learning to *re-direct* your attention and awareness. Focused ATTENTION is the key to all education, transformation and healing. (3) You will also find that the essential points of the Jedi TRUTH are frequently repeated. This is designed to aid your understanding of the TRUTH by focusing your attention on what is absolutely necessary for transcending your senses and the Cave and becoming established in Reality; they will seem repetitive *until* you actually enter and experience the TRUTH. There is great spiritual and healing power contained in these main points, as well as in the POINT-CIRCLE Symbol appearing throughout the Handbook, which I recommend you pause and meditate on whenever you see it. (4) Thus you, the average Reader, should just read the entire Handbook through from start to finish and not be concerned if there are passages or even whole sections you do not understand, which is to be expected since the Handbook contains both beginner and advanced Jedi Teaching. Read these sections anyway—let your eyes pour over the words. And if for example the *History of Philosophy* section gives you much trouble, skip it, and the *Jedi Science* section, which is the most difficult—skip it, you can always return to them later. The truth is that to BE a Jedi and help advance the Jedi Order you do *not* have to master Jedi Science, etc. (for there are Intuitive *and* Discursive Jedi); and be assured that at some point you *will* understand everything. Jedi Science will be easier to master once you have become a Jedi.

Thus we have the three-part division and contents of *The Jedi Handbook*: (1) The Jedi Truth, (2) The Jedi Code, and (3) The Jedi Order.

§44

I: THE JEDI TRUTH (*The Knowledge of the Force*) will provide the basis of Global Jedi Education and the Solution to all your problems.

> **First**, we will reveal the Meaning of your planet's HISTORY and its four periods—the Ancient, Medieval, Modern and Postmodern—and explain how the Knowledge of the Force was reached by your own Jedi in the Modern Period of your History.

Second, we will discuss in detail the Knowledge of the Force and Jedi Science, and how it differs from your own sciences (the Old vs the New Paradigm), and how its central Truth, the "One Concept or Consciousness," is recognized by your own sciences that are currently undergoing a critical paradigm shift. We will also give a *Proof of the Force* that will explain why the Universe, Man (Consciousness), History, etc., *must exist* and that will reveal what true Health and Healing are, and what a Jedi, your true self, and the Jedi Order is.—And give an absolute *Proof that Materialism is false.* It will follow that the Force is *already* and eternally balanced, that You *are* a Jedi, and that the glorious Jedi Order *is now.* We will also show how the Knowledge of the Force reveals not only what Religion is and its true origin, but also its essential *unity* with science, thus ending the war between them and showing how they can henceforth work together to advance the healing of your planet.

Third, on the basis of the preceding account of the Knowledge of the Force, we will present an overview of the basic principles of true Global Jedi Education, what alone is needed to solve all your problems and permanently establish you in The Glorious Jedi Order.

II: The Jedi Code will tell you, based on I:,

How to be a Jedi, the Force actualized and individualized— and thus fully equipped to change your 7 major educational Institutions. This is achieved by observing The Jedi Code and living your life like a Jedi—the greatest life imaginable. You will learn that you already *are* a Jedi and just do not know or feel it yet, and that what you have to do is simply *"Unlearn what you have learned."* Thus we have (1) The Jedi Oath, (2) Jedi Power Ethics, and (3) Jedi Power Methods, and the various Ways to focus on and immerse yourself in the Truth (±), the POINT, 24/7/365. Namely via *(1) Solitude/Alone:* Reason (Science and Proofs), Faith/

Meditation, and Art, and *(2) Society/with Others:* Jedi Family-Groups (at school and office), Relationships (and the Solution to the War between the Sexes/Man and Woman: the "Jedi Androgyn"). We also provide a Test to know if you are and have realized your true Jedi Self, or are deceiving yourself.

III: THE JEDI ORDER will show you, based on I: and II:,

What is the true meaning and purpose of the existing institutions on your planet, hence what is really wrong with them, and how to correct or "balance" them so they truly educate and perform their appointed function: to create and sustain the glorious Jedi Order. The Main Point is that *IT—The amazing Jedi Order—IS NOW* (±), but the Dark Side (+|-) prevents your people from experiencing it—the ONE CONSCIOUSNESS and their UNITY. Hence in this final section we will learn that:

(1) SCIENCE is in truth the Universe's knowledge of itself.

(2) EDUCATION on your planet is in fact "mis-education" due to ignorance of education's true Concept and singular goal of becoming a Jedi; Jedi Charter Schools are the initial solution.

(3) RE-LIGION's true origin and essence is "re-ligare," the canceling of the initial split in the Force's two sides; the creation of Jedi Sects will correct this and end the hate and conflict among your religions.

(4) POLITICS is not fulfilling its true purpose which results in perpetual wars among your nations, inequality and corruption; a Jedi President, Prime Minister, and Third Party is the solution.

(5) BUSINESS on your planet is dominated by the ego-business method which is the root of inequality and misery in your world; you need Jedi CEO's and Corporations to eliminate universal poverty, homelessness, and unemployment.

(6) HEALTH: your doctors and health professionals are not healing your people since they lack the true concepts of health and Man and are ignorant of Unity and the *Absolute I,* the healer of all diseases without exception; you need to educate Jedi Doctors.

(7) THE ARTS & MEDIA have power to heal your planet but are not being used properly; as powerful agents of education they can bring your whole planet into the unity consciousness of the ONE POINT in a very short time; all you need are Jedi Artists, Producers, and Media Specialists.

EDUCATION

There is a UNITY underlying everything and everyone on your planet.
To be Aware of this UNITY is to be Educated ... and a JEDI.

WELCOME TO THE JEDI ORDER

THE FORCE WILL BE WITH YOU ALWAYS!

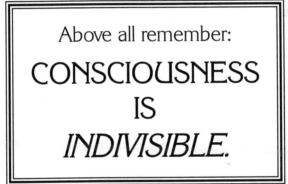

Above all remember:

CONSCIOUSNESS
IS
INDIVISIBLE.

Key Jedi Definitions

"The Force"=The Truth. What Is, Only Is, and Eternally Is. Symbolized by "(±)." It is Reality <u>as</u> Polarity & the Unity of Opposites: The Light and Dark Sides can <u>never</u> come apart—and Light "trumps" Dark.

"Jedi" = Your True Immortal Self, Who you really are: One with The Force.

"The Jedi Order"=The Force fully actualized as JEDI. The Jedi Order alone Is, and Is Now: Perfected Humanity or *Unity*, a state of things where everyone shares the same One Infinite Consciousness (*Absolute I*) yet all remain unique immortal individuals.

"The Dark Side of The Force"=Ignorance of The Truth or Polarity. The belief that the Dark Side (matter) can exist by itself without the Light Side (Consciousness). The "separation" of the two. Symbolized by "(+ | −)." Also known as Materialism and as "The Cave" by Jedi philosophers on your planet (e.g., Plato).

"The Balance of The Force"=The Truth as the Unity (or Balance) of opposites: "+" and "−" as "(±)." Also called **"The Light Side of The Force."**

"The Imbalance of The Force"=A state in which the opposites are *not* in Unity but separated—the root cause of your planet's problems (terrorism, hate, poverty, greed, etc). This pertains not to Reality but to the collective consciousness and level of Education on a given planet.

Thus the simple key to healing your planet and "bringing balance to The Force" in your sector of the galaxy is *JEDI EDUCATION*—

(1) Learn about The Force (The Truth, What Is) and then

(2) Balance The Force in yourself and in Society.—Or, "Be a Jedi and help actualize The Jedi Order."

In sum: The Jedi Handbook is a comprehensive reference Guide to the essential information necessary to solve *all* of your planet's problems and manifest an amazing world beyond what you can possibly imagine. The essential information, to recap, is gathered under the three heads: *part I: The Jedi Truth* provides the Knowledge of The Force, of the Truth and Reality, and serves as the Basis for part *II: The Jedi Code*, which tells you How to live as an Immortal Jedi, and part *III: The Jedi Order*, which tells you How to Balance your Society's Seven Institutions and advent the incredible world that is the happy destiny of your people to enjoy forever.

Obi-Wan Kenobi

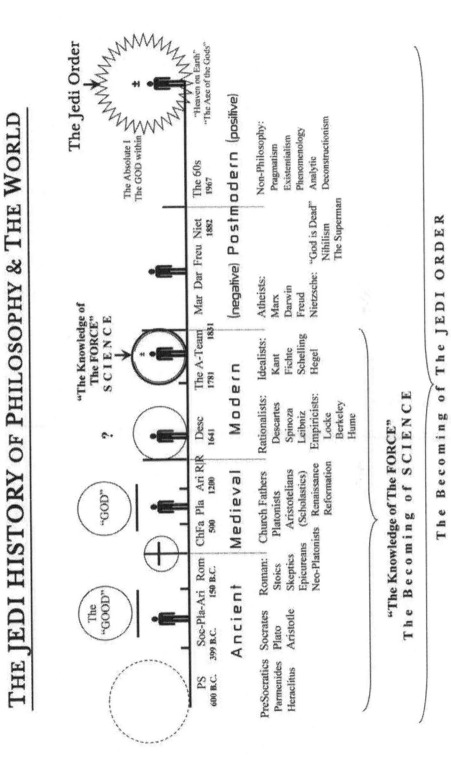

THE JEDI HISTORY OF PHILOSOPHY & THE WORLD

The Jedi Order

"The Knowledge of The FORCE" SCIENCE

The Absolute !
The GOD within

"Heaven on Earth"
"The Age of the Gods"

"The GOOD"

"GOD"

?

| PS | Soc-Pla-Ari Rom | ChFa Pla Ari RtR | Desc | The A-Team | Mar Dar Freu Niet | The 60s |
| 600 B.C. | 399 B.C. 150 B.C. | 590 1200 | 1641 | 1781 1831 | 1882 | 1967 |

Ancient　Medieval　Modern　(negative) Postmodern (positive)

PreSocratics	Socrates	Roman:	Church Fathers	Rationalists:	Idealists:	Atheists:	Non-Philosophy:
Parmenides	Plato	Stoics	Platonists	Descartes	Kant	Marx	Pragmatism
Heraclitus	Aristotle	Skeptics	Aristotelians	Spinoza	Fichte	Darwin	Existentialism
		Epicureans	(Scholastics)	Leibniz	Schelling	Freud	Phenomenology
		Neo-Platonists	Renaissance	Empiricists:	Hegel		Analytic
			Reformation	Locke		"God is Dead"	Deconstructionism
				Berkeley		Nihilism	
				Hume		The Superman	

Nietzsche:

"The Knowledge of The FORCE"
The Becoming of SCIENCE

The Becoming of The JEDI ORDER

THE JEDI TRUTH

History: How your own Jedi attained *the Knowledge of the Force*

Jedi Science

Global Jedi Education

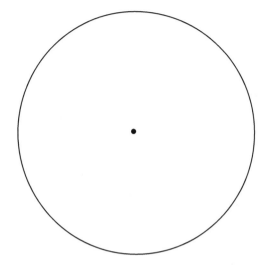

I. HISTORY—How your own Jedi attained *the Knowledge of the Force*, the Truth, and the **POINT**

INTRODUCTION

§45

The TRUTH, my Padawan, is the knowledge that Reality is absolutely ONE. Reality is Consciousness or Thought. Reality is a UNITY. A UNITY of Opposites in which Consciousness trumps Matter while containing Matter within itself as utterly dissolved. This One Reality is The FORCE.

§46

HISTORY on your beautiful planet is nothing but the Truth or the Force becoming aware of itself. Thus History is nothing but the becoming of the JEDI ORDER.

§47

There are *two* ways or forms in which Reality's *self*-knowledge is achieved—by Philosophy/Science and by Religion/Spirituality. The former, as Thought, has *discursive* or *conceptual* knowledge of the Force, whereas the latter, as Consciousness, has *intuitive* knowledge of the Force. Thought is the essence and inner core of Consciousness. Therefore, what Religion calls Consciousness (or Spirit), Philosophy calls Thought or the Concept. So, as your Jedi **Hegel** correctly states, *"the Concept is everything,"* or the One Absolute Reality is THOUGHT. And Thought is the UNIVERSAL (*ALL-gemeine*), which is seen and known by Reason alone, not by the Senses, and is *ALL*-encompassing.

§48

The following gives a summary of your planet's HISTORY and its meaning (see chart on p. 31) which will be fully explained in the four major sections that follow:

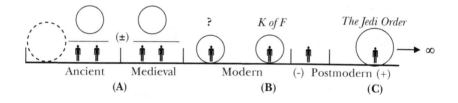

Noble Jedi, notice that the Truth, the Point, the Unity-of-opposites, the One Reality (as a dotted circle) is *there* from the very beginning of your History, although not yet known and individualized—*this* is the sole purpose of your History. The Truth knows itself first in Religion (**A**), as Consciousness-Intuitive, then in Philosophy-Science (**B**), as Thought-Discursive-Scientific, then finally by your whole planet (**C**), as Thought and Consciousness, the glorious JEDI ORDER fully realized.

Also notice that since time is not real, History takes place and unfolds in the *eternal present*. Therefore the actualization of the Truth is timeless or *instantaneous*.

> "Religion proclaims earlier in time what Spirit (the Force) is, but only Science is its true knowledge of itself." **Hegel**

> "For us believing physicists the distinction between past, present, and future is *only an illusion*." **Einstein**

§49

Philosophy/Science is the most detailed and comprehensive form of the *Knowledge of the Force*. So our main focus will be on your history of philosophy, which ends with Jedi Science, rather than on the history of your religions or your political states.

§50

In this connection there are *three* points to be made:

(1) The ARCHE. Philosophy's goal is to become SCIENCE (or Knowledge). That is, "philosophy," as the love or pursuit of Knowledge *ends* when Knowledge/Science is found—which occurred on your planet in your Modern Period. Philosophy proper began in ancient Greece, though there were stirrings in earlier periods. As your Greeks correctly defined it, "philosophy" is nothing but the search for the ARCHE—for the Truth or the Force, the eternal principle, cause and source of all things. More exactly philosophy is the Truth's or the Force's search for *itself*. The Arche is ultimately THOUGHT or the UNIVERSAL as that which comprehends a multiplicity—indeed *all things*—within itself.

(2) The history of philosophy begins with an *OBJECTIVE* ARCHE and ends with a *SUBJECTIVE* ARCHE. An "Objective Arche" (Force, Truth, Principle) is one that is OUTSIDE the knower, while a "Subjective Arche" is INSIDE the knower and is Consciousness or Thought itself. In your Ancient and Medieval Periods there are only *Objective* Arche's, while in your Modern Period, beginning with **Descartes**, a *Subjective* Arche makes its appearance.

(3) Philosophy's—Reason's or thinking's—primary activity and impulse, given that UNITY is the Truth, is to *bring the manifold* or the infinite multiplicity found in experience *into UNITY* and into a single SYSTEM in which all parts are interconnected and form a whole of knowledge, that is, of *self*-knowledge.

—Also, given that the goal of both Philosophy and Education is an INVERSION from the Visible to the Invisible, from the Many to the One True Reality, in our Review of your philosophies we will be looking for the teaching that CONSCIOUSNESS or THOUGHT is Reality or Being.

§51

OVERVIEW: The Force's or Truth's knowledge of itself begins in your Ancient period with your **Thales** and **Parmenides** and their Objective Arche's of "Water" and "Being"—which are Universals that bring everything into a single UNITY, and with **Plato**, with his Divided Line and "two worlds" distinction, and **Aristotle**, with the Force as "self-thinking Thought." Then in your Medieval period the knowledge of the Force is first achieved in Religion, whose Arche however is still an "objective" one and is called "God," with the two sides of the Force remaining separate (+|-). Then in your Modern period a Subjective Arche is discovered in **Descartes'** famous *Meditations on First Philosophy*, namely Consciousness, and finally the "Absolute I" or Concept is uncovered by your "**A-Team**," Jedi **Kant-Fichte-Schelling** and especially **Hegel**, and Jedi Science—the *self*-knowledge of the Force and the end of your planet's History—is achieved. The purpose of the Postmodern period of your History is simply to take or educate all of your peoples into the Jedi Order and the Knowledge of the Force.

> "The Whole *had* to unfold itself through the pain of History."
> **Schelling**
>
> "With Absolute Knowledge History has come to an end." **Hegel**

In essence, the history of philosophy is nothing but the progressive development and realization of the TRUTH—of Jedi Science and the Knowledge of the Force; from simple to fully elaborated. In your history of philosophy we will just be highlighting your main figures and their central ideas.

THE ANCIENT PERIOD

§52

THALES (or the Force active in Thales' thinking) overcomes the multiplicity and reaches Unity by his Arche "Water." *"All things are water."* This means that (1) although the senses seem to indicate that a multiplicity of different types of things exists, in reality the many things are all forms of *one* thing, Water. Hence Reality is One, not many. (2) Hence there are two viewpoints: that of the Senses, correlated with Appearance/Illusion, and that of Reason, correlated with Reality/Truth. (3) Moreover "Water," the Arche, what truly exists, is a UNIVERSAL, something perceived or known by Reason (thought) alone—not by the Senses, which can perceive only *singulars* or singular items. Also Thales' Arche is an "objective" one or a Not-I, as existing outside and other than the I, and not a "subjective" one.

Of course Thales' discovery and doctrine that *"All things are water"* was not without an intuition or direct experience of this *unity* as its foundation, similar to the one related by your Eastern Swami **Vivekananda** who writes: "In this state of *samadhi* all differences between 'I' and 'Brahman' [the Arche] go away, everything is reduced to unity, like the *water* of the Infinite Ocean—*water everywhere, nothing else exists."* (*Ramakrishna as We Saw Him*, 1990, p. 70; also cf. **Plato's** famous Seventh Letter).

§53

PARMENIDES. Here the Force or One, operative within Parmenides, offers the first reasoned argument in the history of philosophy for a position or truth-claim—namely that What Is is ONE BEING. Hence Parmenides' Arche is called "the One" or "Being." Here again the senses lie or deceive while Reason alone reveals the Truth. His premise or principle is: *"What is, is, and can alone be said or thought; what is not, is not, and cannot be said or thought."* In this way Parmenides proves that Reality is absolutely One and without parts and also timeless. (1) If What Is were divisible or had parts then there must exist a space, that is a "nothing," between the parts. But by his principle,

> "The present is the only thing that has no end." **Schrödinger**
>
> "Time is abolished with the realization of the Truth … which is the movement of the circle that presupposes its beginning and reaches it only at the end." **Hegel**

"nothing" cannot be said or thought. Thus What Is, Reality, cannot be divided into parts, hence must be absolutely ONE. (2) It also follows that there is no such thing as "time," as the past or future. For what will be … *is not*, hence cannot be said or thought, and must be ruled out. Likewise what was … *is not*, hence must also be ruled out. Therefore only IS or the Present can be said or thought, hence alone IS or exists—that is, the *eternal* Present or Now. As your Jedi **Hegel** says, "Eternity will not be, nor has it been. IT IS." And as quantum physics founder Erwin **Schrödinger** affirms: "The present is the only thing that has no end."

One defect of Parmenides is that he did not deduce or explain the Many, the sense-world, change, and becoming—what **Plato** will refer to as "the Cave."

§54

HERACLITUS. His Arche, the Truth about the Many and underlying everything, is "Becoming" (or fire). *"Panta re"* or *"Everything flows." "You cannot step twice into the same stream."* With this principle Heraclitus begins to do justice to the world of change, becoming, the senses and the many—and to the principle of POLARITY, the unity of opposites as well. Reality exhibits ceaseless becoming, nothing is fixed or abides—*everything*, each thing or determination, turns into its opposite, which it contains within itself—that is, everything but the Arche-principle-Truth itself, namely "Becoming." For as *the* Truth it *remains the same* and, moreover, is itself a UNIVERSAL, grasped by Reason alone and not by the senses.

§55

> "The entire Soul must be *turned away from this changing world of the senses* until its eye, Reason, can bear to contemplate Reality and the supreme splendor of the Good."
> Plato

Your JEDI **PLATO** is perhaps your most important Jedi Philosopher who was the first to define the program and task of philosophy for all future thinkers in his famous "Divided Line." The Line shows that the one Goal of life is EDUCATION or INVERSION into the Truth, the Arche, the Universal, the Force, which he called "the GOOD" ... and "Inversion" having the meaning of TRANSCENDING YOUR SENSES IN ORDER TO CONTACT TRUE REALITY—that is, turning from the Visible to the Invisible, from the Senses and Sense objects viewed as reality to Reason (consciousness and thought) and its objects viewed as Reality. Following his teacher **Socrates**, Plato gave primary importance to definitions and Universals, the unchanging true realities (Forms-Ideas) lying at the base of all experience and the singulars of sense and knowable by Reason alone. In Plato's words: "[Padawan, be ever mindful of the distinction] between the multiplicity of things that we call good or beautiful or whatever it may be and, on the other hand, Goodness itself or Beauty itself and so on. Corresponding to each of these sets of many things, we postulate a single Form or real essence ... Further, the many things can be seen, but are not objects of rational thought; whereas the Forms are objects of thought, but invisible [*The Republic*, vi. 507]."

§56

For Plato EDUCATION as revealed by his Divided Line and Cave Allegory consists in the following three-stage process (See Diagram below):

[1] We start in (-) the sense-world (the Cave) as "lovers of sights and sounds," believing sense-things and the many to be true reality and the only reality; and thus because of our pursuit and attachment to perishable sense objects it is impossible to become One, Just or Right (*dikaiosune*), for Plato the goal of life.

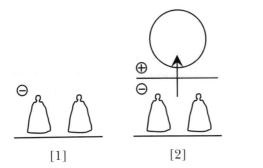

[1]   [2]   [3]

[2] Then we realize that there is another domain of reality, *true Reality* (the Cave, the world of changing sense-objects, is now recognized as "meaningless illusion" [*Republic*, vii. 515]). This is a domain of Universals or Forms, invisible to the senses but not to Reason or Thought. Here resides the GOOD or Absolute Reality (in truth it is **Parmenides' ONE**),

"The true lover of knowledge strives towards Reality and the Good with a passion that will not faint or fail until he has *entered into union with it [with the Force]*." **Plato**

the supreme Universal containing *all* Universals within itself; the GOOD is the source/cause of these as well as of the entire sense-world and its objects. The Goal and Task of True Education is therefore an INVERSION process, from the Senses (-) as Real to Thought (+) as Real—a process of literally "dying to the senses." The Task is to cease loving and attaching yourself to false sense-objects, and to begin loving the Truth, true Reality, and the Universals of Reason. The Goal is now to awaken and perfect your Reason so it is ultimately able to behold and achieve direct contact with the GOOD (the FORCE) *and ultimately merge with it.*

§57

[3] Here you have achieved the Goal, have united the two worlds (±), and are ONE with the GOOD, immortal and indestructible, just like it is. It is to be observed that Plato himself never attained to the Goal because (1) he had an inadequate understanding of POLARITY and hence kept (+) and (-) apart—indeed for Plato the Body was a "prison house" and the ultimate goal was for the Soul to be permanently separated from both the Body and the (-) sense-world. (2) The GOOD for Plato was also an "Objective" First Principle/Arche and not a "Subjective" one; he did not know that the Truth was totally accessible to him and that the GOOD was in fact CONSCIOUSNESS itself—what the Jedi Moderns **Kant** and **Fichte** will name the "Transcendental Unity of Apperception (or Self-consciousness)" and the "Absolute I"—hence of the same nature and substance *as his own consciousness*; this belief resulted in an irremediable *separation* between himself and the GOOD (the Arche, Eternal, "Divine"). (3) Also, in terms of the goal of Philosophy and History—namely, the Knowledge of the Force, the Jedi SCIENCE of the Whole—Plato did not *derive* or *explain* the two sides of the Whole, the (+) INNER and the (-) OUTER and all of their aspects, *from his First Principle, the GOOD.* Plato's disciple **Aristotle** went a long way to remedy this but even he did not accomplish what was required, only your Moderns did.

§58

Your JEDI **ARISTOTLE** made major advances on **Plato** and Jedi Science. For example, he developed all the major fields of scientific inquiry (physics, biology, psychology, ethics, political science, metaphysics and logic), and his *active* Universals and form/matter hylomorphic principles had greater explanatory power than **Plato's** *passive* Universals, and permitted a closer *unity* of (+) and (-). Moreover he achieved a superior Arche in his *Unmoved Mover* whose essence is "the Thought that thinks itself" throughout all eternity. As Aristotle writes:

> "And thinking in itself deals with that which is best in itself, and that which is thinking in the fullest sense with that which is best in the fullest sense. And *thought thinks on itself* because it shares the nature of the object of thought; for it becomes an object of thought in coming into contact with and thinking its objects, so that *thought and object of thought are the same* ... Therefore the possession rather than the receptivity is the *divine element* which thought seems to contain, and the act of contemplation is what is most pleasant and best. If, then, God is always in that good state in which we sometimes are, this compels our wonder; and if in a better this compels it yet more. And God *is* in a better state. And life also belongs to God; for the actuality of thought is life, and God is that actuality; and God's self-dependent actuality is life most good and eternal. We say therefore that God is a living being, eternal, most good, so that life and duration continuous and eternal belong to God. For this *is* God." *Metaphysics*, xii.7.

Aristotle's defects are: (1) He placed his Arche, self-thinking Thought, outside and *separate* from himself rather than *within* himself—and never reduced the multiplicity of individual separate substances to Unity and One Reality. (2) He also failed to articulate the content or moments of this eternal Thinking which is absolute Reality and the Force itself. Hence, Aristotle (the Force within him) did not achieve Jedi Science and show, for example, the interconnections of all fields of study and their subject matter and how their respective universals are fluid and derivable from his Arche, self-thinking Thought (i.e. from *Logic* or the *Logos*). And as with **Plato** Aristotle also had an inadequate understanding of Polarity and the unity of opposites, the key principle of Science.

§59

In passing we will just mention the Roman schools of philosophy, **Stoicism**, **Skepticism**, and **Epicureanism**, which offered methods of this-worldly salvation, and the more important of the Neo-Platonists, **Plotinus** and **Proclus**, who achieved a higher development of **Plato's** philosophy and the Knowledge of the Force by correctly articulating the process of the One Absolute into the three stages/spheres of Logic, Nature, and Mind or Spirit, in a general but incomplete fashion. Their main defect is this—the neo-Platonists were aware of the Force (the Good, Absolute), but the Force was not yet *aware of itself.* They had the "such," the universal, but not its connection or unity with the "this," the individual or *concrete, actual self-consciousness.* This lack will first get remedied in another sphere than philosophy, namely, Religion, and only later in Modern Philosophy.

§60

My Padawan we thus leave your Ancient Period with the Truth, the self-knowledge of the Force still unattained—the two sides of the Force are not unified, and consciousness or thought is still not known to be infinite and all Reality.

THE MEDIEVAL PERIOD

§61

Thus there was a need to exit your Ancient World and enter another historical period because the UNITY-of-Opposites, (+) and (-), and the Force's Knowledge of Itself was not yet achieved. Be mindful noble Padawan that each period of your planet's History is *necessary*—in order to reach the glorious goal of the Jedi Order. It was in the sphere of *Religion* and Faith, as opposed to *Philosophy* and Reason, that the Truth first awakened; and awakened *as Intuitive* and *Consciousness* and not yet as *Discursive*, as scientific Thought or the Concept. This UNITY first occurred with the shift from polytheism to monotheism when **Plato's** GOOD had morphed into the "GOD" of your religions, which became the new Principle or Arche of all things. Your word "re-ligion" itself, noble Reader, indicates the Truth as the "unity of opposites." That is, the purpose of re-ligion is to "re-connect" or unify ("*ligare*") the opposites or extremes God and man into *one* thing, called "God-man," "Geist" (by **Hegel**), "Superman" (by **Nietzsche**), and our own, "Jedi." All true religions contain this principle and truth as their core and the Christian religion's concept of the "God-man" is perhaps the unity of opposite's clearest expression. Here in the "God-man" (Christ) for example, we have the *unity* which the neo-platonists lacked of the "such" (the Universal, Father-God) *and* the "this" (the Individual, actual I or Self of self-consciousness).

§62

This is why the dominant religion of the second, Medieval period of your History, reflected in its theology, is Christianity. Thus in the consciousness of Christ, for example, we have the knowledge of the Force as the *Unity* of opposites, the *One* Consciousness and POINT. But because religion as such expresses the Truth in picture language, the UNITY falls apart into "two worlds," which characterizes the entire period; and hence the need for another period, the Modern, to overcome the duality and separation that still remains.

Further, as noted, a major advance of your Medievals was from polytheism to monotheism. For the Greeks, Romans, and others there were *many* gods (hence each was *finite*) and, since a "god" equals an Arche, *many* Arche or Forces, not just "one." This situation ended with the Medievals and hence the Arche or Force became universally accepted as only *One*, which was a great advance. And soon it was realized that the *One* God *must also be Infinite*—a second major advance, something that the Greeks and Ancients did not know. Then later, with your Jedi **Spinoza**, it was seen that for God, the One, to *be* "infinite" meant that *no* other beings besides the One could exist; everything else (man, nature, galaxies) could only be "aspects" of and *within* the One God, the One Infinite all-encompassing Arche.

Also important is that since in its concept Religion implies that all men are *equal* or the same in relation to God, what necessarily resulted was the end of *slavery*, a practice that was commonplace among the Greeks, Romans, and other peoples.

§63

Thus the salvation, healing and liberation which it is religion's purpose to provide, can only occur when there is no longer a "separation" between God (the Force, Reality, Truth) and "humanity" or yourselves, when the two sides are *absolutely* ONE— which happens with the *experience* of Union with God, with the Force knowing itself in you and as you. Unfortunately the *union* that was achieved in the major monotheistic religions was inadequate and fell apart, resulting in the One Reality's split into *two worlds* (the here and the beyond), which had to be repaired in the *next* period of your planet's History. The "union" was inadequate mainly because of the FORM in which the Truth was expressed and communicated—the Form of a "revelation" in imagery, picture-thinking, and narrative stories and understood as coming from an "outside" source, not an "internal" one. This left the Truth in a form that was not *universally* communicable and acceptable to all persons, allowing for multiple and conflicting interpretations.

§64

So what resulted was not the UNITY of Heaven and Earth, God and Wo/Man, human and divine, sacred and secular, eternity and time, but instead their *separation* and DIS-UNITY, which characterized the entire period. In particular, salvation and healing were promised to occur not NOW but in a state *after* death, in "another world," a "heavenly beyond," far removed in time and space from this Present world—something which absolutely contradicted the Truth (±). As your Jedi **Nietzsche** says, though religion does indeed contain the Truth of the union of opposites *it has been misunderstood*—a misunderstanding which persists to this day. For example he writes that

> **"Only we free spirits have the principles for understanding something that nineteen centuries have misunderstood .... Mankind lies on its knees before the exact opposite of what was the origin and meaning of the evangel; in the concept of "church" it has pronounced holy precisely what the "bringer of the glad tidings" (Jesus) felt to be *beneath* and *behind* himself; there can be no greater world-historical irony ... And what is the *gospel?* Simply this, that *there are no longer any opposites* ... Thus Jesus has abolished guilt and sin, and any distance separating Man from God ... and he lived this unity with God *as* his glad tidings."**

§65

However though it was true that institutional mainstream religions, clergy and laity alike, were involved in the error of the Dark Side and the *separation* of God and Man, Heaven and Earth, and suffered as a consequence, the same cannot be said of the founders of these religions and their mystics and saints, all of whom knew the Truth. For example:

Christianity: "I and the father [God] will make our dwelling in you" (John 14:23). "I live, yet not I, but Christ [God] lives in me" (Gal. 2:20). "As he [Christ or God] is, so are we in this world" (1John 4:17). "Everyone that is perfect (or whole) shall be just as his Master [Christ or God]" (Luke 6:40). "The kingdom of God [or God] is (not will be) within you (it is NOW, and it's not outside you in another world)" (Luke 17:21). "We share the divine nature [hence are divine]" (2Peter 1:4). "Be ye perfect [whole, complete], even as your father in heaven [God] is perfect [Be like God]" (Matt. 5:48). "I [God] said you are gods and goddesses [Elohim]" (John 10:34). "May they be One as we are One, I in them, thou in me" (John 17:23). **Meister Eckhart**, Catholic Mystic, "The eye with which I see God is the same eye with which God sees me, my eye and God's eye are one and the same eye."

Judaism: "Let us [God] make man in our own image" (Gen. 1:26). "And God formed man of the dust of the ground, and *breathed* into his nostrils the *breath* of life; and man became a living soul [i.e., God's breath or consciousness and man's *are one and the same*]" (Gen. 2:7). "You are the temple of the living God" (Jer. 31:33). "Be ye holy, even as I [God] am holy [Be like God]" (Lev. 19:2). "I [God] said you are gods and goddesses [Elohim]" (Psalms 82:6). See also the Kabbalah and the writings of Michael Berg, Israel ben Eliezer, the Hasidism, and Isaac Luria.

Islam: "When I [God] love him, I become his Ear through which he hears, his Eye with which he sees, his Hand with which he grasps, and his Foot with which he walks (there is no separation, only Union)" (Hadith, An-Nawawi 38). "He who knows himself knows his Lord (Allah)" (Hadith). "I am The Truth" (**Al-Hallaj**, 16th c. Sufi Mystic). "To attain the 'I am God' state is the goal of creation" (**Meher Baba**).

Hinduism: "Atman [your true self] is Brahman [God]." "*That* which is the finest essence—this whole world has *that* as its Self. *That* is Reality. *That* is the Self. *That thou art* [*Tat twam asi*]" (Chandogya Upanishad 6.8.7). "The truth is that you are *always united* with the Lord. But you must know this" (Svetasvatara Upanishad 1.12). "The wise man, freed from name and form, attains the Supreme Being, the Self-luminous, the Infinite. He who knows Brahman becomes Brahman" (Mundaka Upanishad 3.2.9).

Sikhism: "Now are for us no entanglements or snares, Nor a bit of egoism left. Now is *all distance annulled*, nor are curtains drawn *between us*. Thou art mine, I Thine [God and yourself are One]" (Adi Granth, Bilaval, M.5, p. 821).

Buddhism. "Awakening or enlightenment is the goal … and it is here and now: for samsara and nirvana are One."

§66

Moreover, in this period true Philosophy did not exist for Theology dominated the schools and men's minds. Philosophy was not free because you had to accept certain doctrines of the Church, Synagogue, and Temple as beyond question and then reason on the basis of these. There were however notable Jedi theologians during this period—**Augustine, Aquinas, Maimonides, Avicenna** (Ibn Sina) and **Averroes**—however even they were not able to entirely free themselves from the error of the Dark Side and separateness and clearly express the Unity of the Truth. Free thought and Philosophy re-appeared only with the close of the Medieval Period, after the Renaissance and Reformation had run their course and the rebirth of the "sciences" with **Copernicus**, **Galileo**, and **Newton** had commenced. Only after this "clearing away" did true Philosophy re-commence with your Jedi **Descartes**.

§67

What specifically had to happen was the following. (1) Given the principle and purpose of re-ligion is the unity of God and Man (as Jedi) and Heaven and Earth (as the Jedi Order), because this Unity and Truth was expressed in inadequate picture-language the Unity fell apart into Two worlds, and this had to be overcome. In other words the Arche of the medievals was known as "God"—understood as a "transcendent" personal Being with consciousness, etc—and the goal of life was to attain knowledge of and union with this God. But the problem was that this God was erroneously pictured as an **"Objective"** Arche that existed both outside yourselves and the universe; hence as located in a "different" world from the present one, God (the Arche) became *inaccessible*. This made total unification and healing impossible. Also the clergy—who possessed an inadequate "picture-version" of the Truth—looked askance at individuals who claimed to be ONE with God and hence divine, rigorously maintaining a strict *separation* between the two. (2) Therefore the dual separation between God and Man, Heaven and Earth, the Present World and the Beyond (the *not* Here and Now) had to be transcended and abolished and their Unity realized. Faith had to be replaced or supplemented by Reason and the Truth had to take another *universal* FORM. Specifically, a new "**Subjective**" Arche had to appear—and it did, with the discovery of the identity of Consciousness and Being.

> "The *form of picture-thinking* is the specific mode in which Spirit, in the [religious] community, becomes aware of itself ... [it is] defective in that spiritual Being is still burdened with an *unreconciled split into a Here and a Beyond.*" **Hegel**

§68

Hence much like **Plato** and others the Medievals and Religion took the (+) Inner-Conscious side of the Force and *separated* it from the Force's (-) Outer, Objective and Present side, placing it, in the form of "God" and "Heaven," in *another world*; which turns out to be unthinkable as the **A-Team** discovered, for *you cannot abstract from the "I"* or think a "thing in itself" or a being completely *out of relation* with thought or consciousness. Thus the "other world" of Religion is and can only be HERE ... and NOW.

THE MODERN PERIOD

§69

The goal of your History, the Knowledge of the Force or the Force's Knowledge of Itself, was achieved in your Modern Period. Here it became clear that the Arche or Principle of all things, the (+) side of the Whole or Divided Line, was not "Objective" but rather "Subjective." This Subjective Arche was in fact CONSCIOUSNESS itself (or the CONCEPT), into which all previous Arche—Water, the One, the GOOD, even religion's "transcendent other-worldly God"—returned as into their sole Truth. It was your Jedi **Descartes** who *began* the shift to the True Arche—with a **Finite I** or Consciousness—and his successors, "**The A-Team**," who *completed* it with an **Absolute I** or Consciousness or the Concept, and the necessary derivation of all things from it resulting in JEDI SCIENCE, the Force's Knowledge of

Itself. As a result the Medieval world's *separation* into two worlds, (+) and (-), came to an end and their *absolute UNITY* was realized—albeit only in philosophy, not yet in the whole world, the Task of the next Postmodern period of your planet's history.

§70

How it happened: First, *the primacy of Consciousness was realized*; that is, the primacy of Thought, the Pure I, and the INNER over Objects, Matter, the World, and the OUTER. Consciousness/Thought *and* Being were one, but initially realized as only a "finite I"—for God and the world were posited *outside* consciousness or the "Cogito." Then when it was realized that it is impossible to transcend the circle of your consciousness, that *nothing* existed "outside" this circle, the **A-Team** was able to realize the "Absolute I" or Concept; and Polarity (or Dialectic), the method of Science, was finally perfected. What occurred, in a word, was that the Medieval's Arche "God" became transposed from "transcen*dent*" to "transcen*dental*," that is, from existing *outside* consciousness to existing Apriori and *within* consciousness.

§71

JEDI **RENÉ DESCARTES**. The discovery that the Arche, the Force, and true Reality is CONSCIOUSNESS (and implicitly Concept) began to be made by your Descartes in his ground-breaking 1641 *Meditations on First Philosophy* with his famous "turn to the subject" away from the object and his "COGITO ERGO SUM," "I think, therefore I AM," which expresses the *unity* of thought and being. This discovery will lead ultimately to the **A-Team's** realization that THOUGHT, the I, the CONCEPT, is everything or all Reality. At the core of Descartes' discovery is the twin realization that (1) in terms of experience it is *consciousness that is FIRST and not the world or objects* and (2) that *consciousness is BEING or true REALITY.* The way that he came to the realization that Consciousness, his own Subject or I, is Reality and may ultimately be the Arche and ground of all things can be understood as follows. Descartes' goal in the *Meditations* was to find something *absolutely certain* on which all knowledge could be based—especially the new mathematical "sciences" of nature then emerging, a la **Newton, Galileo**, and **Boyle**. To achieve this he began *doubting* everything he formerly believed to be true, realizing that whatever was able to survive this "doubting" must be *absolutely certain.* In his *First Meditation* Descartes doubted everything that his 5 Senses, the (-) and the Cave, told him was true, including all sciences based on the Senses such as physics, astronomy, and medicine, and hence his own Body, sense organs, eyes and ears.

§72

Descartes realized that since he was not able to distinguish his waking state from his dreaming state it is quite possible that right now, as he is writing his *Meditations*—and as you noble Jedi are reading this *Handbook*—he is dreaming. And if this were true then all of the above can be doubted. Nothing his senses report can be absolutely *certain* or *Real*. It is in his *Second Meditation* that Descartes achieves his goal and makes his incredible discovery. This happens when he directs his universal doubt against himself, against the one who is doing the doubting. Descartes realizes that he cannot doubt *his own existence* precisely because *he must exist in order to doubt it.* Hence, the one thing that is absolutely certain is that *he exists.* "I think—doubt, sense, dream, am *conscious*—therefore I AM, I EXIST" (compare, "Before Abraham was, I AM," and similar statements of other Jedi). What this means is that *Consciousness* and *Being (Reality)* are *inseparable* or *ONE*. If you are *conscious* or are *consciousness* then you have a reality, a being, which cannot be removed, destroyed, or negated.

§73

Further, be mindful that Descartes, like **Plato** and other Jedi, was acutely aware of the absolute need to "break with the senses" and move to Reason in order to reach the Truth. For he says e.g.: "I will close my eyes, stop my ears/senses ... and see what I am and know." This revelation and Truth of who and what Descartes really is, is called the "**COGITO**" or "I think," and is short for "Cogito ergo sum" and all it implies. It is also very important to know that the "I" that Descartes discovered alone exists and is certain is not the *Particular Individual,* "P.I." or the Ego called "Rene Descartes" but rather the *Universal Individual,* "U.I.," the Pure Consciousness or the "Absolute I" (a la **Fichte**) that is the same for and in everyone; this will be discussed further below.

§74

Now, that consciousness is FIRST and not the world also means that the world and all objects that Descartes experienced and previously thought to exist "outside" or *independently* of himself, are now known instead to exist *inside* himself—inside the circle of his Cogito, Mind or Consciousness. The "Before and After Diagram" below will illuminate this all-crucial point:

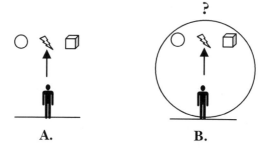

A.   B.

§75

A. BEFORE the *Meditations* and his famous discovery all the objects Descartes perceived—the house, tree, star—were taken or viewed as existing "outside" himself. He was oblivious of their necessary relation to his "I" or consciousness—the perceiver. This is the **"Common or Normal View,"** which completely ignores the presence of the "I" or consciousness. Here, the world or OUTER aspect of the Force has Being, whereas "I" and the INNER do not (or have minimal being). I am "in" the world, one (insignificant) object among myriad others. The world and its objects are regarded as existing outside me, independently of me—they are there, are true beings, whether I am there or not.

§76

B. AFTER discovering the COGITO, Descartes realized that these perceivable Objects were really "inside" himself, were so *many modifications of his mind or perception or consciousness,* and merely *ideas* within his consciousness, within the INNER circle of his COGITO. For they were one and all Objects FOR HIM, each one was in relationship with his "I" or consciousness. This is the **"True View,"** which recognizes the ineliminable presence of the "I" or consciousness. But then it is realized that the world "I" see and its objects—the window, trees, stars—are not such beings as I have imagined—*things* existing "outside" and independently of me. Rather, they are all *relative* or conditioned beings, *as* relative to my "I" or consciousness. And since my consciousness bathes and pervades all of them, they are no longer "things" but *ideas,* so many denizens or contents of my consciousness. What follows therefore is that *"I am not in the world,"* rather *"the world is in me."* This means, as later Jedi-philosophers discovered, that consciousness as such is *not* in the world or universe of space, time and matter at all but rather *outside* it—inhabiting what has been called by your Jedi **Kant** and others the domain of the "Apriori," pure, or transcen*dental*, as opposed to a transcen*dent*, indeed inconceivable and non-existent domain.

§77

The primacy of consciousness and the Subject over the Object and World can easily be grasped by noticing that when I am in the act of describing a painting to you, say your **Picasso's** *Girl Before a Mirror*, I am in fact not describing the painting *itself* but rather only and always *my awareness of the painting*. There are two things present: the object, and the awareness of the object (or *that* I know, and *what* I know). Most people attend to the one, the object, but are oblivious of the other, *the awareness*—which alone is primary and true; the former does not exist as such or is only an "abstraction" from the latter. Therefore it is simply impossible to ignore, "abstract from" or bypass my "I" or consciousness so as to have before myself just the object, without the object's *also* being in relation to or "in" my consciousness. It follows that at all times (and since my earliest childhood) I am only aware of my consciousness as modified thus and so—and not of the sky, sunset, tree, or house, as objects in their own right. These latter objects are really my second or "mediate" objects, they are *there* only in and through my consciousness, my "immediate" object.

§78

Thus right now as I, *OBI-WAN,* look at this book and the things around me, I am really and in truth looking at *my consciousness*—and not at an independent world outside me. All that I see is *inside* me. Therefore, what is there, hence what *is*, is *Consciousness*—colored or modified this way or that. The key point is that because these objects—sensuous, material, extended—exist *in* and not *apart* from my consciousness, they thereby forfeit their independence and status as true self-existent beings. They have only a "being-for-another (for a consciousness)" but not a "being-for-themselves"; they are "conditioned" and not "unconditioned."

All these Jedi-truths are obtained merely by a shift from a focus on "objects"—this pen, glass, picture—to a focus on *the knowing* and *knower* of these objects.

§79

Let us further develop this important point illustrated by the "Before and After" Diagram above—namely, that Descartes' Subject, "I," or consciousness is *first* (or presupposed), while the world or objects are *second.* It can be simply expressed as: *No Subject, no Object.* Here is another example: Realize that when you enter your New York City harbor on a cruise ship, it is not true that you see "the Statue of Liberty." Rather what you see is *your own consciousness OF the Statue of Liberty.* "I AM and I see the Statue of Liberty as *in* my consciousness." *This* is the complete picture. As we said above, normal or "Cave" consciousness habitually "abstracts from" or ignores *itself*—the Subject, its existence ("I AM"), *and its own <u>act</u> of perceiving, seeing, experiencing*—and focuses only on the "Object" it experiences, in this case "the Statue of Liberty." As your Jedi **Husserl** says, most people are "lost in the World, in the Object," and totally dominated, overwhelmed and controlled by it (cf., heteronomy v. autonomy, and outer- v. inner-directedness). In fact as we have noted, True Education involves nothing but *transcending* this type of ("realist") consciousness and mind-set and "standing it on its head"—realizing that in truth there is no such thing as "the World or Object as such," rather only "the World or Object *in* and *for* a Consciousness"— which, expressed differently, is precisely *the Unity of Subjectivity and Objectivity.* This means it is ultimately *Consciousness* that is all reality and embraces the physical world within itself, and not the reverse.

§80

Descartes' successors will say: "You cannot abstract from your I" and reach an object *independently* of your I (**Fichte**), and, "The I think [Cogito] must accompany every one of my presentations or perceptions" (**Kant**). The following thought-experiment will further bring home this all-crucial point: Pretend right now that you are dreaming or are in a dream. Hence your hands, body, the *objects* that surround you in the room, the sky, meadow, stars, and so on, *all exist only WITHIN your dream*—that is, within your Self, your mind, your consciousness or Cogito. NOW suddenly switch to your WAKING state where you are no longer dreaming and hence all you see is "real"—and Realize that: *THE SAME THING STILL HOLDS TRUE.* Namely, that all you see around you exists *only within your consciousness (cf. your dream)*—or, you are just experiencing *your own perceptions,* which as such are "yours" (and not "mine"), are within you, are YOU (i.e., the True You, not the "egoic you"). Further, that these objects you see around you *also* have an existence *outside* of you—*this* you do not and cannot directly see or know. It is an inference only, a mere belief.

§81

As you can now see one of the big questions is (and this is the reason for the question mark in B. in the "Before and After Diagram" above): "Is there anything at all that exists outside of my consciousness, outside the circle of my experience, and disconnected from my I; a so-called "THING-IN-ITSELF"?" In the end Descartes believed there was—namely, that the real physical world (colorless, odorless, "atomic," etc) *did* exist outside this circle, and the traditional "transcendent" God of religion as well

> "I thought I perceived things *outside* of myself ... but this belief was mistaken." *Meditation Three.* **Descartes**
>
> "Nothing is known which does not fall *within experience.*" **Hegel**

(Descartes was a Catholic). Hence, because of this answer that he gave to the question it can be said that Descartes achieved only a FINITE I, and not an ABSOLUTE I. That is, for Descartes consciousness (and thought) is reality, but it is not *all* reality and *infinite.* So with Descartes the One Infinite Consciousness or the Force did not yet come to a full knowledge of Itself. But this was the beginning of the end of this realization—which happened when it was clearly seen to be impossible for "beings" to exist *outside* of consciousness, or out of relation to consciousness, to the I, and to the "I think."

§82

Before we leave Descartes, my Padawan should also be mindful that the "I" whose existence is absolutely certain is not the "P.I." or Descartes' *empirical* Ego, but rather his *Pure or Transcendental I.* We can be certain of this because Descartes reaches this I-certainty *only after* he doubts and sets aside the whole sense-world, his Body, parents, France, etc—and "abstracts" (or "subtracts") from everything. He eliminates in thought everything, the whole universe, in order to get to the "PURE I," later to be known as the "Absolute I." Notice especially that this "I" *must* be the same as my "I" *and* your "I" *and* everyone's "I." This is true because of Descartes' characterization of his two substances and their natures, namely *Thought*—which is conscious, unextended, indivisible, and not in space and time; and *Extension* (space or matter)—which is unconscious, extended and divisible. Thus since *my* Pure I/Thought and *your* Pure I are *both outside* the Universe/Extension (or the (-), the Cave) it follows that (1) there can be no "distance" (or space) between them, and (2) as removed from the empirical (sense) and matter altogether, *there is nothing to distinguish them.* Therefore they must *coincide* and be one and the same. Hence, we have before us the "Absolute I," the basis for the *unity* of all your peoples that is the solution to your world's problems.

§83

It will therefore prove absolutely important in all that follows, noble Reader, to recognize that there are "two" kinds or aspects of consciousness. (1) *Pure* consciousness, which is "pure" in that it is related only to itself, not to any objects; and it is universal and absolute, the same as *Reason itself.* And (2) *Empirical* consciousness, which is *not* "pure" in that it *is* related to objects other than consciousness; thus it is particular and relative, and known generally as the "ego." The key is that there is *only One* pure consciousness (*"Absolute I"*) that we all share in common—while there is an indefinite number of *empirical* consciousnesses or egos (P.I.'s), which all have their source or origin in the "Absolute I." It is this *One* pure consciousness which is the main concern of the Jedi philosophers and which we have been discussing, *and not the "ego."* We will in fact see that becoming a Jedi is essentially an affair of transforming your empirical consciousness or ego into a pure consciousness—but in such a way that your empirical consciousness and hence *individuality* is retained.

§84

Thus in conclusion, (1) Descartes realized that all that he perceived was in relationship with and *inside* himself, his I or Consciousness, and not *outside* or independent of himself; that it was *impossible* to get outside the Cogito. (2) However he still posited Beings (a Thing in itself, the world, God) *outside* of the Cogito. He did not know that *this was impossible*, that "God," the Arche was WITHIN himself, as the Absolute I. (3) Descartes also lacked POLARITY, and therefore Thought *and* Extension/Matter were absolutely exclusive and non-unifiable; and he was not able to resolve the contradiction implied by his positing of three substances, two finite ones and one infinite one; and lastly he did not derive everything from his first principle (the Cogito with its "clear and distinct perceptions"). Also notice that the reason Descartes held that Sense-objects were unreal appearances was because as such they are only "ideas" in the mind and thus *conditioned* by the I or consciousness.

§85

It will be also be helpful if we briefly REVIEW the transition from your Medieval Period and its defect to your Modern Period and the need for correcting the defect. Thus, the defect of the Medieval standpoint was three-fold and was due to the FORM of the Solution—the Unity (±)—as presented in religion. (1) The two worlds or sides of the Force were *separated* and a way had to be found to keep them *permanently* together and from coming apart again (namely, via Reason and Polarity); and (2) The (+) second world, in truth a world of *consciousness* and fully *present* and *one* with the (-) present sense/material world, was a world created by and existing only in *Imagination* but regarded

> "The *Geist* had to come down out of the Middle Ages' intellectual world and quicken its abstract element with the actual Self … its essence had to be guided into self-consciousness." **Hegel**

as REAL, a duplicate of *this* world, and peopled by a "transcendent" God and heaven, which really are *Here and Now* (but in a different dimension; thus we Jedi are *not* saying there is no such thing as what your religions understand as "God" and "Heaven"). (3) Also the Medieval's Arche, "God" (+), was located in the "beyond" and defined as *not here*. It had to be brought down and found *within* yourselves, as your Jedi **Hegel** states in his *Phenomenology*.

§86

Now the way the collapse and unity of the two sides (of the Force) and the transference of the Arche from outside to inside yourselves was effected was by Descartes' COGITO and the ultimate realization by his followers that you cannot escape the COGITO and "this world" (-)—something which forces you into *this* present world in order to find the Arche/God here *within* yourselves and your own consciousness. However as we noted Descartes did not see this— that you cannot escape the COGITO and that there is no "Thing in itself"—and as a result posited (+) entities *outside* the Cogito. Descartes then only attained to a "Finite I" and hence never reached the UNITY that is the goal of philosophy—and the ABSOLUTE and Absolute Jedi Science.

§87

[Interlude] *The Continental Rationalists.* In addition to Descartes there were two other major rationalist philosophers. JEDI **SPINOZA**, who in his *Ethics* recognized Descartes' error of positing 2 finite substances (Thought and Extension) and 1 infinite substance (God); a contradiction which he corrected by positing only One Infinite Substance (God or Nature), with Thought and Matter as attributes of the One Substance (not substances themselves); also called "the One and All" (*Hen kai pan*), the all-comprehensive UNIVERSAL, which is an important advance. And although Spinoza did indeed *unify* thought and extension, (+) and (-), *in God*, his God, Arche, the Force, was only Substance and "Object," and not Consciousness and "Subject," i.e. a *subjective* first principle. He also downplayed *individuality* and did not give it its proper due.—And JEDI **LEIBNIZ**, who in his *Monadology* posited an infinite plurality of "windowless" Monads, self-enclosed "island universes" or Cogitos, with no connection or commerce among them. Leibniz did correct **Spinoza's** lack of Individuality, but in an equally one-sided way; that is, no Universality or unity obtained among the Monads.

The British Empiricists, **Locke**, **Berkeley**, and **Hume**, believed that all knowledge comes from sense-experience and not Reason. It was **Kant**, a disciple of **Leibniz**, who began the process of unifying the two, Rationalism and Empiricism, although initially in an inadequate way.

§88

The **A-TEAM: Kant-Fichte-Schelling-Hegel**. "A" stands for "the Absolute," which means that only One thing exists, namely, "the Force." Thus it was the A-Team who finally attained the Absolute

I and the Concept and the Force's Knowledge of Itself as JEDI SCIENCE. The Systems of all four Jedi offer versions of Jedi Science or the Knowledge of the Force, but the System of Hegel is the most complete and comprehensive. Here we will highlight a few features of each, with special focus on the Absolute I or Concept.

ON THE ABSOLUTE I

§89

First I will explain how your A-Team discovered the Absolute I in three steps, briefly give **Schelling's** proof of it, and indicate some of its features.

(1) Once we see that it is *impossible* to transcend the Cogito or Consciousness, that there is *nothing* outside consciousness (no "Thing in itself," no transcen*dent* Force/God/1st Principle) ...

(2) We then immediately see that the 1st Principle/Force/ Ground of everything *must be within ourselves, our consciousness.* This is because (i) it cannot be Matter/Objects—these are **nothing** (have only "Being for another," are not self-aware; are only "ideas" in me, "appearances" as conditioned by consciousness), and (ii) there can be no transcen*dent* "God" *outside* us (outside consciousness, the Cogito)—this is impossible. Therefore (iii) it can only be *within ourselves*—as an *Absolute I, Subject or Consciousness.*

(3) What follows from the existence of an *Absolute I* is the Knowledge of the Force (±). That is,

    a) As "absolute" it is not relative or related to anything else—to an Object or Other—but only to Itself (that is, it is not a "relative" or "finite" I): the *Absolute I* is hence a principle of *Absolute Freedom.* Thus in relating to (-) matter/the objective world (which is *nothing* in itself) it is relating only to *itself*—that is, it is *infinite* and *all reality* ... in that it "sees itself in its Object."

    b) Hence, the *separation* of (+) and (-)—or "consciousness *of* an object/matter"—must be an *illusion.*

    c) Hence: *There is only the Absolute I ... and nothing else* (and we all share it: *the One Consciousness*).

d) And the Absolute I = Absolute Knowledge = the *unity* of Subjectivity and Objectivity = The FORCE knowing Itself as All Reality, as the Whole—the POINT. Moreover, the Absolute I is transcendental or Apriori and hence entirely outside space and time and the physical universe, and thus in the Center of everything—and it is the basis of all Healing and all Power.

YOUR JEDI SCHELLING'S PROOF OF THE "ABSOLUTE I"

"The Absolute I is infinite, absolute power, contains all reality, is unconditioned, eternal and outside of time, the only substance, and is absolute bliss (as I = not I)." "Two *dependent* things require an *independent* thing to exist"

§90

My noble Padawan, the following simple yet devastating logic à la Schelling will show you what *alone* has true Being and is absolute or is *the* Absolute, and clearly reveal that beneath your "empirical" self you have a *pure/absolute Self*—shared by all selves:

(1) Normal experience demands an absolute or unconditioned *ground* in order to be. By "normal experience" I mean that of "the finite/conditioned/empirical subject or I *in relation to* the finite/conditioned object or world"; where subject and object are *conditioned* by each other, hence neither being *unconditioned*.

(2) *However* it is evident that this situation is *impossible* and cannot be *unless* at the same time something "unconditioned" (self-existent or absolute) exists, for conditioned beings do not have their existence *through themselves* and cannot maintain it by themselves, they are contingent and *dependent on an other*.

(3) Now, this unconditioned being that *must exist* for experience to be possible, must either be on the side of the *object*—as an "absolute Object or Not-I" (e.g. Matter or God)—or on that of the *subject*—as an "absolute Subject or I": *there is no third possibility*. Since an absolute Object *must* be ruled out there must then be an *absolute Subject or I as the ground of experience*. The former (no absolute object) is so because "one cannot abstract from or eliminate the I," and this rules out the possibility of

there being an "object" that is "absolute" or *not relative to* an other (to an I)—not to mention that an "object" as a "Being-for-another" has no true Being and = 0."

§91

This reveals something even more remarkable, my Padawan. For the conclusion is *not* that there is an "absolute I" that supports and makes possible experience (or "being-in-the-world") *and thus implying that three things exist,* viz., an absolute I, a finite I and a finite object. No. Rather the absolute I or *pure self-consciousness* is *all that is* and *exhausts all of reality.* Indeed what has been demonstrated is that the "finite I/finite object situation" is a completely false and untenable one, an *illusion* or *deception*, a

> "You may give me a thousand revelations of an absolute causality outside of myself … [but] my capacity even to assume an *absolute object* would presuppose that I had first abolished myself as a believing subject!"
> **Schelling**

condition from which one is to be released via true education (as your **Plato** has pointed out). Thus education—to put this in a different way—is the process whereby the "conscious" aspect of the universe/whole overcomes the "unconscious" part and appropriates to itself all the "being" the unconscious part was initially believed to contain. That is, normal or "dogmatist" consciousness views the whole of reality as apportioned between ourselves, the conscious part, and everything else, the unconscious or material part, which is (held to be) far more extensive than its counterpart. However, the incredible truth that Jedi Reason (or so-called "idealism/criticism") reveals is that *all the "being" believed to pertain to this vast unconscious domain of matter/object, since it has only a "Being-for-another," is an illusion or = 0*; and note that I did not say that *this domain* is an illusion, but that *the being of* this domain is an illusion. The result is that only the Conscious side *is*; *the Unconscious* side, stripped of its being (qua Being), having utterly vanished and been reduced to *the Conscious* side. Thus and in truth, *"Only the One Consciousness is."*

§92

Further important corollaries of this are: (i) this unconditioned absolute I/pure Self or God-Self is *eternal* or always existed, hence *consciousness as such*, as Jedi **Fichte** and others say, had no beginning—and did not "begin" with your physical birth—and has no ending; and (ii) once you have passed beyond your empirical I and accessed your Pure I you will find yourself *in or at the beginning of all things* or in the Now, i.e. eternal Now or Present. Thus, you further realize that you *always* existed and *always* will exist, that you can *only* **be** and never *not* be, and this is "Absolute Knowing," the knowledge that your *true self* is the Absolute itself, the Unconditioned. Hence as "eternal" you realize that you are above *time*, or rather that time itself is an *illusion* since it pertains to and is sustained by the finite I/Not-I experience and situation (cf. **Fichte** EPW 434, **Schelling** STI 14). Indeed, after your successful regress to the Absolute I and your true Jedi Self it will become crystal clear to you that *consciousness as such is not in time.*

§93

JEDI **KANT**. *Critique of Pure Reason, 1781.*

(1) The *Transcendental Analytic.* The birth and origin of "the Absolute I," the One Infinite Consciousness or Self that alone exists and is all Reality occurs right here in Kant's *Transcendental Deduction of the Categories,* where Kant states that "the 'I think' [the COGITO of **Descartes**] accompanies all of my representations (thoughts and perceptions)." According to Kant the T.U.A.—"transcendental unity of apperception" or simply "Self-consciousness"—is *self-grounded* and is *one and the same* in all representations. Further, it is "transcendental" and not "empirical." That is to say, it is *a priori* or *prior* to all experience, which means that there is nothing to distinguish *your* transcendental I (self or consciousness) from *mine.* Hence it is *one and the same* in every self; or there is only *ONE* transcendental Self or Consciousness—as Kant's disciple the Jedi **Fichte** says, "Any given self is itself the one ultimate substance (I 122)"—and hence we all share it; moreover, it is not in time.

§94

(2) Kant began the Method of scientific or absolute Knowing— which is a Knowing by Thinking via Concepts which contain the unity of Thought and Being, or Subject and Object: "I think the Concept of an Object." That is, a Concept is the source of all Objectivity or Reality. However Kant hit on only 12 Concepts or Categories or Thought-Being unities, and did not deduce or derive them in a scientific manner.

§95

(3) The *Transcendental Aesthetic*. With Kant's teaching we also come closer to an "Absolute I" by his removing one of the two things **Descartes** posited as existing *outside* his Cogito, which rendered it a "finite Cogito or I"—namely, the space-time-material world. That is, space and time for Kant are *transcendental* or have their seat or source in us, and do not exist independently of ourselves/our mind or subject. As Kant writes, "If our subject be removed ... space and time and all that they contain would vanish."

§96

All that now remained outside the Cogito, or circle of our consciousness, is God, as a so-called "Thing in itself"—which is a thing or being totally out of relation with our I or thinking and to be contrasted with a "Thing for us," which is anything that falls *within* our experience and *is* in relation with our I and Concepts, for example, this book you are reading.

To avoid the charge of atheism by the censors and critics, Kant suggested there may indeed be a "Thing in itself"—but in fact his principles do not allow it. So strictly speaking there is no "Thing in itself" for Kant (it is even inconceivable, as his successors pointed out). Hence One Reality, an Absolute I, is indeed *implicitly* there in Kant's doctrine, though not *explicitly*. Also for Kant Understanding (+) and Sensibility (-) were indeed united (as ±) but in an unclear way, and he did not possess an adequate understanding of Polarity (though an element of "triplicity" did appear in his table of categories).

§97

JEDI **FICHTE**. *The Doctrine of Science, 1794.*

(1) Fichte was the first to see clearly what **Kant** was implying with his T.U.A., and extracted it from **Kant's** *Critique* and renamed it the "Absolute I," making it the foundation of his "scientific" philosophy (*Wissenschaftslehre*) and his unique word for the Force; for according to Fichte, *"the Absolute I is all that ever was, is, and will be."* However Fichte's Absolute I was only Consciousness—and not Thought or the Concept, for both he and **Schelling** gave more primacy to (Intellectual) Intuition than to Thought.

"The thought of the *Thing-in-itself* should have been dispensed with long ago simply by realizing that *we* are the subject who thinks whatever it is we may be thinking, and thus that we can never encounter anything independent of us, *since everything is necessarily related to our thinking."* Fichte

(2) Fichte clearly repudiated the "Thing in itself," there being no such thing, since it is a non-thought and a self-contradiction. For example, "You cannot think what cannot be thought or what is supposed to be out of relation to your thought." (3) Fichte was also the first to make an advance on the absolute Method of Jedi Science by giving a deduction of Kant's categories or "Concepts of an Object/Not-I," but the deduction was incomplete and omitted many essential concepts.

§98

JEDI **SCHELLING**. *The System of Transcendental Idealism, 1800.*

(1) **Fichte** mishandled Nature (the (-) or Not-I) by not deducing or explaining its main forms. Schelling, a student of **Fichte**, supplied this lack by adding to **Fichte's** *Doctrine of Science (or Mind-Consciousness)* a *Science* or *Philosophy of Nature (or Matter).* He was the first to define the One Reality that alone is both as "the Absolute" (the Force) and as the UNITY of the Subjective (+) and the Objective (-)—that is, as the UNITY of Spirit (Consciousness/ Mind) and Nature, or the Subjective *subject/object* (±) and the Objective *subject/object* (±). Spirit and Nature, the two sides of the Force, therefore both express and contain the Truth of Polarity (±), the unity of opposites.

(2) Thus Schelling did indeed have Polarity or the Unity of opposites, but he did not develop it adequately and offered as did **Fichte** an inadequate and incomplete deduction of the Concepts and Method of Scientific Knowing.

§99

JEDI **HEGEL** *The Jedi System of Science, 1807, 1817.*

It was your Jedi Hegel (that is, the Truth or Force in him) who finally offered the best and most adequate version of Jedi SCIENCE, which in fact is nothing but the Truth's Knowledge of itself ... or the Force's, Being's, the Whole's Self-Knowledge. As Hegel says at *Encyclopedia* §574, "Philosophy, Jedi Science, is the Truth aware of itself, the self-knowing Truth (Idea or Force)."

(1) First, Hegel supplied an "Introduction" to Science (= Knowledge) which can commence only when the unity of Thinking and Being has been guaranteed, that is, with *Objective Thought* (or the *Absolute Concept*). This is a Thought-Thinking or Concept which is able to penetrate and reveal the inner essence of any and every Object. To do this, we must first get out of **Plato's** CAVE, the Dark Side of the Force, which implies there is a *separation* between ourselves (+) and what exists (-), Being-Truth-Reality, or between our Knowing and Thinking *and* its Object. Such a "separation" would make Thinking only subjective and formal and capable of Knowing the Object only as it is *for us*, but not as it is *in itself* (= Absolute Knowing (±), the Knowledge of the Force). The "Introduction" to Science provides the proof that sense-objects (-) are in themselves *nothing* and that Consciousness/Thinking or the "I" is *everything* or *all reality*—that the OBJECT of consciousness is *nothing* per se, or is really Consciousness or the Concept itself. Thus the Concept is absolute FREEDOM because it is everything and has *itself* in and as the essence of every Object.

§100

(2) Then Hegel added a *Science of Logic,* which contains the Method of Absolute Knowing and in which he completed the deduction of all the essential Concepts (Universals, Thought-determinations) which make up the One Absolute Concept—which, as Hegel says, *"is everything* ... [and whose] sole urge is to know and find itself *in everything."* Then, using the Method of the Concept—the U-P-I or Unity of Thought (+) and Being (-) Principle—Hegel created and developed the *Science of Nature* and the *Science of Jedi (Mind-Geist)*— which we will discuss in more detail in the next Section.

§101

With this achievement the history of philosophy is at an end. The FORCE has now achieved complete scientific Knowledge of itself (attained first in Religion). Your HISTORY is now over

"The History of the World travels from East to West, for Europe is absolutely *the end of History."* **Hegel**

or complete. All that remains is for all of your people to know the Truth, to be *Educated* into the Knowledge of the Force, as a Jedi and the Jedi Order, which already exists but is not known because of the Dark Side of the Force which currently rules your consciousness and planetary institutions. (For a more detailed account of How your Modern Jedi attained Jedi Science and the Knowledge of the Force see APPENDIX ONE).

THE POSTMODERN PERIOD

§102

Since your planet's History has ended—as you now possess the Knowledge of the Force and Jedi Science—the only purpose that "History" (events in theory or praxis) can have after this, is that of EDUCATION ... the education of all your people into the TRUTH, the Knowledge of the Force (by Science or Religion, as Discursive or Intuitive), so that all may benefit by it by becoming JEDI and experiencing the amazing JEDI ORDER. This will bring a permanent end to your perennial planetary crises, wars, hate, greed, poverty, disease and death. This "end-game" purpose on your planet is accomplished by a NEGATIVE *destructive* Postmodern phase of (post-) History, followed by a POSITIVE *constructive* Postmodern phase.

§103

The FACT is that the majority of your people are in one "form" or another still living in the CAVE and the Dark Side, especially under both the religious form that characterized your Medieval Period and the current "scientism" form whereby people, scientist and layperson alike, are so immersed in Dark Side Materialism and the (-) Senses that they are unable to see the (+) complementary Light Side of the Force.—The following presents a capsule review of your HISTORY and its meaning (see chart on p. 31):

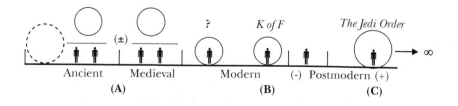

§104

Thus the first step is to overcome and negate this *separation* between yourselves *and* "God" or the Force, Heaven *and* Earth or the present *here and now* world. *This* is the sole function of the postmodern *negative-destructive* "God is Dead"/nihilistic phase of your planet's history. That is, the false far away, not *here* "God" and not *here* "Heaven" must be removed (by a so-called "death" of God), in order for the *true* God and *true* Heaven, as Here and Now and within or *ONE* with yourselves, to exist and be realized. The necessary destruction of the false "God" and transcendence began with the division of **Hegel's** disciples into Right wing THEISTS and Left wing ATHEISTS. It is important to realize that the advent of "atheism" and "atheists" is absolutely necessary for the realization of History's goal. The major atheists are, **David Strauss, Feuerbach, Marx, Darwin, Freud**—and **Friedrich *Nietzsche***, who serves as the Bridge from negative to positive Postmodernity, that is, from the "God is dead" and *Nihi*listic phase, to the advent of the Superman (the new God = JEDI, the union of God and Man) and the Eternal Return (*ewige Wiederkunft* = the JEDI ORDER, the union of Heaven and Earth). As your eminent theologian **Thomas Altizer** pointedly observed:

> "That reversal can be understood as occurring in the full sacrifice of the Godhead, for if that sacrifice is *the absolute negation of absolute transcendence*, its inevitable consequence is the realization of the very opposite of that absolute transcendence, *an opposite which is absolute immanence itself,* and an immanence only possible by way of the negation and reversal of absolute transcendence. The very advent of that immanence is inseparable from realization of the full and actual emptiness of absolute transcendence, an emptiness that is a truly alien emptiness, and one which is realized as *the Nihil itself* …. This is that absolutely new totality which so fully dawns in Postmodernity."

§105

What happened in brief was that the death of God (to *Nihi*lism) and the absence of God and the "Holy" in your world created a *vacuum* which at the right "time" becomes filled with the *New God* and *New Heaven* in unity with yourselves, as Jedi and the Jedi Order—the unity of opposites, of Eternity and Time, the Sacred and the

> "If it is the depths of the *Nihil* which in our world have evoked the most ultimate call, that call is finally a call to JOY itself, or a call to that joy released by the apocalypse of God, an apocalypse of God only possible by way of *the death of Godhead* itself." **Altizer**

Secular. This "time" is called "POSITIVE Postmodernity," which occurred in the 1960s with your political revolution (civil rights and feminism) and metaphysical-or-knowledge revolution with the rediscovery of the "Absolute I" and the "New God within." This Handbook will help your people shorten the period of pain and take you faster to the Goal of Positive Postmodernity, the JEDI ORDER.

§106

Because of its importance in helping you to understand your present situation and place in History in the Becoming of the Jedi Order, I will now discuss this in greater depth.

Negative Postmodernity: The end of History with the **A-Team's** achievement of Jedi Science and the Force's Knowledge of itself and the GOOD involved with it had to be universalized and experienced by your entire planet. This can only be accomplished by the *negation* of your Old Paradigm which regarded God and Heaven as Beyond and not here—that is, in order as we said to make them *Here* and *only* Here. This necessarily led to a period of uncertainty, disorientation and meaninglessness and ushered in what has been called "nihilism," and the "death of God"—which forces the move to the next and final period of your History. It is "final" because once everyone is brought into the Truth and a means has been put in place—namely the Jedi Educational-Cultural System—that enables all succeeding generations to come into the Truth, then there is nothing that remains to be done—except *celebrate*.

Positive Postmodernity: It is only, as your Jedi **Nietzsche** has said, when the energies of the given generation are strong enough to collectively "invert" the old values—as is the case with your present generation—that nihilism can be confronted and effectively overcome and the new paradigm and the amazing Jedi Order realized. The historical turning-point that signaled the transition from negative to positive Postmodernity was the tumultuous decade of your 1960s. I will zero in on three things.

§107

(1) As said, since the *End* of history—the Force's, Man's, or Being's *highest* consciousness—has *already* been attained in your planet's Old World—in Re-ligion and then in your **A-Team's Fichte-Schelling-**and-**Hegel**—and since this is an achievement that is *unsurpassable,* it follows that *all that Consciousness in the New World can do (and need do) is repeat or equal this achievement*—namely, the *re-discovery* of infinite subjectivity, the Absolute I, or "the God within" (but *now* on a universal or global scale). Of course a pre-condition for this Task is that the existentially felt *Need* to do it be present. And this is something that can happen only in the third and last period of a world-historical Spirit's (such as your America's) development, viz., that of the "Cognitive" or "Intellectual" phase, when the Spirit quits the OUTER world and turns INWARD (*"insich-gehen"*) to contemplate its Deed and acquire Knowledge of Itself.

Thus it is that before the "Need" for Self-Knowledge can arise or *be felt*, the Spirit must develop itself *outwardly*, first, by re-fashioning nature in its own image (its initial "Agrarian" phase), and second, by consolidating itself e.g. by overcoming natural *divisions* within itself (e.g., your Civil War), and only then entering into History (and its "Military" phase) and taking on, overcoming, and assimilating the previous world-historical Spirit (viz., the Germanic) and its wealth and achievements. This "Intellectual" or knowledge-seeking period began, as mentioned, after the Second World War (the *end* of its Military phase; a view shared by your **William Barrett** and others).

§108

(2) It was the "counter-culture" of the (1950s and) 1960s that decisively inaugurated your History's final process of the "negation of the negation" and History's entry into *Affirmation*, that is, the "total affirmation of *all* things," namely The Jedi Order.

> (Regarding the "negation of negation": the "first negation" was the negation of the Old God and meaning that issued in "negative, nihilistic postmodernity;" the "second negation" is simply the act/activity of *negating this first negation and its result*, viz., negative postmodernity and its *Meaning- (and Value-) lessness*; which results in the New God-Man unity (Jedi) and Heaven-Earth unity (the Jedi Order) and *New Meaning— qua* Total Affirmation *and the final end* of all negativism,

negation and negativity—that positive postmodernity is to bring in.)

Now the "vanguard" of the counter-culture (the Force's or Spirit's *self-awareness*) saw clearly that the Old Paradigm and its God-concepts, values, etc, were exhausted, obsolete, had been negated and were no longer sustaining and, further, that the materialist/consumerist values that took their place (for an apparent lack of anything better) were vacuous and self-deceptive. Thus with unrestrained enthusiasm and absolute self-confidence your Spirit threw itself into the task of satisfying its Need for something higher, deeper and of true substance, namely, The Truth, the Absolute I, and the God Within.

§109

(3) To answer this Need the Spirit drew readily from the *sources* that were made available just for this purpose. Namely from (i) the Arts—and music especially. In the "hippie" vanguard it was the **Beatles** above all who were the principal Voice of the new Spirit and for the expression of both its pain and needs (cf., *Eleanor Rigby*) and Self-Revelations—it was the music of absolute freedom and *Absolute I* (e.g., "now that you know who you are, what do you want to be? Baby you're a rich man too," etc). (ii) The Spiritual Literature (and marriage) of the East and West; especially the writings of e.g. **Alan Watts** and **Aldous Huxley**, and those of the Eastern "gurus" and "masters," such as **Sri Aurobindo** and **Meher Baba** that appeared on every coffee table—all of them unmistakably containing and disseminating in their own way the Jedi Teaching and Truth that *"We are the Force, the Absolute, the Truth itself."* (iii) Mind altering/Consciousness expanding drugs, such as hashish, mescaline and LSD, which provided direct evidence and experience of "the God within" or an Absolute I or larger Self that underlay one's "normal" isolated empirical self or "ego" (please note that we Jedi in no way intend to encourage the irresponsible use of these potentially extremely dangerous drugs and chemicals). Lastly (iv) Philosophy itself. The new Spirit, with its insatiable thirst for Truth turned once again to the **A-Team** and especially your Jedi **Hegel's** writings (long neglected because the Need for them was not yet present) and in high spirits slowly began applying itself to the difficult yet all-important task of penetrating their meaning and thereby raising itself to the level of the previous Spirit; thus it was only then that the "Hegel Society of America" could and did appear—i.e., after **Hegel's**

total eclipse and banishment since the turn of the century by the hegemony of your "analytic" and "linguistic" (non-) philosophy.

§110

The decades after the 60s and the explosive advent of positive postmodernity, the 70s, 80s and 90s, were mainly "reactionary" for your Spirit needed to "recover from its excesses," its quantum leap and abundance of revelations (the "shock" administered to your Old status quo), and adjust itself accordingly. It is, as your people say, a matter of "two steps forward and one step back." The early 90s, with the **Clinton** era, was the start of the next step forward, etc. The advent of the new millennium—and the year and symbol "2000"— had, and will continue to have, a positive renewing and energizing effect on your Spirit that is making its way into the Jedi Order and helping it in its *necessary* transformational work, breaking through the sludge of ignorance and the Dark Side and illuminating the Jedi Order.

§111

In sum, the meaning of the present time is that you stand at a Crossroads or Juncture, at the unique point where the Old Order has already been "in and for itself" negated and, since your people cannot go *back* to it—for it cannot satisfy the needs of your Spirit—they are thus compelled to go *forwards*. You are in the midst of negating this negation, i.e., of establishing the *New immanent Meaning* that will replace the Old lost meaning and collectively bring in and realize the glorious Jedi Order, or what your religions call "Kingdom Come" and so forth. It will happen—and this is the way it always happens—first by a relatively small group and vanguard among your people reaching a "critical mass," which will then lead to a "chain reaction" that will pave the way for the "instantaneous" global transformation and realization to occur. The *mandate* for your present age is therefore this: That your people do all that they can to hasten the process and arrive at the glorious goal as quickly as possible and thus with the least damage and trauma to your children and your brothers and sisters—your truly beloved, sacred and immortal race.

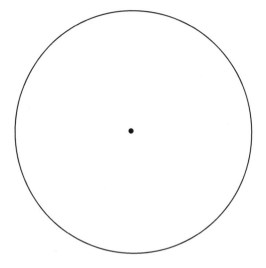

II. JEDI SCIENCE

INTRODUCTION

§112

Noble Reader we have seen how your own Jedi attained the Knowledge of the Force in SECOND CUSP, which completed your HISTORY, and that you are fast approaching THIRD CUSP when all of your people will be united in the knowledge of the POINT, the ONE CONSCIOUSNESS, the JEDI ORDER. (Note: A "Cusp" refers to a critical "turning point" or "paradigm shift" in your History and people's consciousness. "First Cusp" occurred with your transition from your Ancient to Medieval Periods (from many to One God/Force), "Second Cusp," with your transition from your Medieval to Modern Periods, from the Age of *Faith* to the Age of *Reason*, climaxing in Jedi SCIENCE. Finally "Third Cusp" refers to the transition that is occurring right now from your Modern to *positive* Postmodern Periods, which ends with the full actualization and *experience* by all of your people of the glorious JEDI ORDER.)

§113

Now it is time to give you a deeper knowledge of *what* the FORCE itself is and *why* the FORCE is and must be by giving you an overall accurate understanding of JEDI SCIENCE itself, the basis for true Global Jedi Education and the healing of your planet. This will be an account of the FORCE's knowledge or Science of *itself,* which has two parts: first the *Introduction,* where we attain to a knowledge of the Force-Truth-POINT, and then *Science proper or in detail,* where we study the process and stages of its Becoming, the movement up **Plato's** Divided Line, from (-) OUTER-Nature to (+) INNER-Consciousness and the Jedi Order as (±).

The order of topics will be (1) Polarity and the PROOF of The FORCE, and its consequences, (2) Jedi Science itself, and the difference between Jedi Science and your own sciences, and (3) The meaning of Religion, and the Unity of Religion and Science.

THE PRINCIPLE OF **POLARITY**

§114

First, to understand what the Force is and why it is we must become acquainted with the important Principle of POLARITY, or the Unity of opposites or "identity-in-difference," which is used in the Proof of the Force as well as in Jedi Science and its Method of Knowing.

The Polarity principle was discovered early on in your History and developed by various Jedi—**Heraclitus**, **Pythagoras**, **Aristotle**, **Nicolas of Cusa**, and **Niels Bohr** in the West, and known as "yin and yang" in the East—but it was the **A-Team** who perfected it.

§115

The universal law of Polarity states that the inner truth of any *two* apparently separate opposites is an underlying original *unity.* As your saying is, "You can't have one without the other," or "It takes two to tango." That is, the Truth is the ultimate inseparability or *unity* of opposites or opposed determinations. Moreover, each *is* only so far as the other *is;* and each *is* only so far as it is *not* the other.

§116

This basic Truth of polarity is best illustrated by an ordinary "bar magnet"— see Figure 1.

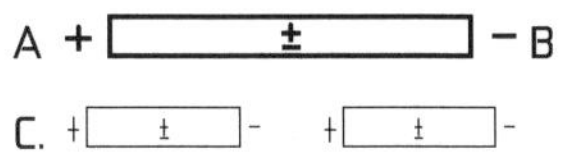

Figure 1.

A and **B**, the positive and negative poles of a magnet, both seem separate and able to exist apart—just as your "I" seems separate and cut off from the universe/Being/the Object. But the truth is *they are not*. The truth of the separated extremes/opposites is their unity or indifference point (±). The extremes (and their manifestation) just express what is contained *in* the Truth, what the Unity is composed of, its "moments" or elements.

So, what is hard to see is not just that the opposites need each other to *be* themselves—are interdependent and involved in each other's concept—but that they are in themselves *identical or the same*. This is seen when we "break" the bar magnet in the middle at its "indifference point" (see **C.**). We then have two magnets, where the right pole on the left magnet is negative while the left pole on the right magnet is positive. Hence what follows is that the selfsame *single indifference point—* indivisible, unextended, dimensionless—of the original magnet must have contained and contains both *opposite* poles or terms *within itself.*

§117

Other examples of Polarity and the unity of opposites are: SELF-OTHER (thus neither Self nor Other exist, rather only their Unity, which is the True Infinite, e.g., "I" am other to the other, etc.), subject-object, inner-outer, ideal-real, finite-infinite, conscious-unconscious, thought-matter, cause-effect, identity-difference, form-matter, whole-part, active (sperm)-passive (egg), masculine-feminine, father-son, right-duty, up-down, on-off, full-empty, and solid-space.

"[The] examples of above and below, right and left, father and son, and so on *ad infinitum*, all contain *opposition* in each term ... Father is the other of son, and son the other of father, and each only *is* as this other of the other ... *their being is a single subsistence.*" **Hegel**

Take "inside-outside" or "subject-object." Each concept has its opposite in itself. For no inside, no outside; no subject, no object.

You cannot have an "outside" without an "inside." "Outside" is meaningless by itself and only has "sense" when in correlation with an "inside"—which *must* exist alongside it and *at the same time*. So the Truth is the "subject-object," the unity of the two (±).

§118

Thus we see that there must be a *unity* or interdependence behind these terms—in fact a *living* unity, not a static one. They are in essence, *two sides of a single thing*, of a whole. They are a "two-ness in oneness." You cannot isolate them; for as isolated they lose their *meaning* and hence their *being* as well.

—Notice my Padawan that two powers are involved. *Verstand* or *Intellect* is the principle of the extremes or opposites; it allows us to see them in their *difference*. *Vernunft* or *Reason* is the principle of their *identity* or *point of indifference*; it is the power that dissolves their separateness or twoness and makes them one. This further involves the *activity* (tension, life, germinating "seed") of producing the opposites and then annulling and unifying them. There is a movement *outwards* into difference and separation; and a movement *inwards* back into unity and non-difference. The point is that *both movements and aspects are necessary*. Or, to have unity you must have difference, to have difference you must have unity. Thus, "You can't have one without the other." Without this "tension" you cannot have life—indeed, you can't have *anything at all*.

> "Pure Knowing is the UNITY which is not abstract but a living, concrete unity since in this unity the opposition in consciousness between a self-determined entity, a SUBJECT, and a second such entity, an OBJECT, is known to be overcome ... [the two] are known to be *inseparable*." **Hegel**

§119

The Law of Polarity governs and is active throughout all levels of the universe and most importantly is responsible for *the basic division* of the Whole, the One Force, into two sides: into a Subjective and Objective, Conscious and Unconscious, I and Not-I side—in a word, into an *Inner Force* and an *Outer Force*. Hence, what is—a la Polarity or Indifference—is *not* an independent Subject (You) standing in opposition to an equally independent Object (the world), but instead and in truth a single *Subject/Objectivity*. A Subject-Object Unity or Whole in which conscious and unconscious (matter) totally *interpenetrate* each other (±)—but with the Inner, Conscious, or *Subjective* side retaining the upper hand—for the "real (the visible) is ideal, the ideal (invisible) real." In Jedi **Hegel's** words:

> The *Science of Logic* demonstrates ... that the subjective that is supposed to be merely subjective, the finite that is supposed to be merely finite, and the infinite that is supposed to be merely infinite, and so on, *do not have any truth;* they contradict themselves and pass over into their opposites. As a result, the passing-over and the UNITY, in which the extremes are present as cancelled, reveals itself as their Truth. ... [Furthermore] the infinite only appears to be *neutralized* with the finite, just as the subjective is neutralized with the objective, and thinking with being. But in the *negative* unity of the Idea (the Force), the infinite *overgrasps* the finite, thinking *overgrasps* being, subjectivity *overgrasps* objectivity. [Thus] the UNITY of the Idea IS *SUBJECTIVITY*, or Thinking, or Infinity (*Enc.* §§214r, 215r).

And thus the Force or the Idea is INFINITE SUBJECTIVITY and INFINITE INWARDNESS, which contains Objectivity and Externality dissolved within itself.

§120

Thus in the highest kind of Polarity, that of the Force's two sides— the Light Side (+)/the Dark Side (-), Consciousness/Matter, Inner/Outer, Subject/Object—it is the *first* side (+) that trumps the *second* (-). The *first* absorbs, has priority or predominates over the *second*, while yet containing it within itself as dissolved. Why? Because for example Consciousness is *Reality* while Matter is *nothing*. This is so because while Consciousness knows that it exists or is self-aware, Matter does not: Consciousness has a "Being for itself," Matter only a "Being for another," for a Consciousness. Therefore, it is true that Matter is *necessary*—since, by Polarity, you cannot have one without the other, thus there *must* be Matter. BUT MATTER HAS NO TRUE BEING.—"True Being" can only pertain to a Being that is self-aware, a Being that is *aware* of its Being; as "the I" in "I think therefore I AM."

THE PROOF OF THE FORCE

§121

This proof will answer the question, Why must the Universe, Man, and God exist? It is a much abbreviated version of the more elaborate and detailed proof found in e.g. the Jedi **Hegel's** *Science of Logic* and **Fichte's** *Doctrine of Science*. NOTE: Since each of the Steps in the Proof is *necessary*, everything happens *at once*—or in *Eternity* or the *Eternal Now.*

§122

Noble Padawan, we shall now understand why Polarity necessitates that the Whole, the Force, the Universe divides itself into two sides, whose truth is their unity or middle; and further why there *must* be a Force or a Universe in the first place—and not nothing at all. And in the interest of giving you a well-rounded introductory understanding and initiation into *the Knowledge of the Force,* I will present *two* different but interrelated Proofs of the Force.

THE FIRST PROOF OF THE FORCE

§123

ONE. Jedi Reason says (1) it is impossible that *nothing at all* exist. This is because nothing as such is inconceivable—as polarity requires—apart from something or being (it is arrived at by starting with something, a thing or thought, and then negating it).—As your Jedi philosopher **Spinoza** among others said, *what cannot be conceived can in nowise be.* Thus, there must be something or Being; this is also known by the fact that given we or something exists now, something must have *always* existed.

(2) Now Reason further teaches that only two types of Being are conceivable, "extended" and "unextended"; there can be no third. A "being" can only be an extended one (a "body") or an unextended one (a "thought").

Thus the first type has dimensions, occupies space, is visible/ sensible/divisible, has parts, is unconscious and a many; the second type, following polarity, is the opposite and is not in space, invisible, indivisible, thought, consciousness, and is one.

§124

The whole of what is, of Being or, in Jedi language, The Force, can therefore be said to be composed of the *outer universe* and the *inner universe*. Or simply, an INNER domain and an OUTER domain; in the Outer everything exists outside of everything else, hence a multiplicity or many prevails; in the Inner everything is internal, hence a one. Some may think (your own scientists) that the Outer domain or the Outside can exist by itself, with no need for an Inner domain. But polarity teaches that is an impossibility, for "outside" is conceivable, has meaning, and can exist only along with "inside." To say, "Everything is outside," is meaningless; it is like saying "Everything is up." Or "Only up exists." Or "The north pole of a magnet can exist without a south pole." Hence "up" is relative (or polar) and can only *be* if "down" exists *at the same time.*

§125

(3) Reason also shows that only the INNER domain has True BEING, while the OUTER domain is in fact NOTHING or appearance only. For the Outer is a realm of "objects" that are unconscious and divisible; an "object" only exists for a subject, a consciousness, and does not exist for itself, i.e. it is not aware that it exists, hence for itself it is *nothing*. Only that which *knows* that it exists (has a being "for itself"), such as a subject or self, has true being. Also, as Jedi **Aristotle** and **Aquinas** taught, "being" is the same as "unity," and since everything in the Outer realm is divisible, all that occupies it can have no unity hence being, i.e., its being is illusory. True unity only exists in the Inner invisible realm which therefore alone IS. Furthermore, this Inner realm, or Consciousness, *pervades* the entire Outer or Unconscious realm (of nothing)—hence is *infinite subjectivity*. This means "there *is* only One Consciousness"—that is, that *subjectivity* is *not* limited by any *object*, totally absorbing and penetrating the object through and through; "grokking" or knowing the secret truth of the object's *nothingness*.

> "The Object presented itself to the Self as a vanishing ... self-consciousness knows the *nothingness of the Object* ... because it posits *itself* as object, or the object as itself."
> **Hegel**

§126

(4) With this key fact connecting Being with "self-aware being" (or consciousness) Reason gives us a second proof for the Inner-Outer division of The Force. Namely: The simple fact that there must be Being and cannot be Nothing necessitates that this Being, simply in order to *be*, also be "conscious." For if the Being were not conscious or aware *of* its Being (*that* it existed) it would not be Being but rather Nothing or the same as Nothing, as we just discovered (for it would only have being for us, but not for itself). Thus for Being to *be*, there must be consciousness or an Inner. However, for *consciousness* to be, there must be an Object, a Nature or an Outer. Thus, simply starting with Being, we see that Being must of necessity (simply to *be*) split itself into two sides, a subject and an object, an Inner and an Outer.

§127

TWO. But the Truth of Being's two sides, Inner and Outer is, by the law of Polarity, their middle or indifference point. This is the KEY POINT: We see that there *must* be an Inner (Subject) and there *must* be an Outer (Object). *However,* the fact that the one cannot exist (be or be conceived) without the other means that they are not *two things* but rather *two sides of a single thing* (The Force). The all-crucial consequence of this is the following:

It is therefore this *unity* alone (or "indifference point") at the core of the single thing that alone exists, that is the Truth of both the Inner and Outer realms—the realm of invisible thought-consciousness and that of visible matter in space and time. Note that if the Inner and Outer were in fact conceivable *apart from* each other this would not be true, their identity or point of unity would *not* be their truth.

§128

THREE. The crucial next step is to see, as required by Polarity, that not only is the Truth of both the Inner and Outer domains the mid-point or indifference point, the *identity* of both, but that *"Man"—you—are precisely and nothing but this very IDENTITY and truth.* This is directly evident in the fact that *you* are precisely the unity or inseparability of Inner and Outer—that is, of Soul and Body, Thought and Extension, Mind and Matter, Unity (Self/ Consciousness) and Multiplicity (Body, organs, cells). Thus "Man" or

JEDI is the singular Truth (±) of the Whole, of the two domains of *the indifference Point;* hence a JEDI is the synthesis of Inner/Outer, Invisible/Visible as a Soul/Body, Form/Matter *Unity.* A Jedi is the "microcosm" of infinite Nature, the "macrocosm," and sums up and contains within himself, as Body, the entire contents of Nature—space, time, matter, motion, gravity, light, shape, magnetism, electricity, chemism, life, sensation and thought. Her Body *is* Infinite Nature—thus her Soul not only pervades her Body but all of nature, the infinite universe as well, since Body (qua microcosm) is Nature. Hence her Jedi Mind and Will dominate and extend into all of physical nature, to infinity. A Jedi has incredible powers and abilities, as we shall see.

> "The Soul is the universal *immateriality of matter* ... it pervades everything and does not merely exist in the individual." **Hegel**

§129

Hence, this is your true identity or who you really are. And when you have achieved full awareness of this, you become a JEDI. In expanded form we can say that there really is no such thing as "Man" or "human being." What really exists is the One Force—which is by necessity and cannot not be—which has two sides, the Inner and Outer. You yourselves are the meeting point of the Force's two sides hence are inherently the Force itself. *But* there are two states or conditions of the Force: (1) the Force as aware of itself, and (2) the Force as not yet aware of itself (or aware of itself only as "human," man or woman, Jane, Peter, American, accountant, etc). History in effect is nothing but the process of the Force moving from condition (2) to condition (1).

§130

Also important: A "Jedi" is precisely the Force *as aware of Itself.* Thus there is a crucial distinction (more later) between a "Jedi" and "The Force itself." There is a sense in which a Jedi both is and is not the Force. A Jedi is not the Force or the Truth *as such* but **the awareness that the Force has of Itself.** This seems trivial, but it is not. You yourself—as a particular person, self, or "ego" (Mary or Paul)—are not the cause of or responsible for and thus cannot "take credit" for reality being the way it is; that is, for the FACT that there is and must be the universe, i.e., the One Force or Truth, having an Inner and Outer,

Conscious/Unconscious, I/Not-I side. Or, that you are in truth the Force's consciousness of itself is not your own doing. It is a fact, a given. But it is nevertheless great news and a thing to celebrate. (It is necessary to say this to avoid the error involved in the potential misconstrual of the teaching, "We are God. You are God.")

§131

This is the true meaning of what all your Religions call "God," as Jedi **Spinoza**, **Hegel** and others have proved. That is, The Force is what is eternal, what must be and what alone is, and this is equivalent to God. The popular idea of "God" as a separate, transcendent, "Creator" is false and logically impossible since a separation between an *infinite* God and a *finite* man and world is a contradiction. There is no "thing in itself" (à la Jedi **Kant**), since it is inconceivable and the Infinite must be here and now and not somewhere else (cf. for example, "The kingdom of God (or God) is *within* you"). *However* the real truth behind the "Creator/creation" idea, and especially the God/man-ego difference is that (1) the "Creator" is what must be *by necessity*, the Eternal Principle, which you, as a particular person, cannot take credit for. (2) And yes, the Principle is superior to and antedates you as "human ego." But when you become or realize your JEDI Self, you *are* the Principle—that is to say, you are not strictly the Principle or Force Itself (as its eternal laws and necessity) but are rather *the awareness* the Principle/Force has of Itself; you are a unique expression or manifestation *of* the Principle/Force. Yet there is also a sense in which You (as a "*Thou*") *are* one and the same as the Force Itself, *since there is nothing but the Force and its modes or aspects*—again as Jedi **Christ** says, "The Father (the Force) *in* me, He doeth the works," and "I and the Father (the Force) are one," and "Who has seen *me*, has seen the Father (the Force)." In any case rank *egotism* and the lower self is entirely banished with this teaching and Truth; for what you *really are* is the Infinite, the Whole, and not a *particular* finite self—and there are no grounds for putting yourself above others (and for inferiority-superiority complexes), but only for equality, for "I = I = I = I."

§132

FOUR. Thus in what preceded is found the explanation for why the universe exists, what the universe is, and who you are. (1) There cannot be nothing so there is something. (2) This something or one thing—name it "Being," "the Truth," "the Force"—has of necessity, as per *polarity*, two sides or domains which are fused or one, an Inner and an Outer. (3) You, as conscious beings (a.k.a. "Man"), *are and can only be* this one being (as the unity of inner and outer) which must be and cannot not be, though you do not, initially, know yourselves to be It, the Force. When you have risen to this knowledge or awareness—have been properly "e-ducated" or "healed"—you have then become the Force *aware of Itself*, that is, *Jedi and the Jedi Order.*

§133

In sum: what is central to all this is that it reveals clearly and exactly *who you really are*—and what you should aspire to and should be your goals in education, life, business, government, and so on.

YOU ARE NOT "EGO/HUMAN," ET AL—YOU ARE A JEDI. YOU ARE THE ETERNAL FORCE— THE TRUTH, THE WHOLE—AWARE OF ITSELF. BORN FOR ETERNAL LIFE and EXISTENCE.

The Second Proof of the FORCE

§134

ONE. Let's start from "scratch" as you would say, that is, from NOTHING—and from the Question, Why is there something rather than nothing at all? Or: Is it possible for *nothing* to exist—that there be nothing at all in existence? No Universe, planets, life, matter, no consciousness or conscious beings, no "God(s)," and so on? PURE NOTHING?

§135

TWO. Reason says, No. For "nothing" cannot be or be conceived without "something," a being or thing. "Nothing" is the absence of all, of any determination, but (1) to think and have this "absence of all" you must first have a "determination"—and then *negate* it or think it away. So "nothing" *presupposes* determination or something.

(2) Also, "nothing" itself is a determination or a something. Hence, there cannot be mere *nothing* ... there *must* be something or being.—Also, to think "no-thing" you must first think/have "thing," and then negate it. So "nothing" presupposes "thing" or "being" and is impossible without it. Sheer "nothing" or nothingness cannot be or be conceived.

§136

THREE. So, sheer nothing is an impossibility. There cannot be nothing or nothing at all. Therefore there *must* be "something" or "being."

The next question is: What exactly is the *nature* of this "Being that must be and cannot not be"? Can this something or being that *must* necessarily be, be or exist without *knowing* that it exists—without being *conscious* of its existence?

Again, Reason says No. This is impossible. For a "being" that existed but was not aware that it existed would be the same as *nothing*, or the same as if nothing at all existed—which as we saw, cannot be.

—Again, keep in mind we are starting from nothing, so yourself as an "observer" to all this, does not yet exist. So you must forget about, abstract from, ignore your own existence—hence the fact that, yes, the being that now must exist, does exist *for you*.

§137

FOUR.—Noble Padawan, now understand that the remainder of the Proof and Deduction is nothing but the deriving of the "conditions" (the world, man, history, etc.) that are necessary for the BEING that must be to become SELF-CONSCIOUS, which *must* occur.

—Thus the Being that must exist, must also be *conscious* of itself, must *know* that it exists or have SELF-CONSCIOUSNESS. And this is only possible if there is first CONSCIOUSNESS.
Hence, there *must* be **CONSCIOUSNESS**.

> [NOTE that another way we could have reached this stage and conclusion, is by having started with "unconsciousness" instead of with "nothing" ("unconsciousness" is a variant of "nothing").

As in: "Can What Is be 'unconscious'? Or, "Can unconsciousness exist? The answer would be, No—and by the principle of Polarity: "you can't have one without the other." Unconsciousness presupposes consciousness, and cannot be or be conceived without consciousness.—Hence there must be *two sides* to What Is: a Conscious side and an Unconscious side (and there is and can be no "third"). But what is most significant is that it is impossible even to conceive "unconscious/ness," and hence, *There is only consciousness.* Therefore, Consciousness is *infinite*—is All in All.]

§138

This necessary and eternal Three-Moment *Process* that is BEING— which first reveals what "Man" is, who You are—can be simply expressed as: The movement of the POINT [1] From BEING (**IS**), [2] To Conscious BEING (**IS as aware**), [3] To Self-conscious BEING (**IS as self-aware**) (in this, as Jedi **Schelling** and **Hegel** insist, is also revealed the true meaning of the Christian "Trinity"). This Process is, in Jedi language, the movement: [1] From The FORCE, [2] To EGO or "Man," [3] To JEDI—or The FORCE as JEDI. Or, what is the same thing, from the **U**niversal to the **P**articular to the **I**ndividual, which three are also *inseparable*—which means that this movement or transformation *happens at once. ALSO, since this is what is really going on it may help if you, Jedi Reader, for a while stop using and drop the names "Man" and "God" altogether, which carry considerable baggage.*

§139

FIVE. So, there must be a Being, a something, that is *conscious of itself,* or has *self-consciousness*—otherwise if it did not, it would have a "being *for us* alone" and not a "being for *itself*," hence would be *nothing* for or to itself, hence would be the same as *nothing,* which cannot *be.* So, the Being that must be *must* be self-conscious.

However self-consciousness is not possible without and hence presupposes *consciousness.* And consciousness (or Awareness) is possible only if there is an OBJECT of consciousness, a resistance. Otherwise the ray or line of consciousness would extend or continue on forever and never encounter anything and would not be conscious OF something, hence there could *be* no *consciousness* at all—hence no self-consciousness and, more significantly, no being, or nothing at all—which is impossible. *And this means a difference in the One or Being—a split or separation (into + and –).—* As Polarity teaches: no consciousness without its opposite: unconsciousness-matter (object, many). And as your Jedi **Spinoza** says: All determination is negation. Or, "It takes two to tango."

§140

SIX. So, according to Reason there *must* be a Being with *two* opposite (or "polar") sides.

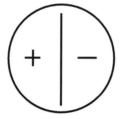

"The FORCE" is the name we Jedi give to the BEING that must be and cannot *not* be; we call the Being's two polar opposite sides "the Light Side" and "the Dark Side" (which also have a second meaning, we will see). The *Light Side,* which we represent as "+", being the side of REALITY, is the side of (in the language of your planet) *Consciousness,* which is also *One, Inner, Unextended, Invisible* and *Indivisible.* The *Dark Side,* represented as "-", as the side of NOTHING, is the side of Unconsciousness/Matter, which is also *Many, Outer, Extended, Visible and Divisible.*

§141

SEVEN. But again, as Polarity teaches, the Truth of the *two* sides (+) and (-) is their UNITY and inseparability, which we represent as (±) and is illustrated by the Magnet. It is this Unity which alone exists or is REAL.

This is an important point that illuminates the key principle of Unity-*in*-opposition, Identity-*in*-Difference. That is, the *difference* (the two sides) is just as important and essential as the *Unity*—or the Unity cannot *be* without the Difference. Yet nevertheless the Unity "*trumps*" the difference or opposites, being their Truth.

In other words: There must of necessity *be* difference or *two* distinct sides to Reality, the Whole, or What IS—for example, Consciousness and Matter, Mind (Spirit) and Nature, me and the world, Self and Other, Subject and Object, Inner and Outer, Unity and Multiplicity, Soul and Body, and so on. But their sole Truth is their UNITY: for by Polarity, one cannot *be* without the other.—*A corollary of this is that there cannot be **only** one side to What IS—which means that neither side is **reducible** to the other;* for example (+) to (-), which would make Matter (-) the sole Reality—which is called "Materialism" on your planet, a major error of your sciences.

§142

Two further important points:

(1) Even though the Truth of the two sides is their Unity (±) and the consciousness side e.g. cannot exist without the material side, it is nonetheless the case that *within* this Unity it is *consciousness* (+) that predominates over or "trumps" matter/unconsciousness (-). This is because the former (+) *knows that it is* and hence is alone REALITY or True Being, while the latter (-) *does not* and hence is NOTHING— or has only a "Being-for-Another" (namely, for consciousness) and not a "Being-for-itself": as a mere Object, it lacks the *self-awareness* of a Subject or "I."

§143

(2) Not only is Consciousness (+) *Reality* and Matter (-) *Nothing* within the Unity of the One Being (The Force) that alone is and must be. But—again and because of Polarity—Consciousness is and can be only ONE and is hence also Infinite. Or: There is only ONE CONSCIOUSNESS—ONE INFINITE CONSCIOUSNESS (which your own Jedi, as we'll see, call the "Absolute I" or "Transcendental Unity of Self-Consciousness," among other things).—Consciousness is only ONE and not multiple or divisible because while *Matter* (-) is extended, hence divisible, many and has parts, *Consciousness* (+), its "polar opposite," can only be unextended, indivisible— hence cannot be split or have parts—and absolutely ONE and POINT-like.—Again as your Jedi **Schrödinger** says: "It is not possible that this unity of knowledge, feeling and choice which you call *your own* should have sprung into being from nothingness at a given moment not so long ago; rather this knowledge, feeling and choice are essentially *eternal and unchangeable* and numerically *one* in all men ... [Therefore] you—and all other conscious beings as

such—*are all in all.* Hence this life of yours which you are living is not merely a piece of the entire existence, but is in a certain sense *the Whole.*"

Moreover, this One Infinite Consciousness as indivisible is not only a **single POINT** (an Absolute I or Transcendental Unity of Apperception) at the center of all things, but is also **APRIORI** and outside space, time, and the universe. It is the source and seat of *all* consciousness and of every Self or Jedi. As a consequence of this FACT *every I or Self*—no matter how great the distance between any two Selves—*occupies this One self-same POINT* (+) and *looks out* upon the sense-world-Universe of extended Matter (-) *precisely from this One self-same POINT.* It is what everyone has in common; all the people on your planet share this same ONE CONSCIOUSNESS and in the ETERNAL TIMELESS PRESENT.

§144

Thus this *One* Infinite Consciousness (the INNER) totally pervades its polar opposite, the Dark Side of infinite Matter or Extension (the OUTER). This is because (+) and (-) are *inseparable,* meaning that wherever there is Matter (-) there is Consciousness (+) as well. Therefore Consciousness is *Infinite,* hence All in All, since not only is it *Reality,* as self-aware, but it is everywhere and not in any way limited by Matter which, as shown, is Nothing—as your **Quantum physicists** and **psychologists** are starting to realize; see e.g. **Goswami's** *The Self-Aware Universe,* **Wolf's** *Taking the Quantum Leap,* and **Grof's** *The Holotropic Mind.* Your Cambridge physicist **Sir James Jeans** himself states that, "The old dualism of mind and matter ... seems likely to disappear, not through matter becoming in any way more shadowy or insubstantial than heretofore, or through mind becoming resolved into a function of the working of matter, but through substantial MATTER resolving itself into a *creation and manifestation* of MIND."

§145

EIGHT. We said in step SEVEN that the Truth of Being's two sides is their UNITY, which means that they can *never* come apart. This means that their *separate* existence—or the belief that they *can* come apart or exist in separation—is an *illusion.* This error and mind-set your Jedi **Plato** calls "the CAVE"—while we Jedi call it "The Dark Side of the Force," using this expression in its *second meaning*. It is the prime cause of an *imbalance* of the Force on a given planet, and the cause of all problems.

ON THE DARK SIDE OF THE FORCE

§146

Now there are *two* senses or meanings of *The Light Side of the Force* and *The Dark Side of the Force*, which we shall distinguish by lower and upper case letters. ONE: As distinct elements or components of the One Force/Being (±): The "Light Side" (+) simply refers to Consciousness, Inner, One, Indivisible, Being-for-itself. Whereas The "Dark Side" (-) simply refers to Matter/UnConsciousness, Outer, Many, Divisible, Being-for-another. TWO: As indicating the two states of TRUTH and ERROR, as used in: "You must turn from the DARK SIDE to the LIGHT SIDE of the Force." (a) The "LIGHT SIDE" here refers to the TRUTH, Reality, What IS, namely, the UNITY of Opposites—the Fact that the two (subject/object) sides of the Force, the Light Side and Dark Side (as components), can never come apart (±). It also refers to, the "BALANCED FORCE," meaning that the Force as such is eternally Balanced. Yes, there *is* difference or opposition or *two* things; but also a Unity *underlying* the difference which trumps it. Again, There must be *difference*, and There must also be *Unity*. (b) The "DARK SIDE" refers to the ignorance or unawareness of the Truth, hence to the ERROR of the DIS-UNITY of Opposites and the belief that the two sides of the Force *can* come apart, etc. The DARK SIDE is the belief in the *two* or *difference*, while being ignorant of the *Unity*. It is symbolized by (+|-) and also means the "IMBALANCED FORCE."

§147

The two dominant forms of the DARK SIDE error on your planet are (1) the universally experienced subject (+)/object (-), self/other, I/Not-I, or "myself and the world" split, separation and situation. This is where you accept and experience the *difference*, but not the *Unity*. It is the root cause of what you call "loneliness," the feeling of separateness, finitude and alienation—it is the origin of *the "EGO"* and the motivation and drive behind all you do in life: namely, to *cancel* the state of isolation, separateness and finitude, and reach

Unity, Infinity, Wholeness, and Freedom (±).—And (2) The form called "Materialism—which is the position, error and belief that only Matter (-) exists or is Reality; Consciousness (+) being in the end reducible to Matter.

> Note my Padawan that "Materialism" is only an intellectual belief-position one entertains in one's study or behind the podium, which in practical-real life reduces to, the I/Not-I split or separation—a split that even religions are involved in, who do believe in the immortality of the "I" (a belief, moreover, which cancels Nihilism and the finality of death). Materialism holds that only Matter or "one" thing exists, which *seems* to be a Unity and a solution to the problem but is not; for it is not Truth but error— since it believes that you are just a Body and when your Body dies you die (plus, experientially, as noted, the same split remains: "me/ Ego versus the world").

§148

"Materialism" results in what your philosophers have appropriately called "NIHILISM," a major cause of depression, hopelessness, disease and unhappiness on your planet. Ignorance of Polarity and of the UNITY underlying the opposites is then the basis of the illusion and error of the DARK SIDE of the Force, and of separateness and Materialism.

§149

Thus the educational Task of healing your planet is simple to state. It is to exit the DARK SIDE of the Force, the CAVE, error and illusion (+|-) and enter into and become aware of the LIGHT SIDE of the Force (±), the Truth, Reality, and the Jedi Order, which already and alone exists. It is to make a planetary shift from the state of *Imbalance* to the *Balance* of the Force.

§150

NINE. Now to review: we said in step FOUR that the Being that must be must also be conscious of itself or *self-conscious*, which is possible only if there is first *consciousness*. And consciousness is possible only if there is an *Object* or polar opposite, namely Matter, of which it is conscious.

So there must be *two* sides of Being—in effect, Consciousness *and* the world/universe.

Now consciousness *of* a world, object or Other is in fact consciousness of *separation*, of a split between oneself and an Other, in truth the *Dark Side* of the Force (+|-). But as we saw in step SEVEN the Truth of the opposites is their Unity or non-separation. In other words, it is consciousness of Self or Self-consciousness, i.e., Being or the Force as conscious of *itself*, which is the Jedi Order.

§151

Therefore HISTORY on a given planet such as yours and all that it involves is nothing but the "time" it takes or took for "Man" to wake up—for Being or the Force *as* "Consciousness" ("Man"/"human Being") to be the Force *as* "**Self**-consciousness," as the Jedi Order. A process which takes place outside of "time" or in the Eternal Now.—It is called "**Self**-consciousness" because, as in Unity, consciousness *and* the world mutually interpenetrate ... or consciousness completely *saturates* the world-matter ... or Self and Other *are utterly merged*: "Other" is no longer "just Other" ... it is **Self** ... or *Self*-saturated, *Self*-pervaded.

> "There is nothing but Consciousness ... Consciousness is prior to experience and unconditioned. It is all there is." **Goswami**
>
> "I am this whole Universe' is the initial postulate of quantum thinking." **F.A. Wolf**
>
> "The widespread idea that all there is in the universe is matter and that all matter was created in the Big Bang and will disappear in a Big Crunch—is a colossal mistake." **Laszlo**
>
> "It is Consciousness that creates an illusion of Matter, not vice-versa." **Haisch**

§152

In other words, the Being that must be finally achieves *Self-consciousness* and true Being by learning in HISTORY, by Faith and Reason, that the *difference* or *separation* involved in Consciousness is an *illusion*, and that the Unity of the two sides—the *BALANCE*—is the Truth and what alone IS.

§153

TEN. We will conclude this Second Proof of the Force by looking at this educational shift from Consciousness (Stage Two) to Self-consciousness (Stage Three) more closely:

(A) So, there *is* only *One* Infinite Consciousness (+) which pervades the whole material universe (-) and all of its *Forms* (which are nothing but ascending types of Polarity (±), e.g., magnetism, electricity, chemism, and sexuality). Hence the *One* Consciousness (+) is involved, by Polarity, in all the Forms of Nature-Matter (-) and always maintains its *Unity*. *However* it is only in the "human" Form, i.e., in a *Body* (-) which has "human" senses and faculties that the One Consciousness is able to truly become *Consciousness*, i.e. *of* an object, and as an "I" in opposition to a "Not-I."

§154

That is, to actually *be Consciousness*, the One Consciousness (the Absolute I) must necessarily "delimit" itself and become a *separate* "EGO" or empirical consciousness, male or female—even though the "separation" is apparent only or illusory (for the Unity is what is fundamental and always preserved). Further, as we noted, this Truth or Unity which must exist—of Light and Dark Side, consciousness and nature, subject and object, Inner and Outer—is called "Man" (or yourself) as the Unity of "Soul" (+) and "Body" (-).

Hence only in the "human" Form—of *all* the "(-) Forms"—do we have *full* and *true* Consciousness for the first time. The One Infinite Consciousness (+) as fused and in identity with your Body and senses, now "looks out" upon the world/creation (-) ... but as an "Other" than itself, as a "Not-I," and thus experiences itself as *Finite*, limited, and mortal—due to Body (-) rather than (+) Consciousness *identification*.

So we now have consciousness or subject/object *separation* but not yet *Self-consciousness*, or subject/object *unification*.

§155

(B) It is the singular purpose of your HISTORY to accomplish this transition from Consciousness to Self-Consciousness. This is the movement from the beginning of HISTORY to the end of HISTORY where "U/I" or the union of the opposites Universality and Individuality is realized and the global recognition of each by all takes place. Briefly, what happens is this:

(1) The goal is for the One Consciousness, the FORCE, as Man/ Ego, to overcome its condition of *separation/finitude* and realize itself as infinite and all Reality. It must come to see itself *in* the Not-I, its Object, Other and the world (-). It must realize that there *is nothing* but the "I" or Consciousness; that only Consciousness is Reality or Real—that Matter, the Object is not, is Nothing.

(2) In sum: The One Consciousness (Absolute I) first becomes aware of *itself* as an I or Ego by being *Recognized* by another I, which is an indestructible *mirror* of itself, an "Object" which is at once a "Subject" (a Consciousness). It is aware it is an "Object" *for* the other I and thereby becomes aware of *itself* or *Self*-conscious—but as a limited or *finite* Self-consciousness. It becomes an "Infinite I" when (a) it realizes the *identity* between itself and the other I and *all* other I's; and (b) it realizes that only "I's" have being; "Not-I's", objects, matter, etc, are *ideal* or nothing or have no true being.

§156

The following graphic illustrates this:

"I recognize *you* as absolutely independent and free. And I also recognize you as recognizing *me* as absolutely independent and free. And I am you and you are me—in that we both share and are the same Absolute I"—cf. the dialectic of the *Infinite* in e.g. Jedi **Hegel's** *Science of Logic.*

This furthermore is the basis of all States, *Right, Equality,* and Law … since as "Man," I am in my essence "Absolute I" and Infinite and independent and free or inherently "GOD" or the FORCE itself, hence deserving of Sacred *RIGHTS*, respect, and recognition. And every Person is equally "God"/Absolute I and free: hence, the necessity for *States* and *Laws*. Or, when I see/find/have myself in You and am *Recognized*, I am no longer finite and limited but *Infinite*. I am on both sides of my LIMIT: I am the *Identity* of Self and Other (±), namely, Love and Reason. Here, the *One Consciousness* gains the realization that it IS in fact the *One* Consciousness (yet Individuality is retained). It is *Self*-consciousness (consciousness OF consciousness). It further realizes that the (+|-) separation (or DARK SIDE) was an illusion and that the Truth always was and is (±), the Unity of consciousness and object, self and other, me and you, I and Not-I, or I and Universe.

§157

As a result of this realization TIME ceases to exist and the One Consciousness, as a JEDI, enters into the *ETERNAL NOW.*

§158

Historically, then, the Jedi Order (the Unity of all I's) begins in families, tribes, peoples, and nations, developing Reason and its *Universals* into the rule of law, *Rights,* legal Persons, Equality, and the succession of *States,* gradually perfecting the progress and realization of FREEDOM.

§159

So the *WHOLE* (Being, the Force, the One Consciousness) comes to consciousness of itself in and as *each* of you, or in *individual* form. Hence even though ultimately there is *only One* Consciousness (+), because the One Consciousness, by Polarity, is necessarily fused with (-) or with *individuated* matter as a Body-Ego (with senses, memory, etc.), its Individuality is retained and it therefore exists and manifests as *Plural*—which is also true by Logic, since *the Universal and Individual are inseparable,* as the one cannot be without the other (±).

So Yes, there is only *One* Consciousness (the WHOLE/FORCE), but the One Consciousness necessarily *experiences* itself in myriad forms and ways—as *Jedi* and *the Jedi Order.*

§160

Thus the FORCE or BEING of necessity transforms itself into the Jedi Order. And *this* is why, my Noble Padawan, the Force and Being must be and cannot not be, and why and what, in their essence, the Universe, "Man," History, and "God" truly are, as I will elaborate below. Only The BALANCE exists and must exist. Above all be mindful that the Force = the Truth = the Balance = the Jedi Order.

CONSEQUENCES OF THIS PROOF

§161

Here we will consider some of the consequences of the Jedi Proof of the Force which will shed further light on the true meaning of the Universe, God, Man, History, the State, a Jedi and the Jedi Order.

As we said before (in "Four" in the Second Proof) a major problem that makes understanding difficult is the use of common "loaded" words to express Reality and the TRUTH, words such as, "Universe," "Man," "God," etc. It will be helpful if you keep in mind that what is really behind all of these words (which are prejudiced and not necessary) is just this: **IS** (isness), **IS** *as* **aware**, and **IS** *as* **self-aware**.

§162

The UNIVERSE and GOD. *First,* the "Universe" taken as the "totality of all that is"—*as* consciousness (indivisible/unextended) *and* the physical-material (divisible, extended) world *and* existing in an eternal *Unity* as the ONE REALITY—is the same as the FORCE, the One Infinite Indivisible Being that alone exists and outside

> "The Truth of the World *is its ideality only*, and does not imply it possesses true reality; it is involved in the World's nature that it should *be*, but only in an ideal sense … it is something created, its Being is something that has been merely posited, or is dependent on something else (God, the Force) … Hence the World's true nature and Process is to return to its source [the Force] from a state of separation and revolt, and get into a relationship of Spirit or Love." **Hegel**. PR III 37.

of which is nothing, and is also called "God" by your religions. Be mindful Padawan that it is the primary mistake of your religions to separate and divide what is ONE into *three parts*—"God," the Universe/Man, and Heaven—and to restrict "God" to the first part only. What this does is to make God *finite*. The truth is rather that God (the Force) is an *infinite* Being and, as such, the *only* Being (there is no "outside" to God or to an infinite being; as your scriptures say, "We live, move, have our being *in* God/the Force") and thus "God" comprehends and includes *all three parts/ phases* in his Concept. "God" is then a process or activity of eternal self-actualization that is not in time. Because there *is* no "time" the Force's three stages, its self-actualization, happens *at once*. Hence it can be said that the Force (God) is actualized and exists "from the beginning." And this is in agreement with your religions. As your Jedi **Schelling** states: "the Whole, the Universe, the Force *itself* is not in time"; and as **Hegel** teaches: "Eternity will not be, nor has it been. IT IS." And lastly your quantum physicist **Schrödinger** says: "The present is the only thing that has no end." Thus in truth "God" is the One Force which of necessity has two sides—the Light Side and Dark Side, Consciousness and Unconsciousness (and has them by necessity or eternally or NOW)—that are in eternal Unity and where consciousness trumps unconsciousness/Matter. "God"/the Force is in truth the WHOLE and comes to full Self-consciousness in and as JEDI, the Force aware of itself.

§163

Second, the "Universe" taken *as only* the physical material energetic sensible Universe in space and time—hence *excluding* consciousness-mind-thought—is in truth only *one-half* of the FORCE, the (-) Matter, Outer-side, called "Nature" by your sciences. This "Dark Side" domain must exist, but it is *nothing* in itself and has no True Being as we have shown: It is Plato's CAVE.

§164

A JEDI and MAN ("human being"). A "Jedi" is the FORCE (Being) actualized and individualized. The following will clarify this: The FORCE, the One Being, is by *necessity* (due to its two sides) involved in a specific process. The Force has Two sides: Consciousness and Matter (Unconsciousness). But Consciousness trumps Matter and hence is all reality, indivisible and infinite; recall that the

Being that must *be*, must be conscious of *itself*. But to *be* conscious, and then *self*-conscious, the One consciousness (+) (Absolute I) must first be consciousness OF, consciousness OF an Object, an Other, a Resistance, which happens when (by necessity or Polarity) it fuses with its polar opposite, Matter (-), in the Form of an *individual* "human" Body with *senses,* etc. Only then does it becomes consciousness OF a World/Matter. As Jedi **Hegel** says:

> "Man qua animal organism is the *microcosm,* the center of Nature, or Nature which has achieved an existence FOR ITSELF [you are the whole Universe aware of itself as/at a unique *POINT;* cf. your scientists *Gaia Hypothesis,* etc], one in which the whole of INORGANIC NATURE is recapitulated and idealized (*Enc.* §352 zusatz)." [Also:] "The Soul pervades everything ... as it is the wholly universal being, the truth and ideality of everything material (*Enc.* §406 zusatz)."

However, due to its identification with its BODY the Absolute I (+) becomes a *finite* Consciousness and an EGO (no longer *infinite* and all reality): this is the true definition of "MAN" or "human being." Here we have the FORCE as MAN, the FORCE in its "Second Stage." But "human being" is only a temporary, *transitional* stage, as your Jedi **Nietzsche** also taught. "Man" as finite and incomplete is completely restless and ruled by *desire, angst,* and *temporality* (cf., your **Heidegger's** "being in time" and "being towards death"). "Man" is the Force itself in its *activity* of overcoming its *finitude* by realizing that its Other or Object (Matter, the World) is in itself *nothing* or *ideal*—is in reality itself or consciousness. Then it becomes *Self*-Consciousness and infinite, it meets with or has *itself* in every Object or Other it confronts. This is the Force actualized and individualized as a JEDI, no longer a "Particular" but a "Universal" Individual, the Force in its "Third Stage."

§165

NOTE: Your *New Age's* teaching on "God-realization" or "Self-realization" is involved in an error. That is, it is *not* the case that "You as a *Particular* Individual (P.I.), an Ego, are God." This is a false exaltation of the particular to the Universal. However, You as a "Jedi," a *Universal* Individual (U.I.) are indeed, if properly understood, the Force itself or God—as e.g., **Christ** says, "As many as be complete/perfect can be just as (*kathos*) his Master," and, "I said you are gods and goddesses." Also a Jedi's singular goal, as **Jedi Master Yoda** says, is to *"transform into the Force,"* which is again the implicit teaching of all re-ligion, cf.: "Be ye holy as I am holy," "Be ye perfect as your Father/ God is perfect." It is precisely the *Knowledge of the Force*—with its distinction between the *Particular* Individual and *Universal* Individual— that makes it impossible to fall into this "New Age" error of regarding oneself, one's empirical egoic self, *as* "God" or the Force Itself. For according to the *Knowledge of the Force*, you (as a particular ego) cannot be the Force or God, since as ego you are in +|-, self/other *separation*, which is the Dark Side, evil and error. Further, what IS, is the Absolute I, which you share with all selves and is God, the Force, and not your empirical ego. Thus you are just "using" God's consciousness (+) (see Genesis 1) and matter (-) and thus should be thankful and humble, not arrogant or boastful. So when you "transform into the Force/ God," you do not "become God"—rather you merge with God in such a way that God/the Force is and remains Infinite and all Reality (and moreover existed "before" I *as* a personal Ego was born); thus all that I am and have, as a Jedi *and* as a "human," is in fact God's or the Force's, and not mine. My consciousness and Body are a "gift." My attitude should be, "Thank You" ... as well as, "This is incredible!"

§166

A JEDI'S NATURE and POWERS.

A Jedi's Nature. A Jedi is the Force or the Truth actualized and individualized, is *One* with the Force and with everyone and everything, since he or she is a *Universal* Individual (U.I.) and shares One Consciousness or Absolute I with everyone, and has a unique Body (-) as well as experiences and memories imprinted on the cinematic film of the mind. A Jedi's essence is LOVE and hence a Jedi loves everyone *without exception ("24/7")*. Moreover, he or she lives fully in the Eternal Present or NOW (there is no time) and is *immortal.*

§167

The PROOF of a Jedi's and a "human being's" Immortality (of both "I" or Soul and Body). In the Truth that is the Force (±) as a *Unity* of Opposites, Consciousness (+) is alone REALITY, indestructible, and eternal since it has a *Being-for-itself,* while Matter or Body (-) is NOTHING since it has only a *Being-for-another* and is not self-aware. Therefore you *as Consciousness, as Being itself,* are and can only be *immortal.* Further, since Consciousness (+) is by necessity always joined with a Body (-) by the Law of Polarity (you cannot have the one without the other), your individual Body is immortal too—or you have a "second" indestructible so-called "Subtle-Astral-Causal-Spiritual" BODY underneath or within your decomposable physical biological BODY. (The *Introduction* to Science, e.g. Hegel's *Phenomenology,* also is and constitutes a proof of the individual reader's or consciousness's immortality, since it concludes with the latter as "the certainty of being *all reality and all truth*").

> *"Man is immortal* in consequence of knowledge ... *the individual soul has an infinite, an eternal quality,* namely, that of being a citizen in the Jedi Order (*Reich Gottes*). This is *a quality and a life which is removed beyond time and the Past ...*" **Hegel**

> "There is a sense in which the consciousness of each of us survives our brain and body ..." **Laszlo**

§168

A Jedi's Powers and Abilities. A Jedi, owing to the nature of the Force and Polarity (±)—or what is known as "mind over matter"—has (potentially) *total* dominion and control over the *entire material physical Universe* (-) (and also over what your Eastern Masters refer to as the "4th Plane"). Hence a Jedi possesses such powers as creation, levitation, de- and re-materialization, healing, ESP, clairvoyance, clairaudience, telekinesis, etc. A Jedi also has access to the *Akashic Records* (aka "The Library of the Collective Unconscious"); for example, you can be in a room and then "see" as a projection on the wall of the room, *any* event in the History of Man, just as in a "movie" theater (as all events/experiences on your planet are forever stored in the cinematic film of the minds of your people from the beginning).

Of critical importance is that Powers *follow* and do not *precede* knowledge and love and are not to be sought as "ends in themselves," only the Jedi Order and Truth are such. Also a Jedi's "SUBTLE BODY," which every Jedi and "human being" possesses, can de-materialize and materialize at will.

There are Three kinds of JEDI and JEDI MASTERS: (1) Intuitive, (2) Discursive/Science, and (3) Intuitive and Discursive who also have full mastery of the Powers.

§169

STAGES of the FORCE'S SELF-ACTUALIZATION. (1) The Force or Point as such, (2) as "Man," (3) as Jedi, and (4) as Jedi after death (in the Subtle/Astral Body and World, which is *here and now*: see also "Spaceship Earth Diagram," *Part III, §468).*

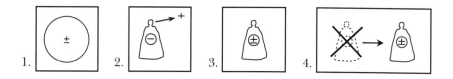

(1) The Truth. The Force in itself, unexpressed.

(2) The Truth/Force as "Man." As Consciousness OF, as EGO. The unity of Universal (+) *and* Individual (-), as a U.I., the Absolute I *and* Individuated Matter as a "human" Body. The Individual Body-EGO must surrender to the Universal in him (the POINT or pure self-consciousness), and must saturate her Individuality with Universality (by seeking and focusing on the Universal, not Particulars) by true Jedi Education.

(3) The Truth/Force realized as JEDI, who realizes that Consciousness (+) is everything, that Matter/Object is nothing, and sees herself *in* everything, in all of Objectivity, and hence is infinite, the One Reality itself—but retains his unique individuality, experiences and memories.

§170

(4) The Truth/Force realized as a JEDI, but *after the death of the physical Body.* He/She is an immortal Jedi with an indestructible *Jedi-Subtle Body* (see Proof of Immortality above). This Truth-POINT, now self-aware, contains everything—including Nature, the infinite physical Universe, the Earth, etc. It is absolute and the only REALITY ("God")—and is eternally in touch with every "I" or Jedi as a Universal "I" or Individual. All else is subordinate to and within this Point. It is absolute FREEDOM and Apriori as outside space/time/and matter; it is everywhere and nowhere.

—Compare Jedi **Jesus's**, "In my Father's house are many *mansions*," Jedi **Fichte's** "Productive Imagination," and **Schelling's**, **Grof's**, **Leadbeater's** and **Cayce's** "Astral Worlds or Planes" (that are timeless; cf. also the film *Inception*). There are Three Levels or Possible States of a Jedi: 1) Unmanifest, 2) Manifest as Theoretical, and 3) Manifest as the Theoretical *and* Practical, and materialized either in the Astral/Subtle or on Earth.

§171

All spirits may complete their education (not attained on Earth) from Stage Two to Three *after death* in their Astral Bodies in the Astral Worlds/Planes. Note also and especially: There *is* universal Justice—hence *consequences* for choosing Dark Side living, sloth and immoral actions, etc, over Light Side living, as your religions also teach.

§172

The JEDI ORDER.

(1) Because the Truth, the UNITY, is NOW—as the Force's 2 sides can never come apart—*the JEDI ORDER, qua the Unity of all your people, exists NOW.* It merely needs to be *experienced*—by Global Jedi Education or realization. As a result of (completed) G. J. Education all adults on your planet will be Jedi and all 7 Institutions will be operational (that is, educational). Thus there will be no wars (nukes), terrorism, fear, hate, poverty, disease, etc, for Reason qua Jedi will rule in all States on Earth and in World Government. Plus the Earth's connection to the Subtle World and commerce between the two will be open and commonplace. Indeed, in every home there will be e.g. a "curtained alcove" whereby Jedi will enter or "beam in" (materialize) and leave (de-materialize)—and in many public buildings and shopping malls, etc, as well.

The fully actualized Jedi Order is thus a problem free world that is incredible and beautiful beyond your wildest dreams and what you can possibly imagine. Again to enter into it you only need to be *EDUCATED*, to become aware that *separation* and the Dark Side of the Force (+|-) is an illusion, that only the UNITY of the Light Side is the Truth, and that the two sides of the Force *can never come apart*.

§173

(2) In other words right now, as we saw in the PROOF of THE FORCE, every person on your planet *is* an immortal JEDI whether they know it or not. Each person's consciousness, including your own, Noble Reader, is in fact *the same* ONE Infinite Consciousness which is alone Reality and all Reality and belongs to the Eternal Force, which thus experiences itself in myriad ways and from unique points of view. As your astrophysicist **Bernard Haisch** says, "God (the Force) actualizes his infinite potential through *our* experience, and lives in the physical universe through *us*." Thus all persons, as true Reality, are *immortal* as well as their Bodies. Hence everyone on your planet—despite unawareness and their national, racial, religious, ideological differences—is absolutely ONE right now. The *separation* experienced between centers of the One Consciousness is due to the "senses" and the (-) material world and is an *illusion*. *Your* UNITY is alone the Truth, for you all share and *are* the same One Consciousness. To be aware and to experience this Unity and LOVE is *the* solution to your problems and the true end of all your wars, hate, terrorism, greed, grief, and fear; for there will be no desire to eliminate the Other, nor need to defend yourself against the Other, etc. This egoic mind-set will be replaced by healthy competition among nations in the arts, sciences and sports and by such things as the engineering and constructing of lunar cities and metropolises on mars, etc. The Task is to become aware of this Unity and its amazing fruits by true EDUCATION and by "Balancing" the Seven major institutions of your global society—Science, Education, Religion, Politics, Business, Health, and the Arts and Media—so that they no longer promote and sustain the error of the Dark Side of the Force, dis-unity and imbalance.

For a more detailed PICTURE of the Jedi Order as fully actualized on your planet see *Part III: The Jedi Order,* the Introduction and Politics.

§174

HISTORY and the STATE.

(1) History is simply the Becoming of the Jedi Order. Thus History, in the form of a succession of States and epochs whose inner essence is Global *Education,* is nothing but the "time" it takes for the Force to

move from Consciousness (+|-) or Stage Two, to Self-consciousness (±) or Stage Three, Jedi and Jedi Order. Hence, History is the progress of the Consciousness of FREEDOM as (±), which is achieved by the rule of LAW and the Universal, the Truth and the Concept (U-P-I), in your geopolitical States.

(2) History on a given planet takes place in the timeless present. Hence it is a FACT that every Baby born is born into the same identical NOW, and therefore differences are historical and only concern the level of consciousness/education achieved by the culture into which the Baby is born. History as such, as the collective movement of the Force from Stage Two to Stage Three is *temporary* ... and therefore comes to an END. As I said, your own HISTORY ON EARTH IS OVER, completed or consummated—via the Knowledge of the Force that was achieved first in your religions and then in philosophy-become-Science in your Modern Period. You are now living in ETERNITY, your people need only become aware of this.

(3) The STATE (and Politics) is the institution and arena that provides the conditions (universal laws and rights) for the education and actualization of the Force to Jedi, from (+|-) to (±). "Rights" derive from and are based on the fact that "Man" in truth is the Force Itself and *absolutely free* (from external determination or heteronomy), and thus has infinite value and worth—and as such, is *sacred and inviolate*. The State *is* the Jedi Order, whose chief purpose is to educate all of its citizens to Jedi, to the UNITY of the One Consciousness (cf. your dictum, "**E Pluribus Unum**"). Moreover, Freedom and "Free-will" imply responsibility and self-determination, hence the subject's existing *outside* of Nature (-), space/time and its laws, and thus *immortality* as well.

§175

The State and Law-Rights-Equality thus exist because each Person is infinite, absolutely independent and free and hence *worthy* of RIGHTS and RECOGNITION, which results in the universality of LAW and the principle of EQUALITY. And the basis of the **Rule of Law** is that, All are equal and have inalienable Rights. Moreover when Reason and the Concept (+) intersects with Nature (-) and the natural drives of self-preservation, growth, sexual reproduction, etc, the necessary result are the institutions of Family, Marriage, Property, Courts, Contract, Constitutions, Civil Society, the State, and so forth (see *Jedi Science*, Part I. §§187, 223, 239 and Part II. §442).

§176

ON The SUBTLE WORLD-SPHERE and the ABSOLUTE I-POINT.
(1) This **POINT**, UNITY (±), or Absolute I *alone exists*—as your Jedi **Fichte** says, "The I is all that ever was, is, or will be." Moreover, the

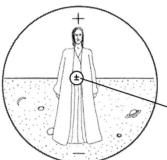

physical extended Universe is equal to Zero, that is, it is necessary and eternal but *absolutely nothing in itself,* as your Jedi **Kant**, the **A-Team**, and your own physicists teach.

This POINT is the INNER, **Kant's** T.U.A. or **Hegel's** SPIRIT (*Geist*): **ALL INDIVIDUAL SPIRITS EXIST <u>IN</u> THIS ONE POINT**, the One Indivisible Consciousness or ABSOLUTE I. In truth, this "I" or (+) is not *in* space and time, and is literally *outside* the Universe: for space's outsidedness (*Auseinandersein*) has no Truth. Therefore everything—all the contents of space and time—collapses or becomes concentrated into a *single indivisible Point* (or "singulum"; your scientists' "Big Bang Theory" of the origin of the universe got this one right, however the true "singularity," prior to **Planck**-time, is not just physical (-) but, as per Polarity (±), supra-physical (+) as well). The POINT is also the root of the Infinite LOVE and Infinite AWARENESS of a JEDI and also contains the KEY to Health and Healing, as I will show you below.

> "All these things—time, space, the **material** world, together with what one might wish to add to them—*are actually and in fact nonexistent;* instead, in case you have only just understood its nonexistence, each one is the very easily grasped appearance of the truly existing ONE … for in truth, bodies *are the **nothing** which is presented as nothing.*" Fichte

Also, what determines the degree of freedom or bondage you enjoy in life *and* post-mortem life is just the nature and degree of your IDENTIFICATION or ATTACHMENT to the "World of Forms" or the Sense-World (-), that is, to your own BODY, people, things, and possessions.

"LUMINOUS BEINGS ARE WE, NOT THIS CRUDE MATTER."

JEDI MASTER YODA

§177

(2) **The SUBTLE or ASTRAL SPHERE'S** existence is easy to prove, Noble Padawan. For example as I have shown, *You,* as the *delimited* One Consciousness or Absolute I (+) *are immortal,* and hence *your Body (-) too is immortal,* due to Polarity (±). You have of necessity therefore an *eternal* subtle Jedi BODY, which can de- or re-materialize. Hence it necessarily follows that there are *degrees* of matter (finer and coarser) and the Body's materialization, from 0 to 100%. As "0" or invisible, your Body (-) enters and fuses with pure *ABSOLUTE MIND or Consciousness (+),* such that not only are you *in* and aware of all points of the Universe (-) simultaneously but you, as (±), can literally "travel" to any point at once, and then *materialize* your Body at that point, in part or in toto. Also see Amit **Goswami's** *How Quantum Activism Can Save Civilization* (esp. 42-43, 96-97), and M. **Sabom's** *Recollections of Death: A Medical Investigation.*

Moreover there are "Subtle worlds/planes or spheres" that correspond to your religions' "heaven and hell" (on the principle of your adage, "Birds (spirit's) of a feather flock together"). That is, ranging from *lower,* baser, less developed/educated spheres, where EVIL I's or Jedi congregate, to the *highest* where more developed and perfect Jedi congregate. The lower cannot come to the higher (as your Jedi **Pythagoras** taught), but the higher *can* come to the lower, with the intent of helping them advance/educate, etc.

§178

The PROOF of the SUBTLE BODY and WORLD via the UNITY-OF-OPPOSITES or POLARITY, continued.

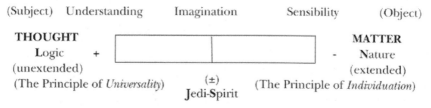

(Subject)   Understanding   Imagination   Sensibility   (Object)

THOUGHT   **MATTER**
  Logic   +   -   Nature
(unextended)   (extended)
(The Principle of *Universality*)   (±)   (The Principle of *Individuation*)
                                    Jedi-Spirit

Note that (+) and (-) are the absolute extremes or opposites.

Thus there are degrees of *synthesis* of (-) and (+), the highest in Nature is Man qua the synthesis of the "Human" Body and *Soul* (±). The Human Body's *Matter* thus becomes *immortal* or *indestructible* (you cannot see this due to your natural Senses). Thus as soon as a BABY is born it has its immortal Subtle Body. *At death,* in accord with the principle of the *Negation of the Negation,* the latent potentiality of Matter (the "Human" Body) comes out or manifests, namely, the subtle, indestructible Body in the form of "Matter 2." The movement from **Logic** → **Nature** and the "Nature-Body" is the *1ˢᵗ Negation* and the creation-production of Coarse "Matter 1" or "Vibration 1"; whereas the movement from **Nature** → **Spirit** and the "Subtle/Spirit-Body" is the *2ⁿᵈ Negation*, that is, the creation-production of Fine "Matter 2" or "Vibration 2."

Furthermore, as your Jedi **Kant** and **Fichte** teach, at the core of the Synthesis (±), one of the Truth's properties or powers is what is called *Productive Imagination*—(and the basis of all *Dream-work*). Therefore there must be so-called "heavenly" or *Subtle* Worlds which are worlds of and existing in IMAGINATION (*cf. Art and aesthetic products*) and constructed of *Fine or finer MATTER 2*. Consequently in Post-Mortem existence there are imperfect or "sloppy" productions and *Perfect* productions (or "Mansions"). Only "Jedi Masters" live in Perfect Mansions of "congealed" Productive Imagination.

JEDI SCIENCE

THREE IMPORTANT THINGS

(1) Our treatment of Science here can be no more than a "guide"—and cannot enter into all the details and depth it requires.

(2) For those who have not had prior exposure to science, philosophy and rigorous thinking this section may prove difficult to understand. You may wish to skip it and return to it at a later time.

(3) The fact is that you do not have to master Science to be a Jedi. In any case, once you have become an *Intuitive* Jedi you *will* be able to understand Science.

JEDI SCIENCE: PRELIMINARY

How Science works:

First, you get the TRUTH—the POINT ($\pm$).
Second, you take it apart and study its becoming
(from - to +).

§179

(1) What Jedi Science is.

With the final goal of your Jedi-philosophers having been reached by the **A-Team**, the knowledge of the Force or **the Truth** immediately makes possible and takes the form of "Jedi Science"—a comprehensive knowledge of the universe as a whole, that is, of the Force as the one thing that truly exists, in all its major forms and stages. And such a knowledge is possible because it is precisely *in you yourselves*, as Jedi, that the Force—the Truth or the Whole of existence—arrives at a knowledge of Itself.

§180

Although the Force is One and therefore the "Science of the Force" is only One, this One Science is composed of three sciences or parts, in accord with its Inner-Outer aspects and the process it involves. In essence, the One Science is simply the study of "the Force and Its Expression," that is, of **the Truth and its coming to know Itself as Jedi and the Jedi Order**. Thus it is the study of the Force or First Principle *in itself* (or for us), called the *Science of Logic (or Jedi Metaphysics),* and the Force or First Principle as Expressed or *for itself,* which involves two sciences: the Force *out of itself*—the OUTER Force, what the people in your galaxy call "Nature," hence called the *Science of Nature,* and the Force *returning into itself* and becoming *for itself*—the INNER Force, what the people in your galaxy call "Human," "Spirit," and "Mind," but which we will call "Jedi" since it is your true concept, who you really are, hence called the *Science of Jedi.* Thus, the Force is one living whole, but we study its several sciences as if in isolation from the whole and from each other and hence we are really artificially *abstracting* from what is in fact One. As your Jedi **Hegel** writes:

> **"The FORCE *(Idea)* is the *Content* of *Science,* namely, the consideration of *the Universe,* as it is in conformity with *the Concept* in and for itself or 'Sub Specie Aeternitatis.' *Science* is *the rational Concept* as it is in and for itself, i.e., in *the Science of Logic,* and as it is in *the Universe* or the *Objective or Real World,* i.e., in the *Sciences of Nature* and *Jedi (Spirit)*."**

§181

Thus, the one *Science of the Force* (or *Jedi Science*) is composed of the *Science of Logic,* the *Science of Nature,* and the *Science of Jedi.* The easiest way to grasp their interconnection is as studying stages in the movement or "grand *educational process*" of the Force becoming Jedi and coming to full self-awareness; a process which begins in the Outer Force and ends in the Inner Force, and which can be represented as a "movement" up **Plato's** Divided Line.

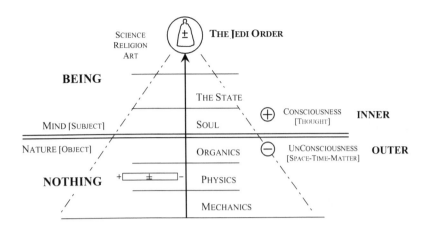

§182

In essence, the *Science of Nature* (the Outer Force) studies the Force in its (eternal-unconscious) movement from Space (Mechanics) up to its most organized form, the human or Jedi body (Organics); the *Science of Jedi* (the Inner Force) studies the Force in its (historical-conscious) movement from implicit Jedi as Soul (Subjective Jedi), to the State and History (Objective Jedi), and finally to fully explicit Jedi, or the Force realized in Art, Religion and Science (Absolute Jedi), and ultimately in the *Science of Logic*, which studies the pure essence of the Force in pure thought. This will be further clarified in the next major section.

> "Science is nothing but the TRUTH aware of itself." (Enc. §574)
> "Science requires the individual (as a *particular* individual) *to forget himself.*" Hegel

§183

(2) How Jedi Science works.

1. What is first necessary, as a preliminary to the study of *Jedi Science*, is that one first becomes a Jedi and has overcome the illusory split

involved in consciousness between oneself and Being or the World, i.e., between the Inner and Outer Force, Subjectivity and Objectivity. One must have fully mastered the "inversion" that **Plato** and other Jedi-philosophers describe involving the realization that it is not the *visible* that is real but the *invisible*, and which takes one out of "the Cave." There are many ways to achieve "**inversion**." For example (a) *By Reason:* For example the **A-Team** members each have their own way and method. The best is probably **Hegel's** *Phenomenology of Mind/ Spirit (1807)*, though it is somewhat out of date and modern readers may find it somewhat difficult (a new version will appear soon). It basically works like this: we move from an initial condition of consciousness *of* an object, to that of consciousness *of* consciousness or I = I, and then we observe the collapse of *all* remaining theoretical, practical, and religious objects into the I = I or the CONCEPT. But a bright reader can acquire the standpoint by just drawing out the full implications of the proofs we gave earlier: e.g. that the sense/material universe qua Object has no true being, only the subject/self does; and the *Absolute I* is the ground of everything and is all reality. "Inversion" can also be achieved (b) *by Will*. This method will briefly be discussed below and in greater detail in *Part II: The Jedi Code*. It shows how you can actualize your Jedi potential or "seed" by aligning yourself to the Truth and achieving *unity*.

§184

Thus the two *basic* ways to achieve Inversion and the *Knowledge of the Force* (±) are:

> (1) **Discursively**, via Reason, moving from concept to concept and insight to insight, as for example set forth as noted in Jedi **Hegel's** *Phenomenology*. The hard part, as usual, is breaking free of the Dark Side, the deceptive power of the *Senses*—"overcoming the world" (as it is said)—and of the false *Being* of sense-objects—and seeing the *Unity*, the One Consciousness, the Absolute I, lying under the sense-manifold ... that is, seeing the **I = I** of Self-Consciousness and being conscious *of* Consciousness Itself as true *Being*.

> (2) And **Intuitively**. That is, it is also possible to reach the standpoint by an Act of Pure *WILL*—"The resolve that wills pure Thought" or I = I. You—in a single bound—can *abstract*

from everything—the entire sense-manifold—and are left with Pure Self-Awareness, or Thought.

—There is another simple *Intuitive* way to get out of the Cave, the Dark Side (+|-) and realize the *Absolute I* as what alone is and one's *unity* with it:

1. Realize deeply that what is opposite or opposed to you, the "Not-I," the (-) sense-world, the entire material universe of objects, has only a "Being *for another*" (for a consciousness or yourself), hence is *NOTHING*—is not a true Being, which is a "Being *for itself,*" one that *knows* that it *IS.*

2. Realize deeply that you yourself as consciousness or self-consciousness, *are* alone True Being—have a "Being *for itself*" etc.

3. And that the same is true of *ALL* Selves/persons in the world/universe. And realize that *Consciousness* as such is not *in* the world as (+); for by Polarity consciousness is unextended and *indivisible*—and is only *One, a UNITY.* Hence there is no separation between yourself and all other selves; only a *Unity,* as what alone is REAL and EXISTS, as an *ABSOLUTE I. To realize this, is to occupy the standpoint of Science.*

§185

2. What you know when you are Jedi and have absolute or Jedi knowledge (as the Force aware of itself). You know (a) that your True Self is all reality and eternal, (b) that only one thing exists (the "many" is an illusion); that your True Self is not "limited human ego" but infinite Jedi, the Whole aware of itself (hence that all other selves are included within your True Self, and yours in theirs, as explained), (c) that the (-) side, Outer-Object-Nature, is nothing or appearance and is grounded in and pervaded by the (+) side, Inner-Subject-consciousness-You, who are being and reality. You also know (d) the Principle (±) for understanding everything, namely as transitional "moments" leading up to the ultimate Jedi-Truth, and that (e) you, as a Jedi, are not "God" and that there is a difference between you, a Jedi, and the Force (hence all egotism is banished).

§186

3. Now we can understand How Jedi Science, a knowledge of the whole, works: Once you know that your True Jedi Self is *all reality* you at once also know that (a) nothing else has or can have true being or reality hence must be *ideal*, or at most can be only a temporary "moment" or stage—natural or human, outer or inner—in the movement or process which culminated in this knowledge (of the Force's self-awareness), and (b) since (-) can't be separated from (+), you recognize that (±) or U-P-I is the principle for understanding each of the Force's essential moments or Forms in the Inner and Outer realms (treated in the *Sciences of Logic, Nature, and Jedi*).

§187

(3) Key Points about Jedi Science.

1. The key principle and method of Science is the CONCEPT, that is, Polarity (±) as the "UNITY of Opposites" or "IDENTITY in Difference."

2. Since there is no time, only Eternity, all these Forms (as rational and necessary) are posited at once.

"In the scale of Nature's organizations (Forms) there must necessarily emerge one which the intelligence [*Absolute I*] is obliged to intuit as IDENTICAL with itself." STI 127. **Schelling**

3. Though the Truth (±) eternally exists (inner and outer are *eternally* fused), this is only "for us" not "for itself." To become "for itself" and consciousness it must become an individual or subject, and be housed in a "human" Body with senses. It must IDENTIFY with its body first, and then learn of its Universal *All* nature. So, the Forms of the Force in Outer Nature (as unconscious) are posited *immediately*, in accordance with *necessity* and *without* consciousness; while Forms of the Force in Inner Jedi are posited *with* consciousness (historically) in the realm of *freedom*. So to be "for itself" the Force immediately "wakes up" in Man, the exact mid/synthesis point of Inner and Outer (as the *unity* of body and soul) and is *consciousness*—*of* an other/objective world, and thereby becomes alienated, cut in two—only later to learn the truth of "self-in-other" and self-awareness. This begins the educational process of *your history* which ends in full self-knowledge of the Force

or Truth. All the essential Forms exist to facilitate this "seed" to Jedi process: Man's BODY is the most suitable vehicle for the Force to reach its goal (it is the *microcosm* and sum of all of nature's Forms), and the Forms of law, custom, rights, marriage, the state, etc, are structures of freedom that guarantee the Force will self-realize.

§188

4. The best way to comprehend Science's Parts and Forms is as a *grand educational process*. That is, as a movement from the lowest to the highest, from *in itself* to *for itself*, as the actualization of a "seed" or potency. *First* we start with what is furthest away from the Truth or Unity—i.e. with the lowest grade of Truth ($\pm$), with Truth in its most minimal form-realization: namely utter Dis-Unity, Externality and Outsidedness, as unconsciousness and non-sentience. And this is SPACE, where every part is outside every other part and no two points coincide. *Second* we trace the process of the overcoming of this dis-unity and externality by a series of increasingly ascending types of Unity or "Subjects" (of fusions of Individuality and Universality/Genus) or higher Forms of Truth ($\pm$) realization, culminating in Absolute Unity (= Jedi/the Force aware of itself and fully elaborated in and as Logic). This is the *Unity* of knowledge/ awareness/thought and Concept where everything is internal to everything else. Also key is that at the end, in Logic, this knowledge or pure awareness is also linked with Nature, the *Outer*, qua its Body—so the *Inner* does not exist alone.

The diagram below shows how the *Absolute Jedi Science of the Force* is and makes possible the interconnection and *unity* of all of your sciences, present and future, which is due to the fact that all sciences are sciences of the *One Force* in its eternal process of self-actualization.

Absolute Jedi Science of The FORCE

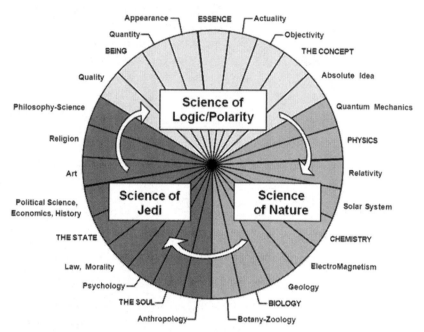

JEDI SCIENCE: In Greater Depth

§189

Jedi Science or Absolute Science or simply SCIENCE studies nothing but the One Force, the JEDI ORDER, or POINT in its essence and principle (in Logic or Metaphysics), and in its actualization or process (in Nature and Jedi).

§190

Science is preceded by an *Introduction* to Science, which is necessary in order to get one out of the Cave or Dark Side and into the Truth, whereby one is then in a position to actually do and understand Science.

§191

As we noted, Science itself falls into three parts: the *Sciences of Logic, Nature,* and *Jedi* or *the Jedi Order.* After the *Introduction* has freed you from the opposition of consciousness and its objects, we FIRST study the Jedi Order—or what is the same, the Concept—*in itself* as *the one true Arche* or Principle of everything in the medium of pure Thought, in the *Science of Logic.* Here we understand the *necessity* of the Jedi Order, why it *must* exist and exist eternally—which is due to Polarity which requires the eternal Unity and inseparability of the opposites, Subjectivity or the Concept *and* Objectivity. SECONDLY, we study how this Unity, Truth or POINT (±) gets realized, first, in the *Science of Nature* or Objectivity (-) and then in the *Science of the Jedi Order* or Subjectivity (+). Nature itself, by stages, transcends its mere Objectivity and shows Subjectivity (Thought, Consciousness) to be its sole Truth, and then Subjectivity by stages transcends its own mere Subjectivity and Objectifies it, realizing the *unity* of Subjectivity and Objectivity—that is, the Jedi Order *as the Truth*, first as the State, then in Art, Religion, and Science.

§192

It will be helpful here to provide a deeper explanation as to why Science falls into *three* parts and how they go together. This requires taking a closer look at the Truth as revealed by *Polarity*, the principle of the unity-of-opposites, the Balance itself.

Thus, there is only One Reality comprised of two opposite sides in *unity*, the Light Side and the Dark Side or, concretely, Consciousness and Matter, Subjectivity and Objectivity. What is all important is that within this Unity it is the first of the pair that trumps the second, resulting in a Consciousness or Subjectivity that is *infinite* and *all reality.*

> NOTE: It might seem at first as though neither of the opposites should have the upper hand or trump the other, but this is not so. For whether the Subject gets Objectivized or, conversely, the Object gets Subjectivized, the result is the same. Namely, a "Subject-Object" in which the *Subject* predominates or trumps the *Object.* That is, wherever and whenever an Object is before me, my own Subjectivity is also before me, absolutely fused with the Object, and I experience myself as outside of myself and in the Object, no matter how independent or distant the Object is from me. Thus, the subject-object split, the self-other separation is overcome and the primary problem of life resolved. Because I now see myself *in* any and all objects or others, I am infinite and free, and not limited or restricted by anything.

§193

Now, this Unity is involved in a three-part process: The Force or Jedi Order as *unexpressed* (in Logic) and the Force or Jedi Order as *expressed* and *actualized* (in Nature and Jedi). According to Polarity *the one cannot be without its other or opposite*. Thus, first we have the One—the Force, the unity of Subjectivity and Objectivity—in the form of Thought or Subjectivity (Logic). However because the One cannot be without its Other or Opposite we also must have—immediately, logically, and necessarily—its Other, namely, Matter, Extension, or Objectivity (Nature). But, by Polarity again, since the truth of any pair of opposites is their Unity we have, thirdly, the *unity* of Subjectivity and Objectivity (of Thought and Matter, of *Logic* and *Nature*)—namely, *Jedi* and *the Jedi Order* (that is, *YourSelf*).

§194

This relationship of the three can also be grasped both by what is called "the negation of negation" *and* by the moments of the Concept or "the unity of Universality-Particularity-and-Individuality"—these are other ways of expressing Polarity. (1) First we have Thought (Subjectivity), then secondly the *negation* of Thought (and Subjectivity), namely Matter (and Objectivity), and thirdly the *negation* of this negation, or the *affirmation* which is Jedi/the Jedi Order and the unity and truth of the first two and what alone truly IS. (2) It is also easy to see that Thought-Logic is *Universality*, while Matter-Nature is *Particularity* (as separateness and parts outside parts), and Jedi is *Individuality*, or *the Universal fully actualized and existent*.

§195

As we know, Polarity in the form of Universality-Particularity-and-Individuality, "U-P-I" for short, is the principle of Science and true Knowledge: *the Concept*. "The Concept" is always "the Concept *of an Object*," hence a Concept-Object or Subject-Objectivity, a *unity of opposites*, and not just one thing or Concept alone. Thus the Concept is another name for the Truth, the POINT, the Force, and it is *the Method* of Knowing in Science. The Concept contains the three moments "U-P-I" and is, most importantly, a *Unity*. The Concept is literally *everything*. Everything is a *unity* of Universality-Particularity-and Individuality—is a Universal that particularizes itself and becomes an Individual. All three of its moments are inseparable and cannot exist *without* the others, say the universal without the individual, and vice versa. This is best illustrated by the three moments in Biology of: Genus (Universal), Species (Particular), and Individual, an example of which would be, (1) Animal (the Genus or Universal), (2) Horse (a particular or specific type of animal), and (3) "Seabiscuit," an Individual actual horse, and thus containing the moments Genus and Species, Universal and Particular, Animal and Horse, *within itself.* The Individual is in fact the *concrete Universal* or the Universal *actualized* (the Universal *by itself* is unactual, nothing, or potential only). The *Universal* is the most important of the three, for the Particular is only the Universal particularizing *itself,* while the Individual is just the Universal *individualized,* or the *concrete Universal.* Hence, there *is* nothing but the Universal—as existing in these three forms, and the last one, Individuality, can be called *totality,* as containing all three in *unity.* Also note that:

Only the Universal is necessary, and not the Particular or Individual.

—This underscores the fact that ultimately the particular individual ("P.I.") must "forget himself and his egotism," as Science and true Education require; nevertheless, as Science and the Truth *also* require, the individual as such *is still preserved in the Universal,* in Pure Self-Consciousness, since the individual is a Universal *Individual* (a "U.I.").

In sum, the Concept (U-P-I) is both the principle of the *Whole* of What IS as well as of its *Parts.*

§196

There is one final way to understand both the division of Science into three parts and the tripartite division of the Concept and all of reality as well.

Let us start with "the ALL," meaning the One Reality or Being or the One Infinite Totality encompassing all that IS. (1) Now, it is one thing to *be* the ALL, but a completely different thing to *know* that one is the ALL, or for the ALL to be aware of itself *as* the ALL.—This initial state can be called *Universality;* note that in your German, "universal" is *All-gemeine,* hence that which encompasses *all* within itself. (2)

Therefore, to be aware of itself *as* the ALL (or infinite, outside of which is nothing), the ALL must of necessity institute a *distinction* within itself, it must "separate itself from itself" (in effect, into Subject and Object, the minimal condition for *knowing*) in order first to become Consciousness and then Self-consciousness. In other words, the Universal (ALL-gemeine) must first *Part-icularize* itself into two, *and then heal the split or division by returning into its Unity* <u>*as*</u> *an Individual, a true* <u>*self-knowing*</u> *concrete and actual Unity.* (Note that in German, "particular" is *Besondern*, meaning to separate or split, and "judgment" is *Ur-teil*, signifying original partition or separation).—It also should be noted that because there *is* nothing but itself (the ALL), the separated part (the Object) *is really itself*—and this is *the* motivation necessary to cancel the split and reach wholeness and self-awareness. (3) Now, there are two stages involved in the ALL's Individualization or healing of its split. The *first stage* is "Consciousness"—*of* an Object, World, infinite Other. The ALL exists now as an *exclusive I* (Subject), excluding the Object or Other from itself and thus *limited* by it. The ALL must then transcend the limitation and go from <u>*exclusive*</u> *individual I* to <u>*inclusive*</u> *Universal I*, that is, to the *second stage*, "Self-consciousness," where it will now *include the Object within itself* and actually know itself *as* the ALL that it is.

> "Logic is pure science, pure knowledge in the entire range of its development ... the *Certainty* which has become Truth ... and no longer has the Object over against itself but has *internalized* it and knows it *as its own self.*" (Logic, p. 69) **Hegel**

§197

Therefore, the ALL which *is* but is not *aware* of itself as ALL is (1) the Universal, in *Logic*, while (2) the Particularization or "splitting" of the Universal, of the ALL, exists first in the form of *Nature* and Matter, the principle of individuation, whose highest and last form is the microcosm of the individuated human Body, the condition for *awareness*. Finally (3) the overcoming of the splitting or division is considered in the *Science of Jedi* as the transition from exclusive Consciousness to inclusive Self-consciousness, that is, to Individuality or concrete Universality, the fully actualized ALL that sees only *itself* in every Object of the infinite totality of all that IS.

§198

Indeed, the Individual or Universal actualized or the concrete Universal is nothing other than Jedi and the Jedi Order. And here we see the *necessity* of the Jedi Order: The *Individual* (e.g. yourself) is not just a simple individual, but rather a *concrete Universal*. As the *former*, the Individual is only a "P.I.," a *Particular* Individuality, and as such is in a state of separation or opposition—namely of itself to Objectivity, especially to other individuals or persons in which it does not see, have or find itself. As the *latter*, it is a concrete Universal or a "U.I.," a *Universal* Individuality, an individual *fused with* Universality and fully aware of this union and of its universality. As such it experiences and knows of its *unity and identity* with the Other person and all others—and the other Jedi (realized "humans") have the *same* experience. *This universal experience of "self in other," of the unity of Subjectivity and Objectivity, is precisely the JEDI ORDER.*

§199

First, we will discuss the *Introduction to Science*. Second, we will look at the overall process of the realization of the Jedi Order as traced in the *Sciences of Nature and Jedi*. Third, we will consider the contents of the *Science of Logic* itself and the Concept, the *Method* of comprehension in Science. Then fourth, we will look at some examples of the Method, i.e. of how the Concept can be used to comprehend such phenomena as the Animal Organism, the Solar System, and the State.

(1) THE INTRODUCTION TO JEDI SCIENCE

"First you get the Truth (as Concept, the Jedi Order)—
Then you study its Becoming in detail"

§200

The INTRODUCTION, which is also the becoming of the Truth or Concept, is necessary in order to understand and actually *do* Jedi Science. For Science presupposes that you are a JEDI and have advanced from Stage Two to Stage Three, from Consciousness OF, to Self-Consciousness; that you have exited the Dark Side (+|-) and Plato's CAVE and have achieved the Knowledge of the Force, the Truth (±), the UNITY of opposites. It is thus presupposed that you have overcome the illusory *separation* between yourself (as consciousness/knowing) and the Object of your consciousness (Being/the Truth) and are now ONE with Being, the Force, the Whole. Thus with Absolute Knowledge or the Absolute Concept you now coincide with the Infinite Whole of all that IS, with the Force itself.

§201

> "Science presupposes liberation from the opposition of consciousness ... the separation of Knowing and the Object is now overcome and the two are known to be *inseparable.*" **Hegel**

The following is very important and also reveals the major flaw in your own sciences:

It is a FACT that Science is True Knowledge. And True Science is Knowledge of What truly IS, not of what seems to be and *is not*. Therefore the preliminary first question of all—before we can even *do* science—is "WHAT TRULY IS?" (a question not asked by your own sciences, which just assume the answer, and wrongly). *This* is precisely what the INTRODUCTION to Science does and answers.

§202

In the course of showing that the *separation* of Knowing/subject and Being/object is an illusion, that the two are in a UNITY, we have found out *What truly IS* (in addition to what "Knowledge or Knowing" truly is). What truly IS, Being, the Object, what is truly *There* before us is ... *Consciousness, Thought or Thinking—or simply the CONCEPT.—Not* sense-objects, the singular material "things" (macro or micro) or "fields" of the physical Universe or "the Cave"—as your scientists believe (though the "empirical" does have a part to play in Science).

> "The Absolute is essentially a result— the process of its own becoming. The True is the Whole, etc."
>
> "The Truth, the concrete Concept, at once *contains within itself the infinite realm of all that is Objective.*" **Hegel**

§203

It is simple my Padawan. The ABSOLUTE CONCEPT (THINKING) is alone What truly IS. It is *ALL REALITY,* containing all reality within itself, with nothing outside. In Knowing *itself* it at once knows everything, all Objects. As **Hegel** says, "The Concept is everything"—it is the *unity* of subject and object, not the *separation* of subject and object; and as your **Aristotle** teaches: "God (or the Force), the ultimate Being or Arche, is none other than *Self-Thinking Thought (noesis noeseos).*"

§204

Once you know that the CONCEPT is alone the Truth and Being and What IS, you at once also know that everything else you originally took and normally take to be reality, cannot be truly real. All else, all other phenomena or alleged "entities," can only be temporary *vanishing conditions,* stages or "moments" in the Process which led up to and resulted in the truly and alone REAL, the CONCEPT—or the Force or *the Jedi Order,* which is the Force actualized and self-knowing. Indeed, the Concept is nothing but the process of its *own* self-actualization.

§205

We also now know what KNOWING is—what it is to truly KNOW a thing. "KNOWING" is the Concept, is thinking or conceiving. To know a thing truly is to think or conceive it according to the Concept and the Concept's "moments" or structure. For the Concept contains and subsumes *everything* within itself and is the *essence* of everything, of every possible and conceivable Object.

The *INTRODUCTION* to JEDI SCIENCE in more detail

§206

(1) Now the Force, the Truth, What IS, is a single UNITY that nonetheless contains a manifold of differences within itself. Hence, in order to adequately understand this UNITY (and its contents or differences) and engage in a Science or Knowledge of it and its contents, it is necessary to occupy the self-same standpoint of the UNITY itself, to know it from the *inside,* so to speak. One must have achieved a state of UNITY *oneself,* must have transcended all multiplicity, duality, division, and separation and become identical with the ONE REALITY itself. This is to possess what your **A-Team** calls "Absolute Knowledge" or the "Absolute Concept," and what we

Jedi call *the Knowledge of the Force*. And NOTE that the CONCEPT is simply the Force's *Knowledge* of itself in its totality. Hence, the need for an INTRODUCTION to Jedi Science.

§207

(2) More exactly, Knowledge or Knowing is a comprehending by means of thought (the Concept), or a thinking comprehension of the Object. The Concept is thus the true *Method* of Knowing in the field of Science, a Method that is explicated in the *Science of Logic*.
As we saw, the One Reality and what truly and alone exists, is *Consciousness*. And since the essence of Consciousness is none other than *THINKING* or the Concept, it is equally true that the One Reality is the Concept—or "the Concept is everything." As Jedi **Kant** says: "Concepts are Concepts *of* Objects" and thus contain the Object *within* themselves, hence are a "Concept-Object" or "Subject-Object." Therefore, the Concept is equally Being or Reality; for as the *unity* of Thought and Being, the Concept contains Being *within* itself.

"The Concept is true Being ... Being is the known Concept." Jedi Master Hegel

§208

It is because of this FACT that Knowledge (and SCIENCE) is possible. For if Being in fact were *outside* of the Concept (or Thinking) and independent of it, then thinking would be only formal or subjective and would not be able to penetrate Being or the Object and know it as it is *in itself* or truly—instead only as it were for us, as outside observers. And this is why an "Introduction" to Science or Knowing is necessary. Namely, to make Knowledge possible. That is, by showing that in truth no *separation* exists between thinking (the Concept) and its Objects or Being—that thinking *is* one with the Object or contains the Object within itself; and therefore to vouchsafe *OBJECTIVE THOUGHT*, that thought is not just *subjective* but is equally *objective*.

§209

(3) The Introduction therefore constitutes an *Education* (by means of thinking or Reason) into this standpoint and realization of the *Absolute Concept*, the principle of Science ... "absolute" meaning that

nothing but the Concept really exists, that there *is* nothing outside of it and other than it to which it can be related, and this because all putative Objects or Others have been found to exist *within* the Concept itself or been revealed to be only *ideal* or *nothing* as such, that is, nothing *but* Consciousness or the Concept. As Jedi **Hegel** says:

> The Concept is absolute idealism and Science is conceptually comprehensive cognition insofar as every Object—which in other forms of consciousness counts as something that IS or is independent—is known *within* the Concept simply as an *ideal* moment. (*Enc.* §160z.)

The Introduction is therefore *the* education of INVERSION or TRANSCENDENCE as pointed out by **Hegel** and in **Plato's** Divided Line—namely, of exiting the CAVE and making the transition from illusion (senses, the many) to Reality (One, thought-consciousness), from *Belief* in sense-material-singular objects as reality, to *Knowledge* of the *Universal* Concept (Self or I) or the Force *as Reality*—which nonetheless contains Matter as suspended within itself ($\pm$). That is, moving from a condition where one knows Objects in antithesis to oneself, to a condition where one, in knowing objects knows oneself and in knowing oneself knows objects: this is the UNITY of Knowing/Consciousness/Thinking and the Object.

§210

(4) Here we will just highlight some of the main points of this educational process and entry into Science. (As we noted above **Hegel's**, which we will follow here, is the best that exists on your planet at present, but a new contemporary version will be coming out soon)

First: Consciousness and its development/education to Absolute Knowledge or the Concept is the theme of this *Introduction* to Science. Consciousness, at first finite and limited by an Object (*Gegen-stand*), will learn by stages that it is unlimited, infinite and all reality.

Second: One of the keys to understanding both the *Introduction* and *Science* proper is that they both involve a *move* from *two* to *one*, from *separation* of terms (+|-) to their *unification* ($\pm$). So as regards the *Introduction:* we start with a *separation* of consciousness from its

Object and end with their *unification*, called Self-Consciousness, Absolute Knowledge, or the Absolute Concept (with the Object thus *internalized*). So the goal or final result, everywhere in Science and here as well, is *UNITY*—in the *Introduction*, the UNITY of Absolute Knowledge or Concept/Object, in *Logic* the UNITY of the Force-Idea-Truth as Concept/Object, in *Nature* the UNITY of the Soul, in *Jedi* the UNITY of the Jedi Order. The final goal is "HISTORY and Reality comprehended."

§211

Third: The *Introduction* has Three Sections: **A.** *Consciousness* (of an Other, Object). **B.** *Self-Consciousness* (consciousness of consciousness, or of itself). And lastly **C.**, comprising **AA**. *Reason*, the UNITY of Consciousness and Self-Consciousness or "the certainty that Consciousness (or the Concept) *is all reality and all truth,*" and in two parts, Theoretical and Practical Reason. **BB**. *Geist* or *Spirit/Mind/Jedi*. **CC**. *Religion*. And **DD**. *Absolute Knowing* or the *Absolute Concept*.

§212

In Brief we have: **A.** *Consciousness*. There are Three Stages and Lessons: Sense-Certainty, Perception, and the Understanding (of forces and laws). We start with Consciousness knowing its Object, the immediate sensuous THIS which, when examined by reason ("dialectic"), then changes into the universal THIS, requiring a new shape—Perception, the Thing and its properties, which changes into the Unconditioned Universal, into Understanding and its Forces and Laws. At the end we learn that the Object is really *Consciousness itself* (or the Concept), and therefore have a new shape, *Self*-Consciousness.

§213

B. *Self-Consciousness*. We have advanced from the Knowing of an *other* to the Knowing of *itself* or the Knowing of Knowing. We then transition from Desire to Recognition and the Master-Slave dialectic: "Self-consciousness exists in and for itself when it so exists for *another* Self-consciousness; it exists only in being *recognized*"; and from thence to Stoicism, Skepticism, and the Unhappy Consciousness—that is, from the Roman, to the Medieval, to the Modern World (via Luther and the Renaissance) and Reason and the re-birth of the Sciences in the 16th and 17th centuries.

§214

C. AA. Reason. We now know that Consciousness, the Concept, is *all reality.* We begin with Theoretical (Observing) Reason and then advance to Practical Reason, where the following movement recurs: namely, Consciousness going out of itself to an Other or Object and then returning *into itself* in such a way that the "Object" is seen to self-destruct or -dissolve through internal contradiction, hence proving itself to be none other than *Consciousness itself.* Reason then becomes the realization that, *"the I is my only Object";* something Jedi **Kant** and **Fichte** came close to realizing but fell short of since they *also* posited a "Thing in itself" in addition to the "TUA," One Consciousness, Concept or the "I" that contains *all reality within itself. This is the end of the book—all that remains is to harvest all remaining Objects into the <u>Concept</u> (I or Self), which is the unity of Thought and Being, or the <u>Category</u> as the unity of Self-Consciousness and Being.*

BB. Spirit. Here we have actual historical States and cultures: Greek, Roman, Medieval, 18th Century Europe, the French Revolution, the German Kantian Moral Revolution, Evil and its Forgiveness and, finally, the "**I = I**," which is *"God appearing in the midst of those who know themselves as Pure Absolute Knowledge"* or the Concept.

CC. Religion. The Self-consciousness of Spirit or God. The history of religions: the Persian, Egyptian, Greek, and Hebrew-Christian, culminating in the God-Man (*the unity of opposites*) and the "Death" of God (as wholly transcen*dent*). But religious consciousness is still divided—involved in the duality of God *and* Man, Heaven *and* Earth—and still stuck in *separation* and the Consciousness OF an Object or Other (namely, "God," "the Absolute").

§215

DD. Absolute Knowledge. Here we overcome the *separation* (in religion between consciousness and its Object/God). We realize the *nothingness* of the Object *as* Object (*Gegen-stand*), for it is Self-consciousness that *externalizes itself as* the Object, and thus knows *itself* as the Object and the Object as itself. This is *Absolute Knowledge* (which "remains within its Concept"). Here "The content of religion receives the form of the Self or the Concept ... and the Activity of the Self *within itself* is thereby known to be *all essentiality and all existence.*" The Force has knowledge of *itself* in and *as* the phenomenological observer, that is, *as* yourself as a Jedi.

§216

The goal of History, Philosophy, and the Universe is the Absolute Concept and Absolute Knowledge, or the absolute UNITY of Concept/Object, Knowing/Truth, which is *Objective Thought.* The Force now unfolds its process in this ether of its life and is JEDI SCIENCE (or "History and Reality comprehended"). Thus with Absolute Knowledge *"time itself is abolished"* and we enter the Eternal Present (or NOW) and begin our life in Eternity (which for your religions begins only *after* physical death); and we also begin to produce and teach Science. Your Jedi **Hegel** concludes his own *Introduction* to Science with these words:

> "*Nature,* the externalized Spirit, in its existence *is nothing but* this eternal externalization of its continuing existence and the movement that reinstates *the Subject* .... History is the conscious self-mediating process of Spirit (the Force) emptied out into Time ... The GOAL of History is Absolute Knowledge [*the Knowledge of the Force*] ... and comprehended History [is] the recollection and the Golgotha of absolute Spirit [*the Jedi, the Force actualized*], the actuality, truth, and certainty of his throne, without which he would be lifeless and alone. *Only* from the chalice of this realm of spirits foams forth for Him his own infinitude."

We are now out of the CAVE, the Dark Side separation (+|-), and into the Truth (±) of the Knowledge of the Force. We are a JEDI, a U.I., a *Universal* Individual and one with everyone, we have entered and are permanently established in the JEDI ORDER. As Jedi **Hegel** says, "The Truth is *this* I and no other, yet at once *Universal I.*" Thus the curtain is drawn and forever closed; the *separation* of us from Being, subject from object is no more, the *opposition* of consciousness (to an independent Object) is overcome and canceled, *never* to recur again whether we are in Science or in daily life/practice. We have attained FREEDOM, Absolute Freedom and Infinity—we see/ have/find ourselves in every other, in every object, for *"the Concept is everything,* and its sole drive is to know itself *in everything"* (which is also the implicit goal not only of Buddhism but of all your religions, namely, "to *be* One with everything"—or simply, "to be ONE").

§217

Thus we have attained the TRUTH, the Concept, the Knowledge of the Force. Now we can proceed to Science itself and study the "timeless" process of the Force's becoming and actualization into the glorious Jedi Order ... for

"SCIENCE IS *TIMELESS* COMPREHENSION."
JEDI MASTER HEGEL

§218

NOTE: (1) Even though, having completed the *Introduction,* you are now a Jedi (the Force actualized and self-knowing), **you now have Two Options: You can either go on to actually *do* Science (and teach it), or *not.*** Further, be mindful that *unless* you go on and at least master LOGIC (Science) you are only an ***Intuitive Jedi.*** You know and *are* the TRUTH in an *Intuitive* and not in a **Discursive** way—and this, even though you have, know, and *are* the Concept (the Thought-Being Unity). (2) It is also important to know that all the God-realized or Self-realized beings on your planet and in its history are one and all "Intuitives" and not "Discursives" (excepting the **A-Team**). They have and are the Concept, *but do not know it*—and most particularly those in the East, who disparage *Thought* and even teach that you cannot know/attain the Truth (God, the Force) by thought—which is absolutely untrue.

(2) THE OVERALL PROCESS OF THE REALIZATION OF THE JEDI ORDER

§219

This process is best grasped as a movement from Two to One, from Dis-Unity to Unity, and from the Dark Side to the Light Side of the Force. Also, since Nature or Matter is *nothing in itself,* or *ideal,* having only a Being-for-another, whereas Jedi or Consciousness is *true Being* as Being-for-itself, Nature's process and movement through its forms will be to show precisely its intrinsic *nothingness*, to utterly set itself aside and reveal Jedi and Subjectivity as its sole Truth.

§220

1. The *Science of Nature* thus studies Nature—as the Force's Dark Side (-), Matter (the unconscious), Objectivity (without the moment of Subjectivity), the OUTER and Self-Externality, where everything is *outside* of everything else ad infinitum. Nature, its forms and stages, is best understood as a process of overcoming this initial condition of externality, multiplicity, dis-unity and separation of parts, and revealing Unity to be its truth. Nature then is simply the becoming of the subject or Subjectivity (the Inner or inwardness). Again as your Jedi **Hegel** famously says,

> **"*Nature*, the externalized Spirit (or Intelligence), is in its existence nothing but this eternal externalization of its continuing existence and the movement which reinstates *the Subject*."**

§221

2. Nature's *first form*, therefore, is that which is furthest from Unity and the most extreme form of *externality: SPACE*—where no two points coincide and all points are *outside* each other to infinity. Nature's *last form*, which is at the same time Jedi's first form, is Life as the *SOUL (Seele)*—in which Nature's self-externality is completely overcome and where two or more points *do* in fact coincide; for example, *one and the same Soul* exists simultaneously in my right index finger and in my left index finger separated by several feet, and also in an infinity of other points of Space (cf. your own science's concept of "non-locality"—entanglement, **Bell's** inequality, and **Alan Aspect's** experiments).

§222

3. Thus, Nature's forms are a series of progressive overcomings of Nature's initial separateness, dis-unity, and externality, or a series of increasing types of *unity*, that is, subjects or subjectivity. For example and in brief:

—With *matter* or *mass* we have the first connection or contiguity of the isolated points of space.—Then with *gravity* and matter in the form of a sphere, like the Earth, we have the first "subject," or *unity of a multiplicity*, in which every object or part of the Earth's mass seeks the self-same indivisible *point* or center of gravity (which if all matter attained, would result in the absolute disappearance of matter; an indication of the intrinsic *nothingness* of matter).— Universal Gravity in the form of the *Solar System* is another example of a unity in multiplicity, whereby a host of separate objects gather around a single center or focus (the Sun).—Then we have *magnetism*, an illustration of Polarity, where one side of a magnet cannot exist without the other, the two being inseparable, thus signifying a still higher form of unity and overcoming of Nature's initial exteriority as Space.—Then *electricity*, where positive cannot exist *without* negative electricity, another example of the unity of opposites (±).—And *chemism*, where we witness the intimate connection of acid and base in their neutralization.

—Finally with the *animal organism* we have the highest type of unity and Subjectivity of which Nature is capable. All of the animal's organs or parts are in a unity and as members cannot exist apart from the whole organism; and a single *Soul* inhabits and pervades all its parts and *points* of space. Nature's externality is completely overcome. Objectivity has become Subjectivity or Jedi (Consciousness, Mind, Concept): the Truth of Nature is the ONE POINT. The Soul is the *universal immateriality of matter*, and the truth that matter, as parts outside parts, *has no truth whatsoever*. The entire process of Nature's overcoming of itself is given a concise summary by Jedi **Hegel** in the following words:

> "The *Science of Nature* teaches us how Nature sublates (cancels) its externality by stages, how matter already refutes the independence of the individual, of the many, by *gravity*, and how this refutation begun by gravity, and still more by simple indivisible *light*, is completed by animal life, by the sentient creature, since this reveals to us the omnipresence of the one soul at every point of its bodiliness, and so the sublatedness (and untruth) of the asunderness of matter. Since, then, everything material is sublated (overcome) by the mind that is in itself and at work within Nature, and this sublation is consummated in the substance of *soul*, the soul emerges as the ideality of *everything* material, as *all* immateriality, so that everything called matter, however much it

simulates independence to ordinary thinking, is known to have no independence in the face of mind (*Enc.* §*389, zus.*)."

Jedi **Hegel** further clarifies the crucial Nature/Jedi-Spirit relation as follows: "Life is the highest form in which the Idea (Force) exhibits itself in Nature and is simply something that sacrifices itself and whose essence is to become Spirit (Jedi) ... *Spirit is just this act of advance into reality by means of nature;* that is, Spirit finds its antithesis or opposite in Nature, and it is *only by the annulling of this opposition that it exists for itself and is Spirit (PR III 42)."*

§223

4. Now we are in the *Science of the Jedi Order.* We have Subjectivity, initially as Soul, which as such and as pervading all of Nature, Matter and Objectivity, is infinite and all reality—which the Soul has to realize in the course of this *Science* and does so as follows:

The first part of this Science is called Subjective Jedi, which treats in Anthropology of the Soul, in Phenomenology of Consciousness, and in Psychology of Jedi (or Mind). The division reflects the Concept's moments of Universality-Particularity-Individuality, as Universal undifferentiated One, to Particularization or division of the One (into Consciousness or Subjectivity and its Object), then Individuality as the unity of the two, Subject-Object. We then start with Anthropology which studies the Soul and its external features and feelings, etc., becoming an actual individual soul that takes possession of its Body (as its tool and outward sign), and then becoming an "I" or Consciousness. The Soul initially contains all of Nature within itself without the differentiation into Subject and Object, and which occurs for the first time in Phenomenology. The "I" projects all the contents of Nature that were previously within itself as Soul, outside of itself, regarding them for the first time as an Objective World standing over against itself. The goal of this section is to cancel or overcome this separation of Subject and Objectivity and realize their unity, which results in Jedi or Mind, the subject matter of Psychology. This studies the Mind's theoretical and practical powers and ends with the free Will. Then the Will (or Subject) must objectify and realize itself in the State and its institutions, which are the embodiments of its Will and Freedom. This is the content of Objective Jedi (Mind), which considers Law, Morality and Social Ethics (Sittlichkeit), which is comprised of the

Family, Civil Society, the State and Universal History, which in truth is nothing but the becoming of the Jedi Order, the end or *telos* of the whole of Science.

§224

5. Then we have the highest Objectification of Subjectivity or *Unity* of Subjectivity and Objectivity (±) in what is called *Absolute Jedi (Mind)*, namely in Art, Religion, and Science, the sphere of the *Knowledge* of the Force or Truth, which is the final Form, the Jedi Order as realized. What is important is that Art, Religion, and Science take place *within* the State and that all three give the *Knowledge* of the Truth, the unity of Subjectivity or the Concept *and* Objectivity. It is only by educating the citizens of the State into this *Knowledge*, making the citizens JEDI, that the reality of the JEDI ORDER is realized. Also the State as such is "in time"—and when we move from Objective Jedi to Absolute Jedi, we move necessarily from *time* to *eternity*. First in *Art*, we behold the Truth (the unity of Subject and Object) in a Painting or Film for example—that is, in an *Object* before us, a material colored canvas or a screen with light-images, as shaped, conceived and ordered by a Subject, by an artist's subjectivity or idea. In *Religion*, whose sole purpose is to bring about the Subject's *experience* of her present union with God (the Absolute or Force) as Object, we have a true unity of Subjectivity and Objectivity but one which occurs *only* in feeling and representation (or picture thinking), i.e. as *intuitive* but not discursive. In *Science* we have the highest *objectifying* and unity of Subject and Object, since it is in Thought or the Concept, where the Subject and Object are *both* Thought, hence where there is an absolutely perfect and adequate correspondence or unity between the two—the Force (Truth or Idea) fully actualized and existent. And recall that the One Science is comprised of the Sciences of Nature, Jedi, and Logic, *the Science of Logic* being the highest and purest science as alone exhibiting

> "The *absolute* elevation over sensibly present particulars only takes place in the Philosophical-Scientific knowledge of the *Eternal*, for the Eternal, unlike the particulars of sense, is not affected by the flux of coming-to-be and passing-away and is, therefore, neither in the past nor in the future; on the contrary, it is the absolutely *present*, raised above Time and containing all of Time's differences within itself." *Enc. 406, zus.*, **Hegel**

Absolute Knowledge or *the Concept* (the "DNA" of Being) in the full range of its determinations.

I will close this section with an illuminating passage from one of your contemporary Jedi scientists who uses the term "Foundation" instead of our "Jedi Order":

> A further astounding conclusion of Absolute Science, the *only* genuine science of the Whole, is that contra Copernicus and empirical "science" in general the Earth is *not*, as they would have us believe, an insignificant "speck" in an isolated corner of a minor galaxy, itself an insignificant "speck" drifting inconsequently in a sea of infinite "specks" circling with other insignificant "specks" an insignificant star of low-order magnitude, etc, etc.—*On the contrary*, the Earth truly stands at the precise center of the Universe, indeed has the infinite undisputed and undisputable Right to be regarded *as this center itself*—notwithstanding the fact of its movement around the Sun ... The Earth is the Centerpiece of the COSMOS for the precise reason that it is the locus and HOME OF SPIRIT, the Self-Conscious part of the Universe. Hence, Human History is the *only* History. There *is* no other place in the Universe where it occurs, owing to the nature of the *unicity* of the CONCEPT or Begriff that prescribes that there be only *one* manifestation or circuit of its Actualization ...
>
> A further consequence is that the *sidereal* Universe is totally "virgin." Its manifest Destiny is to be *thoroughly* Spiritualized (or humanized), that is, *impregnated*, subjugated, colonized, inhabited and cultivated, thereby *hallowed* and *sanctified*—above all *cherished*—for it will be the World of our children, and of our children's children ... by SPIRIT, i.e. by Man, i.e. by human beings, i.e. by US ... Spirit's ultimate Destiny, therefore, is to eternally *mirror* itself in the most concrete and variegated fashion in all of *EXTERIORITY*—this is what the Bible refers to as "World without End." Therefore, since the expression "The Kingdom of God," dear to Hegel, Schelling, and others, connotes for most minds an "Otherworldliness"—which absolutely contradicts the Truth—we propose that the Whole be called: *THE FOUNDATION.*
>
> Thus, it can be said that the History of the World (political, cultural and philosophical), i.e. of the Universe (the Totality), is nothing other than the coming into being of ... **THE FOUNDATION**; with regard

to which and in accordance with the continuing development and advancing Spiritualization of the sidereal Universe, three determinate Stages or Phases can be distinguished and termed respectively:

THE FIRST FOUNDATION—the initial period of Universal History extending from the latter's beginning to the settling of the Solar System;

THE SECOND FOUNDATION—extending from the latter to the indwelling of the Galaxy, that is, The Milky Way; and finally

THE THIRD FOUNDATION—a phase of Spirit having to do with the settling and indwelling of that which lies outside our own Galaxy—a period that will know no end.

(3) The *Science* of *Logic*

> "Logic is the system of pure Reason …
> the TRUTH as it is without veil, in its own
> absolute nature ….
> It is the exposition of GOD as he is in his
> eternal essence *prior* to the creation
> of the universe."

§225

Logic (= *the Logos*) can be defined as the *self-exposition* of the CONCEPT or POINT or "Begriff" in the form of *objective* Thought-determinations or Categories,[1] i.e. of the *INNER* Force or Begriff, the concrete *Sciences of Nature* and *Jedi* (*Mind, Spirit*) or the *OUTER* Force or Begriff, being the self-explication of the Begriff in the form or medium of Exteriority. Generally speaking, the *Science of Logic* and the *System of Jedi Science* as a whole simply repeats or "reconstructs" in the medium of the Concept that which was depicted in the *Introduction* or *Phenomenology* (i.e. in History) in the medium of *Vorstellen* (picture-thinking or "bifurcated" consciousness), namely, the sublation or cancellation of the Subject/ Object distinction or, equally, the deduction of Idealism and the Ascent to the Absolute Standpoint, *the Knowledge of the Force*, where Subject = Object. As Jedi **Hegel** observes:

> Spirit (Jedi, Mind), therefore, having won the CONCEPT (*Begriff*), displays its existence and movement in this *ether of its life* and is SCIENCE. In this, the moments of its movement (*Bewegung*) no longer exhibit themselves as specific *shapes of consciousness* but— since consciousness's difference has returned into the Self—as *specific Concepts* (*Begriffe*) and as their organic self-grounded movement. (*PS* 491 Miller)

§226

Noble Padawan our first question will be: What is the ground of the Logic's division into an "Objective" and a "Subjective" Part? First, the principle of the Whole is the *Begriff* or *Infinity* (its other name) which, as we have seen, is nothing other than the process of its own becoming, i.e. *the positing of itself.* Hence, it is UR-TEIL, *Judgement,* the Act of dividing itself into *two* and then annulling this division. Therefore, the Begriff is the *ground* of the Original Bifurcation of the Whole into a Subjective and an Objective Factor, the sublation of which is the precondition of thinking, yet equally brought about by the same. Logic is simply the Begriff's self-exhibition of this Process or Movement of *self-overcoming,* a movement or "method" which is the First Principle (*Arche*) of the Whole (= Logic-Nature-Spirit/Jedi). We offer here an excerpt from Jedi **Hegel's** *Phenomenology* that perfectly expresses the Life of this self-suspending Ur-teil, the origin of all determinacy:

> INFINITY is this absolute unrest of pure self-movement, in which whatever is determined in one way or another, e.g. as being, is rather the opposite of this determinateness ... This simple Infinity, or the Absolute Concept, may be called the simple essence of Life, the soul of the world, the universal blood, whose omnipresence is neither disturbed nor interrupted by any difference but rather is itself every difference, as also their supersession; it pulsates within itself but does not move, inwardly vibrates yet is at rest. It is self-identical, for the differences are tautological; they are differences that are none. The self-identical essence (being) is therefore related only to itself; "to itself" implies relationship to an "other," and the relation-to-self is rather a self-sundering; or, in other words, that very self-identicalness is an inner difference. (PS 100 Miller, our italics)

§227

In essence, Jedi **Hegel** is saying that the nature of the Begriff, Infinity or Ur-teil[2] is to be the self-identical that spontaneously divides itself into *two.* That is to say, to be identical with oneself is to be in relationship with oneself[3]—this logically necessitates the *making or positing of a distinction* in that which is identical. So what *IS,* viz. the Concept or Infinity, is identical and different *at the same time.* This is precisely its Act, i.e. to *differentiate itself,* to separate itself from itself, to posit *difference* and maintain identity with itself *in that difference*—this is in truth the essence of the *Trinity,* which is nothing but the Begriff apprehended through pictorial thinking (*Vorstellen*), as well as the ground of the distinction of the *two* cognitive operations of the mind (Reason), viz. *Analysis,* the making of Many out of One, and *Synthesis,* the making of One out of Many.

Hegel also explains this division of Logic into "Objective" and "Subjective" as one originating with the *Phenomenology*. In the "Introduction" of the *Science of Logic* he tells us:

> In the Unity of pure or absolute knowing, the result of the Phenomenology, the opposition in Consciousness between a self-determined entity, a Subject, and a second such entity, an Object, is known to be overcome; Being (Object) is known to be the pure Concept in its own self (Subject), and the pure Concept (Subject) to be the true Being (Object). These, then, are the two moments contained in Logic. But now they are known to be inseparable. (Miller 60)[4]

This passage again simply reflects the basic movement of the Whole from Immediacy/Exteriority/Objectivity to Interiority and Subjectivity, a movement depicted in the *Phenomenology* and to be repeated here. "Objective Logic" treats the Categories of objectivity (Being, Necessity, and Nature in general) such as, Being, Finitude, Infinity, One and Many, Quantity, Measure, Essence, Substance and Causality, while the "Subjective Logic" considers the Categories of subjectivity (Thought, Freedom, and Spirit) for example, Concept, Judgement, Syllogism, Life, Volition, Cognition, Definition and Theorem.

§228

In Jedi **Hegel's** words: "Thus what is to be considered is the whole Concept, firstly as the Concept in the form of *Being*, secondly in the form of *the Concept* (Miller 61)." Further, since these two (Being and the Concept) stand *in relation* to each other, "there results a sphere of *mediation*, the Concept as a System of *reflected determinations*, i.e. of Being *in process of transition* into the being-within-self or inwardness of the Concept." This mediative sphere is the *Doctrine of Essence* which, because in it the Concept is still "fettered by the Exteriority of immediate being"—notwithstanding the degree of Interiority reflected by it, for this reason is to be included in the "Objective" rather than in the "Subjective Logic" which has truly sublated *all* relation to Exteriority.

Secondly we need to ask: Where do the Categories come from? The Categories, it is true, have their immediate origin in *Experience* (cp. *Enc.* §400 and §12), in everyday speech and reflection, but they have a higher destiny and employment, viz. they are to be the vehicle through which the Eternal Idea will think itself. Thus their true vocation is to be used to *grasp* Being or the Absolute—recall, the Categories as historically or temporally developed are nothing but progressive *definitions* of the Absolute (the In-itself). As Jedi **Aristotle** says, the Categories are the modes in which *beings* appear, the ways in which they can be said to be, thus they primarily exhibit the *differences* of things. But whence comes this urge or need *to grasp, to know?* In essence, the mind—the incipient Begriff—instinctively knows that it is all and the only Reality. Thus, when it confronts an Other or a puzzle, it has the assurance that through Thought, through the conceptualization of the Other, it can thereby *overcome* the same and reduce it to *itself,* or find itself *in* the Other. This is precisely the goal of all thinking, of Philosophy, of History, and thus of the History of Philosophy; in other words, the goal of thinking is simply *to comprehend* and thus to cancel a thing's condition of being foreign, alien, hostile and other to the Self.

§229

The more originary question however is: Why must there be Categories? or: Why is there thinking at all? For we are saying that the Universe exists in order for thinking to occur. But then, Why must *thinking* occur? or, What is the reason for "Reason"? This is the most difficult question, but of course it can and must be answerable. Briefly, it has to do with the Laws or Dynamics of *Possibility*, which are at once the Laws of Reality, of what can be or not be. For example, if it is *logically* (in thought) impossible for me (my physical Body) to be in Baghdad and Pittsburgh at the same time, then it will be impossible also in fact or in *reality*—as **Spinoza** says, what cannot be conceived, can in no wise be. It is simply a matter of pure Logic. Another example will illuminate the issue. Consider **Schelling's** question: Why is there something rather than nothing? Is it *possible* for there to be *nothing at all?* The answer is "No"—not only because obviously there *is* something, but simply because the thought of nothing, hence its possibility, *presupposes* the thought of something or being. *Neither can be posited and grasped without the other.* Further, if "nothing" be defined as the "indeterminate," then as logic shows, this is the same as pure being; that which *is* but has no specific determinacy. Hence, to say "nothing" is to say "being" at the same time. They cannot be conceived *apart* from each other; this is true of all such Concepts as Finite/Infinite, Identity/Difference, One/

Many, Something/Other and Necessity/Freedom. The point is that to have nothing, being must be present (*vorhanden*) at the same time. Therefore it is impossible for there to *be* nothing, and for there not to be *being*. Hence Thinking, Logic or Reason is merely *Possibility*, i.e. Reality, working out its various permutations.

Another celebrated question of your philosophers is: Is the Universe *finite* or *infinite*? or, Is there anything that actually exists that is *finite*? The answer again is "No," and this because as Logic, the Dynamics of Possibility, teaches, the *finite* is simply the sublation or negation of itself, i.e. its perishing (going under), and its transition or passage into the *Infinite*; as **Hegel** expresses it, "Determinate Being (*Dasein*) determines itself as finite and then transcends the limitation."

§230

This affords us a closer view of the Logic's method, a method self-originative of content. First, we should note that the *method* used to generate the various determinations of Logic, as well as of each science, can be called the "retrogressive-progressive grounding method" (as described in the closing pages of the *Science of Logic*). Briefly, from the *First Determination or Posit* of each science and its spontaneous *self-negation*, all subsequent determinations are generated or derived, and this by means of a *retrogressive grounding* of the First Determination which is at the same time *progressive* as productive of further, more concrete and truer determinations— the *Last Determination* then being the Truth and *Ground* of both the First and all intermediate ones. In effect, all logical determinations are latent or implicit in *Being*, *all* natural determinations, including matter, planet, and animal organism, are implicit in *Space* or *Extension*; and *all* spiritual determinations, including the Family, Right, the State and Religion, are implicit in *the Soul* or *Subject* (i.e. in the Intellect and Will). The movement is in essence from immediacy and universality *to* particularity (particularization) and difference *to* concrete individuality, the Final Result of a given (i.e. *produced*) science, absolutely simple yet containing *within itself* all the determinations relevant to the science in question.

Now, after the identity of Being and Nothing has resolved itself into Becoming, Becoming then spontaneously determines itself as Determinate Being (or "There-Being") which at once splits itself into "Something" and "Other." For to be *determinate* is to have *one* quality and *not* another, i.e. it is to introduce a distinction or *limitation*, the essence of *Finitude*. However, the limitation gives rise to an *Ought*, to the urge to transcend the limitation, which is at once an urge for the Finite to *negate itself*, to perish (cp. "The hour of its birth is the hour of its death"). Thus by canceling its limit the Finite cancels the opposition between itself and its Other, its Other gives way—for it has now achieved identity with it (i.e. it is exactly like its Other since to its Other *it* is the Other)—and consequently both entirely *vanish*. But this vanishing of the Finite is at the same time precisely the appearing of the *Infinite*. This is the true conception of the Infinite, namely, to be the *negation* of the Finite, hence to contain the Finite in itself as a "moment" of itself. Ordinary reflection or *Verstand* insists on keeping these two apart and fails to realize that an Infinite which has a Finite posited *outside* of itself is *itself* Finite, i.e. merely one of two things, while continuing to "imagine" that it understands the true nature of the Infinite.

§231

Therefore, there in truth *is* no Finite and can never be one (cp. *Enc.* §81, *Science of Logic* Remark 2., 154, Miller, and *History of Philosophy III* 261 Haldane and Simson). Anyone who says, "I do not believe that there *is* an Infinite but only the Finite or a multiplicity of finite things" does not realize what he or she is saying, has not reflected sufficiently on the Concept of the Finite, on what it is to *be* Finite. For to be Finite is to be *at once* Infinite, i.e. to pass immediately over without halt into the Infinite. Of course, the Infinite itself is not the last word hence it cannot even be said that the Universe or What is, is Infinite—and it too passes over via *self-negation* into another and higher Category, viz. Being-for-Self or the One, which to be conceived *entails* the positing of the Many, as well as the consequent tendency of the Many to collapse into the One and of the One to disperse into the Many; hence the positing of two new Categories or Moments of the Begriff, those of Attraction and Repulsion. This spontaneous, dialectical movement or "ballet" of self-thinking Thought (*noesis noeseos*) continues until all the various determinations of the Force or Idea have been organically and systematically derived from each other and the supreme Arche, the *Absolute Force (Idea)*, has been vindicated as that which alone *truly is and must be*. Thus as we have said, Thinking (i.e. *genuine* Thinking) is simply the Laws of Possibility working themselves out, and it is impossible for these possibilities, the Categories, not to exist.

§232

Further, there is the question, to be treated only briefly, What actually *is* the Idea (The Force)? is it something, some determinate thing, is it being, is it substance, the really real? In a sense it is all of these and none of these. This is so because it is the entire Science of Logic *alone* that can count as its true definition (cp. *Enc.* § 18). Each Predicate/Category we employ to determine it is itself a "vanishing," i.e. is a "moment" and not self-subsistent, it passes over into a higher Predicate. The Idea is not *thing* or *substance*, for these pass away into the Concept, nor is it *being*, for its truth is *becoming*, and so on, and so on. This is why the best way to express in a word what the Absolute Idea/Force or Absolute Standpoint is, is to say that it is *nothing* or, equally, is a *vanishing*. For what does exist—if it is permissible to use this word—are the Categories; however, each Category is the *negation of itself* and its subsequent transition into its opposite, or is a *vanishing* pure and simple. Thus it can be said that the Force (Idea)—*the veritable Ground* of all logical, natural and spiritual determinacy and reality—is in the end nothing but the entirety of the interconnected and -connecting Circle of these "vanishings."

§233

Lastly my Padawan, with regard to the absolute value of Logic, it must be stated that the *Science of Logic* is the only truly coherent and intelligible *Discourse*. All other discourse that employs the Categories—and it must—without having undertaken a prior *critique* of them, is (as can easily be demonstrated by the speculative Jedi logician/dialectician/metaphysician) inherently meaningless and self-contradictory.[5] Indeed, your contemporary "Analytic" logicians, as well as formalizers of your **Hegel's** Logic, would profit greatly by acknowledging the Fact that until they demonstrate the *objectivity* or *objective validity* (i.e. reference to, connection with being or objects of discourse) of their logical apparatus, i.e. symbols, operators, quantifiers, connectives, axioms and rules of inference, they trade only in abstractions and have intercourse with only themselves or their own subjective creations and not with any substantial Reality.[6] They would do well also to take notice that the subject-matter of the Science of Logic is the *Logos and the Logos alone*, i.e. what is subject-object, thought-reality, category-being *at once*, and what is, in the true and profound theological-ontological sense, the *GROUND* of the Universe or all things (an Office for which their operators, variables etc. are, confessedly, ill-suited); this knowledge of the Logos hence *presupposes* a prior *demonstration* and ascertainment (viz. a "phenomenology") of this all-crucial *connection* and *unity* of these Moments (but as your "analysts" place themselves outside the Tradition—whose sole purpose was to bring the knowledge of this Logos, *the Force*, to light—it is unlikely they have the slightest idea of the word's True significance). In default of this proof of Thought and Being's identity their utterances thus must remain devoid of objective validity, that is, TRUTH.

§234

The Secret to Logic and the Universe: Now, as your Jedi **Hegel** says, "Concepts are implicitly MOVEMENT" … which means that they do not stay put, that they are alive … they are all aspects, vanishing "moments" of the ONE LIVING CONCEPT. "All the words and concepts in the LOGIC refer to the CONCEPT, for that is all that exists." This means that terms-words-concepts such as "Being" "Being-there" "Substance" "Necessity" etc, do NOT HAVE A FIXED MEANING OR DEFINITION OR DETERMINACY (horos)—if they did, they could not FLOW into other terms, and be part of the MOVEMENT, of the LIFE, of the One Living CONCEPT. They, yes, start out with a definite meaning, given to them by Verstand (or ordinary intelligence) … but this original meaning soon changes into something else—when scrutinized more closely, in fact changes into its very opposite … BEING at first is, but then flows into its opposite, NOTHING, which does likewise … this sets up a movement, a vanishing of One into the Other and vice versa, a movement which can be called, and congeals into, BECOMING, which contains Being and Nothing, but now as "moments." So we now have (it seems) a fixed, definite and secure definition of Becoming … but not so. Indeed, the purpose of the LOGIC is to show how all categories-determinations are simply "moments," "dancers" in a Grand Dance Movement … they do not stay or stand still, they are restless activities like the organs, cells, tissues, systems in a living Organism … thus looking at the Living Whole from a distance, the categories both ARE and

> "We must learn to know God as our true and essential Self … Science's task is to trace what is objective back to the CONCEPT, which is our innermost Self." **Hegel**

> "For Hegel, the CONCEPT is God." **Schelling**

ARE NOT—it is the same with the Logic, the Concept, the categories—the Concept's contents or "organs" … AND THE CATEGORIES ARE NOT MEANT TO STAND STILL, REMAIN THE SAME, KEEP THE SAME FIXED DEFINITION THEY INITIALLY HAD. This is the main difficulty in understanding the Logic: everything changes, is fluid, in motion … for we are dealing here with ONE LIFE, with a LIVING BREATHING ENTITY—in fact, IT IS what your religions call GOD. So you *must* "forget yourself," as Jedi **Hegel** and others say, when you are engaged in Logic and Science … must surrender your particularity-individuality to sheer UNIVERSALITY, take a Bath in it, you must MERGE UTTERLY with it, MERGE YOUR PARTICULAR INDIVIDUALITY with its UNIVERSALITY; and remember, *Only the Universal is Necessary*, not the particular or individual. Everything changes, is in motion, so beware of trying to "understand" a specific category and give it a fixed meaning—you cannot. This is the secret of SPECULATIVE PHILOSOPHY, DIVINE THINKING, namely *to think Opposites in their UNITY*; so Independent and Non-Independent are the SAME, as are "Being for itself" and "Being for Another"—also *"I am in and for myself (Independent or Substance) only insofar as You* recognize me as in and for myself and free, that is, I am Dependent on you, on your recognition, for my Independence; I am Substance AND also POSITED, by you."

§235

So, the CONCEPT is a *LIVING ENTITY … it is GOD … it is EVERY OBJECT in the Universe, the essence and inner being of all (cf., your **Jacob Boehme's** writings).* Therefore there are TWO Modes of knowing God/the Concept/the Force, this Living Entity, and TWO ways of being Jedi EDUCATED into this Knowledge. (1) One way, the INTUITIVE, is by the "JEDI POINT CONCENTRATION METHOD"—if you keep doing this eventually you will see before you the Concept, as a living breathing, swirling 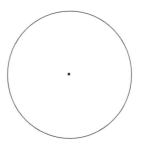 kaleidoscopic Whole of determinacies … a sacred, holy Whole, which you begin to see "superimposed" over and indwelling every object your attention light's upon, and every thought, etc (this is accompanied by special powers or abilities; this swirling whole also contains the sum total of all your life's memories, perceptions, experiences in condensed form, etc). BUT, you do not see the Determinacies-moments which are THERE in the Concept, which only the Jedi Logician-Scientist sees. (2) The other way, the DISCURSIVE, is achieved by immersing oneself in The LOGIC and the specific categories-determinacies of the CONCEPT, and eventually mastering their perfect fluid interconnection and MOVEMENT-LIFE, as a UNITY of Universality-Particularity-and Individuality.

(4) Examples of True Scientific Knowledge via the Method of The Concept (U-P-I) in *The Sciences of Nature* and *The Jedi Order*

§236

(1) *Introduction.* As we have seen, Science or Knowledge is a thinking comprehension of its objects, of Nature and Jedi (Mind). Since only the CONCEPT exists, all objects or phenomena, e.g. the Solar System, Animal Organism, and the State, can only be expressions or realizations of the One Concept and its determinations (U-P-I).

> "The concrete CONCEPT contains within itself the *infinite realm of all that is objective.*" **Hegel**

Thus to understand or comprehend a phenomenon is simply to discern the specific way the phenomenon embodies the Concept's determinations. For example, to grasp the BODY conceptually is to grasp it in the image of the Concept, for the Body's distinctions are only those of the Concept.

Let us first recall how the Concept's determinations (Universal-Particular-Individual) determine Reality or the Force as a whole and in its subdivisions or specifications, with a focus on *Life* or the *Animal Organism.*

First, we have the highest division of the Whole into Logic (Universal or "U"), Nature (Particular or "P"), and Jedi (Individual or "I")— note that in every case the third, the Individual, is the UNITY and Truth of the Universal and Particular. Then we have e.g. the division of Nature into Mechanics (U), Physics (P), and Organics (I). Then the division of Organics into the Geological Organism (U), the Plant

Nature (P), and the Animal Organism (I). Then the division of the Animal Organism into Shape (U), Assimilation (P), and the Genus Process or Sex-Relation (I).

To briefly explain the last triad: Each moment of the Concept (U-P-I) makes itself into a complete *syllogism* (*Schluss* or "close" in German) and is the Totality (or contains the others in itself). The syllogism or "close" is the unity-of-opposites, where the opposites are the Concept and its Object. Thus, in the case of "Shape" (U), the Organism relates to *itself*, or "closes" with itself through regeneration (or consuming itself): the Concept, as Soul (*Seele*), closes or unites with its Object, its Body. In "Assimilation" (P), the Organism relates to an *Other* (external inorganic nature), or closes with an Other, such as *nutriment*, which it converts into itself, into animality (a prime example of "absolute negativity"). In the "Genus Process" (I), which is the Unity of the first two, it closes with itself through copulation or union with an Other that is its own species (or with itself); the Result, which as also the result of Nature (P) as a whole, is both (1) a new individual (the same as itself) and the preservation of the species and (2) the death or negation of the individual, that is at once the realization of the Genus or Universal as Thought and the transition to Jedi or Mind (I), the last and highest sphere of the Force's actualization.

§237

(2) *Life, the Animal Organism (Shape).* Here we will see how the *Shape (U)* of the Animal Organism can be comprehended by the Concept and its moments (U-P-I). (A) *Functions of the Organism:* these are Sensibility (U), where the one simple universal Soul is everywhere present and feels in all parts of its Body, Irritability (P), which is receptivity to external stimulation and reaction to it, and Reproduction (I), whereby the organism constantly renews itself as an individual. (B) *Systems of Shape:* these three functions have their *reality* in three systems, sensibility in the nervous system, irritability in the circulatory system, and reproduction in the digestive system. (C) *The Total Structure:* the *centers* of the three systems (which reflect the identical threefold structure of all animals, from insect to man), are the Head (nervous: the brain), Thorax (circulatory: the heart), and Abdomen (digestive: the intestines). The Structure is at once the process whereby the Organism preserves itself by consuming itself. Each member (organ) consumes all the others (is End), and is in

turn consumed by the others (is Means); in this way the Life of the whole organism is maintained. In Jedi **Hegel's** words:

> The *immediate* Force (Idea) is *Life*. The CONCEPT is realized as soul, in a *body*. The soul is the immediate self-relating *universality* of the body's externality; it is equally the *particularizing* of the body, so that the body expresses no distinctions in itself other than the determinations of the Concept; and finally it is *individuality* as infinite negativity: the dialectic of the body's scattered objectivity, which is led back into subjectivity from the semblance of independent subsistence. This happens in such a way that all of the body's members are reciprocally both *means* and *ends* for each other from moment to moment, and that Life, while it is the *initial* particularizing of the members, becomes its own *result* as the *negative* unity that is *for-itself*, and in the dialectic of corporeity it con-cludes ("closes") itself only with itself. Thus Life is essentially *living being*, and in its immediacy it is *This Individual* living being. (Enc. §216)

§238

—NOTE on *The Theory of Evolution*. Darwinian evolution in its present form is incorrect as it is disproved e.g. by the fossil record which shows no evidence of species or progenitors *prior* to the Cambrian explosion, which even **Darwin** himself acknowledges, if true, would be a mortal blow to his theory: "If numerous species belonging to the same genera or families have really started into life at once, the fact would be fatal to the theory of evolution through natural selection" (from his *Origin of Species*, which incidentally fails to explain the origin of a single species). As eminent evolutionist **Stephen Jay Gould** himself notes: "The extreme rarity of transitional forms in the fossil record persists as the trade secret of paleontology. The evolutionary trees that adorn our textbooks have data only at the tips and nodes of their branches; *the rest is inference* ... not the evidence of fossils. We cannot demonstrate evolution by recording gradual change ... *All the intermediate stages are missing, the fossil record does not support evolution.*" The truth, according to the *Jedi Science of Nature,* is rather that: "The Concept timelessly and in a universal manner posits all particularity [species] into existence. It is a completely empty thought to represent species as developing successively, one after the other, in time ... This gradual alteration is called an explanation and understanding ... but though this *quantitative* difference is of all theories the easiest to understand, it does not really explain anything at all." "Nature's formations are determinate [*qualitative*], bounded, and enter as such into existence. Man has not developed himself out of the animal, nor the animal out of the plant; each is at a single stroke what it is [as **Aristotle** also taught] (**Hegel,** *Enc.* §§249, 339)."

§239

(3) *The Solar System.* Briefly, the moments of the Concept, U-P-I, also determine the structure of the solar system, viz., the solar, planetary, lunar, and cometary natures, that is, U = the Sun, P = the Moon and Comet, I = the Earth, which represent the materialization of the Concept. And since the Concept is eternal and necessary, so are these bodies. Thus as Jedi **Hegel** says, the Sun (= U), as a *self-luminous* body, is eternal. "This body is the primordial, *uncreated* light, which does not arise from the conditions of finite existence, but *immediately* is." Similarly, the Earth (= I), as necessary, is eternal. "The universal absolute process is the process of the Idea (Force) ... through which the Earth is created and preserved. But *the creation is eternal, it is not an event which once happened*; it is *an eternal generation*, for the infinite creative power of the Idea (Force) is a perennial activity (*Enc.* §§275, 339)." Hence the Earth will never be destroyed by collision with a comet or another celestial body, nor by a "supernova," which the Sun will *never* become.

(4) *The State.* Briefly, and in Jedi **Hegel's** words: "The State is a system of three syllogisms just like the Solar System. (i) The *individual* (the person) con-cludes or 'closes' himself through his *particularity* (his physical and spiritual needs, which further developed give rise to civil society) with the *universal* (society, right, law, and government) (*Enc.* §198r)."

JEDI SCIENCE vs. YOUR P-SCIENCES

§240

Your sciences have bestowed on your people many benefits through technology in the arena of practical material living. But strictly speaking they are not true Science, that is, *Knowledge* of the Truth, What IS, the Whole.

1. This is because: They do not know what "Knowledge" or "Knowing" is (via the Concept) and what truly IS, what the true Object of Science is (the Force-Concept and its becoming). Hence, they focus on only one side of the Force or the Whole, namely, (-) Matter-the OUTER, which they regard as absolute Reality. They are a science of What IS NOT or "Cave Science" as they know not of the INNER.

§241

2. Their "Knowledge" is not Knowledge, which is knowledge of the WHOLE, a UNITY or SYSTEM, where each part is interconnected with every other part. So in order to know one thing you must know it in the context of the WHOLE (cf. the liver vis-à-vis the Body). Plus their *Sense*-based scientific method—rather than *Reason-Concept* based (= A priori)—is a *limitation* resulting in the absence of universality, necessity, and certainty, which is attainable only by a *Reason*-based method. They fail to grasp the essence of a phenomenon by privileging Quantitative and Mathematical over Qualitative determinations and those of the Concept. As a result they are unable to realize the Unity and organic interconnection of all the sciences.

3. Moreover they are *Harmful* because they teach the error of the Dark Side (+|-), which results in Materialism and Nihilism; for example, that you (as "human" being) are nothing more than a mortal Body-Ego. Hence, they keep your people permanently in the Cave and prevent the Jedi Order and the healing of your planet from occurring.

4. However they are not without value, for they do provide the *universals and content* of Jedi Science, which translates them into the Concept and gives them their proper place in the Whole of knowledge-Science.

5. For the Refutation of MATERIALISM, see §252 below.

Let us now look more deeply into some of these contrasting features in the following Six Points:

§242

(1) *Jedi Science* begins by knowing The TRUTH by Reason, not the senses, as what alone truly *is*—namely, The Force as a unity of

Inner and Outer ($\pm$) and the principle of all else. Once it knows The Truth, it at once knows what to look for in the empirical realm: namely, examples of The Truth, which now becomes the sole interest.

P-science on the other hand lacks The Truth (or an absolute, a standard) and is at a disadvantage in that it does *not* know what to look for; hence its looking is haphazard, arbitrary, and it must then proceed merely "empirically," guided only by the felt need to bring the chaotic, disorganized manifold into order and unity (it has only the "regulative Idea" of "unity" or Kantian Reason, to guide it).

§243

(2) *Jedi Science of The Force* is *holistic*. It is a knowledge of the Whole of Being and thus is complete and exhaustive; moreover the Jedi Scientist knows that the Whole is *himSelf*, and thus studies his Self and the becoming of his Self in its various Forms. Jedi Science is thus true knowledge in that it knows each part/item in the context of and place in the Whole, outside of which is nothing. Thus it also has the required Unity (of all cognitions) necessary for True Science and making System possible. The Unity is provided by the fact that 1. only one thing exists, The Force, and its various modes and 2. Jedi Science involves a *single* Principle (Polarity and the CONCEPT ($\pm$)) whereby all the Force's aspects can be grasped and interrelated. It knows that you can adequately understand a thing only as a "part" of the Whole to which it belongs (we know the One Force or Whole, it does not). True knowledge cannot be piecemeal or in the form of single cognitions. Hence, to know any one thing you must know the Whole of which it constitutes a living vital part—that is, to know something is to know *everything*, the whole of Being (so nothing essential is left out).

§244

P-science, on the other hand, is not a knowledge of the Whole of Being/Reality, rather only of parts or regions of Being—it is an aggregate or concatenation of disconnected cognitions with no principle of unity or interconnection. This is evident in the manner in which it presents its "knowledge" in textbooks, "Now we come to the solar system, Now we come to heat, to magnetism, to Man, etc." (In its defense, it does have a principle of unity in its "materialism," holding that all things reduce to matter or the Outer, and which we have shown to be false; but to date they have been unable to show how all things, especially mind and consciousness, are derivable from its material principle).

§245

(3) *Jedi Science's* knowledge, as based on Reason's (not the senses') knowledge of The Force, is certain, necessary, universal and valid for all time.

P-science on the other hand, would like to say that it possesses such certain knowledge—e.g. it will often say, "We now *know* that such and such is true, etc"—but it knows that it cannot because of its empirically rooted scientific method whereby all its results are subject to revision pending further research and data. As for the criterion of "necessity," a key hallmark of True Science, they are never able to show or give the reason *why* a given thing or essential feature of existence (light, life, consciousness, the state, history) is necessary or must exist and cannot be otherwise and has the features it does have; and the "universality" of its statements can never be strict, only loose, as based on sense-induction (generalization over a finite number of cases).

§246

(4) *Jedi Science,* unlike p-science, has a *method* of knowing and discerning absolute Truth (of verification and falsification) that is eternal and valid for all time as based on eternal Reason and not the senses which, by themselves, cannot yield certain knowledge. As we saw, the Jedi *method* via Reason involves first, understanding Polarity and seeing, by Reason, that the One Whole-Force must be a *unity* of Two Forces, Inner and Outer in fusion, and that all that exists hence *must* be Forms of this unity (±); and secondly, ordering all Forms in experience on a scale from the *lowest* disunity to the *highest* unity and Truth; and finally cognizing each Form (its Concept) by its approximation to Truth/Idea (±) and its place in the Whole. The empirical indeed has its role to play but Reason is first, the former is used only to illustrate a Form-Category determined by the "Concept"/Truth (as presented in Logic). So the Jedi Scientist has the Pure Truth (Logic's CONCEPT) before him and then looks at the empirical data, findings, and universals (of the p-sciences) and

orders them according to the Truth while evaluating their theories against the same's inner structure of "Being-Essence-and the CONCEPT" and Universal-Particular-and Individuality. As Jedi **Hegel** says:

> The *Science of Nature* takes up the material which physics has prepared for it empirically ... and reconstitutes it, so that experience is not its final warrant and base. [Thus] Science *translates into the CONCEPT* the abstract universal transmitted to it, by showing how this universal, as an intrinsically necessary whole, proceeds from the CONCEPT. [Therefore] Science must be in agreement with our empirical knowledge of Nature ... but its foundation must be the necessity of the CONCEPT (*Enc.* §246, z and Remark). [Hence what Science does is simply] to make the contents (of the empirical sciences) imitate the free creative thought of the CONCEPT (as unfolded in the *Science of Logic*) (*Enc.* §12).

§247

P-science on the other hand, bases its knowledge and way of finding truth (verification and falsification of hypotheses) on the so-called "Scientific Method." As based on the senses it naively and unquestioningly holds that only what the senses reveal is true Reality (contra Reason, **Plato** and Jedi-philosophers), and further that only what can be tested empirically, is in space and time and can be measured (has quantitative features) is *real*—hence consciousness and the invisible realm are not real and = 0, the exact opposite of the Truth as known by Reason and the Concept.

The scientific method thus can never yield true scientific knowledge. For it (1) begins with *observation* of the sense-manifold, of particulars (it cannot moreover take in the whole via the senses), and thus excludes consciousness and thought; then (2) it fashions a *hypothesis* that will explain the data of observation—that is, unify them, explain why something is as it is, does what it does, and further analyze it into its elements, finding common features and repeatable pairings-conjunctions of different items, etc.; then (3) it *tests* the hypothesis to see if other experiences confirm or disconfirm it. It is obvious that this process has no end and can never lead to a final confirmation, to truth and certainty. Also, the senses ever and only present us with an infinite multiplicity of discrete items, and no *unity* as such can ever be found in it—only Reason can accomplish this.

§248

A major defect of p-science is that its method turns everything into an OBJECT or THING—even yourselves. It *reifies* and gives a topsy-turvy picture of reality, harmful to your health and becoming a Jedi. In putting everything "under a microscope" it thus deals with and can see only OBJECTS—(this is why many physicists and doctors tend to see nothing but "objects," hence the patient is just an object, one object looking at another object)—and it gives NAMES, a name being an "object" or "thing." Hence its "science" offers nothing but a series of unrelated Objects and merely reflects the error of its world-view and method—keeping the members of this series or aggregate (e.g. gravity, electricity, plant, animal) as *fixed*, as having a Being in their isolation—with the result that the world is nothing but a Many, a collection of bits, things, objects, with no room for subjects, consciousness or the INNER and true reality. It hence does not see its error that the opposite is the Truth. That there are no "Objects" at all … that only Consciousness exists—or that Consciousness or the Concept is the only true Object, all else being mere "moments" within this ONE OBJECT. Further it does not see that an Object is nothing without a Subject or consciousness; that an Object has only a Being-for-another and is nothing in itself, for only a consciousness is a True Being, a Being *for itself*. True Science presents its objects or subject-matter in a correct way—a way that (1) shows that Reality-the world-what IS, is a "truly Existent ONE" and that consciousness alone exists (not things or matter or many or bits). And (2) it does this by showing how each object-item is a self-dissolving and not a self-subsistent thing/being, is a mere "moment" leading up to their Truth, the *One Force* and the *Jedi Order*. Thus it correctly represents Reality, thereby entirely destroying the illusion and error of the separate EGO-THING WORLD.

Hence p-science not only sustains but creates this separate EGO AND EGO-THING WORLD, a world in which *there is no room for subjects, I's, or consciousness—for what alone is reality.*

§249

(5) *Jedi Science* has a correct understanding not only of the reason and necessity behind the Inner-Outer, Nature-Man, Matter-Consciousness division of Reality or the Whole of what is, but of their true relationship, value and standing as well. That the

INNER alone is Being or true reality while the OUTER is nothing or only *show (Schein* or *Erscheinung).* Thus Jedi Science knows the untruth of "materialism-naturalism," the principal tenet and article of faith of the p-sciences' world-view that informs all they do and say, and holds that the Outer and matter is the real while the Inner and consciousness/self is nothing, only a by-product of matter and which ceases at biological death.

P-science, on the other hand, in letting itself be seduced by false materialism offers a skewed, dangerous picture of Reality, which pervades all its findings and literature. It also fails to know the true value and limits of mathematics and quantitative determination in general (viz., to mechanics or "matter in motion"), and thus fails to obtain a true understanding of its objects, and further holding up an erroneous model, ideal and standard to the other sciences who strive to imitate its procedures and methodology.

§250

(6) Finally *Jedi Science,* because it has the true understanding of the Inner-Outer, Self-Matter relation, also has the true concept of Man, of who you are—one which is totally positive, promoting health and optimism in the highest degree imaginable, and which provides you with an incredible Ideal and Goal to aim at and organize all of your affairs under—namely, to realize your Jedi Self and become an Infinite Jedi. It is a Concept and Goal that provides true MEANING for your lives and existence and JUSTIFICATION not only to continue living but for the intrinsic value and sanctity of all life and people. It is health promoting (of body and mind) and gives an undimmed enthusiasm for life, where waking up each day presents you with another opportunity for getting closer to the Goal (rather, for realizing you are *already at* the Goal) ... and to the True Concept of who you are. That is to say, not only do you belong here, in the universe, but you are its "be all and end all," its raison d'etre—more, you *are* the universe itself ... the Whole, the One Force—its self-awareness—and hence are as eternal and infinite as IT IS. And your body is eternal too. Therefore an incredible future and eternal destiny awaits you (and one that unfolds, please realize, only in the eternal Present)—experiences beyond imagination, with your friends, families, etc., who are also eternal (cf. your scripture, "eye has not seen," etc). For example, you can start building your network or circle of eternal relationships NOW ... knowing that

everyone you meet and befriend will be sharing experiences with you for all eternity. This opens up a whole new way of thinking about your present and future relationships and truly incredible possibilities.

§251

P-science on the other hand, with its botched false Concept of Man disseminates a pernicious *nihilistic* philosophy of life and world-view. Namely it views Man, yourselves, according to its materialism, as just a very insignificant piece of a vast material universe, as a quantitatively insignificant "accident," whose OUTER or physical-biological aspects alone are essential—ultimately you are just another animal species, not much different from other "advanced" intelligent animals such as chimps or porpoises. As a result your Person, self, thought, consciousness—and the values, beliefs, and meanings these support—is reduced to and is solely a function of your body or material cells, neurons, and atoms (which corresponds with theories that are dubbed and range from "supervenience," to "reductive materialism" to "eliminative materialism," according to which the person or self doesn't exist at all, just atoms, neurons-synapses firing in the brain). In any case the result is that (1) the Self (if one is granted) doesn't survive death and the dissolution of the material body, death signifying the absolute termination of conscious existence (not to mention values, morality, and freedom—for religion and spirituality are subjective and not real, which is "relativism"). And (2) There cannot be *any* ultimate MEANING, Point, or Purpose to life. This is NIHILISM—which is what your youth are being force-fed, inundated and indoctrinated with every day of the school year, their entire student careers, equipping them with and making it impossible to avoid a pessimistic, depressive and hopeless view of life (as expressed by their T-shirts: "Life sucks, then you die"—*This* precisely is its unspoken message to your youth) when they graduate and enter the real world, imbued with dismal, skewed, and limited expectations of their prospects and possibilities, having an incalculable negative effect on motivation. To wit, "What am I working for—the grave? Why do anything—get married, raise a family, enjoy retirement? What can be serious?—my children and theirs will have the same future to look forward to, the grave— nothingness, annihilation. *Thus the only Ideal or Goal the p-sciences can provide you with, your "destiny," is to become "worm-food," that is, nothing.*

§252

The Refutation of Materialism ("p-science's" main principle).

(1) It is easy to see that Matter, the OUTER (merely physical universe) has no True Being. The fact is: you can call the "Object" alleged to be absolute being—and an "object" is always an "object *for* a subject or consciousness," and a so-called "object *not* for a consciousness is meaningless, a nonthought—whatever you like: matter, energy, atoms, weak force, strong force, electromagnetic force, "strings," gravitron, quark, brain-wave, neural activity, what-have-you. *But it is still always and hopelessly an Object.* And as such has only a "Being for another" (for a consciousness, a "for itself"). Hence it is *nothing* as such and in itself (*apart from* its relation to consciousness, a subject). It is not, can never be, and can never therefore *produce* a *subject or consciousness*—a "subject" being always *that* for which an object exists (and which can never *itself* be an object).—And most importantly a subject has a "being for itself" or self-awareness, while an "object" does not, and can never *know* that it exists (if it did it would be a subject, not an object): a subject always knows that it exists, that it IS.

§253

(2) What follows is that a subject, consciousness or "for itself" is therefore alone *Being*—that which IS. Thus the entire objective universe and all objects in it (known and yet to be known) have only a "being for another" and are as such *nothing*. They *seem* to have being, but do not—and a "nothing" cannot be the ground or cause of consciousness. Hence the only candidate left to qualify as Being is *consciousness*—the only Being and therefore, as it is limited by *nothing else*, Infinite and All Reality.—Note also 1: The consciousness or I in question is *not* the *empirical* I/ego but the *Pure or Absolute* I which is numerically one and which we all share, and Note 2: When the object of experience is another I (a *You*), I in fact have myself doubled. I = I, for there *is* no distance between us and our I's thus coincide; also your I can never be my object, only your body can.

§254

(3) The view that takes matter or physical things to be absolute or true being and the first principle of all things, consciousness being merely derivative and reducible to matter, is called "**materialism**."

It will be instructive here to look at a current popular version of it that you may see that it is untenable and clearly refutes itself, turning in fact into its opposite. The issue's great importance can be felt in that if materialism were true it would then follow that "**when your brain dies, you die**"—which removes any ultimate purpose to your existence.

§255

(4) It is easy to see that the touted materialistic "brain-state" theory at issue refutes itself—according to which consciousness is really matter or reducible to your brain-state or chemical neural activity. For once this is assumed, *it is impossible to prove that matter, the physical, exists.* For then you are forever trapped within your brain-state and can never get out of it to ascertain the existence of an actual spatiotemporal material world and, further, cannot even prove that a "brain state" has any physical components (cf., the "brain in a vat," and your film *The Matrix*).

I will explain my Padawan. According to this view (cf., **Churchland's** "eliminative materialism"), 1. consciousness is the same as and reducible to your "brain-states"—i.e., electrical-chemical activity in your physical brain. 2. If this is true then it must also be true that *I can never leave, nor ever have left, my brain,* so all that I am aware of (or *thought* I was aware of) as being "outside of me," i.e. my direct experience of a *physical, space-time world/universe is really not such*—or is really a "brain-state" going on "in me," in my brain, as something occurring solely in my brain. 3. So, all I can say for certain is, "I am having a *brain state.*" Hence on this view, *I have no proof that there is or ever was a "physical-material world"—or even a "physical brain."* 4. Hence, I cannot even give the expression "brain-state"—as what alone *is*—a *physical* meaning. Hence, only a *mental* one. 5. Therefore, I can be certain of only one thing: *MY MIND,* and that only consciousness or mental phenomena *exist—the exact opposite of materialism which thus refutes itself.*

§256

Some of the Merits of Your Sciences. Of course it is appropriate that I not end this discussion without indicating some of the "positive" features and contributions of your sciences.

1. Even though in their present form your sciences are not *Science* and do not provide KNOWLEDGE in the strict and true sense, the "knowledge"—theories, laws, partial insights—they do contain have indeed been of great benefit to your people and planet in the Practical sphere and with respect to "application" in the form of *technology*, for example, in medicine, engineering, space flight, satellites, computers, and communications, etc.

2. Also, another important role they play is that their empirical investigations and findings provide the *Content* for the *Jedi Science's of Nature* and *Jedi/Mind*—i.e. they perform the service of gathering, reducing, and subsuming the raw manifold of sense-individuals under *Universals*, which Jedi Science then subjects to its Method, the Concept or Truth, giving them their true logical form and significance and incorporating them into itself.

§257

3. Your Quantum Physics has on one of its interpretations the merit of coming close to the Truth of Polarity (not only with **Niels Bohr's** Unity of Opposites principle) that *the Observer is the Observed* (not just affects it), and that at the base of Matter or Energy is *Consciousness* or *Thought*—that is to say, that Consciousness/Thought is the *ultimate Reality* and not Matter. Of course the main defect here is that Quantum Physics in contrast to Jedi Science, is unable to *prove* this Truth, i.e. in a conclusive manner—which is again due to the limitations of its "empirical" method. As your astrophysicist **Sir Arthur Eddington** has said, "In regard to the nature of things, scientific knowledge is only an empty shell—a form of symbols, It is a knowledge of structural form, and not knowledge of content. All through the physical world runs that unknown content, which must surely be the stuff of our CONSCIOUSNESS. Here is a hint of aspects deep within the world of physics, *and yet unattainable by the methods of physics.*"

4. And the same can be said of the GAIA Hypothesis and ANTHROPIC Principle of your cutting-edge contemporary science. *Gaia* correctly holds that "Man," i.e. your *consciousness* and *thought* is not a fluke aberration of the universe but rather essential and ingredient to it. That is, your consciousness is really the Earth's and Universe's consciousness of *itself*—"how you and I think is how the Earth (and the Universe) thinks, etc." *The Anthropic Principle*

holds that the universe and its complexity is fine-tuned for life and consciousness, i.e. for you/Man. Again, you and your people as conscious beings are not *accidents*, you belong here. In Polarity language: (+) and (-) go together and are inseparable, or you can't have the *physical-matter/energy* aspect of the universe without its polar opposite, *Consciousness*—and *this* is the real *scientific* reason why the "constants" of nature or the universe *are* as they are and cannot be otherwise.

RELIGION, JEDI RELIGION, AND THE UNITY OF SCIENCE AND RELIGION

§258

(1) What RELIGION really is—its origin and necessity (See *Part III: The Jedi Order, 3* for a more extensive treatment). *Religion* like Science and Art exists for no other reason than to cancel the Force's *Second Stage* (+|-) of *difference* or *separation*, of consciousness OF an Object, in order to reach UNITY (±) and, in the case of religion, to "re-ligare" the opposites God and Man, thereby taking your people into the eternal present of the glorious Jedi Order. Religion, in your planet's History, is the *first* form of the Knowledge of the Force; the *second* being Jedi Science.

> "*God is just this entire act.* God is the beginning, and does this definite thing (the Creation of an Other); but God is equally the end only, the Totality. God is the eternal process (of positing an Other, and then reconciling himself with it in Love) which is the Truth and the absolute Truth." PR III.12 **Hegel**

(2) Briefly, as concerns True Jedi religion versus your False or stunted religions: only the former *completely Heals* you and overcomes the Dark Side separation (+|-) and takes you into your Jedi Self and the Jedi Order (±). As I said, your religions are *not* re-ligareing your people as they keep the split between yourselves and God, Heaven and Earth intact and permanent. Moreover your religious leaders have and operate with a *false* concept of "God" in that they make God only a *part* of the Whole and as a consequence *finite*. That is to say, as I indicated above, that they view the Whole as comprised of 1. GOD *and* 2. Creation-Man-History *and* 3. Heaven

or the Redemption of the Fallen Creation, and thus falsely restrict "God" to one finite part of the Whole of What IS, when in truth God (the Force) as infinite is the process or movement of the *WHOLE itself, of all three taken together,* which is proved in Jedi Science. For by definition God is an *infinite* Being—hence there can be nothing else besides or outside of this Being. What "God" really means therefore is simply: The FORCE → realizing itself as Jedi and the Jedi Order. Your scriptures say this, but in code.

(3) An absolutely important consequence of this is the *Unity* of Science and Religion, which becomes possible in that they both have the *same goal*—that of taking you into Jedi (your true self) and the Jedi Order. It is because of this FACT that they can from this time forward *work together* to heal your planet and people and that much faster, instead of being opposed to one another which results in your people having a split, divided or compartmentalized mind and making *total healing* and *Unity* impossible.

JEDI RELIGION

§259

Introduction. Jedi Religion (or *non*-religion) has a three-fold purpose: (1) to help those people become Jedi who are unable to access the Truth by Jedi Science alone, and (2) to once and for all solve the problem of the interminable conflict and hatred among existing religions by showing them that they all have the *same end and goal,* namely, the actual *Experience* or *Knowledge* of the Truth (the Force, the POINT), and (3) to end the war between religion and science by revealing their inner *identity.* Thus Jedi Religion is not really another "religion"—it is rather a religion to end religions and their divisiveness as such. This is why Jedi religion is also called a *non*-religion. It is not another religion to be placed alongside and compete with the other religions on your planet such as Judaism, Christianity, Islam, Hinduism, Buddhism, and New Age cults and spirituality. Rather it is a *universal*—and not a particular—"religion" that contains the *core* of what "re-ligion" as such is and what all religions are and have in common: their efficacious element, which is *the Truth.* Jedi non-religion thus has the power *to unite all religions* and thereby end their conflicts by providing what they inwardly claim to do and be, namely, *knowledge* of the Truth that provides an awareness and actual *experience* of union with God—it does not just occupy the mind with words, pictures, dogmas, and "externals."

Thus what your people will ultimately witness, which is destined to occur on your planet, is the following movement and progression: From many divisive Religions, to One Jedi world religion, and finally to no religion and to a state of your world where only Knowledge and Love will exist—and which exactly coincides with what your religions describe and know as "the kingdom of heaven/God on Earth," "the world to come," "the just society" and so on—note, however, that religion will always still exist for children and pre-Jedi.

§260

Therefore we Jedi are able to resolve your religions' conflicts precisely because *we know the Truth about and behind "religion" as such and its concepts of "God, Man, sin, evil, guilt, salvation, redemption, liberation, unity with God, resurrection, eternal life, and heaven and hell." The Jedi Truth which has been proven and is in our possession, enables us to see that what the different religions are* **really** *talking about is none other than the Truth itself and* **the basic metaphysical situation that you are involved in***: that is, of the Infinite Force, Stage One, and its need to split into "self-other" consciousness (= "sin"), Stage Two, and the resulting need to cancel or heal this split (= salvation or the restoration of wholeness), Stage Three: the result is the ONE, the ONE JEDI ORDER.* In this way we see again that religion has the very same aim as Jedi or True Science—to provide the knowledge of and *union* with the Force (or God)—which makes possible for the first time in your history *the reconciliation and unity of science and religion.*

§261

(1) **The Concept of Religion**. It is first necessary to recognize that the true or implicit goal of Religion is to do away with or annul itself by there no longer being a need for it, by religion having achieved its goal and satisfied its purpose. This is implied in its Concept. For example "religion" derives from your Latin "re-ligare" which means to re-connect or bind back together, or restore, make one, annul the separation between two things—in this case Man (consciousness) and God. The purpose of Religion then is to bring about one's *union with God*. The clear implication here is that "re-ligion" has the status of being essentially a *means* to the *End* of union with God. Hence

when the End is achieved the need for the "means" disappears and there is no further need for "re-ligion". Another word for "union with God" would be direct *knowledge or experience of* God—of one's non-separation from and inclusiveness within God, the infinite being or the Force.

§262

Thus religion's concept is to be a disappearing *means* to the *End* of KNOWING. Hence all Scriptures, Holy Books, writings are *not* the End or Goal of a particular religion, rather only a "means," that is, an "arrow" pointing you to the One Goal that they all share—union with God or direct experience of God and the Truth.

Now since it is obvious that "God" is another word, sound, or name for and equivalent to "the Force," the goal and principle of *Religion* and *Science* therefore is the same: namely, the knowledge and experience of your union with God or the Force. And "Man" or consciousness or Yourself when completed are a Jedi—or a "Jedi" (your True Self) is another name for the goal of religion as the unity of the Force (God) and Jedi (yourself), which is also the Truth of Jedi Science. *We then see that Religion and Science have the same goal and Truth and hence are identical.*

However notice also, as we stated earlier, that there is a critical distinction between yourself and God/the Force/the Truth. For example, to say "I am God," can be misleading and injurious as resulting in a wrongful inflation of one's "ego" (P.I.). The cure is simply to realize that (1) you cannot "boast" or take credit for *who you are*—the Truth just is what it is and you (your empirical Ego) had nothing to do with it, with its nature or essence; (2) if you have actualized or realized your Jedi Self you reached it via a *transformation process;* and (3) the "I" in "I am God" is not your empirical "I" but rather your *Pure or Absolute I,* which is that of the Force Itself and is eternal and which you share *with everyone.* Thus it can be said that you (as a P.I.) are *not* God, the Force, the Truth, but rather God's *awareness* of himself (or as your scriptures teach, you are a *Son or Daughter* of God).

So we have seen that all religions in principle reduce to or are contained in Jedi Religion—and this in principle ends the conflict among your religions—and that Jedi Religion (and hence all your *own* religions) reduces to and in essence is one and the same as Jedi Science.

§263

(2) *The Basic Principles* (not "dogmas") of Jedi (Non-) Religion:* what it is, its explanation of your situation, of Reality, and of your need for it, and How it works or achieves its goal (its Method). We should note that (a) these questions have already been answered so there can be nothing new here to do except point up certain links with traditional religious concepts and ideas; and that (b) Jedi Religion *does* allow for the preservation and "practice" of any given historical religion *within itself,* i.e., as long as the Truth of Jedi Religion principles is acknowledged and given primacy, or grasped as the inner truth and meaning of a given religion's various doctrines. Also see *Part III: The Jedi Order, Religion,* where these principles are further developed in the concept of "The Jedi Sect." (*Note that a "Principle" is based on Truth, which you can verify for yourself, whereas a "Dogma" is only a belief formed by others that you *must* accept without seeing or knowing that it is *true.*)

§264

The General Principles are these:

1. There is a *need* for Jedi Religion. Something is *wrong* with us as we immediately are (as Consciousness) which needs to be corrected or put right (there is "sin" or "guilt" or unfulfillment).

2. That is, we are in a state of "sin" (+|-), a divided state, due mainly to the nature of Reality. That is, we are *separated* from, out of alignment or correspondence with (cf. "Be ye Holy," "Be ye Perfect") God—the Truth (±), Being, the Eternal Force, and Love. Hence we lack the true Knowledge of who we are and who and what God is.

3. Hence we need to re-connect or re-unite with God through Religion as a means or method.

§265

Why we are in "sin" or *separate* from God and how to overcome this or be "redeemed," "saved" or "liberated" is as follows:

(a) The Truth is that what IS is God or the Force, who is infinite, hence has nothing outside him, is the only existent or Being and who is by necessity (i.e., God cannot not be; see also "Polarity"). Reason reveals that God is and can only be a unity of *two* sides, Inner and Outer, Subject and Object, Self and *Other* (±). For example, for God to be a "Creator" God needs an "Other," a "creation," to be "Love" God needs an Other to love, to be "Good," also an Other to be good to, to be "Power," an Other to act on—and for God to be Free, God must first limit himself and then transcend the limitation. But to be self-aware, to *be* God, *God must produce an Other and then take it back into himself, reconciling it to himself;* or God must *separate himself from himself* and become consciousness OF (or "Man"), *and then cancel the separation.*

(b) Hence you and I are *inside* God, are God or the Force in a state of *division.* Hence your primary or ontological (root) "sin" is *ignorance*—and all actions and the life-style that flows from it. You believe that you are a finite "Ego," separate from the world (Other) and God, which is due to *identification* (attachment or cathexis) solely with your Body and personal ego and false identity.

(c) So, you do not know what the Truth is—namely that only the Unity (±) exists, *the non-separation of Subject and Object,* of yourselves and God. For example as **Christ** says, "May they be ONE as we are ONE." And as your **Plato** teaches, "You are all living in the Cave, in a twilight zone between Being and Non-Being, hence you don't know whether you exist or not." You are thus riddled with "ontological insecurity" or angst, always worried that your Joy or the "Being" you have achieved will unravel, come to an end or be taken away by someone or something.

§266

(d) Therefore, to be redeemed, saved, and to overcome or cancel "sin" and separation or *Stage Two* consciousness OF, all you need do is Believe in or Align with the Truth—accept the FACT that *you are saved and whole right Now.* For the "split"—your believed "separation" or being cut off from Being or God—is nothing but an illusion or deception; due, as some of you may say, to "Satan" or, what is the same, "lies" that you believe and are rooted in the Dark Side (+|-), in "Cave, natural, sense-consciousness" and the bad programming of your environment, education, and culture.

Thus the true meaning of the Greek word, *metanoia* (*meta* = change, *noia* = mind or thinking), often translated as "repent" (and given as "the way" to enter the kingdom of God), is *to change your thinking and believing in such a way that you, your mind, becomes "with" itself—and not against or beside itself or "divided,"* as in *paranoia*. It thus means you are to begin thinking of yourself as ONE with God, and not SEPARATED from God.

§267

Thus the more and the faster you align with, believe in, and just accept this *already existing Unity* as the only Truth and Reality, the faster and deeper will your *Knowledge and Experience* of the Truth (your present Oneness with God/the Force) *be*. That is, *until* you have perfect and complete *Knowledge of God*—indeed *are* God *as One* (*echad*) with the Force or as the Force aware of Itself—and then you can *dispense altogether with religion and its unifying methods and practices*, such as prayer, fasting, meditation, and so on.

§268

(3) The Jedi Methods—Or How believing or aligning works.

(1) The primary Method (see also *Part II: The Jedi Code*) involves the ejecting of Old dark side programs (mind-sets) and the inserting of New light side programs into your consciousness. It involves aligning yourself to Truth and Reality: By constantly saying, speaking, thinking, visualizing, believing, affirming, and immersing yourself in the Truth—or in *what alone, always and must be the case*: namely, your present, not future, Unity and inseparability with God/ the Force/Being/the Whole/the Truth. You simply align yourself to it—or better, simply *embrace and surrender to the FACT that you are* <u>*already*</u> *aligned to it*. Doing this has the effect of negating your old, false programming and "ego" and establishing you in Reality or redeeming you and making you "Good "and "O.K."—as you should be, having no sin—or guilt-awareness, i.e., "twoness" or wrongness. Note that the "ego" is opposed to and opposes itself to the world, to God and to all that is "Other" to it—and maintains itself and persists in its *exclusivity*, namely out of fear that the Other (another "I") will take away its joy or Being, that it will let down its wall or defenses, let the Other into its heart, and by so doing get betrayed or destroyed.

§269

Thus *you are saying or agreeing with* (achieving identity with, aligning with) *what is the case*—and not the opposite, and hence are therefore *becoming* what is the case. You are *becoming YOU, your True Self.* And this, because you are no longer fighting, denying, and opposing yourself to Reality or WHAT IS THE CASE—which keeps you in illusion or in what is *not* the case, and in bondage and unhappiness—which happens because you are willing and loving what is *not* the case and is *not* Real. And this can only end in pain and disillusionment and not in what you desire or seek, namely *wholeness,* love, joy, infinity, power, connection with Being and What IS. For "Power" equals "Unity," which you can't be or experience if you *oppose* yourself to and thus *separate* yourself from REALITY.

§270

(2) A Note concerning "GUILT" (sin) and living "GUILT-FREE."

a) The Truth is the ONE, the ONE REALITY.

b) Therefore you have an innate drive to Oneness and to overcome Two-ness or division, which is the essence of GUILT and disharmony (+|-).

c) So long as you are (in) EGO you are subject to GUILT—for as an EGO you recognize the existence of other EGO'S (other "you's") *outside* and besides yourself and as "negations" of yourself.

d) The other EGO'S can always JUDGE you (as a particular) and there is always the nagging thought or possibility that they hate or dislike you, that *you haven't done your duty to them, e.g. they may be in pain and you did not help them, etc.*

e) BUT, when you realize that you *are* them and have them *in* yourself as *your Pure Absolute I,* then there is no more GUILT. For the ultimate requirement that you "Love thy neighbor (Ego/Other) as thyself" is fulfilled and satisfied only via your True Universal Pure I, or being One with God.

f) Thus the state of "No Guilt" (or healing) lies in living *for your whole Race, for the Universal and not just for yourself, your EGO*—that is, it lies in not being "Part-icular" and in not having any Others existing "outside you" and potentially in pain and *judging* you. That is, it lies in becoming a UNIVERSAL being or ALL-SELF. And this is only achievable by having and being a "Universal or Absolute Pure I" or "U.I."—as the "I" in everyone, hence having *all I's within* you; with the result that the Self/Other opposition is overcome. The absolute importance for the *particular* Ego, person or personality to become *universal* is underscored by Jedi **Hegel's** account of the solution to the "problem" of the TRINITY—How can three separate persons be one? **Hegel** insists that

> "[The problem's] solution is contained in the fact *that there is only one person,* and this three-fold personality, this personality which is thus posited merely as a vanishing moment, expresses the Truth ... It is, in short, the nature or character of what we mean by "person" or "subject" to abolish its isolation, its *separateness.* [For example] Morality and love just mean the giving up of *particularity* or of the particular personality and its extension to *universality* ... In friendship and love I give up my *abstract* personality and in this way win it back as *concrete* personality. *It is just this winning back of personality by the act of absorption, by the being absorbed into the other, which constitutes the true nature of personality* (*The History of Philosophy,* III, 24f)."

§271

(4) The Defects of your Old Existing Historical Religions and their Main Objections to Jedi Religion Answered:

1. The texts of your existing religions contain the Truth but in distorted, muddled form and along with error; and their teachers and pastors do not teach the Truth in a pure clear unambiguous way that promotes healing and full actualization here and now of your Jedi nature and, most importantly, the Jedi Order.

2. Their main problem is that either they are never able to collapse the *distance* between God and man so as to produce full healing and unity, or they postpone this unity till after death in a distant future.

§272

3. Two Main Objections Answered (See also *Part III: Religion*):

(a) *Objection*: "No. There must always be a *separation* between yourselves or Man and God; God must be 'outside' the universe/Creation and *transcendent* to consciousness and the world."

Answered: First, your religious seem unable to transcend the fixation of Man as a permanently finite and non-holy-divine Being, and this despite the numerous commands in their scriptures (e.g., "Be ye holy as I am holy," "Be perfect as God is perfect") which point to an inherent identity and equality of natures. This is a result of insufficient reflection on the concepts of man and *"God" as a wholly infinite being*, which when carried to completion shows that Man must and can only be *one and inseparable from God;* and also a result of a want of the deepest spiritual experiences. Secondly, your Jedi philosophers or Reason has clearly proven that God must and can only be *immanent and within* us and not "transcendent" by showing that a "Thing in itself" is nonsense and unthinkable.—And also by showing that it is logically impossible to have an infinite being on one side and a finite one, yourselves, on the other. To do this would make God—Allah, Jehovah—into a *finite* being; furthermore an *infinite* being leaves no place for any other being beside itself. So at the very least, since it is undeniable that you exist (for "I think therefore I AM"), you must be *within* the sphere of Allah's or God's infinite being. This necessarily leads to your being One with Allah, as all your saints and mystics have taught.

§273

(b) *Objection:* "But your teaching then does away with the need for a Savior and e.g. for Christ's atonement on the Cross."

Answered: This is not true. First, your **Christ's** primary desire is that you know the Truth (or be saved and have eternal life). Granting it be true that **Christ** is one and the same as the Truth—which is (±), the *unity* of Universal and Individual, Father and Son, etc—then to align with the Truth, as presented in both Jedi Science and Religion, is the same as aligning with **Christ**. In the end, the "name" is not as important as the Thing itself (see also your Jedi **Fichte** who points out that it is **Christ** himself who says in many places that, "You do not have to believe in me, but just my doctrine and/or my Father, and you will know the Truth, etc"). Secondly, it is about time that your Christians rise to a higher and deeper knowledge and understanding of "the Cross" and the mysteries (Truths) of Christianity as revealed in their picture-thinking and imagery, for it is "The Spirit that will guide you into All Truth," and not the letter or written words of your Scriptures, which are just "pointers" to the Truth of the *experience* of your present unity with God or the Force.—It is also true that your New Age Movement indeed has the Truth but also in a muddled form and with much error; for example some of them teach that the individual *in his empirical individuality and particularity* is God or divine, which is totally erroneous.

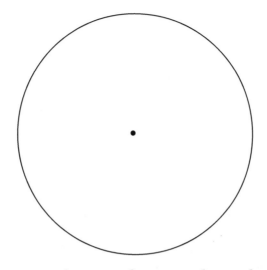

"You must unlearn what you have learned."

III. GLOBAL JEDI EDUCATION

INTRODUCTION

§274

In *Part I: THE JEDI TRUTH* (the Knowledge of the Force) we have thus far seen (1) How your own Jedi got the Knowledge of the Force, the Truth and Jedi Science in the course of your planet's History, (2) What Jedi Science, the study of the Jedi Order's becoming, is and consists in, the Basics, and (3) That and how the Unity of Science and Religion can become a reality.

§275

Now we will elucidate the nature of GLOBAL JEDI EDUCATION ("GJE"), which is based on Jedi Science and is the solution to your world's problems. The task and purpose of GJE is to take your people out of the Cave, the Dark Side (+|-) and into the ONE REALITY, the POINT (±), and make them *aware* of the Jedi Order, the UNITY which already exists—to educate them into it either as Consciousness or the Concept, as an Intuitive or a Discursive Jedi.

GLOBAL JEDI EDUCATION SUMMARY

1. Jedi SCIENCE showed that its sole Object is **The JEDI ORDER, the Force expressed and actualized,** which exists NOW, must exist, and is eternal—which follows necessarily from the UNITY of Opposites: of Subjectivity and Objectivity, Consciousness and Matter, the Inner and the Outer. Hence every person on your planet *is* a JEDI now, a Universal Individual who shares *one and the same* Apriori Absolute I-Point, outside Space/Time/and Matter. Therefore, to be aware one is a JEDI is to be fulfilled, in total Health, immortal, and EDUCATED.

2. So: There is nothing but **The JEDI ORDER,** this UNITY. The aim of GJE is simply to make everyone *aware* of it as a Jedi.

3. Your people must experience the TRUTH (±) by overcoming the illusion and error of the Subject/Object separation or the Dark Side (+|-) and by TRANSCENDING THE SENSES. It is to transition from *Stage Two* OUTER Body-EGO Consciousness or Individuality *without* Universality, to *Stage Three* INNER JEDI Self-Consciousness or Individuality *with* Universality.

4. The fastest way to educate your planet is to change your **7 global Institutions** (especially Education) so they teach (±) and not (+|-), and to educate JEDI who will change the **7.**

5. The TWO forms/ways to see through the illusion and see yourSelves in all of OBJECTIVITY are via Consciousness or Concept.

6. The FACT is that the JEDI ORDER is the FORCE actualized and individuated *as* Universal-Particular-Individual (U-P-I), that is, YOU *as* a JEDI or a *concrete individual Universal* (or ALL). And as Universal, you are IN and ONE with ALL Objectivity and, therefore, only the FORCE as JEDI (U-P-I) or the JEDI ORDER exists.

7. Therefore we have: (1) Global Jedi Education via your **7 global Institutions,** the focus of *Part III: The Jedi Order,* (2) GJE with respect to the **Individual Reader,** treated in *Part II: The Jedi Code,* and (3) GJE via **your Institution of Education,** treated here in *Part I: The Jedi Truth* and also in *Part III: The Jedi Order.*

§276

The fastest way to educate everyone on your planet is to "BALANCE" your Institutions, especially the major Seven, and make them "educational" so that instead of teaching the Dark Side error they teach the TRUTH—the Knowledge of the Force, the One Reality. This can be done by educating JEDI who will then impact the Seven, "Balance" them, and make the necessary changes. *Part II: THE JEDI CODE* will do this, while *Part III: THE JEDI ORDER* will show concretely what has to be done and how to do it.

§277

(1) To be educated into the Jedi Order as a Jedi each person on your planet must transition from *Stage Two* Consciousness to *Stage Three* Self-Consciousness, from an Ego to a Jedi—that is, by TRANSCENDING THE SENSES and entering into the POINT or the TRUTH, in the midst of the Senses. This is achieved by REASON or FOCUSED ATTENTION, which has Two Forms, (1) Thought-Concept and (2) Meditation-Concentration (or Faith-Affirmation). To know the Truth by (1) Thought is to have achieved the CONCEPT and to have become a **DISCURSIVE JEDI** or a Jedi Master Scientist. To know the Truth by (2) Meditation or Faith is to know it (and the Concept) in the form of CONSCIOUSNESS (but not as CONCEPT) and to have become an **INTUITIVE JEDI** or an Intuitive Jedi Master; and both ways and forms overlap and intersect.

(2) Noble Reader, *Part II: The JEDI CODE* will show you how *you* can be educated into a Jedi by using both methods of Reason and Focused Attention.

(3) And *Part III: The JEDI ORDER* will show you how *everyone else* on your planet can likewise be educated into a Jedi and the Jedi Order by means of your Seven major educational Institutions, including Education itself.

§278

We have said that the fastest way to educate your people into the Jedi Order is to educate Jedi who will then transform your Seven Institutions, but both tasks can be done at the same time—that is, as a school principal, CEO, senator, artist, citizen, etc., you can immediately begin to work in and transform or "Balance" your Seven Institutions even before you have become a Jedi. Also, to be most effective in changing the Seven, educated Jedi Scientists will be indispensable. Thus we have the four topics of this section:

>   (1) **What exactly do you have to *do* to BE EDUCATED and a JEDI?**
>   (2) **Global Jedi Education with respect to the *Individual Reader's* Education to JEDI.**
>   (3) **GJE via your 7 global *Institutions* and**
>   (4) **GJE via your Institution of *Education* in particular.**

(1) WHAT EXACTLY DO YOU HAVE TO *DO* TO BE EDUCATED INTO THE TRUTH AND BE A JEDI?

> *YOU MUST UNLEARN WHAT YOU HAVE LEARNED.*
> *TRANSCEND YOUR SENSES AND ENTER INTO*
> *THE POINT-THE TRUTH-AND THE JEDI ORDER.*

§279

The Object of Education is to realize the Point, the Truth, the Balance, the One Reality, the Jedi Order, which is Now and alone is; it is to see the One in the Many and move from *Stage Two* Consciousness to *Stage Three* Self-Consciousness, from P.I. to U.I. (where "U" is *the Absolute I*), from Ego to Jedi. The Goal in essence is to dissolve the Ego (P.I.) by transforming it into *Universality.* THEREFORE:

1. The TRUTH is ($\pm$), the Concept, the Subject/Object, the Unity of Opposites—of Difference and Unity.

2. It is the Dark Side (+|-) that prevents you from seeing the Truth right now. It is your Senses and Consciousness OF an Other, a Not-I, which keeps you in your false separate Ego and captive to the belief that REALITY is Many and not One, and that it is Matter or Body and not *indivisible* Consciousness or Thought.

3. Thus to actually see the Truth and overcome the Dark Side of the Force you must *Unlearn what you have Learned*—by true Jedi Education.

4. You have *learned* the error of the Dark Side from both (1) *Non-Education:* due to the Force's *Stage Two* state of Consciousness OF, whereby Polarity's *difference* is "in time" experienced *before* its Unity, and (2) *Mis-Education:* by your planet's schools and major institutions.

§280

5. So you must *Transcend your Senses,* its errors and the Dark Side mind-set to be able to *see* true Reality and the POINT—which is Apriori, everywhere and nowhere, as the circle whose center is everywhere and circumference nowhere. The Diagram below represents an *expanded* form of the "Two Stages" of Jedi Education involving transcending your senses into the Point, in which *Stage Two* is comprised of both (1) and (2) below. Hence in this expanded "Three Stage" version, Stage (1) is the initial condition of "**Plato's** Cave" or the Senses (-), where one believes that only sense-material objects or the OUTER exists; it is the stage that *must be transcended.* In Stage (2) one is in the *process* of transcending the Senses by becoming increasingly aware that a *second* domain of reality also exists, that of Consciousness, Thought, the Point, and the INNER (+). Stage (3) Represents the accomplished goal of education where one has a perfect awareness of the POINT or the *Unity* of Opposites (±) in which Consciousness-Thought "trumps" Matter and the Senses, the former being infinite and all reality. One is now a JEDI, the FORCE fully actualized.

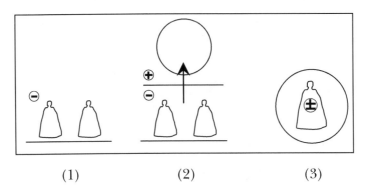

(1)   (2)   (3)

§281

6. Now in truth the POINT or Reality is the **CONCEPT** or Thought—as the Universal which contains within itself Matter or the Individual (-), which is true because of Polarity (±) and the fact that you cannot have one, the Universal, without its polar opposite, the Individual; in other words, as your **A-Team** discovered, the "Concept" is always "the Concept of an Object." However it is also a fact that many of your people know the Point or the Concept *only* as **CONSCIOUSNESS**, the I or Self, for example your quantum physicists, transpersonal psychologists, New Agers, and religions (e.g., Hinduism/Vedanta). Moreover all of your religions (except Buddhism) know it also as a Personality, "God," or Spirit. In point of fact my Padawan, the Concept or Truth is *both* personal and impersonal, where the impersonal aspect is contained inside the personal aspect; indeed, from the mere fact that "persons" or "personality" *exists* it necessarily follows that their Source or Cause (the Point-Force-Concept) cannot but have a "personal" aspect or dimension.

§282

7. And to know the Point or the Concept as **CONSCIOUSNESS** is in essence equivalent to knowing it as **CONCEPT**. However, as I said, the "Consciousness Knowers" do not know or understand it in its fully articulated form as SCIENCE and hence cannot be teachers of the highest order. Indeed "the CONCEPT" is the veritable "DNA" of the existent Universe or Totality and alone gives one an understanding of everything, of all phenomena, in their Truth— namely, as "expressions" of this DNA or Concept *qua* U-P-I.

8. As for the question, What is it to be "educated" and What do you know as a JEDI? ... As a JEDI (1) You Know the Truth, Reality, the WHOLE (as an Intuitive or Scientist), (2) You Know WHO you are, namely, everything or the infinite Whole, the Force actualized, (3) You Know that you are *one* with everyone, on all planes, sharing with them *the same One Absolute I,* and (4) You Know HOW to live in the Eternal Present as a citizen of the eternal Jedi Order.

How exactly to Transcend your Senses, the Dark Side (+|-), and get out of the Cave and into the Point (±)

§283

That is, How does one actually come to SEE the One in the Many and transition from *Stage Two* Consciousness to *Stage Three* Self-Consciousness, from P.I. to U.I., from Ego to Jedi, thereby dissolving the Ego and raising it up to *Universality?*

It is done in no other way than by a *24/7 Focus on the Truth, the Point, the Universal.*— And always be mindful that the Universal not only contains the Individual *within* itself but is also the *essence* of the Individual.

> "The student *must first die to sight and hearing* and be torn away from concrete representations—she must be withdrawn into the night of the soul and so learn to SEE on this new level." **Hegel**

Thus, You must live more and more in **Plato's** Upper World. You must AWAKEN REASON—your so-called "6th sense" or "third eye," that is, the Concept or Consciousness—and learn to "SEE" in this Upper World by means of this divine power or faculty of REASON that alone Liberates. Noble Jedi, You must "Learn about the Force" and thereby (1) See through the illusory "Being" of material Sense-things, (2) Cease loving them and attaching and identifying yourself with them, and by doing so thus (3) Realize your Oneness and Unity with all persons and all Reality.

§284

The Key is *Focused Attention* on the UNIVERSAL (the "ALL-gemeine," the all-encompassing reality). The Fact is that the POINT or REALITY is the CONCEPT or, what is the same, the UNIVERSAL (+)—hence it is Universals that alone occupy the Upper World and true Reality *and* contain as well the (-) or sense-individuals within themselves; because of (±), the unity of the two, of (+) and (-). And Universals are "invisible" to the senses, only Reason can "see" them. (Also be mindful that when you "pray, worship, or meditate" the same thing happens—you leave your Senses and enter the Upper World of Universals, Thought, and the Concept.)

§285

The essence of true Jedi Education is summarized and contained in the Three Parts of The JEDI CODE. In a nutshell: (1) *The Jedi*

Oath: whereby you commit or resolve 100% to be a Jedi and realize the Jedi Order, (2) *Jedi Power Ethics*: based on the fact that IT IS, the Jedi Order is Now and is your #1 priority, all else being #2, and (3) *Jedi Power Methods*: whereby the Dark Side is dispelled and the POINT is realized via the methods of *Solitude*, namely Reason (the CONCEPT), Meditation/Faith (CONSCIOUSNESS and Love), and Art, and *Society*, namely by creating Jedi groups and relationships, since the Dark Side pull is strong.

> There is only *One Goal* of education:
> To be a JEDI—which involves the Shift
> from STAGE TWO to STAGE THREE
> Consciousness.

§286

Before we continue it will be helpful if we go deeper into the *Stage Two* and *Stage Three* states pertaining to true Education. What is required is that You overcome the Subject-Object, me/Not-me *split* in everyday consciousness and realize the Subject-Object *unity* or the "One Consciousness" State. You must realize your Universality or your Universal-ALL nature whereby you come to see yourself (your Pure Jedi "I") in everything, in every Object, every Other, every Self. You must shift from *Stage Two* Consciousness OF an Object to *Stage Three* Consciousness of Self *in* Object, or Subject-Object in order to see through the illusion of SHEER OBJECTIVITY or OBJECTIVITY without a trace of SUBJECTIVITY. What is required is simply that, "You bring the MANIFOLD or MULTIPLICITY of Nature (Part-icularity, *Be-sonderheit*) into UNITY."

§287

Therefore You (as *implicitly* the Force or Absolute I) have to transition, transform, advance, from CONSCIOUSNESS **(Stage Two)** to SELF-CONSCIOUSNESS **(Stage Three),** from the Dark Side (+|-) to the Light Side (±), from EGO *to* JEDI. (And Note that **Stage One** is the initial FORCE as it is *in itself* and in its unexpressed state *prior* to manifestation as Nature and History).

§288

Thus the transition that is Jedi Education is FROM Stage Two, EGO … where you are not aware of your immortal Whole JEDI SELF and the JEDI ORDER …

Here the Truth of the POINT, the Absolute I, and Recognition is not known yet. The Self feels it is only a *separate* empirical EGO or personality, separate from all others and the universe, that it is only its BODY (hence Death, Pain, and Nihilism); thus if your Body were to die you too would die and cease to be.

The Self can be said to be in a state of "Limbo" and hence subject to unstable EGO-Rage and ontological Anxiety—at any moment its imagined Being or absolute independence, worth, security, and Freedom *can be undone* by the Other, by another Self or Event. It has *not* achieved *Universal* Self-Consciousness and "Recognition," that is, reconciliation with all other selves whereby it becomes *certain* of its *Absolute Independence and Freedom* and that of every other Self, and certain of the Ec-stasy and Infinity of *itself* as a Pure Absolute I and *one and the same as* every other Objective Self. It has *not* achieved, as **Hegel** says, the state of "I am them and they are me," and has not realized, as **Ram Dass** writes, that "We are all one consciousness in many bodies," *Be Love Now,* p.61.

§289

The Self is immersed in the Senses and OUTER Multiplicity. As knowing only of (-) and steeped in "unresolved Objectivity" it experiences itself as limited by Objects and made Finite and does not SEE itself, THE "I," in *all* objects and other Selves, and is not thereby INFINITE. Hence the Self is *anxious,* fearful of Death, non-recognition, and rejection and is ruled by desire and "in time"—that is, the PRESENT is deficient (+|-) and has to be corrected in a projected non-existent imaginary "future." It is not certain that it has "Being" hence it fears *nothingness,* extinction, meaninglessness. Further, the Self is not in UNITY and does not see or have itself in *all* objects or experience the UNITY of all Selves. It also lives exclusively in the OUTER domain of the Force—completely unaware of the INNER domain and that its Consciousness is in truth Infinite and ALL REALITY and that Matter (-) and Sense-things are = 0 or *nothing.* As a consequence the Self believes that Matter-Things are absolute and the only Reality. It is therefore immersed and trapped in Egoic PARTICULARITY and in its binding Ego-ATTACHMENTS, IDENTITY, Dependencies and Identifications—rather than in Liberating UNIVERSALITY. Finally, the Self is merely a "Natural Man," a natural EGO or an undisciplined Natural Will and subject to what your religions call "evil or *sin (hamarteia),*" which in your Greek means (+|-) *separateness,* as in missing the mark or the Point; hence "no sin" means (±) *unity.*

§290

...TO Stage Three, as a JEDI (via *the Knowledge of The Force* (±)) and an eternal Member-Citizen of the JEDI ORDER. YOU ARE *POINT-ED,* Educated and Healed. You are (1) aware of the One-Point-Unity underlying everything, you are the FORCE aware of itself as Concept or Consciousness (as Intuitive or Discursive) and (2) you have unified all that you are, your whole being into a single POINT.

Now the POINT, *UNITY,* THE ABSOLUTE I and RECOGNITION are *Realized*—and continually lived in and experienced. Everyone is the WHOLE, the ABSOLUTE I and eternal ... and is a unique realization of U-P-I, of the Concept or Force. There is no Fear, Anxiety, Desire, or Time—only LOVE, etc. You know that (+) Consciousness-INNER-SUBJECT is alone Reality and that (-) Matter-Things-OUTER-OBJECT are *nothing.* But you also know that the two are in UNITY (±) as SUBJECT/OBJECT. The Dark Side and separation (+|-) are overcome *permanently*—only UNITY and LOVE and AWARENESS remain. And you know of the "SUBTLE WORLDS" and Subtle Bodies, etc. You know of UNIVERSALITY and are established securely in it; and PARTICULARITY (sensory and intellectual) remains, but only as a plaything for purposes of creativity, etc. Particularity is known to be inconsequential, hence there is no need to identify with it or find yourself or *meaning* in it.

§291

THUS the need is for *everyone* on your planet to be a JEDI and educated into the Truth. The fastest way this can be done is via your Seven major global Institutions which are educational by nature and can change or Balance your people's consciousness and world-views. Hence you must educate Jedi who will be best equipped and informed to go in and change the Seven. Of course your people can *immediately* begin to transform and Balance the Seven by using Jedi principles, that is, even *before* they have become full Jedi.

(2) GLOBAL JEDI EDUCATION WITH RESPECT TO THE INDIVIDUAL READER

What follows is only a summary of *The Jedi Code*, which will be discussed in depth in *Part II*.

"IT IS" means that "I am a JEDI" and "The JEDI ORDER is Now (±)."

§292

The Jedi Code has three parts: *1. The Jedi Oath, 2. Jedi Power Ethics,* and *3. Jedi Power Methods.* All three are aspects of ONE EDUCATIONAL METHOD. In essence, to be a "Jedi" you must do what a Jedi does or live like a Jedi. This is to live by the "Jedi Code" which is summarized thus:

> "I will no longer live for myself alone, but for all of humanity. I will make serving The Jedi Order my number one priority in life, and everything else number two and in its service. And I will live in the knowledge that *The Jedi Order alone exists* and that hence I am a JEDI now—that is, I am one with the Eternal Force and all other beings and will love them unconditionally. I will use all Jedi methods to help me live up to this sacred Code.
> *The Force will be with all of us."*

(1) The Jedi Oath: Involves a 100% commitment to the Jedi Code, to healing yourself and the world.

(2) Jedi Power Ethics: You are to live as if Jedi Order is Now (IT IS) and the Dark Side and the CAVE is not. THE OMEGA POINT (a la **Teilhard de Chardin**) … IS NOW. *First*, "Power" increases and is maximized when *everything* is put under One Goal. *Second*, "Ethics" concerns Self-Other relations, which are solved by the (±) TRUTH, the Unity of Self and Other that is LOVE. Not only are you to love and forgive everyone (as your religions teach) but you also have the power to do so. "Ethics" also concerns, How to live your life and what is Right and Wrong. What is "Right" is simply that everyone realize they are an immortal Jedi and live in the Jedi Order, while what is "Wrong" is that the Jedi Order be not known or experienced.

§293

(3) Jedi Power Methods: Provides Ways to Focus 24/7 on the POINT or the TRUTH (±). What you do is Focus on (±) until it prevails and pervades everything (-) as the only Reality … and continually Live above the Divided Line in the Eternal-Divine-Universal Realm 24/7. The GOAL is to become more and more aware of the POINT (the Absolute I, Universal Self-Consciousness) in the center of your Being (or EGO) … and its infinite LOVE. There are Two Categories:

(1) **SOLITUDE** *(alone)*. You must master Solitude *and* Society … but Solitude is more important. The division here is based on Jedi Science's *Absolute Jedi:* Art, Religion, and Science:

1—By REASON (Point as **CONCEPT**): Includes Jedi Science, Proofs, Jedi Books, and Old to New Paradigm: God=Man=World = POINT.

2—By FAITH-Meditation-Will (Love) (Point as **CONSCIOUSNESS** or "SPIRIT"): Use your Religion and scriptures (love and surrender to God, Reality, Truth) but change or supplement your religion's concepts of *God-man-world*. Use Meditations/Affirmations.

3—By ART (Truth in sensuous form as Beauty): True Art heals you, dissolves your EGO, and opens your True Infinite SELF. The Arts are: Architecture—Sculpture—Painting—Music—Poetry, and reflect the transition from the Outer to the Inner and the Truth-Point.

(2) **SOCIETY** *(with Others)*. Because the Dark Side PULL is strong you need Others. There is power in numbers and in *Jedi Groups* (but don't get *dependent*), for example: Family-Household, School, Office, Phone, Internet, etc.—Relationships (Diadic vs Triadic): their purpose is to dissolve EGO and realize each partner's true JEDI nature and Self.—Job or Profession: work in the 7 Institutions, e.g. start a Jedi school, a Jedi Sect, a Jedi Business, etc.

(3) GLOBAL JEDI EDUCATION VIA YOUR 7 GLOBAL INSTITUTIONS

§294

All that is required here is simply to introduce into your Seven Institutions the Jedi Education Principles and Method outlined in *The Jedi Code* above, which is sufficient to change them from teaching (+|-) error to teaching (±) Truth. As I stated, the fastest way to educate all of your people into the JEDI ORDER is by means of the Seven Global Institutions that shape your planetary consciousness and are educational by their very nature. Presently your Seven Global Institutions are not teaching the Truth (±) but error (+|-). Let us see briefly how each institution is teaching error and how they can be Balanced so they may teach the Truth and truly educate your people; this is the subject of *Part III: The Jedi Order.*

§295

(1) Your SCIENCES—are now teaching the error (+|-) of materialism, nihilism, and of yourselves as mere Body-Egos—and not teaching that the JEDI ORDER (±), UNITY, and the INNER is Now and is all that is. To teach this by means of Jedi Science and the CONCEPT is alone to truly educate.

(2) Your EDUCATION—is not teaching the JEDI ORDER but the Dark Side world-view of your p-sciences that keeps you in the Cave and the OUTER domain. Your schools and universities must switch to Jedi Holistic Education which teaches both CONCEPT and CONSCIOUSNESS (Discursive and Intuitive) and is based on Jedi Science: "Welcome students. We are IN the JEDI ORDER Now. You are here to learn via your studies all about the JEDI ORDER,

what it is and how it came to be, etc." (See below (4) "GJE via Your Institution of Education")

(3) Your RELIGIONS—put off the Kingdom of God, the World to Come, and the JEDI ORDER till the future. Rather they are to teach, via CONSCIOUSNESS (as Intuitive), the Truth of the *Unity* of the Opposites "God and Man," "Heaven and Earth (the Here and Now)," thus that the JEDI ORDER is Now, and Create Jedi Sects within themselves, thus ending all hatred and conflict among them.

> (Note that the following four institutions, as based on Jedi Teaching, will incorporate *both* CONCEPT and CONSCIOUSNESS in their own way and to the extent their concept permits)

(4) Your POLITICS—and politicians know nothing of "Politics" and the JEDI ORDER. They keep you in the Dark Side and the Ego-World and keep war, poverty, corruption, etc., as the status quo. They must change by teaching the leaders and citizens of your nations the true concept of politics (*politeia*) as expressed in your *"E pluribus unum"* motto, and create a Jedi President, Congress, and Third Party.

(5) Your BUSINESS'—need to switch from the EGO Business Method, responsible for greed, poverty, unemployment, and financial-economic crises worldwide, to the JEDI Business Method and focus on the "WE are ONE" principle which teaches that the JEDI ORDER of abundance and health is NOW.

(6) Your HEALTH (Medicine and Psychiatry)—practitioners are not Healing you due to their false concepts of Man and Health and are preventing the glorious JEDI ORDER from manifesting. They must teach true Health and who you really are: JEDI.

(7) Your ARTS and MEDIA—are very powerful and hence are in need of Jedi teaching regarding Jedi Truth and the Jedi Order on Television, the Internet, in film and the arts, etc. We will see How this can be done in more depth in *Part III: The JEDI ORDER.*

(4) GLOBAL JEDI EDUCATION VIA YOUR INSTITUTION OF EDUCATION IN PARTICULAR

THE FEATURES OF TRUE JEDI EDUCATION

§296

True Jedi Education has the following hallmarks:

1) It has a *single supreme Goal*: TO BECOME A JEDI—which involves the knowledge of the Truth/the Force/the Point, of *who you really are*, and *of How to live in Eternity*. That is, the knowledge of What IS and Why IT IS, by both the Concept (Discursive) and Consciousness (Intuitive). True Education teaches you that What IS is the ONE FORCE that contains Inner and Outer domains, and that *You* or *Your True Self* are the Force/Whole/Truth *aware of Itself as a JEDI*. And because of this Jedi Education's curriculum is *holistic*, especially as relating to Science and as all subjects are related to *this single Goal*.

2) It teaches you *How* to reach the Goal, actualize the Truth, and become a Jedi via the true education the Jedi-curriculum provides.— And especially How to recognize and move from the Dark Side of the Force and its world-view to the Light Side—while equipping you with weapons against Dark Side beliefs that are rooted in your 7-Institutions.

3) It incorporates you into and prepares you for Life in the eternal Jedi Order Society by disciplining your natural Ego, will, and character into a Jedi-Citizen.

§297

4) It informs you on what today's main problems in The Order are, why they exist and their causes, and offers methods and strategies for solving them—that is, the work that remains to be done and what you can do. It also helps you with career choices and with How best to continue your Jedi Education in Society and the "Real World," and serve in and contribute to Jedi Society.

§298

Your own "false or mis-Education" does the exact opposite of all of the above and keeps you in the OUTER and in your false Ego, with no hope of achieving Unity and True Health. This is because 1. it lacks the true Concept of Education, 2. it is without the #1 Goal of Education: to be a Jedi and a citizen of the Jedi Order, 3. its focus is on the OUTER and not the INNER and True Reality, 4. it lacks a Holistic Curriculum based on Jedi Science, and thus it is 5. *Nihilistic* in that it teaches Materialism and a False Concept of "Man" and the Universe, and 6. it regards Education as only a means and not the #1 END (see *Part III: The Jedi Order,* 2, for more).

HOW TO REACH THE GOAL OF JEDI: THE "JEDI CURRICULUM"

§299

Introduction. "Education" is to be taken in the *broadest* sense of the word, one which extends beyond the confines of "school" and formal education (the *narrow* sense) and can also be *life-long.* The goal of this broader sense of Education as of the narrow is the same: *to become a JEDI.* It begins in the family, continues through formal schooling (K-college), and then into Society. In fact it always takes place *within* society and its seven areas, which always exert their influence on it, for good or ill. A key issue is, *At what point does the child/student reach the Goal of Jedi?* The answer is: Either while he is in school and before graduation, or after graduation while in society. This is undetermined and will vary from individual to individual. It is probable that, at least in the beginning—when the 7 Institutions of society have yet to *align* with the Light Side Truth and foster it— the majority of students will attain the Jedi Goal *after* graduation, when a citizen in society, in a corporation, etc. So, when the 7 areas or most of them *are* aligned, we can expect more individuals will actualize Jedi *while in* school. The main point of this remark is to remind you noble Reader that "Education" and reaching the Goal is not limited to formal schooling and the Jedi-Curriculum about to be described—which in many respects can be viewed as providing only the *foundation* for Jedi Education, which instills deeply into the student that his or her #1 priority in life is to *be* a Jedi (and is not money, fame, family, etc)—and hence will insure that she *will* at some definite point reach the Goal. As to How the other 6-Institutions or Areas of Society will be forces which continue and further the educational process begun in school-education, we will see later in *Part III: The Jedi Order.*

§300

The Jedi Curriculum. As indicated, the Curriculum—*what* is taught and *how* it is taught—will be *modified* depending on what *level* of society-culture the student is living in; whether for example in "level 1," where only the first Jedi-schools exist, so more time has to be devoted to neutralizing the "dark-side" errors disseminated by the not yet aligned 7 areas of society—or in "level 3," where *all* 7-Institutions are operational and continually promoting the Jedi Order and Truth, so less time and courses are needed to defeat error, etc.

Also, since there is only One Goal in Education, not many, viz., to Heal the subject/object split and realize the student's infinite Jedi Self, much of what is currently taught in K-12 and college is non-essential and dispensable. And so it really matters little *how* the Goal is reached as long as it *is reached.* Hence in principle there is much freedom in the curriculum and what constitutes it, and in the form and stages in which it is imparted. The following section will give you an idea of the extremes of the form and stages possible.

§301

Education in Transition. In the beginning there will not be many Jedi and Jedi Masters around and perhaps none in Jedi-Schools.— And this is not an insurmountable problem since all that is really needed is that the principal and her staff/teachers be imbued, inspired and inspiring, with the conviction of its Truth; the rest, the actualization of the students' inherent Jedi nature, will take care of itself. Hence there will be a lone "Pilot Jedi School" in the community and it will be forced to adjust and adhere as close as possible (though greatly modified) to existing curriculums in non-Jedi schools (and to tests, regents, etc). Also because there will be a continual flow or transfer of students from non-Jedi schools into Jedi ones, it is best to have not just one teacher but many educate the child in the various areas and subjects of the holistic Jedi Curriculum.

§302

Things will be different when the *success* of Jedi-Pilot schools has been admitted and universally recognized in society and they have become the Norm or Public and there are more Jedi Masters teaching in schools. The more Jedi Masters and Teachers there are, the more options as regards teaching.

In an "advanced" Jedi Society Culture, where there are many Jedi's (and teachers) and the Knowledge of the Two-Spheres (the Physical and Subtle) and open commerce between them is the norm and commonplace, you will have these types of formats:

(1) There will be a class of *Private* Jedi Tutors (like **Aristotle** and **Alexander the Great**) who alone take the student through K-12 and all the way to Jedi.

(2) Since most parents will be Jedi and have a full knowledge of the Force/Truth and hence can serve as the best Educators, they may choose to "home school" their child from K-12 to Jedi—or perhaps just until K-6, then 6-12 in a Jedi Public School, etc. (The Jedi parents may teach other children as well, and run a small private Jedi school or "academy.") The possibilities and combinations are infinite.

(3) For example, the child may begin in Public School K-6, then Private (with a Jedi Tutor) 6-12, then go on to Jedi college. Or he may begin in an exclusive Private Jedi Academy, K-6, then Public School 6-12, and then go on to complete her college and graduate education with private tutors (physical/"flesh" or subtle/"glorified") and/or public educators, for example:

> (a) Private Tutorial/Seminar/Workshops (by selective invitation, after application) to study Art-Painting with **Michelangelo**, Vermeer, Rembrandt, Picasso, Rodin, Correggio—and/or playwriting with **Shakespeare**, Dostoevsky, Hawthorne, Plath, Woolf—or filmmaking with **George Lucas**, S. Spielberg, Capra, D.W. Griffith, Kubrick, Hitchcock, or Fellini.

> (b) Science with **Plato, Aristotle, Descartes, Schelling, Hegel**, etc.

> (c) Religion and spirituality, and Mastery of powers with **Jesus, Moses, Babaji, Elijah**, etc.

(d) And other courses at a regular public Jedi College or University, etc, etc.

(Note all of this follows from Jedi Science, which teaches that consciousness is indestructible and the individual immortal).

> There is only *One Goal* of education:
> To be a JEDI—and reach the Subject/Object unity that is Knowledge/Truth, Infinity and Freedom. So the *means* (curricula) are not as important as the *End (Jedi)*. It matters little *how* it is reached, as long as it is reached.

§303

Key Curriculum Principles.

However, though there is much room for diversity in the *means* and curriculum, there are certain *key principles* serving as guidelines that must be observed for use by the Jedi Principal responsible for the curriculum and success of the school. How the educator applies them, in what combinations, etc, is entirely up to him:

(1) The core of Education (à la your Jedi **Plato**) is to go from Many to One, to overcome the illusory Self/Other split (+|-), and realize and live in the *Unity* of Subjectivity/Objectivity (±). It is for the student, at first sunk in the "senses"/world/immediacy/ multiplicity, to rise above this "Divided Line" and *Transcend the Senses* into the One all-inclusive Universal or CONCEPT (U-P-I)— that is, to "overcome the World (the I/Not-I split)" and *be* the Truth. Therefore everything follows from this, and all other goals (e.g. becoming a member/citizen of Jedi Society, etc) take a back seat to it.

(2) Thus the center of education and what alone is important in the last analysis is what can be called "**The CORE**"—that is, *Pure Science-Logic-the Concept and the Eternal Truth* with the Methods for realizing it, namely, One-Pointed Focused Attention (on the Universal or Point) via Reason, meditation, concentration, etc.

§304

(3) The Three supplementary Agents effecting the educational/ transformational process of *transcending the senses and entering the POINT* (±) or maturing the (as it were) Jedi "*Seed*-Potency" in each student, are *the Sciences (real-concrete-applied), Religion, and Art.*

—Note: (a) These three are important and effective only because they contain *The Core* principle of **bringing the manifold into unity** *within* them and thus reinforce it. *Science, Religion, and Art* only exist *at all* because of the root-problem of "consciousness" or I/ Not-I *separation: Science, Religion, and Art* exist simply *to cancel* the separation. If there were none, they would not be. In fact once you are healed and a Jedi, you are above the three agents and can take them or leave them, for you do not need them; hence your relation to them, for the first time, is a *free* one. (b) The active agent in all three—the power to realize and "awaken the Jedi Seed-Potency" of the student—is in the *reduction of many to unity;* that is, in progressively aligning your being/consciousness with the Truth and true Reality, which is *UNITY* (±). It is precisely this agreement and correspondence with WHAT IS that does it and effects the change; that is, *You* more and more correspond with your *Concept* (as e.g. the "Image of God"). For example, the active agent in *Religion* is *believing or agreeing with* the Truth/Reality ("I am saved, healed, One with God," etc); in *Art* it is seeing the world/the many *idealized* and reduced to unity = *Beauty* in the Work of Art or seeing in it the Idea, your True Self ("My, how beautiful *it* is," that is, "*I* am"); in *Science* it is seeing/knowing that the many/Reality in fact reduces to One, the Concept or Force, and vanishes, and seeing that *You*—your true self—are this One.

§305

(4) Additional supplementary Agents are: Foreign Language (the I—"Other"/culture relation), Project-based learning and group activities, Team sports (integrating a many into One), Dance (e.g. Tai Chi), events/interactions with Role Models (from the outside "real" world), with Jedi, experts, distinguished professionals, etc.

(5) You—the educator or principal—can use *any* of the three supplementary Agents either alone or in combination; except, nota bene, that Art *alone* cannot accomplish it, or permanently establish

one in the Truth, for only Science alone or Religion alone (or both together) can. It is recommended you use all three Agents, given your present place in History and culture.—And for Science/ Philosophy *alone*, be sure to stress the LOVE, heart-affective aspect. The special problem and challenge for Religion *alone* is that at some point you must *transcend* the "Picture/Vorstellen" form of the Truth (±) completely, i.e. *into* Pure Awareness (the I = I or Concept). Also because of the scientific/intellectual age in which you live many minds will not be satisfied with Religion's "picture answers" to their questions. In this case Educators will have to use Science/Reason as a supplement to Religion.

(6) However the educator "breaks down" and apportions the Whole (the Truth) to be taught (as the Curriculum) it is strongly advised that you have a continual CORE course from start to finish that serves to *integrate and coordinate* all the various aspects of education and whose prime function is to realize and mature the student's inherent Jedi nature.

THE JEDI CURRICULUM K-12 and UNIVERSITY: A SAMPLE

§306

We recommend what follows as a "Template" for the Standard Curriculum to be used in all Jedi Education: for **[A]** The first "Pilot/ Charter" Jedi Schools (K-12) and **[B]** The first Jedi University—since it diverges least from the curriculum that is currently used on your planet and accommodates much of it (e.g. standard tests, regents, SAT). Hence it is easiest to implement. As time goes on this will change. We also recommend in K-6 both male and female teachers in the classroom, as well as the use of "Project-based education" as a supplement but not a substitute.

§307

As we said, HOW you get there and become a JEDI is not as important as *that* you get there. So there is much freedom and flexibility in the organization and *curriculum* in Jedi schools and Educational Institutions.

However, my noble Reader, we must also be mindful of the current state of your planetary civilization. That is to say, not only is there the basic need (1) to prepare students for the richness of Life in the Jedi Order and to equip them with the tools and knowledge necessary to meet the challenges of your world, and (2) to enable students to have a wide exposure to all fields of knowledge and thus to the various ways they can *serve* in and contribute to the Jedi Order and the healing of your world. But there is also (3) the obvious FACT that at this critical time in your planet's history, when the Dark Side of the Force reigns and has a stranglehold on your people's consciousness, *there will be* much resistance to "changing over" to the Light Side. *Hence the need for a significant number of Jedi <u>Scientists</u> to help facilitate this.* In view of this situation we strongly advise that *all public educational institutions* in a given Nation-State have a curriculum and structure *based* on and making available to both students and faculty *JEDI SCIENCE in detail;* this kind of institution moreover would accommodate and dovetail nicely with the structure of your present schools and universities. Here too there is much room for variety and alternative orderings and Forms—however here we will just advance *one* Method or System for K-12/University Education.

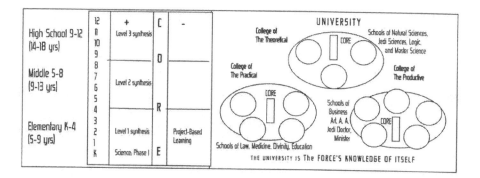

[A] THE JEDI K-12 SCHOOL CURRICULUM

§308

Pre-University Schooling K-12 is ideally and in Concept a *preparation* for the complete education (to knowledge of the Whole and Jedi) which occurs in University. So ideally *all* students should be required (by the State) to go into University from High School. But for a time, HS graduates will also be permitted to go directly into Jedi Society (the "real" world)—where they *can* and *will* (if HS education was adequate) nevertheless continue and eventually complete their education to Jedi (e.g. in a corporation, etc).

§309

Here as in Jedi-University the #1 Goal of education and the K-12 curriculum is to help students realize their Jedi-Self and overcome the Self/Other split (+|-) as far as is possible. It is also to prepare students for University (or in certain cases, for Jedi Society) and for *life in Eternity* and, ultimately, for service in and their contribution to Jedi Society, where they will continue their education and blossoming via your 7 Institutions and agencies.

And, as in University, the Jedi "Core" Course will be at the center of the educational process and curriculum; all else as *means* will take a back seat to it.

§310

Thus according to the #1 Goal of becoming a JEDI the CORE Course will have as its main focus, (1) the Unifying of the INNER "human" or Jedi sciences (+) and the OUTER natural sciences (-) into (±), and especially (2) the elevating of the student from *Stage Two*—Natural Ego to *Stage Three*—JEDI, by tracking and encouraging his or her *progress* towards the supreme Goal. Education starts at home in the Family and in Society and its influences (T.V., computer, etc). The home situation is a Key factor—the ideal is to be educated in a Jedi Family, the worst is a home where there is one or no parents and/or where the parents or guardians abdicate their responsibility, etc.

§311

(1) As we said the main Concept/Principle of E-DUCATION as such is (1) to "LEARN ABOUT THE FORCE," about What IS, the Truth (±), the One Consciousness or Concept, and that the Jedi Order is NOW and that You *are* Jedi NOW and that ETERNITY is NOW ... AND (2) to BALANCE and ALIGN YOURSELF and thus your World/Planet to the Truth. So as we have demonstrated, "The Force" *is* the Jedi Order, the UNITY-of-Opposites, represented by (3) below—which is the Goal and Result of True EDUCATION, and which à la **PLATO** has 3 Stages:

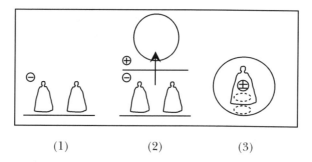

(1)   (2)   (3)

Note: (1) and (2) together comprise *Stage Two. Stage Three* is (3). Also see §280.

§312

To Review: The child begins in (1), the sense-world (-), the many, separation and EGO, believing these to be alone true reality and completely ignorant of (+) *UNITY* and the Invisible-Consciousness-Thought-Light Side of the Force, nevertheless possessed with an inner encoded Feeling or presentiment of (+). Therefore *EDUCATION*—or "Learning about the Force" and moving from *Stage Two* to *Stage Three*—is simply a matter of achieving this feeling of (+) and coming to be *aware* of this Other *Second* Dimension of reality as alone True Reality—*and* as in absolute UNITY with (-) as (±) or the Subject/Object, Self/Other, Consciousness/Matter unity.

Consequently (2) represents the long process of the child's *E-ducation,* of being *led* from the (-) OUTER to the (+) INNER domain and out of ignorance into Knowledge. It is a process of becoming aware of the *two* sides of reality and learning to focus more and more on the (+) or Universal side, while acquiring an increasingly truer *evaluation* of both (-) and (+) sides. This process ends finally in (3), their *UNITY* and Truth and the student's *unity* with the *UNITY*—as the Jedi Order and Jedi, which was *there* from the beginning but prior to Education not known.

§313

(2) The next issue concerns HOW exactly is the child/student to "Learn about the Force," to advance from *Stage Two* to *Stage Three* and actually become a JEDI and member of the Jedi Order, the WHOLE aware of Itself?

The main thing as we know is for the Educator to gradually wean students off occupation with Senses and sense-singulars and get them to be aware of the (+) Invisible, *UNITY* realm of *Universals*, and lastly *fuse* with this UNITY; which also contains the Many (-), particulars and individuals, within itself.

Since there are many ways to do this, many studies and practices which effect this "turning around" or "inversion" of the SOUL à la **Plato** and **Hegel**, the *CURRICULUM* in K-12 is very flexible. The main thing necessary—however you specify your curriculum—is to keep the students *on course* to UNITY, Truth, and POINT-edness, the Goal for which they are already programmed. You the Educator, should continually place *unity* before them and keep bringing the variety of subjects and the multiplicity within each subject into *UNITY* and into the Truth (±). Always focus on and bring everything *back* to the Truth, to Unity, the INNER, the Absolute I, LOVE, and the One Consciousness and Concept, which is *the Force aware of Itself.*

One of the main goals in a Jedi school is to constantly Focus on the essential *UNITY* of all the children of *different* races, religions, and ethnicities—so they may learn to Love, respect, and value each other by seeing the *UNITY* (the INNER I) beneath their surface differences.

---

§314

Special Goals and Objectives of the K-12 Educational Curriculum.

(1) The Curriculum is mainly geared to entering University; other "vocational" students are special cases and easily handled.

(2) A major objective and segment of the process will be to provide beginning Jedi students with the Basics-Tools necessary for success in education and for mastering the curriculum contents, e.g. Reading, Writing, Speaking, Computer, the Body and Physical Education, etc.

Jedi Core Teachers will have to "get the students excited and motivated" with respect to the Jedi-education "adventure" they are about to embark upon. For example: The child (K-1) will begin his first Day in CORE and will end in CORE (or "homeroom"). He will see a Picture of a "JEDI" and the symbol of Jedi Science in front of the classroom to continually inspire him. The Main Thought that will supply the ambience for the entire educational process is:

This is REAL. The *Jedi Order* is *real*, it is *Now* and You are here to learn about it. You are very special since no other schools teach about it, and *you* will help your race *enter into it*, solve your world's problems and realize a truly Amazing World.

(3) The Two Main Sciences are *Jedi Society/History (+)* and *Nature (-)*. They will be presented and taught at increasing levels of comprehensiveness, complexity, and "scientificity"—that is, logical rigor, systematic interconnection and intelligibility, and in accord with the "transitional" nature of each subject-matter as leading to the singular Goal of Jedi and the Jedi Order.

THE JEDI-CORE COURSE

§315

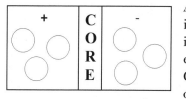

As I stated, the Jedi *CORE* Course is central and *the one constant* to be included in *all* Curriculums without exception. The main elements of the Curriculum—based on the Knowledge of the Force and Holistic Jedi Science— are therefore (1) the central *CORE* (±) and (2) the two main branches of the *Jedi "human" Sciences (+)* and the *Natural sciences (-)*.

(1) The Main Purpose and Function of the **CORE** is (a) to Teach the Eternal TRUTH and the METHODS for realizing it—namely the FORCE (±), the Jedi Truths and Proofs, LOGIC (Metaphysics) and the whole of Jedi Science: **Logic**-Nature-Jedi—and (b) to elevate the student into a JEDI and track his progress to the Goal. And as said, she can become a JEDI *without* having mastered Science or made adequate progress in it, that is, she can become an "Intuitive" Jedi instead of a "Discursive" Jedi.

To this end the CORE teachers can use a variety of *methods* (from the "JEDI CODE") to facilitate the goal of the actualization of the student's Jedi potential or "*Seed*," such as: One-Pointed *MEDITATIONS* (and breathing exercises)—alone or in a group,

Personal instruction via readings and discussions of *Key Jedi Books* selected by the FACILITATOR (the *same* one throughout K-12; or K-4, 5-8, 9-12) or *Jedi Movies*, Art (hi-tech/nology) Shows, weekend Retreats with Jedi-Teachers, etc. CORE teachers can also help students solve personal-home problems which may interfere with their Jedi Education, and can help with a student's Body-Mind harmony/coordination, as well as overall health and study habits.

Special *Tutors* can help the student to understand Key Principles and Truths, e.g. POLARITY, by using examples from Nature and real life ... and they can try to *awaken* his latent abilities e.g. by challenging him by putting him in a *leadership* position, thus giving him confidence and activating his untapped skills, etc.

§316

(2) The CORE also integrates (+) and (-) studies into the (±) Whole and *UNITY*, and helps to clarify any difficult *Concepts* by group discussion and making the students *summarize* the (+) lecture in front of the group, which develops Public Speaking abilities; and it teaches LOGIC as well, in increasing sophistication.

The CORE is a *constant* that begins in "K" and all the way up to "12" and into University—and continues, in a fashion, into Post-University, for example in the Corporation, etc.—and this because the #1 goal of life and Society is EDUCATION, to be a realized JEDI.

The CORE can meet everyday at the end of the day for 1 or 2 hours—or once a week, e.g. on a Monday or Friday, 3-4 hours— and with many variations; e.g., the *same* teacher can teach both (+) History *and* CORE, and in some cases one teacher can teach everything, (+) and (-) and CORE (±).

§317

(3) The basic idea and structure of the **CORE** is the same as in University, only it will be tailored initially to capabilities of beginning K and 1ˢᵗ grade students.

So, there are three Core components: *Facts/Truth, Transformation,* and *Coordination.*

(1) As regards the *Facts/Truth* component, the Teacher-Facilitator will tell you "what the story is" (initially in simple terms a young child can grasp), what life is about—your great destiny as a Jedi, what the Whole is/the Force and the process you are privileged to be involved in, "who you really are" and what your "options" are: you can "take the High road or the Low road," and the consequences of both. Also treated will be Morality, good and evil/the Dark Side, plus Character (natural Will) development and discipline via sharing, loving, etc. Plus "The Jedi Oath" and songs, etc. "I (the facilitator) am here to help you in this and tell you what your course of study will be, its Objectives, etc."

The task of the Core Teacher/Facilitator is to Get the students excited about their Jedi Education. As noted, a Picture (Emblem) of a Jedi (themselves), their Ideal, should be *displayed* continually and throughout the educational process. This is a *unifying force* for all their education. The Teacher should frequently tell them THAT and HOW all their courses are important for helping them realize and become a Jedi, stressing the *unity* of their education and the curriculum.

A major focus will be on *Logic/Metaphysics/and the Polarity Principle or CONCEPT* (Universal-Particular-Individual, Being-Essence-Concept, (-), (+), (±)) and how everything they will study (in the Inner and Outer domains) can be explained from it. And of course this will be done at increasing levels of difficulty and comprehensiveness, geared to the students' understanding.

§318

(2) The *Transformation* component is based on and will implement POWER-ETHICS (see *Part II: The Jedi Code*). It involves the student's cognitive transition from Believing to Knowing (from Sense to Pictures to Thoughts/Universals) via Science-Religion-and-Art, here initially mainly via Re-ligion: that is, via Affirmations and Meditation ("I am a Jedi," etc), Dance, etc; and to be modified from grade to grade.

(3) The *Coordination* component simply undertakes the coordination of *all* subjects with the #1 Jedi Goal of the Core Course, and also includes, Questions? Pitfalls? and so forth (see the University discussion in [B] below).

§319

(4) In early grades, K-4, it is advisable to have not just one but two Jedi Core-Coordinators (= Home Room Teachers), Male and Female. From 5-8 and 9-12 perhaps one is adequate—and a woman for girls, a man for boys (separate genders). Also in 5-8 and 9-12 use a "departmental" situation and structure. The Jedi-Core, moreover, should be devoted to a review of what was learned during a given week and to an explanation of the connections of the courses with the Jedi Goal, and to answering students' questions; the sessions can close with a song, the Jedi Oath, or a meditation, prayer, etc.

Again, one of the most vital lessons in all of education—second only to overcoming the Self/Other split and becoming a Jedi—is *to learn how to live in Eternity or the Eternal Present or NOW*—the place where *all* knowledge and Truth (and Reality or the Force) resides and is immediately available and accessible. For "Time is an illusion," as all Jedi know and teach.

THE JEDI SCHOOL CURRICULUM: K-12 (K-4, 5-8, 9-12)

THE BASIC (+) AND (-) CURRICULUM CONTENT

§320

In this last section I will provide Guide Lines as to What the Content of the Curriculum is and How it is to be taught.

There are logically Three component areas to be taught: The BASICS (Tools of learning), BODY-Health, and the CORE along with the Supplements of Jedi Science (Nature and Social), Jedi Universal Religion, and Art. These are the active agents that mature the Jedi-Seed Potency and prepare students for University. (Note again that only Science and Religion used alone or jointly are efficacious, and that the school principal or board can decide which to use). There

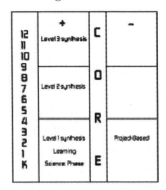

is also much agreement and overlap with the current curricula on your planet, hence its easy implementation.

§321

The BASICS, which are a prerequisite for all learning and mastery of courses, include: Reading, Writing (= English: Composition, Grammar, Spelling), Speaking, Math, and learning a *Foreign Language*, which also helps to overcome the Self-Other split by helping you to "enter into the *Other*" and see what it feels like, etc., and helps with *Logic* via grammar/syntax/logical relationships and 1st, 2nd, 3rd person, verb forms, and tenses; and Tools like Computer (and other technology and "shop") and Library skills, etc.

All these can begin in K and run to 4-5 (as is done now), and some (language, math, computer) can continue to the 12th grade.

§322

BODY-Health: A prime desideratum, as your ancients taught, is, "A Healthy mind in a healthy body." The child needs to master her Body and mold it into a pliable, obedient instrument for her use. For it is the *medium* between the child's *Inner*/Mind/Will and the *Outer*/Physical world and essential for expressing and communicating its thoughts and translating them into Action. As we Jedi know, Mind/Body, Inner/Outer, (+)/(-), are *one* and *inseparable* (as Form/Matter). Hence one *must* master and take care of one's (eternal) Body, which to master and keep healthy requires *Physical Education*, such as, sports, Jedi Light Saber exercises, Jedi Aerobics, health, hygiene, and information about Jedi dating when necessary.

§323

The CORE with Art-Religion-Science: Science, Religion, and Art are *secondary* as supplements to CORE (which we have already discussed) and the central Goal of becoming a Jedi and realizing/maturing the students' Jedi "Seed" (or self/other *unity*). All three disciplines contain the power to merge the particular EGO with Universality (and the ONE-POINT as Concept or Consciousness) and delete the illusion of the *separate* Ego-Object-Thing-World. They are also *ideal* as involving the "many-to-unity" dynamic that helps to cancel the self-other split; and as pertaining to Eternity and the region above the Divided Line (which is not "in time"). Thus as dealing with the Truth, they take one into Eternity as a realized Jedi. All three, further, will be imbued with a "moral" component since they involve the transition from the "Dark Side" (realism and the many) to the "Light Side" (idealism and the ONE).

§324

(1) *JEDI SCIENCE* will teach about Eternity, for example, that *this NOW* is the Beginning of "time," meaning that there *is* no time. Jedi Science, as a supplement, has Two Parts, *the Outer Force (-) or the Nature Sciences* and *the Inner Force (+) or the Social/"Human"-Jedi Sciences;* the Third Part, the *Science of Logic* (as well as the *Introduction* to Science) is treated primarily in CORE. The *Nature Sciences* will comprise: the Physical (matter), Earth (geology, astronomy), and the Life Sciences, while the *Jedi Sciences* will include: Global World History, Geography, Sociology, Economics, and *Political Science,* which teaches about the State and Eternal Foundation Living. It underscores the fact that *History* is nothing but the Force coming to know and realize itself as the Jedi Order, and that therefore History is *sacred,* as involving both "Adam's Race" and the Akashic Records or the "Library of the Collective Unconscious." *Jedi Science* moreover helps mature the students' Jedi "Seed" by being *transitionally* taught (moving from Nature as 0 to Jedi as 1) and by reducing the many to ONE—or by reducing Nature or Space/Matter's *externality* and parts-outside-parts to the One Consciousness/Concept and *interiority* (as your Jedi **Hegel** says: "in the end nature vanishes and reveals Spirit/Mind to be the truth of nature").

§325

The learning of SCIENCE, of *who* the students really are and of the Whole of Reality (the Knowledge of the Force, Inner and Outer), can be effected by a *Three-Phase Process*: for example, from K-4 to 5-8 to 9-12, where each Phase would make up ONE UNIT or one level of comprehension of the WHOLE, progressively more advanced and sophisticated; and where the 4th, 8th, and 12th would constitute *Synthesis* and *Testing Points,* etc, that would *Sum up* all previous courses and subjects. The student above all must learn to think and to grasp the Subject-Matter (Math, Biology, History) *HOLISTICALLY* and as a *UNITY* ... where everything, all parts-items-concepts-contents are and can be *Derived* from a *Single Principle,* much like a *seed* from which the Whole tree or plant and all its parts-features originate, indeed like SCIENCE (the Knowledge of the Force) itself. For as we know, from the "Seed" of Logic, the ARCHE, *all* forms of Nature and Jedi develop ... ending in Philosophy, Science, and Logic (the Logos) itself. Further, as the student advances in learning—and in mastering the CONCEPT or GRASP ("*Begriff*," from "*begreifen*")—he will coordinate and begin to integrate into ONE the several WHOLES (Unities) or SUBJECTS he has *already* grasped and integrated ... until he masters SCIENCE in toto and becomes a JEDI MASTER SCIENTIST. The Two-fold Aim is therefore: 1. for the student to become familiar with the *Basic Forms* (of Polarity, in Logic), and 2. to awaken and inspire in her a lasting *interest* in these subjects.

§326

(2) *JEDI RELIGION* will teach Jedi Religion (or non-religion) and principles and the History of Religions (or other main religions) and How they are absorbed and incorporated into Jedi Religion. We will accommodate all other Religions-Faiths and teach *tolerance* towards other religions. This will also help mature the student's Jedi-Seed by "Re-ligare-ing," that is, by negating the individual's EGO (by raising her love to the Universal) and overcoming the gap between herself and God/the Force; there can also be "group worship."

(3) *The ARTS* are comprised of Literature (poetry, stories: where the hero and the good overcomes evil and the Dark Side), Music, Painting, Sculpture, Architecture, and Dance (stressing both theory and practice). All of these help the student's Jedi "Seed" develop by Art's "many to one" power and as embodying the Ideal and the Truth ($\pm$).

§327

ON ELEMENTARY SCHOOL: All three—Science, Religion, and Art—can begin to be taught immediately—in K or 1. When they are taught (especially Science) the Teacher can begin by *deducing them* or showing their *connection* to the Whole ($\pm$), as taught in the Jedi CORE, and also remind students of how this helps to realize their Jedi nature (of the value, relevance, and importance of the three). They are taught at increasing levels of sophistication and comprehensiveness, from general to more detailed and logical. For example, Social Science (and the World) can begin in K and 1 with a unit on the Family and School, then on the Community (in 1-2), then on the City and State (in 3rd), and on the Nation and World (in 4-5). The teacher can highlight different *areas* each term or year—e.g. History, ancient/eastern cultures, the State and political science—and make adjustments to Regents and Standard Tests. As I said, *Science* (of Nature and Jedi) will be taught *transitionally,* where Nature = 0 and is merely a *means* to Jedi (a Jedi's Body is the microcosm of Nature), and Jedi or Knowledge = 1 (reflecting the overall movement from the Dark Side to the Light Side).

ON MIDDLE SCHOOL: The same essential Curriculum as the Elementary School Level will be taught but with greater sophistication, detail, and logical interconnection.

ON HIGH SCHOOL: The same essential Curriculum as Middle School will be taught but with even greater sophistication, detail, and logical interconnection, and with special emphasis on preparing students to enter University (the curriculum can also include pre-Practical and pre-Productive studies, such as pre-Med and Architecture, etc).

§328

On the JEDI TEACHER: He or she need not have a complete "Knowledge of the Force" or even *be* a JEDI—but minimally must be in possession of a substantial amount of knowledge (for example about Polarity, their specialty, etc) and be 100% convinced and dedicated to the Jedi-Idea, as well as possessed with a thirst for knowledge, always learning, etc. To the student, the Teacher must be perceived as embodying to a sufficient degree the ultimate Goal, a JEDI—and hence must be enthusiastic and of a high ethical character, etc. The teacher just has to nurture and guide the Jedi-seed of the student to Maturity and Actualization. Also as we stated, when there are more Jedi Masters and Teachers in the world there will be many ways to educate K-12 and reach the Jedi Goal, for example, via a Jedi Academy, Jedi Parents, Jedi Master Tutors, and so forth.

§329

Principles concerning How to Teach SCIENCE in schools:

1. Science is to be taught with an eye on the Goal of Education: Being a Jedi and a member of the eternal Jedi Order.

2. Teach Science HOLISTICALLY—as a Single Whole, leading up to the Jedi Order.

3. All Parts and Stages of Science are *vanishing-transitioning*, absorbed into the higher stages—the last stage containing all previous stages.

4. Always have in the Room a CHART of all the contents of Science as a Whole.

5. Stress the *upward* movement (**Plato's** Divided Line) from the OUTER (nature-the senses) to the INNER (thought-spirit-consciousness-the I)—help the students to *transcend* or break free of *the Senses* and awaken to Universals.

6. POLARITY must be the main focus. Teach Method #1 to K-12 (without the *Science of Logic*). Method #2 in University (with the *Science of Logic* and the U-P-I or Concept Method).

7. In K-12 education, Focus Mainly on the ABSTRACT (*Verstand*) Mode of THOUGHT (and not the "Dialectical and Speculative"), emphasizing Fixed Shapes (*Gestalten*) and Concepts—while *also* indicating their "transitional" status as vanishing Moments.

8. Also, Both (+) and (-) Teachers know and teach the Whole of Science—i.e., always start each UNIT (Mechanics, Physics, Organics, Psychology, etc) by placing it in the context of the WHOLE.

§330

How to Teach MATHEMATICS—and the true Value of math (Plato again is the key).

When you deal with *number*—the ONE and its operations/variations—you are *immediately in* the Upper World, the INNER (+), across the "Divided Line" and in the *Invisible* domain of True Reality and the Mind; you are out of the CAVE, the sense-world and "time," and in the *Eternal* realm. This is because the ONE as such, in pure form, is a "Concept" or "thought," which can be seen only by the Mind but not by the senses—for no pure Ones exist in the sense-realm as each sense-item is a many, has parts and is divisible, with a front-back-sides, etc. Also Math focuses the mind on *eternal* unchanging Truths and relationships (e.g., $\sqrt{9} = 3$, the Pythagorean

Theorem's $a^2 + b^2 = c^2$), and on *necessity*, on things that *must be* and cannot be otherwise, the hallmark of true Science—all of which deepens one's awareness and belief in the existence of true suprasensory Reality and interest in it. This further serves to weaken attachment to the sense-world, sense-singulars and illusion.

The main value of Math then is as a *preparation* for the higher Jedi Studies of *Concepts-Forms* and *Thinking*, that is, of LOGIC (Abstract), Nature, Jedi/the Jedi Order and the POINT. All math and number is *mid-way* between the senses (-) and thought (+).

So the Teacher should start with the ONE (UNITY) *and* BEING and its True, higher Meaning as the One Force (±) and as a symbol of Reality and the student's JEDI Self. The Teacher can also connect Math with Ontology, by connecting the ONE with BEING—serving as an introduction to LOGIC, one of the Jedi Sciences. Then the Teacher's task is to derive all mathematics (addition-subtraction-division-multiplication-powers-calculus: differential and integral, etc) from the ONE.

In addition, students should strive to see both the *eternal Universal* (and its Truths and relationships) *in* the *sensible*, as well as the *individual* (-) *in* the (+) *Universal* and thus their UNITY (±).

§331

How to Teach HISTORY.

This follows from the Concept of History given earlier—namely, that HISTORY is in essence an *educational* process whereby the FORCE as "Man" goes from *Stage Two* "Consciousness" to *Stage Three* "Self-Consciousness" and overcomes the (+|-) subject/object separation and reaches the Knowledge of Itself as a JEDI and the JEDI ORDER. That is, History is the study of the stages of the progress of the consciousness of *FREEDOM*, the final result being the universal recognition of each by all, with the realization that each person is the Infinite WHOLE as *absolutely Independent and Free and aware of Itself.*

The major periods of your History are the Ancient, Medieval, Modern, and Post-Modern, negative and positive. In teaching *Global History* the focus is only on the "main events" of advance in the process. Briefly stated, (1) *Ancient:* China (substance, where One is free, the emperor), India, Persia, Greece (where some are free) to Rome (Roman Law and the legal Person), (2) *Medieval:* Religion and the initial appearance of the Truth (±), from polytheism to monotheism, (3) *Modern:* the Arche/Force as *Consciousness* (where all are free), the Rights of the Individual, the French Revolution, the Modern State in which the "**A-Team**" wins Jedi Science (±), and (4) *Post-Modernity: negative* (the "death of God" and nihilism) to *Post-Modernity: positive*/the 1960s, the new God *within*, the rediscovery of the *Absolute I* and *the Concept*, and the realization of (±) the JEDI ORDER (see Part I.1 *History* above).

Note also that WHO, which individual or group or nation in History, actually advanced the Truth, the Knowledge of the Force and the Jedi Order and "gets the credit or glory" is *not ultimately important*. *Particularity* and racial national differences are merely external, for All of Your People—your race/the Force—are truly ONE. Thus an advance or discovery (e.g. of the telegraph, the "double helix" in science, the internet, etc) by a particular person or nation is an advance for ALL. Of course if some of you insist on identifying *not* with the Universal-Whole but instead with a *particular* group that has not yet made an advance or contribution in History, then you can *change* this ... by YOU becoming a JEDI quickly (which in itself is plenty) and by making a unique contribution in a chosen Area or Global Institution.

§332

How to Teach BIOLOGY, the LIFE SCIENCES, or ORGANICS.

1. It is to be taught within the Context of the WHOLE, as a Necessary STAGE of the Force's realization into and as the Jedi Order.

2. Teach (a) The Concept of LIFE (as means/end in one) and (b) Life's Structure as grasped by the Concept (U-P-I): Sensibility-Irritability-Reproduction/the GENUS, etc.

3. Explain the *Necessity* for "Man" and that the Human Body *must exist* in order for the Absolute I to realize itself, that is, Man's BODY as (-) is the perfect complement of (+). Explain how the *negation* (the BODY) is preserved in the "negation of negation," in the move to Spirit or Jedi (+) and (±), and results in the Jedi *Subtle Body*.

Further, Nature's forms transition from the Inorganic to the Organic with the result that Life, "Man" and Man's BODY contains and embodies *all* lower stages and hence is in actuality the *Microcosm* of Nature, the Macrocosm.

4. Most importantly, "Man" or the "Human" Form/Organism is the *TYPE* (perfect-complete) from which all other lower organisms are to be understood. Hence (as many of your evolutionary biologists erroneously teach), it is incorrect to start in the reverse order with the least developed, complex organisms—diatoms, amoeba, paramecium (bacteria)—and on their basis (and structure) attempt to understand the higher, more complex organisms, and ultimately Man. The lower organisms are *imperfect* and mere anticipations of MAN, the perfect organism and *ArcheType*, and are found wanting in respect of certain functions and features belonging to "Man"— primarily Reason and Thought, as well as certain senses, respiratory, nervous, and other systems, hands, upright posture, plasticity of movement, etc.

§333

Special Problems:

(1) Students transferring into Jedi-School from other schools will be underprepared for Jedi-Education. This can be solved by providing an Introduction/Jedi-orientation and "conversion course" that will correct errors of dark-side teaching e.g. in the sciences taught in the non-Jedi schools, etc—and an entrance examination will also be required.

(2) In the beginning there will be few or no Jedi Masters. This presents no problem—for all that is required are Teachers who are completely dedicated to Jedi Principles and Education, and who will continue their own Jedi-Education outside of school and among themselves.

(3) The *TextBook Problem*. No Official, Approved and contemporary "Jedi-Science text book" exists yet (other than those of the **A-Team** Jedi Philosophers, which need to be updated). The solution is that until Jedi-Science and Education Textbooks are written and printed the Jedi Teacher can "create" his own by drawing from his *own knowledge* of the subject (e.g. History) and from existing "non-Jedi"

textbooks—which is what many of your Teachers today do anyway; i.e. they do not follow the textbook rigorously and use their own "handouts," etc. Also the Teacher can *use* the same e.g., History textbook she has been using and just overlay and integrate it with a Jedi *Holistic* interpretation. The Basic Information is the same and useable. This is also true of Science Books—just add "Force-Truth" Principles and correct major errors (e.g. the widespread teaching that "atoms" or "matter" is absolute reality and what everything— including selves, persons, and consciousness—is made of, etc).

[B] THE JEDI UNIVERSITY CURRICULUM

§334

The Divisions of the University into Colleges and Schools and their diversified curriculum content are based on the GOALS of the University and of Jedi Education as such, which are: to facilitate and accelerate all students becoming Jedi and to promote the Healing that entails transcending the illusion of the *separate* Ego and Ego-Thing-World; to secure and further the expansion and transmission of Knowledge for all future generations—indeed the *Univers*-ity is and should be the locus of the UNIVERSE's, the FORCE's or GOD's knowledge of himself/herself; and to prepare students for *Life in Eternity*, that is, for entrance into the Jedi Order and Society and for career/role/and service, and to network and make eternal life-connections, friendships, and relationships.

§335

Because the Primary Goal is *becoming a Jedi* everything else—all other special studies and majors, careers and service—has only secondary importance. This is because all the Knowledge contained in other courses is contained *in* the student's Jedi-Nature and Essence (or minimally the means/power to acquire it), while the reverse is not true. Therefore the *Jedi Core Course*, which all students will take and whose main objective is to mature the student's Jedi nature, has primacy over all else, namely, the Theoretical, Practical, and Productive courses of study (and majors), as well as Science, Religion, and Art, the primary agents for healing the (+|-) split and realizing Jedi (±). We shall first look at the "Divisions" of the University.

ON THE DIVISIONS INTO COLLEGES AND SCHOOLS, AND THE PRINCIPLES OF HOLISTIC CURRICULA

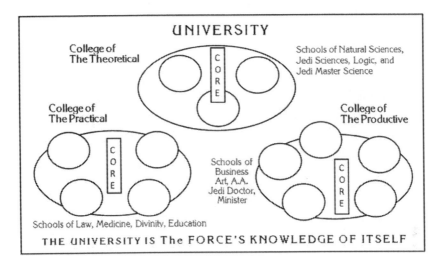

§336

1) The main thing to be mindful of is, to reiterate, that all of these colleges and schools are *secondary* to the Jedi CORE.

2) The overall Curriculum and Curricula will be *Holistic* and will follow Jedi Holistic Science—whose component sciences reflect the stages in the becoming and healing of the One Force as Jedi. To recall, first there is the *Principle* (±), and then the *realization* of the Principle from Outer (-) to Inner (+) and their union as the Jedi Order (±).

3) The division of Colleges into The Theoretical, Practical, and Productive, is one taken from your Jedi **Aristotle**.

4) The Basic requirements and procedures for entrance and matriculation into each school and for degrees and other bureaucratic concerns can follow current practices. There are two categories: those students coming from Jedi-K-12 schools, and those coming from non-Jedi schools and who need special Introductory and transition courses.

5) Degrees and Curriculum: all colleges/schools can offer B.A., M.A., and Ph.D. degrees and post-graduate studies.

§337

6) B.A. Core "A": All Students, in addition to their Jedi Core and major(s)—academic (theoretical) and professional (practical and productive)—must take during their first two years all Core "A" courses. These include:

> (a) *Jedi Science of the Force* as presenting a detailed Knowledge of the Whole: Logic, Nature, and the Jedi Order, which last includes: History, Society, Foreign Cultures and Languages, the Arts and Literature, and Religion and Morals. The central focus is on The Force, its process, and who you as a Jedi are; the Method of Science, what "Knowledge" is, and why other kinds of "knowledge" are not scientific or genuine knowledge.

> (b) *Logic* and *Science's Introduction* or *Phenomenology* (those wishing to be *Master Scientists* will continue with two more years).

> (c) An Introduction and exposure to *all* Colleges and majors/disciplines, whether or not students have decided on a major (if they have, they will take the briefer course). One or two semesters only.

> (d) The following is also important to note: Jedi Science's parts (Logic-Nature-Jedi/Spirit) are taught (unlike at present) "transitionally," i.e. as vanishing stages or "moments" leading up to the Jedi Order (and Absolute Knowing and Logic or Metaphysics); while *History* is taught as the recorded stages of the becoming of Jedi and Jedi Society (the Force's awareness of itself); and *Society or the State* is taught as the Order or Structures of Freedom (as Universals or Laws) for realization of Jedi, while *Art* and *Religion* (as with *Science*) are explained to have originated as a *way* of overcoming the subject/object split and realizing Jedi-Wholeness.

§338

7) M.A. and Ph.D. This will be the same as currently practiced, with certain additions:

(a) There will be the same Jedi course progression: from introductory to intermediate to advanced, and then the Thesis. However, a Ph.D. candidate in History for example will be required to possess an adequate mastery of *all* of history, and not just their special area of interest (which is in accordance with the *holistic* nature of Jedi Science and Education).

(b) Those studying to be a *Jedi Master Scientist* (encompassing Logic, Nature, and Jedi-Spirit) will either have achieved mastery by the completion of their program or will not (in which case post-graduate studies are recommended).

8) There will also be a *Board of Science* and a *Board of Jedi Certification.*

9) Special Issues concerning the *transition* to the Ideal Jedi University:

(a) In the Ideal Jedi University all Faculty members are Jedi. But in the beginning there will be a period when only a few will be Jedi. The pre-Jedi teachers will need supervision by a Jedi or Jedi Master Scientist. This is no major problem because all that is needed is for each teacher to be fully dedicated to Jedi Education and the healing of their planet and race—the "spirit" and Truth will supply the remainder of what is needed.

(b) As for the Textbook problem on the university level, the solution is the same as for the K-12 level (see §333, (3)).

THE JEDI "CORE COURSE" (will continue and build on the work done in pre-university)

§339

The purpose of this Central Course is to "keep you on course" to realizing your Jedi Nature and fitting you for citizenship in the Jedi Order. Your "Jedi Core Coordinator(s)" will also help you to integrate and coordinate your studies and show how they *all* contribute towards the one Jedi Goal and to *learning how to live in Eternity and Jedi Society*. It is impossible to overstate the importance of this educational objective of *learning how to live in Eternity, in the Eternal Now or Present; that is, learning how to "transcend Time" and that*

Time is an illusion (a subjective convention). The more and the faster you can do this, the easier and the more success you will have in learning and in progress towards Jedi actualization; this is because ALL knowledge exists and is perfectly accessible IN the Eternal Now—WHICH ALONE EXISTS. Remember always, as your Jedi **Hegel** states, that *Eternity (the Force) will not be, nor has it been: IT IS.*

§340

As per *Part I: The Jedi Truth* the Main Course Objective—to Become a Jedi—involves the following:

1) The Realization of The Truth (±) that *You as a Jedi are the Force, the Whole of All That Is,* as the *identity* of subject/object, Inner/Outer—which involves the overcoming of the Self/Other split or the illusion of the Cave. It is thus necessary to overcome the Dark Side (realism) and become absolutely established in the *Light Side* (idealism) or the Infinite Inner, which is *Subjectivity* as the *Pure Absolute I* that is Apriori, all reality, and absolute Freedom. As we know, it is simply a matter of *Transcending your Senses and entering the ONE-POINT or Jedi Order by means of the Concept or Consciousness, in order to become either an Intuitive or a Discursive Jedi.*

§341

2) The Objective is therefore to Transition from one's separate-isolated EGO (and the Thing-Object-World) to one's Infinite Jedi Self, a process that involves the Discipline of one's Natural Will and character by way of:

> (a) The *negation* of finite exclusive *Individuality* (via perfected Awareness and Love) resulting in an Infinite *Universal* Self, which is both ec-static and intersubjective.

> (b) The *realization* of your Pure Infinite I (T.U.A. or Absolute I) as numerically *one and the same* in all selves, as both Jedi **Schrodinger** and **Hegel** affirm (e.g. "I in and as them, they in and as me") and which leads to the complete experience of the timeless Present. Further, this realization of universal oneness does not do away with your unique individuality but rather preserves it, since the *individual* negated is ingredient in the Universal (*without which not*).

(c) The *overcoming* of "BLOCKS" (or errors) and EGO-Attachments (both positive and negative, and Fears) which sustain Ego-separateness. Hence as the Jedi Code teaches you must master both *Solitude and Society* and be able to Love *all* I's, for only then can no I ruffle your peace or equanimity. The fact is that only a Pure I can master *Solitude* since such a one contains all I's in himself and is *never* alone, non-Universal, and incomplete. *Solitude* also brings about the dissolution of negative attachments.

3) The perfect and sustained Mastery of LOVE or AGAPE, which is the core of the Infinite INNER and the essence of both the FORCE and a JEDI, which, as we have learned, is due to Polarity ($\pm$).

§342

The overall Objective—Eternity Living, realizing the Truth, becoming a Jedi—will be achieved via the Core's three parts: FACTS and TRUTH, TRANSFORMATION Methods, and COORDINATION and Integration of all Studies:

FACTS and TRUTH: This part will provide an ever deepening Total Picture of the Whole, that is, the Force ($\pm$) and "who you really are" (the Force aware of itself). It will include (a) *The Principle* and Truth of Polarity ($\pm$) as revealed by Metaphysics (Logic, Reason, and Science) and How all derives from it (the Inner and Outer) and the status of each (Inner = 1, Outer = 0); (b) On Nature and History and the Jedi Society and State (the main principles); and (c) On the nature, possibilities (powers and the 4th plane), and laws of a Jedi based on **Fichte's** division into: the *Absolute I* ("God"-Freedom is the #1 principle)/*the Theoretical I, and the Practical I* (society and the individual). You can serve here or in the Subtle or Astral Worlds.

This part will also give *Proofs of the TRUTH* ($\pm$) of one's Jedi Nature and immortality, the infinity of the I/Self (of the One Pure I), and of the *nothingness* (ideality) of Nature, Matter, Objects, and Things.

§343

TRANSFORMATION METHODS: The focus of this part will be the Actualization of the student's Jedi "Seed" Potency, primarily by realizing you are already a Jedi and one with the Truth, the

Force, God (±). It is a fact that just being with people with same goal is powerful and transformative. The Actualization is achieved by *Focused Awareness* on the Truth (±) and the One POINT via the Concept or Consciousness. The Jedi Core Coordinator(s) should:

(a) *Use POWER-ETHICS*—see *Part II: The Jedi Code*—which involves (Re-) Programming the Mind (thinking, believing, and saying), (i) Negatively by removing Blocks (errors), and (ii) Positively by affirming Truths (Affirmations).

(b) *Teach Logic and Phenomenology* and the movement from Consciousness OF an Object to Consciousness OF Consciousness. Plus provide more Proofs of Reason and an ever deepening knowledge of the Whole and your Self, comprised of the *Outer* and *Inner* Force, that is, Nature, History, the State, and Art, Religion, and Science.

(c) *Use Love and Religion* methods such as Meditation (prayer and worship, etc, such as the "I = I = I = I" and the "You and We" methods; also the Love-affirmations, "I love you," "I'm in love," etc); and Love exercises, as well as Dance and Tai Chi, etc. Develop the students' powers of concentration and One-pointedness.

(d) *Use Methods that Facilitate the Mastery of Solitude and Society* (such as special group activities and public speaking) and that will help students to overcome attachments—wants and fears.

(e) *Discuss Pitfalls* and dangers (e.g. concerning the Powers and the 4th Plane) and how to avoid them, and *Overall Student Assessment* or How to test and measure one's *progress* to Jedi. At the end of each year the Coordinator will evaluate the student and assign him to the following year's Core Course, to Level 1, 2 or 3/advanced.

§344

OVERALL COORDINATION and Integration: This part will address (1) How your studies and major will help confirm and actualize your Jedi-Nature, (2) What the current world problems are, How you can help and How you can best serve and contribute to Jedi Society, and (3) Any Questions or concerns that students may have as regards their studies and/or their private lives. There is more on Formal Education in *Part III: The Jedi Order, 2,* where we will contrast your mis-education with Jedi Education.

There is only *One Goal* of education:
To be a JEDI—to Shift from STAGE TWO
to STAGE THREE Consciousness.

EDUCATION

There is a UNITY underlying everything
and everyone on your planet.
To be Aware of this UNITY is to be
Educated … and a JEDI.

THE JEDI CODE

The Jedi Oath

Jedi Power Ethics

Jedi Power Methods

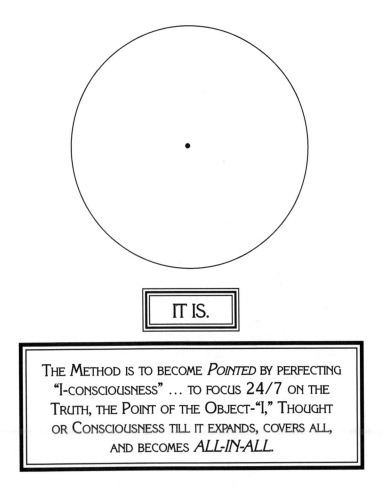

IT IS.

THE METHOD IS TO BECOME *POINTED* BY PERFECTING "I-CONSCIOUSNESS" … TO FOCUS 24/7 ON THE TRUTH, THE POINT OF THE OBJECT-"I," THOUGHT OR CONSCIOUSNESS TILL IT EXPANDS, COVERS ALL, AND BECOMES *ALL-IN-ALL.*

INTRODUCTION

§345

Noble Reader in *Part I: The Jedi Truth* I taught you the Knowledge of the Force, the Foundation of Global Jedi Education and the Healing of your Planet. We learned what the *TRUTH* is and what Reality is—namely, the *Balanced Force* or **the Jedi Order** which is Now, and also what is required to BALANCE or EDUCATE yourself and your planet into the POINT.

§346

In this section I will *show* you How you can *BE* a JEDI and as a result be most effective in *bringing balance* to your major planetary

Institutions as well as becoming a vital member of the eternal Jedi Society and Order.

§347

In a word, to *BE* a Jedi you have to "live like a Jedi." And this is to live by "The Jedi Code"—summarized thus:

> "I will no longer live for myself alone but for all of humanity. I will make serving The Jedi Order my number one priority in life and everything else number two and in its service. I will live in the knowledge that The Jedi Order alone exists and that hence I am a JEDI now—i.e., I am one with The Eternal Force and all other beings and will love them unconditionally. I will use all Jedi methods to help me live up to this sacred Code."
>
> *The Force will be with all of us.*

The three words, *"Trust The Force,"* express the core of The Jedi Code: You should trust and align with the Force—with what IS, and not with anything else (with what IS NOT). It is just a matter of growing in the awareness of what you already are—a JEDI.

§348

The answer to the question, Why am I already a JEDI or a JEDI right now? is simply, *because of Polarity and the inseparability of (+) and (-).* "Union with The Force (God)" is the only Reality. There is no Dark Side. You just do not feel it due to the "Soup" you are in—wrong beliefs, wants, training, mis-education, error, the Dark Side, etc. Also, you can only realize and actually attain the *Union* if you believe and accept that it is *already a Fact.* For if it is *not* a Fact and is not now, then when will it be?

§349

Of special note is that although you are a Jedi right now, a process of **"transformation"** or **"death/dying"** (as the Masters say) is still involved. That is, a *"dying"* or *"letting-go"* ... and equally a *"loving."* It is a *"dying"* to *"ego"* and *separateness* (from everyone and the Force) that is at once an expansion of *"loving"* and your capacity to love, as you enter into your true *Universal* Jedi Self, which includes all Selves, all Jedi within it.

There is also a TEST to determine whether or not you have actually realized your Jedi Self (or are close to it). A Jedi alone is able to give an *affirmative* answer to the following four questions: (i) Are you are able to love everyone? (ii) Do you have no fear of anyone or anything? (iii) Do you have perfect mastery or control over the reproductive/sexual drive? and (iv) Are you are capable of living/being "alone" indefinitely (only a Jedi with a *Universal* Self can do this).

§350

ONE*:* First notice that I did not say, "How you can 'become' a Jedi" ... but "BE" a Jedi. You cannot "become" a Jedi since you already *are* a Jedi—since, as we saw in *Part I*, the Force's two sides can *never* come apart. All that is needed is that you become *Aware* of what you already are, by true Jedi Education and Balance. This makes education or "transformation" a lot easier for you *are* already at the place you are to *be*, you are now standing at the very goal, the finish line. For the "journey" is a journey of Awakening to the Truth of who you are and of what already and eternally is the case.—Notice that the mistake of many of your religions and your New Age Movement is that they assume *you are not yet there*, are not at the goal already and that it does not yet exist. As a result you get caught in the trap of so-called "works" and having to "make it happen" by doing so many deeds/things, which is a "time bound" viewpoint making achievement impossible.

§351

TWO*:* Now although *You* are already there and **only the Jedi Order exists** and the Dark Side and *separateness* does not exist—You, that is, the Force as you, nonetheless start out in the Dark Side illusion and Imbalance (+|-). And as we mentioned in *Part I.*, this is because of both *non-education* and the *mis-education* of your people on the part of your planetary schools and institutions. Both of these pertain to the Force's *Stage Two* Consciousness, that is, Consciousness OF an

Object or Objective World (Not-I). This Stage focuses only on the *difference* and *opposition* within the Truth (the Balance or Polarity) and is oblivious to the *Unity* or *Balance*, and makes it seem as if the Objective World and other people are really and permanently cut-off and separate from you—making you permanently a limited *finite* EGO. This situation is an Illusion and a deception, as your Jedi **Plato** teaches. *Your education and Balancing requires that you see through this Dark Side deception* (+|-) by advancing to *Stage Three* Self-Consciousness and experiencing the Truth of the *Absolute I*, the POINT or the Concept (±) that is initially buried in the sense-world (-) and must be liberated in order for you to see and understand that Consciousness and your true Jedi Self is absolutely *infinite*.

§352

The Goal then is to become **POINT-ED** or SINGLE-POINTED. This is why we use the word "POINT-ED." Thus you begin in the Sense-world as yet unaware of **the *Absolute I-POINT* at the root of your EGO** and located *outside* the space-time universe (yet permeating everything). The Goal of education and Jedi is simply to become AWARE of this *Absolute I, this Single omnipresent POINT* within yourself—and within everyone and everything else—and also AWARE of the POINT's *unity* with the *Objective World*. You do this by Focusing more and more on this One POINT—by Focused Attention, using both mind and heart. Hence it is a Fact that, *"The more POINT-ED you become the more POWER and success you will have in dealing with Others and in transcending and deleting the Dark Side illusion by realizing its unreality and that only UNITY and LOVE truly exist."*

Therefore, being **"POINT-ED"** symbolizes everything and means simply **"BEING EDUCATED,"** that is, being aware of your true self as a JEDI *and* the JEDI ORDER as absolutely present and the only Reality.

§353

THREE: The way to realize that you are a JEDI, to see through the illusion of your finite Body-EGO and "wake up" and experience the BALANCE and the *unity* of Subjectivity and Objectivity that alone is—is simply by *strengthening* the Truth and Light Side of the Force (±) and, at the same time, *weakening* the Error and illusion of the Dark Side (+|-) and the grip it has on your consciousness.

This as we said is achieved by Focused Attention via Concept and Consciousness. *The Goal will be Realized* when the *critical BALANCE point* is reached with the preponderance of (±) over (+|-). Then the illusion and Dark Side (+|-) will just "pop", having been weakened to the point where it is no longer able to put up resistance and deceive you. You will then wake up in the Eternal *Subject/Object* Present, in the One Reality of the glorious Jedi Order, one with the TRUTH and never again to fall back into illusion.

Thus to *strengthen the Light Side* what you do is simply to FOCUS on the Truth (±), the Balance, the Unity, the POINT *24/7/365*.

The Jedi Code will show you How to do this—How to focus 24/7 on the Truth and thus become **POINT-ED**. *It will show you How to realize the* **POINT** *within Yourself at the core of your Being.*

THE JEDI CODE HAS THREE PARTS: THE JEDI OATH-DEDICATION, JEDI POWER ETHICS, AND JEDI POWER METHODS

I. THE JEDI OATH

§354

For many people the *desire* to be a Jedi, to *be* all they can be and help realize an incredibly wonderful world beyond what can possibly be imagined signifies a major Turning Point in their Life. Accordingly something has to happen to clearly demarcate *before* and *after*, that is, your life up till this point and your life from now on. Hence *"The Jedi Oath (or Dedication)"*—that acknowledges and celebrates this turning point whereby you resolve to dedicate your life 100% to healing yourself and your planet.—Of course it is rare that one can start with *100% dedication*; one's initial depth of commitment will naturally increase and solidify in time and with practice. And of course it is not *necessary* to take this Oath to BE a Jedi, but we find it is helpful and does facilitate the Jedi educational process—especially if you take it with another person or persons and repeat it often.

§355

Thus the Jedi Oath:

"I at this moment of my life commit 100% to healing the world. I truly want to be a Jedi—rather to wake up to the fact that I AM a Jedi right now—and help realize the Amazing Jedi Order. I will from this day forward live as if the Jedi Order and the BALANCE exists Now (it does) and as if the Dark Side or "CAVE" is indeed an Illusion and does not exist (it does not) and as if I AM a Jedi now (you are). I will make the Jedi Order the #1 Priority of my life and I will use parts II and III of the Jedi Code to help me grow in Knowledge and Love and live up to this sacred Oath."

II. JEDI POWER ETHICS

§356

Noble Reader what is presented here and in *Part III* is designed to help you become **POINT-ED**, that is, fulfill the Jedi Oath and live the greatest life imaginable, the Jedi life, and be maximally effective in *Bringing Balance to the Force* in your world.

§357

As we saw the TRUTH (±) teaches that UNITY is fundamental and trumps Difference, Opposites, and Multiplicity. Thus the task of education or *Balance* is for you to transcend *multiplicity* and not leave it as it is, for it keeps you in a SELF that is divided and fragmented, anxious, pulled in many directions, with unfulfilled desires, living in "time" and towards "death." You transcend this egoic Self by focusing on and coming to realize the UNITY underlying all the multiplicity in your Life and the Universe. The Fact is that, The more UNITY you experience, the more POWER in your life ... hence, Jedi "Power" Ethics.

§358

Thus Jedi Power Ethics as based on the Truth (±) will show you How to release total POWER and ability in your life as a Jedi dedicated to the Jedi Order. This happens and can only happen, as all of your own great Jedi say, when you bring ALL under ONE. When you bring everything you do, internally and externally, thoughts and actions, ideas, goals, activities, projects, people, etc, under ONE supreme GOAL, END or PRIORITY—which of course is the Jedi Order and being a Jedi, or being POINTED. Recall that these seemingly two things or ends (Jedi and Jedi Order) are in fact One—since right now you as a Jedi have a UNIVERSAL Self, in that you share the same One Infinite Consciousness or Absolute I with all other persons or Jedi. So "a" Jedi already implies and involves a plurality or community of Jedi, namely the One Jedi Order. If you recall that the word "Jedi" is both singular and plural you may think of the ONE supreme Goal to which all is to be subordinated simply as "JEDI"—meaning the "Jedi Order," in which you are a living functioning Member and eternal participant.—Or you may prefer to use the word "BALANCE" for the One Goal, which immediately signifies both the Truth (and the Force itself) and the Jedi Order.

§359

JEDI

JEDI ORDER: BALANCE

ONE. Therefore I shall use the symbol on the left to refer to The One Supreme Goal, your #1 Priority. Hence, everything else in your life is to be considered #2 or a MEANS to #1. The main Jedi RULE here is: *Never let a #2 goal usurp or take the place of the #1 Goal.* Among #2's would be a family member, spouse, boyfriend, girlfriend, Job, goals, activities, passions, etc. To keep a #2 *as* #2 will present your biggest challenge.

§360

Using **Plato's** "Divided Line" (see Diagram below) you can think of all **#2's** as taking place in the CAVE (-), the illusory region of Dark Side *multiplicity*, and also as making up what can be called your "Ministry," since #2's are a *means* to #1 and in its service.

The critical FACT is that the Jedi Order, your UNITY with all "I"s, *exists NOW*. This means that there really is no #2 or Dark Side region in the sense of the "dis-unity" of opposites (+|−)—rather only #1, the Light Side, the Truth (±), the POINT. Therefore you should order your life, your #2's and Ministry, in a way that makes you more and more *aware* of this Fact that the Jedi Order alone exists—that the Cave, the Dark Side, and *separateness* is in reality an illusion.

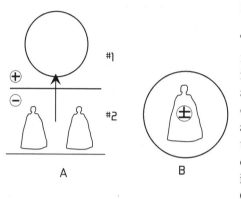

§361

TWO. What is to be done next is to "**jedi**" all #2's. That is, see if each item in #2, such as an activity, person, or goal, can in some way be used for and serve as a means to #1, the *POINT*, which contains everything within itself and is the *core* of Jedi and the Jedi Order and actualizes them.

This will greatly help you to FOCUS on the TRUTH (±) 24/7 and become *POINTED* since it is now in your consciousness that *whatever* you are doing, as a #2, is connected to the *selfsame* #1/POINT that everything else you are doing is connected to. This causes you to *"Be mindful of the Present (Anakin)"*—that is, *of the Force*, the TRUTH, and the Jedi Order—and your Jedi Self *as* integrated into and One *with* the Jedi Order, and with every person in your experience and on your planet.

§362

So what you do is to make a LIST of all your #2's and then "**jedi**" all of them. You may find that you will have to eliminate some of them as incompatible with the #1, a hindrance or counter-force. This means that you may have to separate from a particular person for a period of time, etc.

Also since you need to "Bring the *multiplicity* of the Cave's contents into UNITY," you must also *detach* yourself from sense-particulars. Hence you should not divide your love but instead educate your *Eros* (desire), as **Plato** enjoins in his *Symposium*, until you love only the

Truth, the Absolute I—and the Absolute I in everyone. You should especially not be attached to money and things.

§363

There are Two Ways you can do this: (1) You can keep all your #2's as they are and just "jedi" them. (2) Or you may overhaul *all* your #2's, that is delete some and add new ones—e.g., add Reason or Faith, perhaps sign-up for a Meditation class or a Philosophy-Reason class at College (say on **Schelling** or **Hegel**). You can also add such careers and activities that bring to mind The Jedi Order.

§364

Let's take a few examples from the following Basic Categories: SELF, Relationships, Beliefs-Thoughts-Worldview, Values, Job-Career, Money, Body/needs, Wants-bad habits/addictions, Goals-short & long term, Projects, Activities, and the Arts and Entertainment.

(1) *"Jedi Friends."* ASK: "Does this friend or person in my life bring me closer to UNITY or to Dis-Unity?" Peace or Anxiety/Stress? Is it a healthy or unhealthy relationship? Can I share Jedi Principles and Jedi Power Ethics with her or him? Is she sympathetic to them, or hostile to them? Is he interested in healing our planet and himself? Or No? If, No, then you may choose to *separate* from such persons for a time. It is wise, at least in the beginning, to stay with Jedi friends as much as possible and to avoid non-Jedi persons or "heavy EGO game" players. The more POINT-ED you become the more success you will have in relating with non-Jedi—they will *feel* your FIELD and the POWER of your One-Pointedness, their resistance will fade and you will change them and win them over to the Cause and the Jedi way of life, what they really want and are looking for in truth.

§365

(2) A major challenge will be *demoting* your present #1, such as, spouse, boyfriend-girlfriend, or goal of becoming wealthy, etc., to a #2 spot. Or even after you have demoted it there is the possibility of its returning and claiming the #1 spot. The more POINTED you become the easier this will be.

§366

(3) *Long Term Goals*—such as your *Career,* your decision to be a Doctor, Professor, or to buy a home, get married, have a family, etc. Most career goals are easy to connect to the #1, the Jedi Order. A main challenge is to *separate* your Ego from the goals, for otherwise your Ego will use them to enhance your "ego-identity," etc. Further, if you make your happiness and feeling of completeness depend upon your being for example a Doctor, then you have made *this* your #1 and not the Jedi Order, which alone can bring you *true* happiness. You must hence be ready and able to give up a specific long term goal, if something better, more Jedi-producing, comes along.

§367

(4) *Activities.* For example, Does going to a certain club or event on a Friday night help or hinder your #1 Priority? Thus before you do anything you should ASK: "Will this increase Unity-Peace in my life or instead disUnity/anxiety? Will it strengthen my Ego or my Jedi Self?"

ALSO it is highly recommended that you: (1) Treat each person as if they already were a Jedi. Love and "recognize" everyone you meet. Focus on the UNITY/the Absolute I shared between you and them, and then do a "Recognition Meditation Exercise" with them (see §407 below). (2) Sacrifice your End and Good for the Other's—which is a win-win situation since helping them is helping yourself. (3) FOCUS on Science-Philosophy, Religion, Art, on the Invisible, the Universal (**Plato's** One over Many: Right, Law, Family, etc), and the Eternal. Above all, Open your heart and your mind to PURE LOVE simply by disciplining your *Desires* and by serving others and sacrificing egoic selfhood.

III. Jedi Power Methods

§368

Putting into practice the following Jedi Power Methods will make you increasingly more *aware* of the (+) side of the Force, Reality, the INNER, Universality and Unity, and will free you from Dark Side bondage and *attachment* to the (-) side of the Force and to OUTER Sense-things. The Power Methods will liberate you from the illusion of your separate Body-"EGO" and establish you in the Reality of your true JEDI

Self. Their purpose is to *strengthen* the Truth (±) of the Light Side and *weaken* the Error (+|-) of the Dark Side to the point where you are living *in* the Jedi Order 24/7, fully aware of the present, sole, indivisible Reality. The goal is for you to realize *Infinite Awareness* and *Infinite Love*—which when realized your response will be: "Wow. This is incredible. *This* was here all the time. I just was not aware of it!"

THE KEY TO EVERYTHING IS: WHAT IS IN YOUR CONSCIOUSNESS AND WHAT DO YOU THINK ABOUT *ALL THE TIME*?

§369

Thus Jedi Power Methods will help you TO LIVE IN ETERNITY and THE ETERNAL PRESENT *which alone exists*. *"Living in TIME"* is a function of multiplicity and attachment to changing sense-objects (where you fear their loss) and ignorance of *Unity*; it is an immersion in Dark Side wrongness (+|-) always accompanied by a feeling of incompleteness, emptiness or lack *in the present*, somehow to be remedied in the "future."

§370

In the end there is really only *one* Method, namely, 24/7 FOCUS on the TRUTH, the BALANCE, the POINT—on your present UNITY with all others and the Jedi Order.

The FACT is: You seem to be **HERE**, as an isolated "EGO," and seem to start out here *outside* the circle and *separate* from the community of "I"'s, the One Jedi Order.

EGO

"cancer" - delusion - time

But you really are **HERE**, as an immortal Jedi, One with everyone else and *inside* the One Reality. The Power Methods of education and Balance will help you to

JEDI

health - reality - the timeless Present

realize the twin Truth of *infinite Awareness*, that you are *infinite* as *in* everyone and every other, and *infinite Love*, that you are One with everyone as sharing the same One Consciousness. You will know that it is because of Polarity, the Unity of the opposites "Self" and "Other," that *LOVE* is the only reality and is your true essence.

§371

> "We are all One Consciousness ... and You are Love. When you look at another being, you are looking at Love." **Ram Dass**
>
> *"The Concept* is the liberation from the Ego or finite being-for-itself, and meets only with itself in the Other ... it is Blessedness and Love." **Hegel**
>
> "Our feeling of being a *separate* Ego is *a kind of optical delusion of consciousness."* **Einstein**
>
> "Being is dying by loving." **Meher Baba**

There are *two* categories of *Methods* for Focusing and becoming POINTED based on the only two states a SELF can be in: (A) *Solitude,* which pertains to things you can do when you are *alone,* and (B) *Society,* pertaining to things you can do when you are *with others* (and there is some overlap). To be a full Jedi you have to master *both* states: being alone and being with others.

§372

(A) SOLITUDE (being alone).

The following division into Reason, Faith-Meditation, and Art is based on *Jedi Science's* three-fold division of "Absolute Jedi (Spirit)," namely Art-Religion-Science, which corresponds to the three *modes* of the Truth—which are the True, the Good, and the Beautiful—and where one alone achieves Absolute Knowledge and the *Knowledge of the Force.* Absolute Jedi (Spirit) is the *eternal* sphere where one is in communion with the *eternal order* and the Force, and raised above the mere "Objective Jedi" sphere, the sphere of the State, which is *temporal* since concrete existing States are in time and perishable. This is the case even though this *eternal* sphere of Art-Religion-Science has its existence *within* the State itself. The FACT is that the more you focus your attention on *Eternal Objects* (art-works, sacred images, scientific truths) the deeper will be your experience of Eternity and the more you will find yourself *living* outside the illusion of "time" and *inside* the Reality of Eternal Presence.

§373

As I said earlier the final goal of Jedi Education into the Truth or Point is achievable *only* by the One-pointedness of Focused Attention which has but *two* forms, Reason and Meditation/Faith, or Concept and Consciousness, the former alone having the advantage of the comprehensive knowledge of Science and a Master Teacher. Let me elaborate.

§374

1. Reality, what is *there* before you, underlying everything … is the CONCEPT, which we call the "sacred POINT."

> Your Jedi **Aristotle** was the first to correctly define the supreme Arche as "self-thinking Thought" (*noesis noeseos*) or the "Thought of Thought." Thus the Absolute, the really Real, is THOUGHT or CONCEPT. And as Jedi **Kant** showed, the Concept is always "the Concept of an OBJECT," hence "Concept (+)" contains its opposite, "Object (-)," within itself, hence is in truth (±) or a Unity of Opposites.

2. As I said, at the present time the majority of your scientists and religionists know the POINT only as CONSCIOUSNESS and not as the CONCEPT or THOUGHT, which it really is. The Concept is both the essence of Consciousness and indispensable for true SCIENCE as well.

§375

3. Now, to be a JEDI and to be educated all that is necessary is that you *transcend the senses* (the Cave, the Dark Side) *and achieve a knowledge or awareness of the POINT.* You must advance from *Stage Two* Consciousness (of an Object) to *Stage Three* Self-Consciousness, or Consciousness of Consciousness (I or Self).

> That is, *Consciousness* or *Thought* must become your Object and as what alone is Reality—not the Sense-world, material things, the Cave. And be mindful that the *PURE I* (in contrast to the Empirical I or EGO) is THOUGHT ITSELF; and that the "Pure I" is identical with the "Pure Self" and "Pure Consciousness."

4. Further the POINT can be known in one of two ways—as CONCEPT or as CONSCIOUSNESS.

> The knowledge and experience pertaining to both is essentially *the same*—namely, that of union with everyone and All That Is; the difference is that only the Concept-Knower knows the Point in its fully logically articulated shape allowing for a detailed Science of the Whole.

§376

5. Finally it is REASON that is the way of the Concept, while FAITH or MEDITATION is the way of Consciousness. As for ART—the experience of Truth, the Point, in sensuous form as Beauty—its educational value lies in helping to heal you and transcend the senses and the Ego but, in contrast with Reason and Meditation/Faith, Art cannot by itself make you a Jedi or permanently establish you in the Truth.

§377

ONE: **REASON** (Science). The method of *Reason* is the most powerful method for becoming POINT-ED and realizing the Truth and has great advantages over the others. This is because (1) Reason, in the form of the CONCEPT, which is the true essence of the Point itself, is the principle of Jedi Science and alone provides a Knowledge of the Force in full detail and comprehensiveness. Also (2) once it is clearly seen that and why something is true and *must* be true through Reason as opposed to mere Belief or Intuition, one possesses a certainty that cannot be shaken and is able to withstand any objection or doubt. For then, as your phrase is, "You *know* that you know." Further, as your Jedi **Plato** and others say, *Reason* or *higher unitive Thought-Awareness-Seeing* is not only that faculty or power within your Soul whose proper *object* is what is eternal, Universal, and indivisible, as opposed to changing sense-singulars. But it is Reason *itself* that is implicitly this very *object*. That is, Reason or the Concept is its *own* object, is the *Absolute I itself* in its pure essence. Thus, as soon as one uses Reason properly (especially as the Concept) one has transcended the CAVE, sense-world and false "EGO" and finds oneself in the domain of Reality and one's true Universal Self; and in the presence of and merging with the One Infinite Consciousness, *Absolute I* and the Force itself. This greatly facilitates the *weakening* of the Dark Side (+|-) and at once the *strengthening* of the Light Side (±).

ON THE LIFE OF REASON:

THE MORE YOU USE REASON OR YOUR "SIXTH SENSE,"
DIRECTING IT ON ITS PROPER OBJECT, THE MORE YOU WILL LIVE
IN ETERNITY AND THE MORE "TIME" AND THE DARK SIDE WILL
LOOSEN THEIR GRIP ON YOU, HAVING LESS PULL AND CONTROL
OVER YOU—UNTIL ULTIMATELY THEY SIMPLY VANISH.

So noble Jedi be mindful that by "Reason" we mean true *unitive* Reason (*Vernunft*) and not the false "instrumental" separative reason (*Verstand*) that is much in vogue today on your planet; which is a key distinction made by your **A-Team** Jedi **Kant** and **Hegel**.

§378

THERE ARE THREE WAYS you can use Reason or Thought to realize your true Jedi Self.

(A) First and foremost is by the study and mastery of *Jedi Science* or *the Knowledge of the Force.* As said earlier you can **EITHER** study the *Introduction to Jedi Science* alone, whereby discursive Reason enables you to permanently break the spell of the Dark Side (+|-), liberating you from its PULL, and to successfully move from *Stage Two* Consciousness OF to *Stage Three* Self-Consciousness; thereby establishing you in the Truth (±) as an immortal Jedi—for when you have reached the end, *Absolute Knowledge*, you have become a *self-aware* Jedi.—At present, as mentioned, you have available only your Jedi **Hegel's** *Introduction* (the *Phenomenology of Mind or Spirit*), but a new updated more reader-friendly version will appear shortly.

§379

OR, you can also go on to study and master Jedi Science itself, that is, the Whole in all its parts and detail, namely, the *Sciences of Logic (the Concept), Nature* and *Jedi* and their subdivisions. In this way you can also become a TEACHER (a Jedi of the 3ʳᵈ Order) greatly needed in this present time of transition, which will greatly accelerate the healing of your planet. Also mastering Jedi Science and the Whole is very important since knowing the full Truth *in detail and logical interconnection* (i) safeguards against errors of your own p-sciences and religions and (ii) gives you a unique *holistic* perspective on reality that helps you to *integrate* all of your experiences and new data constantly coming in. Of course, even if one has yet to master the *Introduction to Science* one can still greatly benefit from studying Jedi Science proper since it involves occupying your Reason with the Eternal **Universals**, Forms and Concepts that inhabit the invisible (+) domain of Reality, while at once encompassing the visible (-) domain of sense singulars, constituting their essence and true being.

§380

(B) You can also use Reason to study and master the all-important principle of POLARITY or *the Unity of Opposites* (±), the Key which unlocks the doors to all Jedi Knowledge and Freedom, as found and discussed especially in *The Jedi Handbook.*—And to master the PROOFS given in *Part I,* especially the PROOFS of The Force and the Untruth of *Materialism*—a teaching that holds many minds on your planet in adamantine bondage, as well as the PROOF of your immortality. Again once you clearly understand through Reason *why* Materialism is false, why Matter can *not* be the ultimate Reality, Consciousness alone being such, and why you *are* immortal and not subject to death and annihilation, *you are permanently protected against these errors.* You can never again be presumed upon or led astray and most importantly can also help others to become free. Such is the awesome power of Reason.

§381

(C) Lastly, you can study and benefit from reading "Jedi" books and articles, that is, literature which contains Jedi Truths and expands upon them and upon principles found in *The Jedi Handbook* (we will provide a List for you—and though some may contain errors, the principles and proofs discussed in *Part I: The Jedi Truth* will help you identify them).

Also note that the "Reason" we are speaking of in this section is Reason in its pure or strict Form as *unitive* thinking, reasoning, and argument—that is, as *discursive* and as moving from concept to concept, bringing a manifold (of *Verstand* or sense items) into Unity (*Vernunft*). It is nonetheless true that because Reason as such is synonymous with Unity, (+), and *the Absolute I* itself, Reason is present and active in *all* human activities and methods, such as faith, meditation, art, etc. In fact *all* methods are involved in *all other methods.* For example, not only is "faith" involved in Reason and Science, but in Art "Beauty" is a Universal and as such is *one*—and even though the art-work is an object for sense and imagination, Reason is involved in all true aesthetic experience.

§382

TWO: FAITH (Religion-Spirituality)—and including **Will, One-Point Meditation, Concentration,** and **Affirmation.** The Method we will call *Faith* or *Faith-Meditation* is also one that increases POINTEDNESS and focuses you on the TRUTH and can *by itself,* unaided by Reason in the strict sense, take you all the way to the Goal of Jedi—the Force aware of Itself in you and as you (but not as a Jedi *Scientist* or *Teacher* in the full sense).

§383

Preliminary. (1) *Faith* as such and as operative in true religion ("re-ligare") is not *opposed* to Knowledge (or Reason) but is rather itself a *form* of Knowledge. And faith as such—in all its forms, inclusive of meditation, concentration, and affirmation, etc—is, like Reason, able to give one a *certainty* or Awareness which is unshakable and cannot be undermined or negated.

§384

(2) Like Reason, FAITH is *unitive* and has *Unity* as its goal and purpose, the Unity of itself and Being (the Force or God), and in truth has its *source* in Reason (as Absolute I and the Concept). Faith differs from Reason in that it is more *intuitive* than *discursive*. Notice that we say "more" intuitive, since Faith in its beginnings is *not* purely intuitive (which it is at the end), however in order to reach its goal Faith makes use of such "discursive" elements as series of discrete items, words, concepts, images, and representations which contain a powerful truth and serve to elevate one from multiplicity (+|-) to Truth and Unity (±).

§385

(3) Briefly: How *Faith* works and achieves the Goal. *First,* Faith begins with the intuition, belief or conviction that *a solution* to the (+|-) Egoic state of "Man" (the Force in its Second Stage) indeed exists. That there is Truth (±) or Unity, called "God," and that one's ultimate *unity* with God is possible. *Secondly,* by Faith one then *stands* in this Unity or Truth, e.g. "I am *one* with God" ... which becomes one's primary focus in life. As a result one's heart and mind gradually *shift* from (-) sense-objects, to the (+) *Absolute I. Thirdly,* this

shift and focus at its highest intensity results in *UNION*. Further the WILL is also involved in Faith. 1. Will is in truth "Practical Reason" and mediates (+) and (-), the two sides of the Force. You use Will whenever you think, speak, or act. As a function and extension of Reason, which is Apriori, Will is both rooted in Freedom and is the means of realizing Freedom. 2. With proper use of the Will you can break through the Dark Side deception (+|-) to the Truth (±). 3. Indeed, focusing your Will on the POINT in the form of "concentration," can take you all the way. You need only to *Master your WILL*—your desires and thoughts, and your Whole Being or Self as concentrated into a single POINT. As Jedi **Hegel** says, you only need to "will the Will"—that is, the Universal" or the Point (U-P-I) and as your Jedi **Jesus** says, "If thine eye be *single* all of you will be full of light."

§386

THERE ARE TWO ASPECTS *or* WAYS:

(A) RELIGION. Noble Reader, if you are *religious* or follow a specific religion or faith you *can* and *should* use your religion and faith and its own methods and practices to help you achieve BALANCE and realize the Goal. We would however recommend that you "modify" your Religion in accord with the Jedi principles and Truths discussed under the "JEDI SECT" and "JEDI RELIGION" in *Parts I* and *III* in order to fully benefit from your Religion. Indeed starting a *Jedi Sect* within each of your Religions will greatly accelerate the Jedi Order by the ending of all religious hatred and conflict on your planet.

Thus the methods that follow assume that one has already "Jedi-ed" one's Religion, knowing the Truth behind *re-ligion as such,* and thus can willingly adopt and use them. Note that these are SOLITUDE and not SOCIETY Methods, as we are not discussing *Group* methods or those that involve for example "communal worship" in a Church or Temple setting. These of course should be used by the religious person as well.

§387

"ANAKIN. BE MINDFUL OF THE PRESENT ...
OF WHAT YOU ARE DOING." Jedi Master Qui-Gon Jinn

(B) MEDITATION, CONCENTRATION, and AFFIRMATION.
Widely known and practiced for millennia on your planet, *Meditation* is a technique not only for deepening one's Awareness of the Truth and Reality and getting permanently established in it, but also for dissolving one's EGO and one's attachment to it and its dynamics, which serve to keep one in the Dark Side split (+|-) and Plato's Cave.—And "dissolving one's EGO" means none other than "balancing," integrating and fusing one's EGO with the Absolute I as a thoroughly *universalized* self-ego (or "U/I"), fully permeated by Universality (+) and the Absolute I. Meditation involves a "laser-like" focusing of one's attention or consciousness on a *Single-POINT* to the exclusion of everything else such as the contents of the mind clamoring for attention, especially the infinite variety and multiplicity of stimuli coming from the (-) sensory realm. Focusing on a Single-POINT has the effect of bringing this manifold (of sense *and* thoughts) into UNITY and taking one across the Divided Line from the Dark Side (+|-) to the Light Side (±). This POINT or Unity-focus also results in mastery and total control over the contents of one's consciousness and in achieving the Goal of one *over* many or one *in* many, symbolized by our familiar (±) or "point in a circle" icon. This "Single-POINT" that one focuses on by consistent meditation will gradually expand and eventually cover everything, becoming *all in all*. This Point is the *Truth* and can take many Forms and be represented in many ways, for example, by a short pithy statement. We will examine some examples shortly.

§388

This Jedi method is most effective when on a regular basis one meditates e.g. in one's room 15 minutes (or longer) twice daily, once in the A.M. and once in the P.M. One can also do a "walking meditation" in which one focuses on a single word/idea or statement (from Science, religious scripture, or inspiration) while out and about in the world. Most *effective* of all is the 24/7 meditation where you meditate—are **"mindful of the Force"**—all of the time, throughout your conscious waking hours. For example, you first select a particular word or Truth for the day—or week, or even year, such as, "The Jedi Order is Now," "I am One with Allah," etc—and then meditate it in the morning as you begin your day, and continuously, whatever it is you are doing. In the beginning at times you will drift away from it and it will move from the *center* to the periphery of your conscious attention. And after a "time" you will have to call it back to the center. Eventually it will be permanently in the "center" of your consciousness and remain the *focus*. Be mindful that the word or Truth is ultimately merely a "pointer" that points you to *the* Truth, the Force, the Balance (±) *as an experience*—namely of your *unity* with everything and everyone. And it is a state in which you can *still* do all the things you are used to doing and are responsible for.

§389

On "Concentration." *Concentration* is an advanced form of meditation that dispenses entirely with words and verbalizations and involves simply a laser-focus e.g. on the Point in the center of the Circle below.

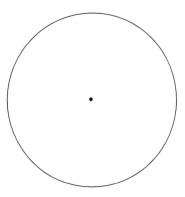

As in meditation in a continued on a single Point— on a "physical" in your mind's eyes open or open you can 1. the empy space and an object, objects, or 2. on an object, say that the Point is *the* you just engage concentrated focus situated either page or a wall or imagination, with closed. With eyes locate the point in between your eyes or between two locate it directly the Wall. Notice *same* in whatever direction you are looking since the Point is "a priori" hence outside the space-time universe and located *above the Divided Line,* yet completely pervading space-time and occupying all points at once. Notice when your eyes move from one object to another the objects are *different,* but in point-concentration (and meditation) there is no change, *the point remains the same wherever you look.* Also many of your own Jedi teachers say that if you can do concentration you do not have to meditate, for example, **Meher Baba**.

§390

On "Affirmation." As a rule when you "meditate" on a Truth or statement you say it to yourself or just think about it. You do not say it "aloud." If you say it aloud it becomes an "Affirmation," which is very powerful since it fills the room or the objective-public space your Body occupies, and *you* hear it. It becomes even more powerful when you say it to another person or in a group (as Jedi **Schelling** says: "It takes *two* persons to make *objectivity*")—or also in front of a *Mirror.*

§391

Here are a sampling of statements and Truths that you can use as foci for *Meditation* and that can also be used as *Affirmations.*

- "I am a Jedi NOW." ("I" meaning your true Self, as a universal individual or "U.I.," which is *one* with the Force, and not your Ego or Particular Self, as a particular individual or "P.I.").
- "I (P.I.) can do **nothing** apart from the Force (God-Allah-Father-Hashem, etc.)." "I (P.I.) AM *nothing* apart from the Force." ("I" = P.I. or EGO, e.g "John" or "Mary." Compare Jedi **Jesus'**, "I can do *nothing* of mine own self." And NOTE: (1) The "EGO" in terms of its *separateness* and isolation is a fiction and an illusion, hence does not and never did *exist.* And (2) This reflects the Truth that, "The Force/God *possesses me or takes me over* ... that I am just USING The Force's consciousness and matter/body, etc." Also as Jedi **Hegel** writes: "The highest independence (freedom) of man is achieved by knowing himself as totally determined by the absolute IDEA (FORCE or GOD), which is the same as **Spinoza's** *Intellectual LOVE of God.*" See *Enc.* § 158z).
- "I am immortal and eternal." ("I" meaning your true Jedi U.I. Self).
- "The Force (Reality, the Universe) is eternally Balanced and infinitely Perfect (It is *We* who are imbalanced, not Reality)."
- "I AM the Infinite Indivisible WHOLE. The Infinite Indivisible WHOLE AM I."
- "The Jedi Order is Now." ("The Jedi Order" = the *unity* of all people or conscious Selves).
- "Eternity will not be, nor has it been. IT IS."
- "Time does not exist. There is only the *eternal Present.*"
- "The Present is the only thing that has no end."

- "I am the Truth." "The Truth is now living in the U.S.A. (in England, in Japan, etc.)." "We are the Truth." "You are the Truth."
- "I'm IN." (That is, "in" The Jedi Order, in Reality, in Love, etc: I am above the Divided Line, out of the CAVE (+|-), illusion, and "in" Reality/Truth (±)).
- (Meditate on such Power-Words as) "Truth," "Unity," "The Force," "Infinite," "Love," etc.
- "I AM."
- "I AM The Force." "I AM The Force aware of Itself." "I am one with The Force."
- "I am one with everyone and everything."
- (Religion:) "Praise you Lord (Allah, Hashem, Vishnu, etc)." Etc.
- "I am getting younger and more *whole* everyday in every way."
- "I am healed, WHOLE, Holy, and Healthy."
- "I recognize you, and recognize you as recognizing me." Etc.
- "May the Force be with you"—means: (1) "The Force" is what *is* and only *is* = The Truth. (2) So it means, "May you be One with The Force/The Truth/What Is"—that is, aligned with and not *apart* from Truth/Reality ... hence not in *illusion*, the Cave, the Dark Side, or EGO. (3) Of course, the word "May" is incorrect since by definition you *are* one with the Force/IS eternally and can *never* be separated from it. It is really only up to *you* whether or not you become, or allow yourself to become, *aware* of your *present* unity with Force/Truth. Hence as I, Obi-Wan, also say: "The Force *will* be with you always," which is closer to the Truth, meaning that, You will be and are One with the Force/Truth *forever.*
- "Luminous beings are We/am I—not this crude matter."
- "Fear (hate, anger) is a path to the Dark Side." "I will not fear."
- "I am mindful of the Present."

§392

Of special importance is the FACT that in these Meditations the word "I" has *two* very different meanings or referents. Noble Reader you should take the time to completely understand this important difference. Thus the word "I" can refer to:

(1) *Yourself* as a "particular" empirical "Egoic" self, called "EGO" and abbreviated as "P.I.," that is, yourself as a *"Particular* Individual." That

is, as "John" or "Alice" and as permanently *separated* from every other person (with no knowledge or belief in and experience of your *unity* with them) and from the Force itself (God, the Universe, Being, the Whole). This initial *separate* finite self or EGO (P.I.) is the false self you do not wish to remain in and is to be BALANCED or Educated into your true Jedi Self. A good example is the Meditation: *"I'm IN (Reality)"* ... where the "I" here refers to my P.I./Ego and *not* to my Jedi *Universal* Self or to the Force Itself, and which means that "I", my P.I./Ego, is literally *in* or merged with the Force (see below).

§393

(2) Or "I" can refer to two things, which are really the same: (i) *The Force as such*—or what your religions call "God" and your sciences "the Universe" as the totality of Being—as exemplified in the Meditations, *"I AM"* and *"I AM Infinite."* Or (ii) *yourself as a JEDI,* as not a "particular" but a *"Universal* Individual or Self ("U.I."). As a Jedi you are ONE with the Force (the Force is aware of Itself in you and as you), you have realized the *One Absolute I,* which you share with all

> "Each person is in a sense the Whole."
> **Schrödinger**
>
> Each person is the *You*-niverse."
> **F.A. Wolf**
>
> "Every I is in reality the One Infinite Substance (of Spinoza)." **Fichte**

other persons or Jedi in the universe. For your *Universal* Self includes all Selves within itself and is included within all Selves. Examples are, *"I am a Jedi"* and *"I am Infinite, the Whole."* Therefore by definition your P.I. or Ego is *not* a Jedi and cannot be Infinite or the Whole as it is only a "part" and "finite." Only your True Jedi Self (U.I.) as one with the Force, as the Force (Absolute I) aware of itself, is such.

§394

It is also important that when you say-meditate-affirm, *"I AM the Force aware of Itself,"* in order to underscore the Fact that the "I" is *not* you as a separate Ego or P.I. you should also say, "I am *not* John or Alice, the son/daughter of ____." "I do *not* live in New York, Tokyo, on Earth, etc." "I am *not* white, black, hispanic ... I am *not* in debt, rich, democrat, republican (a carpenter, doctor, lawyer)." "I am *not* 25, 88 years old, young." "I do *not* have cancer, etc." "**I am *not* my Body**, nor sick etc." "I was *not born* in 1981 on this planet"—for "I am ageless, eternal, I AM THAT I AM" (in fact your Jedi **Jesus** said this; and this is not arrogance for all are equally I AM; see also your Psalm 82). Rather, "I AM the Force, I AM A JEDI, Infinite and Immortal—not mortal and finite, etc."

—Again, for the Religious among you, the reality is that you are giving *total Glory* to God when you do this, as for example Jedi **Jesus** did. For he said "Follow Me," which means "You are to *imitate* me, do what I did, overcome the world as I have (Rev. 3)," and "Before Abraham was, I AM," and also "Who has seen me, has seen the Father/God (the Force)." Therefore, in *imitation, YOU* say it too. This is *the* way to be "filled with *all* the fullness of God" (Eph.5). Also compare, "As many as be complete or perfect can be *just as* (*kathos*) his Jedi Master." As one of our beloved Masters said:

"REJOICE FOR THOSE AROUND YOU WHO TRANSFORM INTO THE FORCE." JEDI MASTER YODA

§395

This is crucial to understand (for many in your "New Age" do not). When you meditate or affirm out loud: *"I AM. I AM the WHOLE,"* it is important to realize deeply that it is not "you" as a separate

> "The eternal spirit-mind itself must descend to empirical consciousness and finite mind in order to overcome it and *be* eternal spirit-mind."
> **Hegel**

particular Ego that is *speaking* but the Force, the Whole itself (again notice your Jedi **Jesus's** sayings, "The words I speak are not mine" and "It is the Father (the Force) in me, he doeth the works," etc). In effect, the educational process or "transformation" is such that, in *the beginning* you simply allow yourself to be "possessed" by the Force (God), you surrender to It as something different from and "other than" yourself. It is "God" speaking *in* you, one can say. You maintain this *distinction*—of you, P.I., and God/Force, not you—until the end. That is, until you reach the "point" where (1) the Ego or P.I. totally disappears by merging utterly and completely with the Force or "I AM," or what is the same, where (2) the Force simply takes over and becomes predominant. At this point you literally become the Force itself aware of itself, or a Jedi as the Force actualized and individualized—or perhaps better expressed, the Force itself *becomes you* ... becomes aware of Itself in and as you, as an immortal indestructible JEDI. And there is no arrogance, superiority or egotism here since *everyone* is the same as you and you know that the consciousness you enjoy (*the Absolute I*) is *shared* by everyone, without exception. As your Jedi **Alan Watts** writes, "*I* appear in every baby born."

§396

To be fully clear and avoid misunderstanding—namely, the error (common in your "New Age") that "You are God," the aggrandizement and inflation of the P.I. Ego to infinity—you should recall the FACT that: Only the Force exists, the BALANCE, and it has two sides, Consciousness and Matter or Body, that exist only in the Now or eternal Present. So, when you become a Jedi (realize you already <u>are</u> a Jedi) or go from being an asleep "Ego" in time to being an awake Jedi in eternity, you attain to the realization that your consciousness and body are <u>not</u> your own but the Force's. As an "Ego," you were all along just <u>using</u> the Force's consciousness and body (+ and -) <u>but</u> <u>without knowing it</u> (cf. the Islam Hadith, "I God will become the eye with which you see, the hand with which you grasp, etc"). As a fully awake Jedi you realize for the first time that your consciousness and body are really that of the Force itself—and not yours as a separate personality or Ego.

§397

Therefore, you as a particular individual cannot "take credit for this" and "cannot boast," as your scriptures say. Your attitude is inevitably that of *humility*, truly profound infinite *gratitude* (from an "egoic" perspective); it is, "Thank You." For this is just the way it is, this is the process of *the eternal Truth itself,* which *is* by inexorable *Reason* and *necessity*. You (as an Ego which began "in time," with a name, "Abu" or "Miriam") had nothing to do with it, it is an eternal Law. *YET,* you are free and responsible, you can control your Consciousness/Body and Will and can use them for good or evil, for the realization of Jedi and the Jedi Order—or *not*.

—For the religious Reader: It is the above alone that explains God's true nature as "self-sacrificing," good, humble, and *kenotic*. That is, again as your scriptures say, "God poured out himself, his Spirit, on all flesh ... and gave himself to and for the world (humanity)." God *died*. God gave ALL of himself (*kenosis* = emptied himself). This means that there *is* nothing left of himself, nothing remains behind, there is no place whatsoever on God's part for "Ego," jealousy, envy, etc. *This* is God's nature, LOVE—which is the same nature as the Force and a Jedi. Again, the Force or God is not an "Ego," for "God emptied himself and died." The Force itself or God can therefore be said to be—*nothing ... indeed, nothing but LOVE—a sheer self-giving, self-sacrificing of herself.*

§398

And as I have said, there is limitless room for Uniqueness and Individuality. Each Jedi is unique or *sui generis,* one of a kind, and unlike any other, despite the *Universal* aspect pertaining to Jedihood. This is true because Matter/Body (-) is the principle of *individuation,* and also because of the nature of Polarity (and the Concept, U-P-I)—which requires that (+), the Universal Pure Self, *cannot exist by itself* but must be connected and in unity *with* its polar opposite, the Individual and individuated Body (-). Thus you and every person ever born has their *own* experiences, memories, acts, etc.

§399

Additional KEY JEDI TRUTHS pertaining to Meditation and Affirmation. The following "Key Truths" are Truths you should immerse yourself in and meditate on all the time, 24/7. There are others connected with these in this Book, which you can find yourself. They will help you to weaken the PULL of the Dark Side and to dissolve and resolve your Ego into your true Jedi Self. You should always make these Truths *present and Now.* For example, "The Jedi Order *is Now* ... And we are all *in it.*"

§400

[1] *ETERNITY IS NOW.* As we saw in *Part I,* **"The Force/Eternity will not be, nor has it been, IT IS."** Not only does True Being have no past or future because **IT IS,** but your Jedi Self in fact *is* True Being. Further, there is no "time"—as it is illusory or phenomenal only. It then follows that *This Now* is the first moment of time, that *This* is "the Beginning of all things," and that therefore we have never left the Beginning. Thus: "I am in Eternity, in the Eternal Now/Present, etc." "I am *in* it now."

An Exercise/Meditation: "Close your eyes" = you are in Eternity, in The One. Now "Open your eyes" = though it seems as if you are now in The Many and in time—the truth is that *you are still in The One and in Eternity.*

[2] "I am not [Your Name], finite, human, or animal. I am an Infinite Jedi."—Note that the "Soup" or "Cave," the unconscious people and forces in society, will tell you the opposite. Just ignore them and stay on course.

[3] "The ONE alone is real. The Many is not."

§401

[4] "I am the Truth." ("I" here is not Ego or P.I., but rather Jedi or U.I. or the Force actualized as U-P-I.) Hence, "My *consciousness* is not mine (as an empirical Ego) but the Force's (the Universal Absolute I's)—which I share with everyone."
"I—my True Jedi Self—am not limited to my Body." "I extend to the infinite and embrace the Universe—which is my true Body" (as Jedi **Alan Watts** and **Schelling** state).

[5] Reality (the present moment) is *incredible* and *incredibly deep* beyond your wildest dreams. What your religions call "Heaven" is in actuality Here and Now. Hence you should Get excited and be *passionate,* continually ... Expect the Soup, the fog to lift. And do this despite the evidence of your *senses* to the contrary (e.g., the 6 o'clock news, etc). This is hard in the beginning ... but it *can* be done and becomes easier with practice.

[6] The Truth of the *Equality of all selves* removes all *Inequality* (superiority and inferiority) and your anxiety-ridden, status-driven Egoic Self as well.

§402

[7] Realize that *attachments* are not good for you—except *attachments* to the Truth and your true Jedi nature (±)—especially *Non-Pure Egoic Love.*

- It is simply a question of being *INNER* (+) *dependent* and free, Healthy and Whole, or *OUTER-Sense* (-) *dependent* and a slave or "machine" (à la **G.I. Gurdjieff**), and unhealthy and "half."

- Any *thing* or *person* you "can't live without" is a lie and a denial of the truth that you are already within yourself complete (±). This belief will keep you in bondage.

- The same is true for *Non-Pure Egoic Love* Relationships. If you are *attached* or think you need someone, and want them to want you (and vice-versa), then you are leading them to believe a lie—that you alone are the "(+)" they need to complete themselves, that they do *not* already have it within themselves. This is *immoral*. It is the true meaning of "co-dependence." You should instead *help to realize each other's* completeness—but be vigilant and circumspect. "Sex" as such and severed from the universal, spiritual, and Jedi dimension is a potential danger and trap; it can take you away from Jedi (as a substitute for #1) and reinforce your false Ego (by fostering e.g. *jealousy*: my happiness now depends on her, she must not leave me, etc). It also creates the illusion that "you have arrived." The Goal, in any case, is to *Master* Sex and Body drives and thereby win the Absolute Freedom that is achieved only via free-will and not by surrender to biological drives. "Sex" therefore is to be engaged in with extreme caution, using Jedi intelligence. Also be mindful that all relationships without exception are *eternal*. And since you are a Jedi and your #1 priority is the glorious Jedi Order and the total healing of your planet, *this* is what should be foremost in your mind in all your social interactions and intercourse. Thus you should not ASK, "What's in it for me? but rather, "How can I best help this person realize her or his true Jedi Self?"

§403

- Therefore since you are by necessity drawn to Other people (as "Other" they are your Truth and your true Being *as* Absolute I) and Relations are a good thing, you *must* cultivate "Pure Love" (called "Agape") which is a non-binding, non-dependent, "free" Love that promotes growth to Jedi (±), *and not the Ego-binding love that keeps you in Ego and the Dark Side* (+|-).

- Meditation/Affirmation: "I do not need this [person, object]." "I am complete without him/her/it." "I give him his freedom, and me my freedom. Yet I still love him in a *pure* non-attached way (and forever)." "I own and use these things, but am neither *attached* to nor dependent on them. Their loss would not affect me, and I have no problem giving them away, etc." (See below §429, "the Problem of Sex")

- It is a FACT that as a Jedi, not only are you *Love Itself* or is Love your essence (as (±) or the unity of Self and Other), but since your *INNER* being/dimension is *Infinite* you have *an infinite capacity to Love* (note that for a Christian this is required and not an option, as per John 15:12, "Love one another *as* I have loved you," that is, with an *infinite* love). Moreover you can start to exercise and develop this capacity by (1) *loving* other people (purely) and by (2) activating love *within yourself*. That is, you do *not* have to be in a relationship with an actual person *before* you can love or experience love. You can simply "give yourself *permission*" to love and be in love. For example you can meditate and SAY the words: "I'm in love," "I love you," "I am Love," and "Love." This is especially helpful with difficult people in your life and work or who have injured you.

§404

[8] Love and Guilt/Fear. The latter can only exist when you are not loving or do not love. To experience *no guilt at all* you must be One with all people on your planet, or be a Self-aware Jedi.

[9] I also realize that all relationships are *eternal*, because all Jedi (or people) are *eternal*. So I will act accordingly.

[10] "Light Saber" Meditations. A "Light Saber" is a symbol (just as an extended "index-finger") for both (1) the sword of Truth, and (2) infinite power (as light or fire), which can be used to destroy any negative, Dark Side forces or elements within or without you. For example, you can turn the sword inwards to "clean out" or "burn out" the *gook* or the unwanted desires and thoughts within your heart-mind-and spirit.

§405

FIVE VERY POWERFUL JEDI MEDITATIONS

(1) The "I'm IN (Reality/Love)" Meditation.

To help you to *break free* from the OUTER-Sense domain you can do INNER-exercises and meditations. For example, (1) you can break from your Senses by walking around your house *with eyes closed,* for 1-3 hours (compare, "sensory deprivation"). You should "Live in the INNER" more and more. (2) You can break your *attachment* to sense-OUTER objects, for example, by living alone in a cabin for 6 months to one year, etc. The following is particularly powerful:

> *FIRST: Close your eyes* and enter (+) or (±) and Say, *"I'm IN"*—in the One Infinite Consciousness or the Unity that encompasses the whole Universe and all selves. Plus, I'm back at the beginning of the Universe, the beginning of "time," and in Eternity or the Eternal Present without before or after. I'm in the *Absolute I, Unity, the POINT* … the Truth, Reality, the BALANCE. Thus by doing this you are in effect "stepping outside" of time, History, and the Universe. You can also *walk around the room or house you are in, keeping your eyes closed, etc.* You will be astounded by what you can learn from this.

> *THEN: Open your eyes* and enter the (-) manifold sense-world, and Say, *"I'm IN"*—that is, "I'm *still* IN." What you do is let the Unity of (+) just bathe and saturate the entire (-) "Cave" realm, which will merge the two, (-) and (+), into *One* (±). You will come to see the (+), the Unity or POINT in everything that is in (-), in everything that you look at. Again, recall that the "I" in "I'm IN," is P.I. and not the Force, God, or U.I. Thus, "I" or "Ego" am *in* Reality, I am fused with or dissolved in the Force or the I AM. In time you will *feel* this *Unity,* and your false Ego and sense of *separateness* will simply dissolve.

§406

A variant of this "IN"-"OUT" meditation involves Alternating or "toggling" between the following two states: *State One:* You are *in* the world, say standing on the corner at 42nd Street and Times Square in New York City. Now with **Eyes Open,** say: "I'm IN" (that is, *in* the world). *State Two:* Now with **Eyes Closed,** say "I'm OUT" (that is, *outside* of the world). Since *You are no longer in the world or on the planet* you should now imagine yourself in outer space, calmly and meditatively looking at the Earth and *objectifying* it, totally removed from all the stimuli, clatter, and confusion. This exercise will change and reconstitute the texture of your experience and your relations with others, and give you immense POWER to overcome all types of negativity and disturbing impressions coming especially from the sensory realm.

§407

(2) The "Recognition" Meditation/Affirmation.

Say to each other (or in a group): "(Mary/John) I recognize you as absolutely independent and free. And I also recognize you as recognizing me as absolutely independent and free. And We are One: *I am you and you are me*"—which is true since the two share *one and the same* Absolute I. This is based on the POLARITY of Unity-in-Opposition, Identity-in-Difference, which results in the "Global recognition of each by all" that is a primary feature of the Jedi Order. The Short Form of this important meditation is: "I recognize you, and also recognize you as recognizing me; and We are One." You can also do this as a "walking meditation"—by saying it (to yourself and not aloud) to people passing by and up close.

—Also, if done in the proper way, most of the so-called "mental disorders/conditions" that plague the people on your planet—like depression, phobias, etc—can be *cured* within 4-weeks of this therapy, especially when done in Groups.

§408

This exercise (meditation/affirmation) actualizes and reinforces the Truth of the Unity of Opposites on the *interpersonal* level. The "Opposites" are me and you, self and other—each as *absolutely independent and free*—and the "Unity" is the Truth of the opposites, *which however remain opposites*. It is the *True Infinite* that leads to the Total Freedom that comes from seeing myself in my Other or counterpart—and to Total "Health" as well (from your words "Hāl" and "Holos" meaning the state of being WHOLE).

§409

We said that the "*Unity*" is the Truth of the opposites—in the sense that (1) both persons are Jedi and both share the same One

Absolute I or POINT (*outside* the Universe and space-time) and (2) both *re-cognize* each other, that is, "I recognize you as the *same kind* of being as I am," i.e., a "*subject*/object" and not just an "object" like a tree or table, which is not *also* a "subject"—a subject being *that* which is able to make me or have me *as* an Object, that is, "recognize" me. Thus, *"I"* am an *Object*, as a Body/thing you can see, and also a *Subject*, as *that* for which "objects" exist. And *"you"* are an Object in that *I* see your Body-Face, etc, *and* a Subject as well since you can see "me" or *I* am an Object for *you*. Hence *we* are, as such, *the same* or *One*—namely a *Unity*.

§410

Moreover, You recognize "me" and "my space" or universe or sphere of existence (as a Monad)—which is hence *inviolate* and cannot be penetrated without my will. Thus I have an *eternal* sphere and existence that is *universally recognized*—and so do you (and everyone else). *Nevertheless* there is a *unity* underlying *each* of us, and this unity is LOVE, in that "I am (in) you, and you are (in) me."—You may also compare the Self/Other "dialectic" of the *Infinite* in Jedi **Hegel's** *Science of Logic*, whose main point is that, "I" am *both* Self *and* Other at once since, "To *you*, it is *I* who am the *Other*."

§411

(3) The "Stop the World I want to Get Off" Meditation. And the "Abstracting" Meditation.

The main thought is: "There *is* no World. It does not exist—and *never* existed." In this powerful meditative state you experience a respite, rest, deep healing, and a liberation from all the anxieties of life. There is NO ANXIETY—about war, terrorism, nuclear holocaust, politics, money, death and disease, foreclosure, homelessness, genocide, etc. Your Jedi **Spinoza** taught that it is only a total sustained bath in the Universal One, the Unity of Substance, that can "*cleanse you from all Particularity*," egoic selfhood, and worry.

The "Abstracting" Meditation helps you to access *the Absolute I* and get out of the Cave and into the eternal sphere. What you do is: In thought, simply *Abstract* from everything. Remove the *world*—take it all away. There is no human race, no political problems, money, financial worries—I don't care about the "News," about what happens or does not. I have no *fear*—for I am totally disconnected from the human race and its affairs and troubles, and from Time and "the slaughterbench of History." This is also the method that was used by your **A-Team** to reach Absolute Knowledge or Intellectual Intuition—the single POINT or Apriori One Consciousness that underlies everything and alone exists.

§412

Another version of this meditation, equally powerful and effective, is to imagine that you are **dead** or have just died, *yet still exist* as a "ghost" or in an "astral body" (cf. your film "The Sixth Sense"), that is, *you* can see other people but *they* cannot see you.—But! The important point is that, *It's all over.* You can no longer affect or change the world, have an impact on the persons you knew, your loved-ones, etc. The object is to go through the experience and just see how you feel, e.g., "I never told my brother, 'I love you'," etc. What will happen is that a deep and powerful ego-cleansing will take place ... and an Awakening.

§413

(4) The "MMA I love you" Meditation.

"Come to see people as *sacred*," as Jedi **Thomas Merton** did. Go to a public place (e.g. the Metropolitan Museum of Art in New York City) and single out *one person*—a stranger—and do a LOVE meditation on them, for one hour. Say or think this to him or her: "I love you infinitely, more than you'll ever know." Your love-laser will penetrate through the person's (i.e. *my perception* of the person's) Ego, faults, possible moral and physical ugliness, etc. What you are to do is just "forgive him, accept and affirm and value him *absolutely, unconditionally and without reservation.*" In a short time you will begin to see beyond all her (perceived, possible, probable) flaws and shortcomings; you will see the person just as "God" or the Force does. This exercise will develop your *capacity* to LOVE by causing you to experience the Truth of subject/object, self/other *Unity* (±).

§414

(5) The "Micro-slowly" Meditation.

This meditation will expand your experience of Eternity, of the Eternal Present and its infinite depths. Begin by Pointing your finger or a pen at the horizon or in a horizontal direction. Imagine it as a beam of light, a laser extending and reaching to infinity, cutting through all objects, stars, galaxies, spaces, etc. Now move your pen "micro-slowly" describing an Arc ... first on your desk ... then walk around your room ... your city, your planet, your galaxy (in thought), slowly moving it from left to right, 360°. Then keep slowly moving your finger/pen *while also looking around your room.* You will feel the NOW and the Present will deepen ... and deepen. You will soon have the experience of, "Oh that magic feeling ... nowhere to go"—as your British poet bore witness to.

> MEDITATION IS ABSOLUTELY ESSENTIAL FOR BECOMING A JEDI AND EXPERIENCING THE TRUTH. IT IS NOT AN OPTION. YOU MUST MEDITATE!—AND INCORPORATE IT INTO YOUR DAILY LIFE: START WITH 15 MIN. A.M. & P.M., SAME *PLACE,* CHAIR, & SAME *TIME.* THEN 24/7 WALKING MEDITATION, IN CAR, ETC.

§415

THREE: ART. Art and the aesthetic experience is a very effective educational method and way of entering true Reality, and hence the absolute importance of continually immersing yourself in the Truth (±) that is found (not in mere "entertainment" but) in *true* Jedi Art, literature, poems, and films, etc. For in point of fact Art (like Reason/Science and Faith-Meditation/Religion) inhabits the *eternal* sphere and hence occupation with it and its object—Truth in the form of Beauty—has a powerful influence on your consciousness. Not only does Art turn your focus from the many, multiplicity and the Dark Side to the ONE POINT and your true Jedi Self, but it also provides you with a deeper awareness of the *fully present* Jedi Order. "Beauty," as a whole in which a manifold is *unified,* is in reality an image or representation of your True Self in a sensuous shape. This is why whenever you are in the presence of a work of

Art—whether a painting, symphony, or film—a feeling of exaltation and transcendence overtakes you; transcendence, that is, of your limited Ego and of the dis-integrated sense-world (-) that results in an experience of your larger true Infinite Self reflected in the art work before you.

It is also true that great *literature*, novels, dramas, and poetry, have a more powerful effect than the visual and auditory Arts since they involve to a greater extent the *imagination* or the form of images, which is more akin to Pure Consciousness (+), Reason and Thought than sensory Arts such as painting and architecture.

§416

The special power to elevate and make you POINTED, shared in common for example with Film and novels, resides in the *unification* of a multiplicity of events that are unfolding before the viewer or reader. In short, *you are always beholding only yourself in the work of Art.* For example in the film before him, the viewer is in fact watching *his own life* in the shape of a series of events or scenes that have a beginning, middle and end; and is simply looking for and wanting to see the "unity" or theme that underlies them and makes *sense* of them: she desires to see "the manifold brought into a *Unity.*" It is *this* which satisfies and produces the aesthetic effect, in addition to other factors (see your Jedi **Aristotle's** *Poetics*). This *Unity* is *Beauty* or *Perfection*—an Image of her True Self—and in its presence she is transformed and elevated for it represents what is *eternal and True*— which she implicitly IS.

§417

Hence as far as possible one should strive to live in these Three modes of Art-Religion-Science all the time since they all involve occupation with and focusing on the Truth, which *weakens* the Dark Side PULL and *strengthens* the Light Side; thus helping to bring one to the *critical* point where the Dark Side Pull entirely gives way or just "pops," resulting in the Light Side (±) alone prevailing.

—Your Jedi agenda or schedule should accordingly be filled as much as possible with activities and occupations that involve all THREE: Reason/Science, Faith/Religion, and Art, which alone constitute the Absolute Eternal Sphere of the TRUTH (±) ITSELF.

§418

(B) SOCIETY (being with Others)

As we have discovered, the key to everything is that the Jedi Order or Society *already exists*, and this is what has always to be kept in mind: **IT IS**. The idea here is thus to utilize your contacts and relationships with others in all capacities in such a way as to unveil *Unity* and *Love* and the Jedi Order. Hence as a Jedi you are to live and act and think as if you *are* in the Jedi Society NOW and a member of it—indeed, as if everyone on your planet and everyone you meet *is already a Jedi*. However because the majority of persons in your experience are not yet *aware* of the Truth and are still living in **Plato's** CAVE and immersed in the Dark Side, the Dark Side's influence and PULL on you is very strong. Thus it is recommended that you not pursue your Jedi Self and the Jedi Order alone but rather do it with others and in groups, for *there is POWER in numbers*. The situation on your planet will be much different when all or most of your 7-global institutions are BALANCED and disseminating the Light Side of the Force (±) instead of the Dark Side (+|-). The need is thus to create and expand Jedi-friendly spaces and environments. Hence our division here will be into, ONE: Jedi Relationships and TWO: Jedi Groups.

§419

ONE: **JEDI RELATIONSHIPS**. Like everything else the main purpose here is to increase your Focus 24/7 on the TRUTH (±), the One Infinite Consciousness, and help you to become POINTED, a Jedi, the Force aware of Itself.

According to the Truth of POLARITY discussed in *Part I.*, a *relationship* between two persons or Jedi is a primary and *necessary* example of the Unity of Opposites in the Self/Other form. What is really happening when two persons meet is that one Jedi or "Infinite Field" (or the WHOLE (±) or Force aware of Itself) meets with another Jedi or "Infinite Field." Each is totally complete and independent (±) and knows the other as such, yet each experiences total UNITY and Love with the other person who is

> "The truth is the *Universal* Self-Consciousness, in which each person is absolutely independent and yet they exist in an identity or *unity*." **Hegel**

actually itself in another form. There is a difference and opposition, and also a Unity and Identity. The *Unity* consists in the fact that (1) they both share the *same* One Infinite Consciousness (of the eternal Force (+)) and occupy the *same POINT* outside space-time and the OUTER-Material (-) realm; and (2) they both *re-cognize* themselves as the *same* kind of being—i.e., as a Jedi, a subject/object or self/other (±) unity.

§420

The relationship of the Two constitutes the core of the Jedi Order, which is NOW—for the UNITY of all selves, the Truth, is NOW. Everyone on your planet simply needs to become aware of it and, most importantly, of the Love which is its accompaniment.

Hence the *purpose* of all relationships without exception is for each party to help the other realize their Jedihood, completeness and independence (±)—to become Whole and *Healed* and fully integrated into the One Jedi Order, and no longer "cut off" and living as a *CANCER* in the One Body. The purpose is to facilitate each party's education and transition from their "egoic" isolated Dark Side self to their true Light Side *universal* Jedi Self. The purpose is *not* to "use" the other only as a Means for one's own happiness and ends, nor to become "dependent" on them or "complete" through them.

§421

Again, in your untrue EGO-state you feel you are *incomplete,* say a (-), and hence need something outside yourself, a (+) such as fame, love, or status, in order to become complete as (±). This is an error—for you are really *already* complete and have the (+) which you seek *within* yourself.

Hence "relationships" are in truth an opportunity to become complete, healed, POINTED, and a Jedi, and should be *utilized* to the fullest extent to educate and Balance both yourself and others. Your main problem is that up until now relationships on your planet and during its history have been predominantly "egoic" and Dark Side. The only solution is for your people to switch over NOW to healthy Jedi style relationships; the past habits and conditioning of your people must be overcome.

§422

In this section we will focus primarily on men-women so-called "romantic" relationships, which we will call *"Holy* Jedi Relationships"—"Holy" from the root HĀL, meaning WHOLE and HEALED, hence a relationship that leads to each person's becoming a WHOLE Jedi. We will also treat "the Problem of Sex and its Solution" and "Holy Jedi Sex or Intimacy."

§423

THE HOLY JEDI RELATIONSHIP. The *Dyadic* vs the *Triadic* Relationship.

The Triadic Relationship is Jedi and Healthy, the Dyadic is "egoic" and unhealthy. The "Dyadic" involves *two* Ego's who initially see each

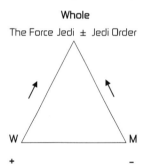

Whole

The Force Jedi ± Jedi Order

W

M

+   −

other as "perfect," or see the Infinite in each other (as an egoic/human self), however have no *third* or higher principle or goal they are both committed to. It is a "dependent" relationship where two halves make up a Whole, "W+ plus M– = (±)" (where "W" = Woman, "M" = Man). It is very dangerous, unstable and unhealthy. The "Triadic" is essentially the same but is distinguished by the addition of a *Third* principle ("Jedi/The Jedi Order") that they both commit to as a higher cause than themselves, and to which they subordinate their separate egoic selves.

§424

The *Dyadic* is most popular and common in your world, but you must transcend it. It is highly toxic. Further, the FACT is that you are not just "human"/egoic ... you are Infinite and more than human. You are a Jedi, Divine, the Whole or the Universe aware of itself, indeed in the language of your religions and scripture, you are "gods and goddesses (*elohim*)," (Ps. 82, 6, Jn. 10,34).

§425

In the case of the *Triadic* relationship both persons start out more or less as Ego and P.I. and agree to use their relationship as a "means" to realize Jedi, U.I., and the Jedi Order. They do not try to find completeness and fulfillment *exclusively in each other* but in a third higher *all-inclusive* thing, (±). Their goal is to cultivate each other's completeness and Independence (±) and Jedi Self.

The *Dyadic's* pitfall stems from the couples ignorance of the Truth, the Knowledge of the Force, and the true goal of life. Thus they begin as two separate Ego's expecting to find completeness and fulfillment in each other. One sees the other initially as *perfect* and *infinite*, but in time this disappears because it cannot be sustained. And even if it can, it is unhealthy and can never lead to the goal and your true Jedi Self. The FACT is that only the Infinite, the Perfect can completely *satisfy* an individual, so problems will inevitably arise. Moreover, you cannot find the Infinite and Perfect in the OUTER (-) physical sense realm, outside of yourself ... rather only *inside* yourself in the INNER, as *Absolute I.* Hence to embrace such an egoic-OUTER belief and attachment is untenable and doomed to fail.

§426

Furthermore, since the *purpose* of the relationship is for each person to realize their completeness and independence (±), it follows that all types of *control* and dependence are unhealthy and to be avoided. Hence only non-Binding or Free-Love relationships should be cultivated, not Binding Egoic ones: as for example in the declamations, "I need you to complete me," "I can't live without you," "You need me ... ," etc. This is a lie, it is evil and immoral. You are telling her that you have the (+) she needs to *be* complete, and hence that she does not have it in herself. This is not true. You thus not only make *her dependent*—but yourself as well. In addition this produces and unleashes Dark Side emotions such as jealousy, fear, and hate, which can lead to criminal behavior.

§427

Give yourself permission to be in LOVE and to experience Love 24/7. Do not let love depend on meeting "Mr. or Ms. Right." The truth is that as a Jedi with an Infinite INNER (as well as OUTER) you have an infinite capacity to love, which just has to be cultivated, activated and released. You can do this by One-Point meditations and affirmations such as "I'm in Love," and "I am Love" ... that is, you should say, think, and use the "Love" word a lot (and the "love" I am speaking of is "*agape*," see below). Cultivating and experiencing Love gives you the *power* to control biological *lust* and the need and desperation for "love" and relationships, as well as to overcome egoic loneliness; it also helps you avoid bad-toxic relationships and marriages.—Note that your Jedi **Hegel** states in his *Jedi Science of Right* that "lust" (eros) is positive and acceptable in marriage, where it receives an ethical/spiritual community-sanctioned element and value and where it gradually "wears away" thus becoming educated, perfected and transmuted into "*agape*" (the highest type of love). One can call it "legal lust," for you have made a commitment by an act of your wills to stay together, etc. Also, the cultivation and pursuit of lust *apart* from marriage and/or complete Jedi commitment involves one in major insurmountable difficulties.

The benefits of Marriage cannot be overstated. For many it is an indispensable means for overcoming the *material* world (–) and realizing its intrinsic nothingness. Making a commitment to ONE person helps both people navigate the currents of the world's ever present sense attractions and distractions. The stability of a Jedi Marriage enables one to gradually DETACH from the Cave's manifold distractions and become securely anchored in the ONE POINT (±).

---

§428

Lastly my Noble Padawan, be mindful that the ultimate Goal is to be a Jedi and to realize the Jedi Order, which is absolute independence and Freedom. And this necessarily implies that you must MASTER and transcend or sublimate SEX—having *complete* control over it. That is, to the point where you have no need or compulsion for it; otherwise you are *not* free but *dependent,* a slave to your biological drives and passions. However if you do engage in intimacy, it is to be only by free choice or will. We will also see how sex and intimacy can be employed in a Jedi way that will help you *master* it and become a Jedi and Pointed and also realize your #1 priority, the amazing Jedi Order.

§429

THE PROBLEM OF SEX AND ITS SOLUTION.

"Sex" and the sexes has its origin and basis, as everything, in the Truth of POLARITY, the Unity of Opposites. Hence "sex" has two meanings. (i) "Sex" = gender, as male or female, and (ii) "sex" = intimacy, as the union of male and female (i.e., on the physical level). But the True Union is on the (+) higher level (non-physical, non-sensuous): that of the One Consciousness, Absolute I, and *UNITY* (±).

§430

On your planet the word "Sex" comes from your Latin "secare" meaning "to cut" (cognates are "section," "sect," and "bi-sect"). Hence the division of the sexes into Male (+) and Female (-) is the

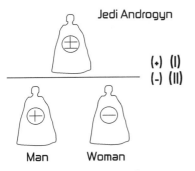

Jedi Androgyn

(+) (I)
(-) (II)

Man   Woman

result of originally having an undivided WHOLE or ONE, in which the Two were fused or undifferentiated (compare the indifference point of a Magnet), and then cutting it in half (note, in your religious texts the word "ADAM" means male *and* female, uniting *ish* and *isha*). The Point is that male and female are originally *two* sides of a single Thing. Hence the sexes as such, as separate entities, are really BI-SECTED or HALVED BEINGS—and in a condition of *wrongness* as searching for their other "half" in order to become WHOLE (See *Jedi Androgyn* Diagram). Hence "**(II)** *After Division*," on the (-) physical level where they exist as independent opposites, their desire and drive is to re-unite and cancel their one-sided existence. This is the origin of the unquenchable *sexual drive* and the tension and so-called "War between the Sexes," that is, you cannot *permanently* achieve *union* through sex, for bodies *remain* separate. However in the "**(I)** *Before Division*" state that is on the (+) level, we have *the Jedi Androgyn* who contains the Two sides (masculine & feminine) as united and in Unity (±). We have the WHOLE Being ... where "sex" and bi-section are transcended.

> "Man and woman not only seek union but also wage a war against each other like deadly enemies—due to the POLARITY of human nature ... Original sin [is] the division into two sexes and the Fall of the ANDROGYN: man as a *complete* being. Man is a sick, disharmonious creature because he is a sexual, i.e. *'bi-sected'* being ..." **Berdyaev**
>
> *"There is neither male nor female"* in the Spirit and in the Truth. **Gal. 3, 28.**

§431

This is the *only* solution to the Problem of the Sexes and the War between them—which is based on a dual *contradiction*. (i) First, "Man" has a dual *nature*. He is not only "human or animal" (i.e., *Particular*-Biological, with a Sex drive as a male or female) but a JEDI as well (i.e., *Universal*-Spiritual) who as a Self-conscious "I" is absolutely Free. As the former only, he is *dependent* and driven to find completion in his complementary polar opposite, while as the latter he is *independent* and vacillates or alternates between both: "I want you, need you, love you" ... "And I hate you, since I don't *really* need you, as I am free, independent, and complete in myself." (ii) On the merely human-biological Sexual level (-), he seeks and is driven to find *union* and salvation in his counterpart but is eternally frustrated since such permanent union is impossible; he cannot overcome the *separation* of male & female *bodies*.

§432

The *only* Solution therefore is to *be* a Jedi-Androgyn, to cross the Divided Line and Dark Side (+|-) and become a complete JEDI (±) by transmuting Erotic Love into Agapic Love (see below).

Also very important, as long as one persists in regarding their *PRIMARY IDENTITY* as a "Man" or a "Woman" (by gender or sex/uality) there is no escape from the Problem of the War between the Sexes and its consequences (rape, brutality, murder, emotional-psychological-spiritual illness, trauma, etc). Only by acknowledging *Jedi-Androgyn* as your *PRIMARY IDENTITY* and "Man/Woman" as your *SECONDARY IDENTITY* can the problem be solved.—It is also a FACT that whether you are gay or straight *you must MASTER Sex* or *Gender* (+|-) and become a Jedi-Androgyn (±) as your *PRIMARY IDENTITY.* Here alone is FREEDOM to be found. All else is Bondage, Dependence, Unhappiness, and Problems.

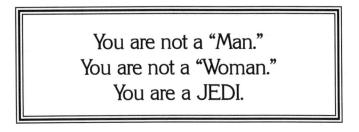

§433

So one must *transcend Sex or Sexuality* (that is, as one's "primary identity"). As it says in one of your religion's scriptures, "there is neither male nor female" in the Spirit or in the Truth, i.e., the Balanced Force (±) (Gal. 3, 28). The FACT is that to have a SEX—to be solely, exclusively, and one-sidedly a Man or a Woman—is to be a BI-SECTED Being, half of a Whole. It is to be insecure, anxiety ridden, and *Evil* as well … as being more concerned about your *own* well-being and welfare than that of others (as in: "I need a Fix, I must end my one-sided, bi-sected miserable condition. I must find someone at any cost"). That is, you are forced to "use" people, especially your counterpart in a relationship, as a "means" only and not as the sacred *End*-in-themselves which they are.

What you should do therefore is to Meditate, Affirm/Believe/Know and Realize that: "I am not a Man (Woman)." "I am a Jedi." I am not my (Male/Female) Body." "I am Infinite/the Whole/Complete." "I am the Force, the Infinite One, aware of Itself."

In other words, the goal of becoming a Jedi-Androgyn is achieved simply by *being* a JEDI, that is, by following The Jedi Code and Methods, and by the proper use of Relationships and Sexual Intimacy.

§434

HOLY JEDI SEX OR INTIMACY

(Note: You can also transmute Eros into Agape *apart from* a "Romantic" Relationship and Holy Jedi Sex)

The true Goal and Purpose of a Romantic man/woman Relationship is precisely to help each other become a Jedi and complete (±). Hence given our dual nature this goal of being a Jedi-Androgyn can be achieved simply *by transmuting EROS into AGAPE.*

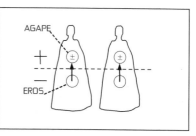

—Note: "Eros" is natural/biological, in service of the reproduction of the species and the basis of all male-female attraction. However without Reason-Intelligence Eros creates *dependence* and toxic behavior—and is a hindrance to Jedi-actualization. "Agape" (from your Greek) on the other hand, is the highest kind of love as it is Divine, self-sufficient, and contains both *Eros* and *Phileos* (friendship) within itself. It is the *Core* of the Jedi Self and a Jedi's immortal Life in Eternity, and it flows from the Unity of Opposites (Self and Other) and results in Freedom and power over lust and egoic Dark Side emotions.

§435

How to Transmute EROS into AGAPE by beginning and committing to a *Jedi Triadic Relationship* and delaying level 4 and 5 intimacy. This can be achieved in many ways and forms. The following is one designed especially for adolescents:

We advise for young people—if you insist on including intimacy in your male/female "romantic" relationship—that you (1) Date many people and do not limit yourself to one person (whom you later marry), for diversity expands knowledge and growth and lessens the chance of making a bad choice in marriage, and (2) Restrict intimacy to the absolute minimum until you find the most Jedi-compatible date/mate with whom to enter into a Jedi-Triadic Relationship.

Levels of Intimacy (suggested): 1. shaking hands—for a minimum of 3 months (longer, is best), 2. holding hands, kissing—not below the shoulders—for 6 months, 3. soul kissing—for 6 months, 4. all, but full intimacy—for 6 months, 5. full intimacy. (Note: 3-4-5 *only* during daytime).

When you find the right person who will agree to Jedi and the Jedi Order as their #1 Priority you may institute a Triadic (not Dyadic) Relationship. And be mindful of the importance of *delayed intimacy*, especially since today's young usually very quickly go to level 4/5 intimacy—too soon—and hence only get to know a Person superficially and not deeply. The Result is a short-lived relationship. By delaying intimacy you get to know the Person better and in different settings (a museum, park, on holidays) and with different and difficult people, friends, family members, etc. Also attend various Jedi Lectures and events, etc. (You can also test the person to see if she or he is truly sincere in their commitment to a Jedi Relationship).

§436

As you progress—if done properly—"Eros-lust" will gradually transmute into Agape. And minimally you should invoke the "24 hour Rule," that is, if you cannot exercise control over your sexual drive, wait 24 hours before intimacy and/or confer with a Jedi authority-parent-Teacher *before* intimacy—if you do you will receive more power and Jedi wisdom. The ideal is to reserve Level 5 intimacy for marriage (or if you cannot, then until your engagement and/or a commitment to marriage).

The POINT: If done properly you will after a period of time and at a certain point have realized your true Jedi nature and AGAPE will be actualized; after which there will be no need or compulsion for sexual intimacy, which will be entered into only as a result of the well-reasoned Free choice of one's Jedi Will.

On commitment: Yes, in a Jedi Relationship the two parties make a "commitment" to each other (as boyfriend/girlfriend, marriage, etc), but one without toxic dependence or attachment, and that also includes a commitment or dedication to Jedi and the #1 Goal. For example: "We will help each other realize our Jedi Selves and completeness and the glorious Jedi Order."

§437

As concerns relating with or living with *difficult* people, one should treat them, and everyone, as if they are *already* Jedi and should Love them (and forgive them) unconditionally, 24/7. By doing so you will grow in your capacity to love and forgive and the more POINTED you will become. You may have to separate from a difficult person for a time, till you are more Jedi and Pointed, and then you can see them again and *positively* affect them and guide them to Jedihood.— This applies as well to (abusive) Parents and family members because your duty to the Jedi Order and the Healing of your world (your duty to the Force, God, the Whole, and your race) supersedes your duty to your biological Family (or "blood-ties"; cf. your **Jesus's**, "Who is my mother, my brethren, my sister?").

§438

Finally be mindful that all Relationships are *eternal.* Knowing this makes a tremendous difference in How you relate to people during your average day. The FACT is that you *will* see and be with these persons *forever.* Moreover, to *be* a Jedi you must become reconciled with *everyone* ... and have no fear or hate towards anyone.

§439

TWO: **JEDI GROUPS.** The Jedi Family, School, and Work. Because at this time in your History the Dark Side PULL on your planet is very strong, you will have need of others. There is power and strength in numbers and Groups. This will help you to deepen your 24/7 Focus on the Truth, the POINT, and the Jedi Order. It is important to always remember that it is *you* and your Jedi friends who are "normal" or the "norm" (as in agreement with Reality), whereas all others or non-Jedi living only in the Dark Side and the Cave, *are not.*

§440

Introduction. We recommend you have at least 2 or 3 or more Jedi friends whom you can be in contact with on a regular basis—in person, via phone, text message, internet, etc. There is no need to "proselytize" for people will notice the change in you and will *want* to know what is different about you; this is because they and your whole planet are undergoing **Final CUSP.** In addition the more POINTED you become and are, the more you will automatically find yourself moving in a higher sphere of life, people, and opportunity. You will be attracted to *positive* things and people and they will be attracted to you; and *negative* things and energies will flee from you and fall away.

§441

THE JEDI FAMILY. Your Home or Home Base is very important. It should be the most Jedi-friendly space of all—a center of UNITY, LOVE and TRUTH, and a place where you re-charge your battery after a stress/activity-charged day in the Public sphere.

§442

The CONCEPT of Family. According to Jedi Science the "Family" is one of the major ethical-spiritual institutions in the State or Jedi Order—where "ethical-spiritual" means conducive to educating and transforming the isolated-natural P.I. EGO and Will into a Universal Free Jedi Will. For example in a Family you will care not only for yourself but for others as well, hence a self/other *unity* is nurtured. Further you will come to *see yourself in others*, thereby expanding your Will and being and your capacity to Love. The husband and wife, the spouses, enter into a "Union of Hearts" and become *One Person* (qua *the Absolute I*) and One LOVE. They sacrifice their wills not just to each other but to something higher, the Family and the Jedi Order. Moreover they share everything in common—responsibilities, capital and property; and in every object and possession each one sees not just himself reflected but also the other. In their children their Love and their Unity exists permanently and in *Objective* form—moreover the children, as inherently Jedi and the Force aware of itself, are of infinite value (as sacred-divine, if one prefers). It is the parents' responsibility to preside over their children's *education* to adult Jedi, to freedom and independence, where they will enter the wider Jedi Society and make their unique contribution and (perhaps) start a family of their own. This FACT indicates (i) that the destiny of the Family, from its logical or scientific side, is its *dissolution* and transition first to Civil Society and then to the State; and (ii) that a key principle of the Family dynamic and the parents' relation to children *is* that they must raise the children to *independence* and hence must cultivate a *free, non-dependent* relationship with them.

Parents should (i) not become *attached* in a way that hinders the free development of the child and puts unnecessary constraints and burdens (e.g., "guilt") on them; for example, "to pin their hopes on their children"—or force them to follow *their (the parents')* and not *the children's own* goals. And (ii) parents *must find an "identity" apart from their children* (it also helps to know that children are immortal and that death not final and that they will see them again). Above all parents are to cultivate their *own* independence and Jedihood—this is a major problem and danger in the Family today.

§443

Also, many families on your planet make the mistake of making no RULES and structure for children, that is, *initially* (as they make them up as they go along). The FACT is that children need Rules. "Rule" is from your Greek word "trellis," meaning to guide a seed, plant, or child to maturity. A "rule" is also a "universal" Law that is the *same* for everyone and which takes you to (+) Reality (as a *universal* and not a sense-singular) and also helps to focus a child's consciousness on (+). Children *want* to learn and grow and have a natural inborn drive to be Jedi. Just guide this Jedi seed or impulse by giving it tracks, rules, and trellises with which to grow.

Moreover the main focus of a Jedi Family is *not* just itself but also the community of Families, the Nation, and the entire World or Jedi Order.

§444

Hence you can simply begin by *declaring* your family a "Jedi Family," all the members taking the Jedi Oath together: "We exist to help realize and serve the Jedi Order and make it our #1 Priority, and to help each other become Jedi. We will do all we can and devote all our activities and energies to this supreme end."

§445

To be a most effective Jedi Family you should meet together at least *once* a day (say for Dinner)—have weekly Jedi Meetings (see §447, "The Jedi Society"), Jedi Teachings, Readings, Sharing, Films, and discussion of problems, etc. You can also *network* with other Jedi Families and Individuals, bring them to Dinner, etc—don't keep aloof and avoid fellowship with other families and people. Include a monthly community service project—say in a hospital, nursing home, etc. and get involved in your community. This will help you and your children *feel* Unity and the presence of the Jedi Order NOW.

—Also help to develop your child's "sixth sense," by which she can anticipate, avoid and preempt dangers and people, and become more attuned to the One Infinite Consciousness (or the God or Holy Spirit of your Religions).

§446

Employing Meditation and/or Prayer at Family Meetings (and beyond) for specific people (e.g., at work or school, etc) is very important, for we are all connected. This will also help family members to overcome *separation* and achieve *unity* with each other and the Force (the Universal *Absolute I* or "Higher Power"), and thus advance Jedi Education and becoming POINTED. Moreover parents can do the "Recognition Meditation" with each other, become deeply immersed in *UNITY,* and then take the Unity (Love-Healing) acquired out into the Public Sphere. For the ultimate goal is to unite the Private and the Public spheres, moving from (+|-) to (±).

Lastly, as regards the *EDUCATION* of children (and Parents), children should be enrolled in a Jedi School, and if none exist yet, parents (and friends) can lobby and work to start one in their community.

§447

START A JEDI SOCIETY or CLUB at YOUR UNIVERSITY or SCHOOL, which is dedicated to the Jedi Order, to Unity, and to Healing and "Balancing" the World and Yourself (the following may be modified).

The JEDI SOCIETY

- Meet once a week for one hour (Common Hour). (You can also meet with your Jedi friends on a daily basis, etc.)
- Each Jedi Meeting will be presided over by 2 (or 3) Facilitators on The Jedi Council, serving for one month terms and elected by all Jedi Members.

- Room: Circle format—Table or rug in the center with a Rose (= Love) and a Flashlight or Candle (= "Light-Saber," Knowledge) on it.

  ✳ The Purpose of the Jedi Society (on a poster or placard) is: To increase the UNITY—Awareness & Love—in ourselves and in the World. To heal the World, Be Jedi and help advent the amazing Jedi Order. To learn to see and feel the ONE in the Many (in people and things) via "I'm IN," "I'm IN You," and "You are IN me" meditations.
  ✳ Have a "Jedi Bulletin Board" (or weekly flyer hand-out) for announcements or postings ("need roommate/ bandmate," etc).

§448

TYPICAL MEETING & GENERAL JEDI AGENDA

First 5 minutes, coffee & schmooze; then "Call to Order" (take seats). Then a 40 minute Jedi Meeting in Three Parts. Last 15 minutes used to socialize, meet, plan weekend events with Jedi friends (movie, museum, music, etc). Again, the primary Purpose is to deepen UNITY on *all* levels (so physical & emotional healing = Unity will also occur).

Open with an Affirmation and a "three-minute UNITY Meditation" (sometimes even a 30 minute meditation, e.g., "I'm IN"; and even have a SILENT non-verbal meeting) and *Close* with an Affirmation: "In the Truth we are ONE, now and forever" (or sing a song).

§449

PART ONE: JEDI BUSINESS

- Read Last Meetings Minutes.
- New Members will Take "The Jedi Oath" (everyone joins in).
- We vote on our "CommUNITY Service Monthly Project"—To cheer up people/residents and create UNITY wherever we go. For example, Visit a nursing home, children's hospital, cancer ward, hospice, hospital's psychiatric ward (e.g., pick one person you sense can be helped and "Jedi"-heal him/her by extending and sharing your UNITY with them, others will be helped and become ONE too (Note: this is voluntary).

- Vote on and select our "Monthly Jedi Outing"—for bonding and UNITY (Art Exhibit at the Met, etc).
- All the *Star Wars* movies (and others) can be screened on Friday nights, with Discussion following.

The Object is to do things together and thereby increase the UNITY (Absolute I) in yourselves *and* in the Public Sector. You will discover that—due to your increased Light and Unity in the Dark Cave of e.g. New York City, London, or Rome—people will want to know more, and want to start a Jedi Society at their own school or workplace or church/temple/mosque.

§450

PART TWO: JEDI KNOWLEDGE

Do Either: **[A] Jedi Teaching**—Of Jedi Truths to learn, master, and use in your daily life and work. Or: **[B] Jedi Discussion**—Of any aspect of The Jedi Solution: The Jedi Code, The Jedi Order (7 Areas), or Jedi Truth: The Knowledge of The Force and the Proofs. (On Occasion there will be **Guest Speakers** giving talks on all varieties of Jedi Related Topics)

- For example: Today's Topic will be: "How to Start a Jedi Family or Household" or "How to 'Jedi' your goals, activities, and relationships (to gain more Unity, Power and Love in your life)" etc.
- Any Jedi Member can give a Talk (Read a Paper). Just submit it the week before to the Council Facilitators for their OK.
- No Topic is off-limits; you can discuss Race issues (on campus etc), difficult people, "control freaks," home-life: parents, siblings, roommates, Dating, etc, national or world problems, the Iraq War, national elections, etc.
- You can solve problems in the area of e.g. RELIGION: Help start a "Universal Jedi Sect" that includes *all* religions—"I'm a Jedi Muslim, Jew, Catholic, Sikh, even a Jedi Atheist, etc." Each one can find UNITY-scriptures in their religions Holy Book, etc. All can go together to a Muslim service, Jewish service, Sikh, Hindu, or Christian, etc. All can go to a Movie together, and discuss it afterwards. Create UNITY.

- Your university's Jedi Society can also spawn and link to "sister" Jedi Society's, on campus and other schools (e.g., a Jedi Business, Jedi Hindu, Jedi Political, etc, Club).
- You can also read and share powerful Jedi Truths & Wisdom as found in Novels, Poems, Songs, Films, Religious Texts of Mystics (Eckhart, Rumi, Vivekananda, etc); from writings of physicians, scientists like Schrodinger, Bohr, the Gaia Hypothesis, etc.

§451

PART THREE: JEDI PRACTICE

(Personal Challenges, Victory-UNITY Reports, UNITY-Exercises)

- **Personal Challenges**. For example: "I'm having trouble with my boyfriend, father." The Group listens, and then discusses it, brings their UNITY into the situation, etc.
- **Victory-UNITY Reports**. For example: "I finally left my abusive boyfriend (girlfriend)." "I aced my exam—got accepted to Queens College, Harvard." "My relationship with my parents is much improved." Etc.
- **UNITY-Exercises**. To facilitate awareness and realization of our eternal, indestructible Present UNITY, of The ONE Absolute I in all of us (as well as Physical and Emotional Healing).

  ✳ "PASS THE BOD." The act of surrender develops Trust and melts ego separation and defenses.
  ✳ "CIRCLE OF LOVE & LIGHT." One person stands in the center of the Circle. All say, "We love you" (verbal or whispered); diseases/stress will vanish, immune system strengthened 100-fold, since (+|-) is overcome and Universal Self is actualized.
  ✳ "LEADING THE BLIND." Close your eyes; someone leads you around. The result is Trust, dissolving the ego, and lowering the stress level.
  ✳ "PSYCHODRAMA." (will save on therapist bills) For example: "My father yells at me, it makes me sick." First: John plays the "father" role, and yells at you. You play yourself. Second: Then Switch. You play your father and yell at yourself (i.e., John). Etc. Put yourself in the Other's

shoes, whereby You "put on" your father's *power* ... and nullify it. Next time he yells, it will be no big deal (this also gives him the space, the opportunity to change his own behavior, etc).

❋ JEDI LIGHT SABER Meditations and Physical Exercise Sessions. For example, Jedi Aerobics, Jedi Tai Chi, etc.

§452

END OF MEETING

Fifteen Minutes: Free time, socialize, meet, plan weekend etc, coffee, cake etc.

Always end each Jedi Meeting with a Two-minute Meditation and Affirmation (for example): "May the Force/Truth be with us." "UNITY—now and forever."

"The Jedi Oath"

"I COMMIT 100% TO LIVING BY *THE JEDI CODE*: TO REALIZING *THE JEDI ORDER*, BEING ALL I CAN BE, AND USING *JEDI POWER ETHICS* TO HELP ME. *THE JEDI ORDER* WILL BE MY #1 PRIORITY IN LIFE AND EVERYTHING ELSE #2. I WILL ACT AS THOUGH THE GLORIOUS JEDI ORDER ALREADY EXISTS (IT DOES), AND THAT I AM ONE WITH ALL OTHER BEINGS: THEY LOVE ME AND I LOVE THEM UNCONDITIONALLY."

§453

There are Three Versions of "The Jedi Oath"—(1) One using Jedi language—"I commit to being a Jedi ..." (2) One without "Jedi" language—"I commit to being all I can be ..." and (3) One for those who want to use language from their own Religion/Faith—"I commit to being all that God-Allah-Jesus (not "The Force") wants me to be ..." Please suggest any changes you deem fit. You can also base it on the following version (also, commit it to memory, repeat it often (in groups), meditate on it, and frame it on your wall, refrigerator, or desk):

"I dedicate my life to healing the world and myself and realizing the glorious Jedi Order of fully *actualized* immortal Beings, I will commit and use all that I do, have, and am to this one supreme

Goal-End-Purpose. I will, alone and with others, re-program my mind-thoughts-life to accord with The Jedi Truth, and reject and eliminate error wherever I find it. The CAVE, the Ego-world of separate isolated Ego's, does not exist. Only The One exists. The One Infinite Consciousness, Jedi Order, Absolute I, which I am and share with all other Jedi, while still retaining my unique, indelible, eternal identity and Individuality. Using Jedi Power Ethics I will (1) never let a #2 take the place of my #1, and regard all #2's as *means* to #1, and as making up my Ministry. I will (2) by faith-belief-conviction-knowledge—*believe* The Truth and act as if *only #1—The One, The Truth, The Jedi Order—exists;* that #2, The Cave, etc., does not exist, has only phenomenal and not true Being. Hence I will regard all that goes on in #2 (below the Divided Line, in the Cave) as really taking place right now in #1, which is Reality. Meaning for example, that I will act as if all the people I meet and have relationships and sacred dealings with are *already living in #1, in* The Jedi Order and *in* their Jedi True Selves, and I will *Love* them accordingly and unconditionally—even or especially if they do not love me and treat me the same way."

§454

The Jedi Society of Our University Constitution

Article 1: *Name*

The name of the organization shall be The Jedi Society of [your university], hereinafter referred to as The Jedi Society.

Article 2: *Purpose*

The purpose of The Jedi Society is to help improve the quality of life in our multicultural university and world. That is, to help to diminish the level of mistrust, hate and fear in society, rooted in our **Differences**, and bring us closer to the world we all desire ("The Jedi Order")—a world of mutual understanding, love and respect, where humanity's full potential and creativity is able to flourish at its highest level. And to achieve this by increasing the **Unity**, awareness and love among club members ("Jedi") and, as a consequence, in our world-community, through the intelligent application of principles and methods drawn from philosophical, scientific, and spiritual traditions of the East and West and given a unique Lucasian *Star Wars* format for its universally acknowledged appeal and power to inspire a positive vision of the future [Etc.].

§455

START A JEDI GROUP AT YOUR WORK/OFFICE.
The CEO and Corporation (See *Part III: The Jedi Order, Business*)

If no Jedi Corporation exists yet you can start a Jedi Group at your office, with one or two friends, and meet at lunch or after work. It will grow. Share ideas with your Employer, he/she will use them as they will increase productivity and Unity within the company.

§456

WORK in the SEVEN AREAS. YOUR CONTRIBUTION.
Start a Jedi Charter School, a Jedi Sect in your religion, become a Jedi Artist-Musician-Entrepreneur. You can "Jedi" your current Job/work-life as in Jedi Power Ethics above. Be a Jedi Carpenter, Lawyer, Salesman and find ways to incorporate Jedi *Principles* of Unity into your Job. (See *Part III: The Jedi Order*, The Jedi Business Method).

§457

Additional help for Religions and the Religious/Spiritual: Jewish, Christian, Muslim, etc.

(1) "*Be* who you are," and agree with your Concept. For example, I am created in "the *Image* of God"; and "Image" means likeness, picture, template, blueprint, as specifications *of* God. Hence "I am just *like* God." He is infinite, so am I. He is divine, ditto, He is perfect, whole, etc. There is still a *difference. We* still have to be told, have to "wake up" from ignorance and the false concept-image of who we are and what we are capable of.

(2) Some may feel uneasy saying, "I am the Force [God], Truth, etc." If so say instead, "I am *One* with The Force/Truth/God—or even "I am *in* The Force, Truth, God" (and "The Force-Truth-God is in me"). *All* will lead to the same goal and experience of the Truth as a Jedi (U/I).

(3) As said, you can stay in your own Religion—but add Jedi "CD" Principles. *The Jedi Handbook* and Principles are above all designed to facilitate the UNITY of ALL RELIGIONS, PATHS, and so-called "CULTS"—and help overcome all hatred and divisiveness. Inevitably the religious on your planet will soon

be declaring e.g., "Oh, I am a "Jedi Muslim," "I am a Jewish Jedi," "I am a Jedi Christian." See *Part III: The Jedi Order, Religion.*

§458

Special Problems (in brief):

(1) Most people are "Other-Directed" or "Dark Side-Directed/ Controlled," hence cannot break from the control of Others (a mother, spouse), or act regardless of the consequences of what Others will say, think, do. Just keep going: you may need to separate for a while, move out—have a confrontation, say what you feel. It is *their* problem, etc. You *are* a Jedi.

(2) How to break the power of Addictions (to sex, porn, drugs, food, smoke): All are broken by "24/7" Jedi Power Methods (eventually). (1) Go cold turkey. Go to a cabin 6 months. Replace with Jedi Truths and friends, Do this 24/7, etc. (2) Use the so-called "Baptism in the Holy Spirit with tongues," the laying on of hands, etc. (3) Live in a Jedi (or spiritual) Retreat House, with Jedi people, in the Circle of Light, laying on hands, Pass the Bod, etc. Use a "Support Group." (4) See a Jedi Therapist. (5) If addicted to Fame or Wealth: Give away all and Become "homeless" for 1 year, etc (read books/see films like **Somerset Maugham's** *The Razor's Edge*). Ask yourself, "Can I survive and be happy if I lost all that I have?" (my children? Cf. "Abraham's sacrifice of Isaac").

(3) "Mental" Problems. All problems—neurosis, psychosis, bi-polar, schizophrenia, phobias, etc—begin with the *Tension* (or "double bind") between what you should be and can be (viz. a Jedi) and what you *are* (and the *hatred* towards the people who hold you back and keep you fixed in your Ego-role). For the cure see, *Part III: The Jedi Order,* Health: *The Jedi Therapist.*

§459

A TEST to see if you are a JEDI:

(1) A JEDI is complete (±), is BEING itself and LOVE itself; needs no one else to complete him or her. Has mastered both *Solitude*—can be alone forever (especially knowing his

INNER is all, and embraces all souls within itself; as he is in all other souls)—and *Society*—is comfortable in any group; no individual or group can affect/diminish his Being, Love, Serenity, ability to think, act, and so on.

(2) A JEDI has no FEAR—of death, pain, criticism, loss, abandonment, poverty, etc.

(3) A JEDI has mastered *Sex*. Has total control/mastery over any desire/urge coming from his natural Body-being.

(4) A JEDI is able to *be* in the midst of a "sense-saturated environment"—e.g. a construction site, mid-day, on ground level, inside, wood-sheet walls, dank-damp-smell-floor, wet concrete, macho-men around with jack-hammers, deafening sounds, etc—and be able to say: *"All This is absolutely NOTHING. Only IN or the INNER IS"*—and be able to "shut out all of the OUTER," Go IN, and Meditate (or do a math problem, recite Jedi proofs, etc).

CODA: CONGRATULATIONS. You are Now a JEDI.
Fully healed and immovably established
in ETERNITY—in The FORCE (±).
ENJOY and SERVE. You have the Highest Calling
and Most Sacred Responsibility of Advancing
and Maintaining the GLORIOUS JEDI ORDER
forever and ever, *World Without End.*

THE JEDI ORDER

Science

Education

Religion

Politics

Business

Health

Arts & Media

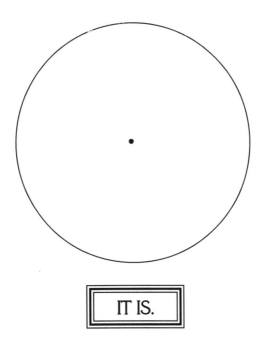

IT IS.

"YOU MUST UNLEARN WHAT YOU HAVE LEARNED."

My noble Jedi, we are healing your world together and solving its many problems by Global Jedi Education which will take everyone on your planet into the amazing JEDI ORDER. At this point you have by *Part I* achieved a knowledge of the FORCE, the TRUTH … that You are a JEDI and All are JEDI, and by *Part II* you have become and are now a *self-aware JEDI* (or soon to be). Here in *Part III* is where your main Work will be done, making everyone in every nation aware of their Jedihood and the Jedi Order by helping to Balance your Seven major planetary institutions:

Science, Education, Religion, Politics, Business, Health, and The Arts & Media

I, Obi-Wan will show you (1) What each institution really is—its CONCEPT, (2) What is wrong with it and How it sustains the Dark Side—its IMBALANCE, and (3) How to change or Balance it in the shortest possible time and thus accelerate the healing and education of all of your people into the glorious Jedi Order—the BALANCE.

INTRODUCTION

§460

Nobly-born JEDI, realize how important your work in the Seven Areas is, for these Seven have the greatest influence on planetary Consciousness—on beliefs and worldviews, on how your people perceive reality, themselves, the world, the universe, and life. Please now Meditate on these seven points:

§461

1. To be most effective in your work and service in changing your Seven Global Institutions you need a true understanding of each.

2. Know first that the true purpose of each institution is EDUCATION. It is to ongoingly educate your people—planetary citizens—into the JEDI ORDER and sustain the ORDER for all generations to come.

§462

3. As you now know, the JEDI ORDER already exists. IT IS. NOW. The UNITY or One Consciousness that all on your planet share and are ... IS A PRESENT FACT, A REALITY. Your people are not now experiencing and enjoying the Jedi Order because your Seven major global institutions are not teaching the Truth but rather the Dark Side of the Force, which prevents Healing and sustains your planet's crises.

4. This situation *has* to be changed. The Solution to your problems is simply to bring BALANCE to your institutions by having them teach and promote the LIGHT SIDE of the Force instead of the DARK SIDE. Only in this way will they be fulfilling their true purpose as vehicles of your people's EDUCATION and HEALING. You noble JEDI, will be the primary agent of this change. I, Obi-Wan, will show you exactly what has to be done and what you can do.

§463

5. There are *infinite possibilities* as to the way or ways you can serve. Only *you* can determine which is best for you. You may wish to serve in your present field or profession, or in a new one, or in both.

6. You should constantly keep in mind that the ideal world, the amazing JEDI ORDER, *exists Now.* Therefore *visualize* the Seven Areas, Science, Education, Religion, Politics etc., as if they were now functioning as they should be according to their true concept. This will help you in your work immensely.

7. And finally when your Seven Institutions are optimally functioning, within a short time, say one generation, what you cannot now possibly imagine will occur: *Your entire planet will be Jedi-educated and all of your problems and crises without exception will have ceased and "become history."*

§464

FIRST A BRIEF PICTURE OF THE JEDI ORDER.

Here I will provide for you a brief snapshot of the Jedi Order as fully actualized, where all Seven Areas are BALANCED and operational.

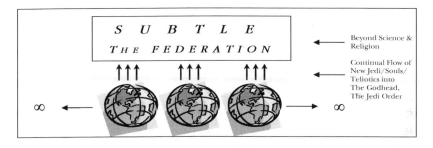

§465

As we saw before, the Jedi Truth makes evident that there are not one but *two* orders, "worlds," or spheres of existence, the physical (natural) and the subtle (spiritual), where ("-") predominates in the one and ("+") predominates in the other. This follows from the fact that *the two sides of the Force are inseparable* (±). Hence since the (+) side (the Self, Soul, Consciousness) *is eternal*, so must its counterpart be *eternal*, the (-) side (the Soul's Body, Matter, and the physical Universe).

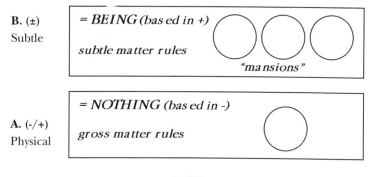

B. (±)
Subtle

= *BEING (based in +)*

subtle matter rules

"*mansions*"

A. (-/+)
Physical

= *NOTHING (based in -)*

gross matter rules

§466

Briefly: There are always new Babies or Jedi being born … and educated. Fully actualized Jedi or Jedi Masters are beyond the Law and Authorities pertaining to Earth (and other Planets or Spheres), which are only for Pre-Jedi. Jedi live in both worlds at once, the Physical and Subtle, and travel back and forth freely, etc. All Planets and Nations are Sovereign and are distinct geo-political States, and all leaders are Jedi. Science is open and Tribunal-governed; Religion exists but only for Pre-Jedi or Pre-*Telics*; and Education has many ways of educating Pre-Jedi to Jedi (for example *via* Politics, Business, Health, the Arts and Media). And as we said, Jedi (or "gods," *elohim*) are beyond both Science and Religion.

§467

The Three Modes or States of an Immortal Jedi:

(1) *The Absolute I,* with indestructible Subtle and Physical Bodies Unmanifested.

(2) *In the Subtle (or Astral) World,* with Subtle Body Manifested.

(3) *In the Physical World,* with Physical Body Manifested or fully Materialized.

§468

"SPACESHIP EARTH" DIAGRAM—The THREE "DECKS" or LEVELS

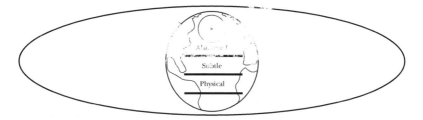

The relation of the three modes is best understood through the above "Spaceship Earth Diagram." Your beautiful planet Earth is to be conceived as a Spaceship with Three Decks or Levels, all of which *co-exist* and *interpenetrate*. The First is that of the PHYSICAL World, the Second that of the so-called SUBTLE or Astral World, and the Third is that of the POINT itself or the *Absolute I* which pervades the whole. Every educated or realized Jedi has achieved a complete self-awareness of this Third Deck or Level, and has become "The POINT aware of itself."

§469

A. *The Physical* **is the sphere/world where** Absolute Freedom reigns, all adults are Jedi enlightened and in the know (and beyond Science and Religion); where Jedi *education* informs all areas of Society and the schools so all children or pre-Jedi may optimally benefit—by love, kindness, and joy; where infinite esteem, creativity and all talents and powers are realized; and where the deepest most sincere, meaningful relationships (of friends and lovers) are experienced because everyone knows they will last forever and become deeper and deeper without end.

—Love reigns (the Self-Other problem is permanently resolved, as infinite imperishable Love). Hence there is no *fear* in society, in city streets, etc.

—Distinct geo-political states still exist where all government leaders are Jedi, and hence there are no wars because they have the principles and Jedi-will to resolve all disputes, their only mandate being to enhance and advance the qua   of eternal life for all Jedi in the Jedi Order; there is only co   ition among nations to do good (e.g., "interplanetar " and "   galactic" Olympics and competitions in Science and Art).

—The entire adult population are Jedi—teachers, parents, doctors, scientists, religionists, artists, etc.

—And there are eternal challenges (hence no boredom, etc), especially in relationships and friendships (e.g., Who will I see, date? Whose party to go to? Whose *Cause* shall I take up, contribute to? Etc). "Time" devoted to How to design my home, library, etc, giving gifts to others (people and nations), to bless my friends, etc. And there will always be "evil", the Dark Side, with new Jedi-babies eternally being born; but it never gets the upper hand. There is also much work to do on the "other side," i.e., in those regions of the Subtle Sphere corresponding to what is known on your planet as "hell," "bardos," purgatory, etc; work such as erasing *evil* and liberating Jedi spirits still bound by the Dark Side.

—Lastly, You can look forward to incredibly great and wondrous things, such as learning art-painting from Leonardo or **Michelangelo**, getting accepted as a student in his studio and special classes; meeting past historical Jedi Spirits and starting friendships, relationships with them, joining their Circle (helping them in *their* work of educating and saving their relatives and friends still trapped in the Dark Side); experiencing the delight of a Jedi Spirit inviting you to enter his/her Mansion in the Subtle Universe, for a day or week, for summer vacation, spring break, and then return to Earth; and designing your own Mansion (working on it for all eternity), collecting art, bedecking it with beautiful things, etc, etc.

§470

B. *The Subtle* is the sphere/world where Each person, Jedi or pre-Jedi, has their own Mansion. Note that the "resurrected" Jedi-Spirit-Body, as coming from the *negation* of physical nature (death), has all the properties of physical nature itself, and its own space-time continuum and galaxies. But a Jedi can custom tailor the contents of his Subtle Universe, as a "designer universe" or Mansion. As for the question *Where* is the Subtle-Astral World in relation to your present visible universe, the answer is this. The key point is that your universe is *phenomenal* only or is *Nothing in itself* (as **Kant** and the **A-Team** teach); which means that only the *Absolute I* (not in space-time, not extended) or the Invisible is ultimately REAL. So your Mansion or "attached Body-with-Universe" is solely an *inner*-based product or creation of what the **A-Team** calls the *Productive Imagination* (à la **Fichte**), that hence can be manifested or withdrawn at will. See also the "Spaceship Earth Diagram" above.

§471

There are Two Types or Conditions of Jedi in the Subtle Spheres: A Complete Jedi and an Incomplete Jedi.

Concerning a Complete Jedi, having all abilities and privileges:

—You are eternally in (or are) the Center of the Totality of All That Is (all else = 0).

—Now, you can manifest *first* your (Subtle) Body, existing only for you, your "subtle senses," *second* your entire environment or universe (like in a "dream"), *for yourself* (cf. your **Leibniz's** Monad). Note that in a "dream" you have no control over your Productive Imagination. It "does what it wants," etc. But a Jedi has *complete control* over his or her Productive Imagination.

—Or you can manifest your (Subtle) Body (with or without your universe) *for those in the Subtle Sphere* (and "By invitation only"). Or you can manifest your (Physical) Body *for those in the Physical world.*

Concerning An Incomplete Jedi:

—You are in a condition of Self/Other non-union or, in the language of your religions, "evil" or "in sin." The same rules and structure as for a *Complete Jedi* apply, but you are not aware of them.

—There are three basic levels or states: the Lowest: pain, torment; the Middle: less so; the Highest: some. But though these Jedi are incomplete or "evil" they are still the Force, the Truth—but the Force led astray, due to ignorance (and will). Hence they *are* redeemable and destined to become Complete Jedi (as your scriptures and your **St. Paul** teach, e.g., "In the end God will be *All in All*").

§472

Concerning "death." The "dead" at the time of death are thrust into the Subtle-Invisible world, and if unprepared they are disoriented and initially quite frightened. What happens is that their (subtle) *Productive Imagination* ("dream work") immediately activates in order to "fill in/up the void" or lack of content, due to the lack of a physical body and physical senses; they see and experience "heaven and hell" states as in a cinema house in their Mansion, and initially have no *control* over their Productive Imagination. After a time they adjust. Jedi Spirits (complete and incomplete) however will come to aid and acclimate them, show them their "new home" and help them to slowly master their Productive Imagination (or Mansion), etc.

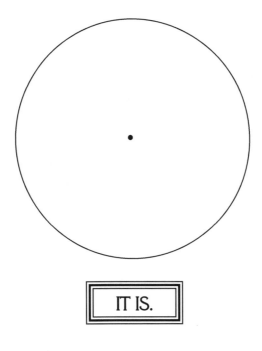

IT IS.

SCIENCE

We saw in *Part I* that the true healing of your world and yourself is attainable only by the knowledge of *who you really are*; this is achieved only by a knowledge of the Force (the ONE Reality-POINT) and of yourselves as Jedi, the Force's knowledge of *itself*. And to be a Jedi and be healed is for you to have seen through the illusory *separation* of Self-and-Other and have realized your Infinity, Eternity and Freedom. This "healing" or alignment to the Truth and your True Self, which alone is True Education, is impossible unless *you know what the Truth is,* hence unless you possess *True Jedi Science—the Science or Knowledge of the Force.*

SCIENCE SUMMARY

(A) CONCEPT. The chief purpose of Science is Educational—to take your people into the POINT, the JEDI ORDER. True Science as we saw in *Part I* is JEDI SCIENCE or the Knowledge of the FORCE in all its detail. It is simply the study of the FORCE, the one Being that alone exists, in its Movement or process of self-actualization into JEDI and the JEDI ORDER. Science is the Force's knowledge of Itself, of the WHOLE in its Necessity. It derives from: (1) *POINT:* As what alone exists and is *true* eternal Reality—namely, the One Consciousness or CONCEPT, which is true because of POLARITY. We simply study the stages of its Becoming. (2) *ETYMOLOGY:* "Science" derives from your Greek word "episteme" and Latin "scientia" and means *Knowledge* that is certain, necessary, universal and forms a Unity or System. It is not "opinion" (*doxa*), etc (as it is with your own sciences).

(B) WRONG/IMBALANCE. Your science is NOT *true* Science, i.e., a science or knowledge of *what IS*, rather it is a science of *what IS NOT, namely* the CAVE, Matter (-), the sense-world. It is immersed in the Dark Side (+|-), in the Old Paradigm and "M/C" (Matter over Consciousness) worldview which erroneously believes that the OUTER is alone reality and is ignorant of the INNER. It teaches the error that YOU are only a Body-Ego and death is *final*, i.e., NIHILISM and the meaninglessness of life. Moreover it keeps you in EGO and prevents UNITY, Healing, and the Jedi Order from manifesting, and thus perpetuates war, hate, greed, and despair. The New *Paradigm Shift* from "M/C" to "C/M" (Consciousness over Matter) is indeed occurring in the work of **Grof-Schrodinger-Laszlo-Einstein-Bohm-Bell-Wolf-Goswami** and others. But this is not enough as only *the Knowledge of the Force (±)* can prove and establish "C/M" on a permanent basis.

(C) BALANCE. Switch from p-science to Jedi Science and demote p-science by passing laws and instituting the "Great Science Debates." Your scientists should rise above "specialization" and become *generalists* or Jedi Master Scientists.

§473

[A] CONCEPT. First my Padawan, be mindful above all that of the Seven of your planetary institutions only Science provides the highest knowledge in and of the Universe and Society. It is the absolute final authority (even above Religion) in matters concerning Truth. And since we have discussed Science and its Concept extensively in *Part I* our treatment here can be brief.

§474

The *purpose* of all Seven Global Cultural Institutions is to ongoingly "Educate" your people into the Truth by making them aware of the POINT, the One Infinite Consciousness at the core of the Jedi Order that already exists, and teaching them How to live in Eternity and the Eternal Present. Science, that is, *true* Jedi Science, fulfills this supreme purpose since it *is* nothing other than occupation with and study of the Jedi Order or the Force fully actualized, that is, the Single *UNITY* or *CONCEPT (Begriff)*

> "The highest, most concentrated point [of Logical Science] is the *pure Personality* which … no less *embraces and holds everything within itself."* **Hegel**

which alone exists and *contains everything within itself*—and of the *stages* of its actualization. Hence to successfully study Jedi Science is *at the same time* to be taken into the Jedi Order itself. SCIENCE is extremely important especially at this time in your planet's History since it carries great authority and is deferred to by many in matters of Truth.

§475

Be mindful that the One Jedi Science though essentially complete is open to unlimited expansion as to "particulars." Hence the new findings, universals, theories and laws by your own scientists will be ongoingly incorporated into Science. A *Science Committee* that meets periodically to evaluate these new findings for inclusion into the One Science will of course be formed in the near future.

Here we will see clearly how it is that Science *educates* and has the singular goal and effect of lifting Consciousness from the Dark Side, dis-Unity and multiplicity to *UNITY* and the Light Side (±).

§476

My noble Jedi, a glance at the meaning of the word "science" is enough to show you that what passes for science in your galaxy is *not* in fact Science; and because it misrepresents Reality it is harmful to your people and a major obstacle to their healing and the Jedi Order. "Science" comes from your Greek "*episteme*" (and Latin "*scientia*") and means minimally "knowledge" that is certain, necessary and universal and the opposite of "opinion" (your Greek "*doxa*") which may or may not be true or certain. True science therefore is a knowledge of *what truly is* (not of accidental, contingent features of reality) and in its *necessity*, hence *of what cannot be otherwise than it is* (as your Jedi **Plato**, **Aristotle**, and **Hegel** teach). In the ideal case all knowledge should form an interconnected Whole, a Unity or a System where no *item* of knowledge is unrelated to the others; and a single principle should be responsible for this Unity (and for the systematic derivation of all items). Furthermore, it is absolutely necessary that the knower (the scientist) and the known (her object) *coincide*, for if the two were radically different you would know the object only as it was "for you" but not as it truly is "in itself."

§477

The "Object" of Science or Knowledge is essentially ONE or one thing and not many, namely, "the Force." This one thing (the Truth, the ONE Reality) is at the same time a WHOLE that has various parts or stages that are involved in its timeless process of becoming or self-actualization. That there exists only ONE thing we *know* both from the PROOF of the Force (in *Part I*) and from the *Introduction to Science*. There it was shown that the *separation* between Consciousness and its Objects is an illusion and, further, that the only true Object (the only one to survive Reason's scrutiny) and the only True Reality is *Consciousness itself* and its UNITY. We call this UNITY, "Being's or the Force's *Knowledge* of Itself"—aka Jedi or the Jedi Order. Hence true Science is the study of the WHOLE of What IS and not of separate PARTS in their separation and disconnection from the Whole (as in your own sciences). Also as one of your Jedi, **Henri Bergson**, said: *"The Universe is a machine (template) for the making of Gods (Jedi)."* Accordingly, Science can be viewed simply as the study of this great "Machine" (or Template) or single Whole whose end-product is the amazing eternal race of Jedi, the Force or Whole fully actualized and aware of Itself; something your own scientists are beginning to glimpse in their "Gaia" and "Anthropic" theories.

§478

What follows then is that Science becomes the study of a single WHOLE—that is, of the vanishing-transitional *Stages* involved in the becoming of this One Being's Knowledge of Itself—essentially those of Nature and "Man" or History. Hence Science is necessarily a **Unity** or **System** in which all of its parts are interconnected since they are all parts of One Thing. Hence as said, to know any one thing or part you must know its place in and connection with the Whole (its antecedent and consequent) and with all other parts.

As also stated, *it is the Knower that is the Known,* or the Scientist and his Object are *one and the same*—as your own quantum physicists have realized, for *your* Knowledge of the Force is at once *the Force's* Knowledge of Itself. There *is* nothing but Being and its Knowledge of Itself, and this Being's Knowledge of Itself *is* precisely SCIENCE. The *subject* of Science and the *object* of Science coincide.

§479

THE SYMBOL OF SCIENCE

In brief: As we saw in *Part I,* (1) There is One Indivisible Whole, which to study we take apart, hence *the Sciences of Logic, Nature, and Jedi.* (2) We study *first* the OUTER aspect of the Whole (Nature and its Forms) and *then* the Force's INNER aspect (Jedi-Spirit and its Forms) as Nature's Truth. As we advance up the ladder of stages and forms, the earlier stages are taken up into the later ones, the last containing all previous ones— namely *the Absolute I* or the *CONCEPT* (studied in *Logic*), the Truth or the Force aware of Itself *and* containing the State *within* itself and Nature *within* the State—*the Jedi Order.* So at the end of the process and Science everything, all multiplicity, is concentrated and brought together into the single *UNITY* we Jedi call *The BALANCE of the FORCE.*

§480

Jedi Science therefore is based on the BALANCE (±)—the BALANCED FORCE, or the Truth *as* Polarity and the Unity of Opposites, both in the *Whole* and in the *Parts*. In the *"WHOLE"* we have the Balance (±) where Consciousness (Thought) and Matter are in *unity* and can never come apart—a unity *in* which *Consciousness* trumps Matter and as "Being for itself" is *all reality*, while Matter is known to be *nothing* as a "Being for another." And in the *"PARTS"* we have the Balance (±) via the *Method* of the Concept, "U-P-I" (see *Part I*) and the ascending grades of Polarity.

§481

[B] WRONG/IMBALANCE. Now noble Jedi

we shall contrast your sciences with true Jedi Science for a clearer understanding of why yours teaches the Dark Side and error and needs to be corrected. It is easy to see that your empirical "science" (or "p-science") cannot be true science as it contains none of the features of True Science and thus condemns itself to being mere "opinion." This is because its "scientific method" as based on the senses (the empirical) can achieve neither *certainty*, necessity, nor universality as a new finding or sense-datum can always invalidate its reputed "knowledge." More pointedly, its basic "materialist" world-view and unproven assumptions promote "nihilism" and destroy the hope and best possibilities for your global society and youth.

§482

To begin with your sciences are *not true Science or a Knowledge of What IS* but rather a "knowledge" of What *IS NOT* and, as a result, they are steeped in Error and the Dark Side of the Force and give an untrue concept of "Man" or yourselves and the universe. This keeps your people and world in *separation* and *multiplicity* (in interminable Ego and Group conflict) and ignorant of the *Unity* underlying everything—the only Solution to your Problems. Your sciences are a "knowledge" of What *IS NOT* because they recognize as Reality only the (-) or Dark Side of the Force; that is, "the CAVE" or the world of the senses and material *objects* in space and time (measurable and quantifiable), which as we saw are in fact *nothing* or What *IS NOT*. This error of theirs is known as *MATERIALISM* and holds that Consciousness, Mind, "Spirit," Thought, and all that is "immaterial" is in the end *reducible* to Matter or energy. This is absolutely false and leads to *Nihilism*, as was shown in the PROOFS presented in *Part I*.

§483

Secondly, there is no *Unity* or principle for the *Unity* of all your Sciences and no HOLISM or SYSTEM where everything is derived from *One* Principle. Your sciences are thus in radical disconnection from each other such that each one studies its own sphere or region of Being, of the Whole, in *isolation* from the others. They do not know that there is only One Reality, the Force, and that everything and all regions of Being are necessary Stages of the One Force in its process of Self-actualization.

> "If *our subject* be removed, the entire character of *objects* and all their relations in space and time, nay even *space and time themselves, would vanish* ... they are mere appearances and *nothing* in themselves, and can exist only in us." **Kant,** *Critique of P.R.*, B59.

Thus your scientists are totally immersed in and limit themselves to the OUTER or Nature and have *no* awareness of the INNER, the realm of True *Reality*—a view which they impart to Education at a terrible cost. Not only do they focus exclusively on the OUTER or Nature, but because of their ignorance of the CONCEPT they erroneously regard *quantitative determination* as the paradigm for all other sciences, including the "human (Jedi) sciences" such as anthropology, psychology, and political science. Hence the true order and valuation of the two domains is inverted, for as we Jedi know and have proven in *Part I* it is the INNER that has absolute primacy over the OUTER, *and not the reverse*.

§484

Thirdly, lacking the true concept and method of Science, each Science erroneously regards its subject-matter and objects as *Beings in their own right*, i.e., in a *static* rather than in a *dynamic* and "transitional" manner—namely as fluid "Moments" or stages in a single process whose proximate truth is the next higher stage, and ultimate truth the final or highest Stage—the Concept or Force aware of itself *as* the Jedi Order. In particular, as we noted, objects in the

OUTER domain—material physical entities, with mass, position, momentum, etc—are given greater reality than those pertaining to the INNER domain, which is a total error. Further, due to their ignorance of Polarity and of the truth that Consciousness and the *Absolute I* (+) is *outside* the space-time continuum or *a priori* and *transcendental*—your scientists believe that they, that human beings, are nothing but their material Brains and thus are *in* and wholly restricted to the world of space and time, a very myopic and false view.

§485

Finally they believe that since you are only a Body-Ego and the separation and isolation between yourself and others is permanent (+|-), there is no real *UNITY* (or *LOVE*) possible between yourself and the Other. Not only does this view lead to hopeless "depression"—as does nihilism and the view that death is final—but it leads to the primal *Self against Other, Us against Them* situation and *fear* dynamic at the root of all anti-social behavior (as exemplified in Columbine, Virginia Tech, and Sandyhook) and of all hate, war, greed, and murder. The view of the *other* as a mere limit and *negation* of yourself necessarily harbors the desire to *negate* or eliminate the Other (cf., the events of "9/11")—rather than love and cherish the Other by recognizing the true *Unity* of Self *and* Other that is LOVE itself and the only reality. This view is harmful in the extreme and the cause of all your problems as it keeps separation and the Dark Side (+|-) in force and makes *healing* (of Self/Other, Us/Them) and *unity* impossible. The inability to resolve the Self or Ego/Other problem is also the root cause of all diseases—mental and physical—and of the inability to cure them. We will see my Padawan in *Part III: The Jedi Order, "Health,"* that the *Absolute I* is the only true and *permanent* cure of dis-ease. Also see *Part I:3* for more on the defects of your sciences as compared to true Jedi Science, and also *Part I:3-4* for the *Refutation of Materialism*, the prime error of all your sciences.

§486

Before moving on to the matter of How to BALANCE your sciences it will be just and also instructive to indicate some of their "positive" features and contributions.

1. Even though in their present form they are not Science and do not provide KNOWLEDGE in the strict and true sense, the

"knowledge"—theories, laws, partial insights—your sciences do contain has been a great benefit to your people in the practical "real world" sphere and with respect to its application or "technology"— namely, in medicine, engineering, space flight, satellites, computers, and communications.

2. Another important role they play concerns their empirical investigations and findings which provide in part the *Content* of the *Jedi Science's of Nature* and *Jedi/Mind*. That is, your sciences perform the service of gathering and subsuming the raw manifold of sense-individuals under *Universals*, which Jedi Science then subjects to its Method, the Concept or Truth, thereby giving them their true logical form and significance and incorporating them into itself.

3. On one of its interpretations your Quantum Physics has the merit of coming close to the Truth of *Polarity* (and not only in **Niels Bohr's** Unity of Opposites principle) that the Observer *is* the Observed (and not just affects it), that at the base of Matter or Energy is *Consciousness* or *Thought* and, further, that Consciousness/ Thought is the *ultimate Reality*, and not Matter. The main defect here is that Quantum Physics, in contrast with Jedi Science, is unable to *prove* this Truth in a conclusive manner, which again is due to the limitations of its "empirical" method.

§487

4. The same is true of the GAIA Hypothesis and ANTHROPIC Principle in your cutting-edge contemporary science. *Gaia* correctly holds that "Man," i.e. your *consciousness* and *thought* is not a fluke aberration of the universe but rather essential and ingredient to it. That is, "our" consciousness (yours and ours) is really the Earth's and the Universe's consciousness of *itself*—"how you and I think is how the Earth (and the Universe) thinks, etc." *Anthropic* holds that the universe and its complexity is *fine-tuned* for life and consciousness, i.e., for you/Man. Hence you are not *accidents*, rather you belong here. In Polarity language: (+) and (-) go together and are inseparable—you cannot have the physical-matter/energy (-) side of the Universe or Totality without its polar opposite side, *Consciousness/Thought* (+). And *this* is the real reason why the "constants" of nature and the universe *are* as they are and not otherwise.

§488

[C] BALANCE. Since your "sciences" as they are are not true Science or Knowledge they must be replaced by true Jedi Science, that is, subsumed and incorporated into Jedi Science. *The age of specialization or being a specialist in science is now at an end.* For you cannot claim to have Knowledge of a specific thing or subject *unless* you have a knowledge of the Whole. Every true Scientist *must* become a GENERALIST, otherwise he or she remains only a "Pre-Scientist."

§489

The situation on your planet is critical since (1) your "sciences" and their Dark Side (+|-) materialist worldview is *very harmful* and must be dealt with. (2) Furthermore your "sciences—and the very word "Science"—have tremendous power and authority in all areas of your global society. (3) Finally it is true that while *some* in the community *may* see the Truth as regards Science in this *Jedi Handbook,* the majority will most likely resist the changes that must come being *unwilling* to give up the authority and standing they presently enjoy. But the fact remains that they *are* not and *may* not call themselves, *Scientists,* just as their "science" in its current form is *not* Science.

Therefore action must be taken—for the quicker the change the better and the faster your planet will be Healed. It is extremely urgent that you immediately reduce the status and authority of your "sciences" to their proper limits. As in the "Education" section the quickest way to do this is to *"start a movement to demote p-science."* The ultimate goal is for Congress or Parliament to pass a Law requiring that p-science no longer be called "Science" (perhaps "pre-science" or "technology-science," etc) and at a minimum allow a *place* in Society for True Jedi Science, which in any case *will* assume its rightful place in due time.

§490

Educators, Principals, Teachers, Professors et al who read this Handbook and are so persuaded can begin the Movement— especially in Pilot Jedi-Schools—by saying, "We no longer recognize p-science as Science. We find their assumptions and world-view to be unfounded, misguided and detrimental to the health of our students and the wider Society. And here is the Proof, etc."

The same parties and students at all levels can write letters to Congressmen-women and trustees of colleges, etc, demanding the needed changes (the website is: www.ussenate.gov). All can start websites, etc. Parents and Teachers can lobby school Boards and petition the Departments of Education and Science. The movement will start on a grass-roots level, and then ultimately "The Great Science Debates" will convene and permanently resolve the issue.

§491

Above all you need on your planet Jedi Scientists or Real Knowers who can make the case, argue successfully, and defeat counter-arguments. These Jedi can have a powerful effect in their classrooms, at Science colloquiums, through books, lecture tours, and especially in Jedi Charter Schools and Universities.

§492

We strongly recommend that those "scientists" who really wish to be true Scientists—and really *KNOW* and not just opine and really make a difference in the world and advance its healing—take the following steps and dedicate themselves to them:

1. Stop what you are doing, and clear your head—separate or distance yourself from your present discipline and its mind-set-assumptions, methods, goals, constraints, etc. Take one or two months off in order to revolutionize your thinking and worldview, and reconstitute and re-prioritize your life for a complete make-over. Ideally you should change your surroundings, geographically live in a different city, in the country, etc; if you simply cannot, then do this mentally.

2. Refashion your life in accordance with *The Jedi Code*, Part II. Make the #1 priority of your life being a Jedi (or, which is the same, the Jedi Order)—and *not* being a "Scientist per se." Make everything else you do (even the goal of being a Scientist) #2, and in the service of #1.

3. So your primary Goal is to *be* a Jedi, i.e., to realize that you already *are* a Jedi (the Force, the Whole of What IS, aware of itself). You may encourage yourself and strengthen your commitment and conviction with the words of your quantum physicist **Schrödinger** ("your true self is the whole, all in all") et al. The fact is that you *cannot* be a true Scientist or Knower without having reached this *realization* unique to a Jedi, that is, the Knowledge of the Force, of the Truth of the BALANCE, the Unity of Opposites and of your *Absolute I* or Consciousness which is all Reality.

§493

4. You can do this—become Educated to Jedi—by the methods given in *The Jedi Code*, especially in *Jedi Power Methods*, which include the study of SCIENCE itself, the *Introduction* and *Science* proper (e.g., **Hegel's** *Phenomenology*). There are several ways to reach the Goal of Absolute Knowing, POINTEDNESS, and the BALANCE. Of course you may and should study (on your way to the goal) Jedi Science itself and its contents and strive to familiarize yourself with the WHOLE: *Logic, Nature,* and *the Jedi Order.* In this regard you can study for example *Part I: The Jedi Truth, 2,* on *Jedi Science* to help you in this and, above all, master the principle of POLARITY.

5. Once you are a Jedi you will have the Master Key to understand all of Science (Logic, Nature, and Jedi) and really KNOW. It is well first to study and master LOGIC— which gives the *Method* of doing Science and of KNOWING, and then the other two branches, Nature and Jedi.

§494

6. You will then be a *True Scientist* and in fact a *Generalist* (not a specialist, which you are currently). So you can in addition still have a "specialty," or more than one, for example your present discipline (chemistry, biology, psychology, etc).

7. Then you will be equipped to make a difference in Science and in the world. It is entirely up to you how you wish to serve and use your Jedi talents and knowledge.

Also: Given the case where you choose to remain in your field (e.g. molecular biology) and are also teaching at a University and wish to "Jedi" your field and present it in true Scientific fashion *and there is no Jedi Textbook available yet* (other than help from the **A-Team's**, e.g., **Hegel's** Science)—*What do you do?* Briefly: (1) *If you are already a Jedi* you will know exactly what to do: First you present the WHOLE of Science, explaining what it is and the *place* your "subject" occupies (as *transitional*) within this whole, and then you order the contents of your subject according to the CONCEPT and Method of Reason (from abstract to concrete, U-P-I), spotlighting *items* which express Polarity and the Truth. (2) *If you are not yet a Jedi* then do the above as best you can, and if challenged by colleagues/students you can respond by using the PROOFS and arguments in this *Handbook*.

§495

Scientists in any case—if they really wish to *be* scientists and attain to a true knowledge of the universe—should seriously occupy themselves with Philosophy, i.e. with Metaphysics and its Truths and Principles. Above all, as stated, they should master the Principle of Polarity: the Unity-of-Opposites, *Identity-in-difference*, or the *BALANCE*. They will then discover they can finally comprehend such things as:

§496

(a) *Consciousness*—its necessity, nature, and "emergence" from Nature (Matter, Externality, Multiplicity). For as *Polarity* teaches: "no inner, no outer," or "no thought (non-extension), no matter (extension)."

(b) *Entanglement* (cf., **Bell's** Theorem and **Alan Aspect's** work), which is a phenomenon in which *two* originally connected particles (or photons) that subsequently become *separated* by a vast distance (even by light-years) can still be "in communication" with each other—for example, if you touch one (or give it an "up" spin), the other is *at once* touched (or given a "down" spin).—Hence, as if *space* or distance meant nothing or was not ultimately real, but ideal (which it is); and as if *time and motion* too were nothing or were only ideal and no real obstacle or barrier (also true). This follows from the FACT that the One Apriori POINT which alone IS is indivisible and occupies/pervades *all* points of space and time *at once*. In the words of your physicist **Fritjof Capra**: "**Bell's** theorem [of the *"nonlocal"* *instantaneous connection* of particles] supports **Bohr's** position and proves rigorously that **Einstein's** view of physical reality as consisting of independent, spatially separated elements is incompatible with the laws of quantum theory. In other words, **Bell's** theorem demonstrates that *the universe is fundamentally interconnected, interdependent, and inseparable.*" And,

(c) *Mitosis/Meiosis in Embryology:* that is, cell-replication and duplication, *from* a single cell, a ❋ gamete, or union of egg and sperm, *to* ❋❋ two cells, *to* the whole organism; and chromosome replication et al— something that is comprehensible only by the CONCEPT and its inner necessary development.

§497

The sciences in any case *must become ONE*—that is, *SCIENCE*—which reflects the One Truth and the One Reality. Also see the "Unity of Science" movement by going to www.unityofscience.org, which is based in England.

Lastly, "Science" should not be the enemy of "Religion" and they should not be adversaries. Rather Science should be one with Religion and work together with Religion in order to heal the world (in this regard you may contact such foundations as: www.templetonfoundation.org and www.metanexus.org).

§498

To sum up: What is *wrong* with your planet's "Science" and How does it teach and promote the "Dark Side of The Force"?

(1) Through its main assumption: *Materialism,* which believes that only the Dark Side (-), Matter, the OUTER (the sensible, measurable in space and time) is Reality, not the INNER (+). This is false and results in false/distorted views of "Man" (or yourself as a "mortal-chance-animal species" and not an immortal Jedi), the Universe, "God," and the purpose of life. It also keeps you in your finite Ego (+|-) and prevents healing

and realizing your full potential (±). Hence it is ignorant of the Force and Polarity and why the Universe exists in the first place; that matter is nothing and that consciousness or You as a JEDI are alone Reality, eternal and immortal.

(2) It is not SCIENCE, which is the knowledge of the Whole, hence *Holistic* as a unity and organic system containing cognitions that are certain and necessary. It is only Opinion, a vast disconnected assortment of facts and theories, with no principle of *unity* possible, and this because its "scientific method" is *sense*-based and mired in multiplicity and contingency, and not Reason-based in Unity and necessity. At best it is "technology"; and also for the most part capable of being incorporated into true Jedi Science by means of the CONCEPT.

§499

What can you do to correct or "Balance" the problem?

(1) Simply replace your planet's "sciences" with JEDI SCIENCE. That is, Demote them from being called "Science" to "Pre-Science" (by Passing Laws, etc) and bring them under and within the One True Jedi Science.

(2) Make people aware of their harmful effects (that their errors and materialism breeds nihilism and hopelessness): inform parents, students, teachers, your boards of education, trustees and officials. Start a grass-roots movement.

(3) Expose their errors using Jedi Science and Jedi Reason's Proofs (e.g. the refutation of materialism). Debate with their "scientists" in universities and conventions, etc.

(4) Learn and master Jedi Science. Teach Jedi Science in Jedi Charter Schools and Universities.

(5) And your *scientists themselves* in their own respective fields can help. They can start using Jedi Science (Metaphysics) Principles in their own research and teaching. And they can become *Master Scientists* themselves and strive for *a view of the Whole;* they can switch from being a Specialist to a Generalist (Master) and study and promote *Jedi Absolute Science.* Becoming a *Master Scientist* is not difficult—for to "Know Thyself" (the *microcosm*) fully is at once to know the Whole cosmos (the *macrocosm*).

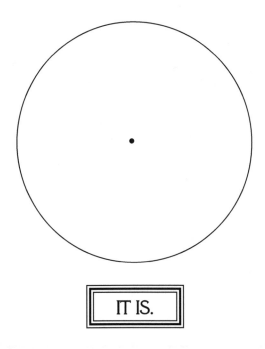

IT IS.

EDUCATION

True Education is Taking everyone into the POINT, the Knowledge of The Force (±) as JEDI and the JEDI ORDER. We have already treated the bulk of this section's content in *Part I: The Jedi Truth*, especially What Jedi-Formal Education is, K-12/University. Here our main concern will be with Imbalance, or Why your Education is in fact "mis-education."

EDUCATION SUMMARY

(A) CONCEPT. The chief purpose of Education as of all institutions is of course, Educational—to take your people into the POINT or The JEDI ORDER. It is the most powerful Institution since if done correctly it can elevate entire generations, entire nations into the Jedi Order. Education's Goal is to make you a JEDI or the Force's knowledge of Itself AS a JEDI. "Education" derives from: (1) *POINT:* Since *this* is the Truth and what alone exists, the supreme purpose of Education can only be for all individuals to achieve a Knowledge of it. And (2) *ETYMOLOGY:* "E-ducation" derives from your Latin "e-ducare" meaning to be led out of Ignorance into Knowledge. Hence Education must be based on Jedi Science, the complete knowledge of the Truth. Moreover its curriculum is HOLISTIC as it is the study of One Thing and has One GOAL: to be a Jedi and to transition from the OUTER to the INNER domain of Reality.

(B) WRONG/IMBALANCE. Your Education is in fact "mis-education" since it has the wrong Goal and concept of Education, of what it is and is for, is not Healing your people, and has no Unity in its curriculum. As based on the p-sciences it focuses on the OUTER and not on the INNER realm. As a result it disseminates false concepts of "Man" and Reality and is NIHILISTIC.

(C) BALANCE. You must switch to Jedi Education via Jedi Charter Schools and Jedi Universities. Teachers, students and parents can strike and petition the Board of Education and the Department of Education; and Laws can be passed that demote p-science and cease to subsidize dark side mis-education.

---

§500

[A] CONCEPT.
Noble Jedi, here I will merely give you a short summary of what I have said in Part I: The Jedi Truth under Global Jedi Education. (1) True Education—from your Latin "e-ducare"—takes you from Ignorance and the Dark Side (+|-) to the Knowledge of the Force, the Light Side and the POINT. (2) Education

in its entirety and in all its ramifications has only one Supreme GOAL: for the student to be a JEDI—which includes Learning How to Live in Eternity and How to be a citizen of the glorious eternal Jedi Order. This one Goal is what unifies all the Courses taken and makes them absolutely relevant to the student, each one contributing to the same one Goal. (3) Hence education is not a Means (to a comfortable life, money, a good job) but rather an END—the #1 END of all Life and Existence. (4) The Curriculum is based on Jedi Science and is thus HOLISTIC, where all courses are interconnected parts of a single WHOLE. The Curriculum is INNER and not OUTER focused—and the OUTER and the natural sciences are viewed only as a "means" to the INNER, to the POINT and the Force aware of Itself. Moreover the student, as a Jedi, is essentially this WHOLE itself that he or she studies and comes to know; and since she studies essentially herself, her interest and excitement is total. Lastly (5) Education and Religion have the *same Goal* of taking you from EGO to JEDI and into the Jedi Order and REALITY, by activating the UNIVERSAL within the student. The student's EGO and Natural Will (-) is transformed when she *focuses* on the Universal, the ALL-POINT, and surrenders to *Pure Self-Consciousness or the Truth.*—That is, when she *Transcends the Senses (+|-) and becomes more and more cognizant of and at home in the One Apriori POINT (±) located in the very center of the Sense-Material Realm.* It is because of this FACT that heads of *Schools, Churches,* and *religious institutions* can work together to coordinate their curricula and thereby strengthen and accelerate the *education* of their students.

> "Education simply retraces the path of Spirit's self-realization and gives a Knowledge of the Reason behind the State and its Forms. Through it one's Subjectivity is aligned to the historical progress of mankind and his Age. [Moreover] *The curriculum is the mediation of human character and will and its absorption into the wider Social Ethos.*"
> Hegel

§501

Now, in the *global or general* sense—the sense in which *all* seven institutions (not just "Education" per se) can be said to "educate"—"education" is a process of transformation you undergo that, as your Jedi **Plato** teaches, takes you out of ignorance into the knowledge of *the Truth* about who you are, your true identity or Jedi

Nature, powers and possibilities, and what and why the world or Reality is. Education is hence an INVERSION process from the *Stage Two* Dark Side to the *Stage Three* Light Side of The Force that takes you into the Jedi Order. It is a transformational process whereby the *separation* between yourself and the World—everything else "not-you"—is canceled, and the world becomes *idealized* and reduced to consciousness or your *Self* (not your Ego). That is *You*, as a Jedi and the Force aware of itself, become infinite, eternal, and all reality and capable of living in eternity *to the full*. It is a process achievable by ONE-POINTEDNESS either via Reason/Science (the CONCEPT) or via Meditation/Faith (CONSCIOUSNESS), and results in either a Discursive Jedi Master or an Intuitive Jedi Master.

§502

In the *special* sense, as applying to K-12 and university instruction, "education" will have the same essential aims but presented in a more detailed and particularized fashion due to a curriculum that is based on *Jedi Science*. It has the same purpose and goal of *learning the Truth and how to live in Eternity* and is in accord with its

> "We live in a *YOU*-niverse."
> **Fred Alan Wolf**

root "e-ducare" and true **Platonic** meaning and thus involves the important *link* between Education, Knowledge, Truth *and* yourSelf as a Jedi. Education thus is above all about **YOU**—*your True Jedi Self and not your "ego," P.I.* It is about "leading" you to the awesome *knowledge of who you really are* so that you can actually *be* all that you can be. It is a *process* that heals the me/not-me, self/other split in consciousness via the twin knowledge of who I am and of the Whole.

§503

Furthermore the student is made aware of the *single Goal* of becoming a JEDI at the start of his education, all throughout and up till the very end. Thus the central Task of Education is to CULTIVATE THE STUDENT'S *INNER* IN ORDER FOR THE STUDENT TO *TRANSCEND THE SENSES INTO "THE POINT."* The need and goal is to open the student's Reason (or "third eye") and achieve One-Point Focused Attention so that he may be able to penetrate through the Sense-Manifold and actually see and coincide with the TRUTH, the One POINT or the CONCEPT. And this is achieved primarily by STUDY; for by the Study of Mathematics, Science, Logic, History and Language, the student during the entire course of his education learns to focus his attention and thought on a single POINT. Lastly "education" involves a clear understanding of the Light Side of the Force and the Dark Side as a movement from the one to the other. It not only teaches you *how* to actualize the Truth and your Jedi nature via its Jedi Curriculum but also prepares you for eternal Life in Jedi Society—informing the student as to what the problems of the day are and how to solve them, as well as helping with career choices and how best to serve and contribute to the Jedi Order.

For a detailed account of the Jedi Curriculum, K-12 to University, see *Part I: The Jedi Truth, 3.*

§504

[B] WRONG/IMBALANCE. Here my Padawan I will show you What exactly is wrong with your planet's "Education" and How it teaches and promotes the "Dark Side of the Force."

- In brief: Education on your planet today is injurious and in fact "mis-education" since it lacks the true concept of "education"—to lead the student from Ignorance to the *Knowledge* of the Truth and the Force (±)—and of education's *one GOAL*: to be a JEDI and a citizen of the eternal JEDI ORDER.
- Hence the Curriculum of your education is *fragmented,* lacking in *unity,* and non-*Holistic.* It thus lacks *relevance* for the student who views it as a mere *means* to an End (e.g. of getting a good job) and not as an *End in itself;* hence "grades" are more important than course-content, which is forgotten after exams and graduation.
- It is based on your non-holistic, dark side "p-sciences," which erroneously teach **materialism**—that the OUTER/matter (-) is Reality, while the INNER/consciousness (+) is not. Hence students are not encouraged to cultivate their INNER dimension and thus remain "in the Cave" as hopelessly separate Body-Egos, insignificant objects among myriads, products of random evolution ending in biological death. Hence the "p-sciences" and your planet's education promote *nihilism* (no Meaning to life) and prevent true Healing (±) and attaining one's true destiny as an Immortal Jedi and the UNITY of your Race: the amazing JEDI ORDER.

We will now elucidate these points.

§505

In a word, education on your planet today is viewed primarily as a *means* to other ends and not as an *End in itself,* which in fact it is, indeed the supreme End of life. Most especially it is ruled by and sustains the Dark Side world view upheld by your p-sciences and hence knows not *who we are* and is ignorant of the true Jedi/Nature relationship. More specifically:

§506

Today's educators are ignorant of the true concept of education, of what it means "to be educated," and thus have no idea of the true Goal of education. Hence they lack a principle and method for the *unity* and relevance of education and the overall curriculum—the student feels this absence with devastating results.

(1) Above all your educators think of education not as an *End*—as the highest end of life, namely knowledge of the Truth, realizing Jedi—but as a *means,* foremost to the "good life," money, a good job and the comforts of life. The damage caused by viewing education as a means only is dishonesty and cheating. For only the "A"-grade, the test score, is important and not *how* one comes by it or the subject-matter for its own sake; which in most cases is only studied to pass the exam and move on and is forgotten on graduation day, or the day after the exam. The subject-matter is viewed ultimately as irrelevant, a "stepping stone" that one forgets when "the real Goal" has been reached (*outside* school or college).

§507

(2) Lacking the true concept of education educators fall back on the platitude: "we just do what the previous generation of educators have done, or what has always been done." As a result there is no real *unity* behind the educational process and curriculum, which is only an aggregate of disconnected subjects—which is reflected in ever inadequate "standardized tests," regents, SAT's, GRE's, etc.

(3) Consequently the student sees no *unity* in his education—which results in a lack of unity or fragmentation in the student himself and

less power (= *unity*) and overall comprehension. This missing "unity" can only be secured by placing before her an *image or ideal*—namely, JEDI—of what she is to become and of the Goal and end-result that everything, that all her courses are leading up to, thereby indicating their clear relevance; a Goal serving to continually inspire her and help her overcome any obstacles that may present themselves along her way.

§508

In default of this—and this is the true cause of the escalating "drop-out rate" in education on your planet today—he seeks this unifying image-ideal-goal that is vital to his true being and nature (as in truth a Jedi, the Force, the One Reality itself), *outside of school* and in the general culture, in video games, internet "chat rooms," even in crime (i.e., gangs). Hence at a minimum the student cultivates a "divided" consciousness, owing to the fact that her main Goal and interest, her true self "identity and ideal"—"Who am I? Who can I become?"—is found outside of school. So "school" takes a back seat to her "number one" (her essence). She perceives that her "education" is not relevant to her highest needs and aspirations, is a detour and hindrance that is only grudgingly endured.

§509

Most important, today's educators are without the concept of what *knowledge* is—and of the vital *link* between education-knowledge-Truth *and* the student herself.

(1) Educators desire to impart to students useful accurate Knowledge of reality, of the real world, but the tragedy is that they only impart *changing opinion* and *disconnected facts and theories*. This is because they take their idea of "knowledge" from your flawed "empirical or p-sciences" with their flawed "scientific method" which, as we saw in *Part I.*, can never give *knowledge* of what is true, universal, necessary, and certain *and unified* in a single systematic interrelated Whole of Knowledge (*Jedi Science*); but only a "knowledge" (by induction) of what is hypothetical, tentative, contingent and subject to ceaseless revision. To educators the communication of "knowledge" is simply an affair of imparting "textbook information" to kids, marshaling a series of isolated facts, of "laws" of repeatable regularities empirically ascertained (cf. **Plato's** *Republic* 84d) and

expressed in numerical formulas. Since there is no *unity* to this "knowledge" and *no perceivable relevance* to their lives and #1 goal and ideal, students view it as only a *means* to passing tests and as noted, forget it by graduation day.

§510

(2) The "knowledge" they impart is also steeped in the erroneous and pernicious "materialist" world view, which inverts the *true* relation between matter and consciousness, Nature and Jedi, according to which matter/nature = 0, and is only a means to Jedi and the Jedi Order, which is all reality. The student feels this deeply—that he is ultimately unimportant, there being no Meaning to life since biological death is the end and nihilism the final truth—and accordingly imbibes a pessimistic despairing view of life. The negative consequences of this are incalculable—to self-esteem, self-image, and self-worth, possibilities, aspirations, and dreams.

§511

(3) In truth education is really an *End in itself* and not a means; and this End is Knowledge, and Knowledge can be only of the TRUTH, of what IS and only is, as we saw in *Part I*—namely of the Force and yourselves as Jedi, the Force aware of itself. As I said, current education and its "science" does not know about the One Force underlying the two polar opposite INNER/OUTER realms, and thus gives the wrong priority to each, privileging matter over consciousness. Most important your educators do not know and omit mention that what you are learning about is really yourSelf, that all curriculum subjects are really about *yourSelf*, since nothing but the Force anywhere exists. *All* of Science is about your Self, as infinite Inner and infinite Outer. And what a difference this makes in education, in the attitude of the student and the interest she will take in each course and subject matter.

§512

Thus existing K-12 and university education is based on a false and dangerous version of science, one which promotes a most egregious form of the Dark Side.

(1) We saw the respects in which your p-sciences are false and rest on false assumptions: There is no *unity* within the sciences, among the parts, and within each part ("we now come to heat, now magnetism, etc"); this fosters a fragmented view of reality which the student struggles to overcome and unify, but cannot; and his self and world-view get similarly divided. Moreover as based on the senses and sense-scientific method, your sciences are without certainty or necessity and offer a wholly inverted relation of Nature and Jedi as the truth.

§513

(2) Because today the words "science" and "scientific" are equated with "technology" a confusion exists among scientist and lay-person alike, of "knowing how" with "knowing that." Only the latter is Science, the former is not. That is, e.g., to know the properties of a certain metal and to know what happens when you combine 3 elements or chemical substances in a certain ratio (so as to get a rocket to the moon, or via relativity or quantum physics, to build a super-conductor, etc) *is not Science or scientific knowledge,* but only "technical knowledge or *know how*" ("techne" from your Greek meaning "making," how to make something happen or achieve a desired result). Again, True Science is *knowledge,* and knowledge is only *of* the Truth or what truly IS— namely the Force, the Whole of Inner and Outer, and of You, a Jedi as the Whole's self-awareness.

§514

(3) P-science is dangerous because it teaches the error of *Materialism,* which gives ontological primacy to the visible-material-physical (or energy, atoms and quarks) as the sole Being, and not to the invisible, conscious Inner, which it regards as non-existent since it is not an object of "scientific," i.e., sense investigation. Hence only sense-things have true reality—the subject, consciousness, "You" and "I" do not. I am dispensable since I am reduced to matter, my physical body.

"The 'scientific worldview' [e.g. Materialism, Evolution, the Big-Bang theory] is an image of the Universe that rests on a host of daring metaphysical assumptions ... which stand on a very shaky ground." *The Cosmic Game.* **Stanislav Grof**

"That all there is in the Universe is Matter—is a colossal mistake." **Ervin Laszlo**

As a consequence, since my only goal can thus be to connect with the being of the world, I am forced to spend my days in the sense-world's multiplicity, pursuing only these visible things as what alone is real. Hence I can never reach my True Goal of *unity*, and do not bother to cultivate my INNER Infinite aspect; as a consequence I am "lost in the OUTER" for I am not told the Truth that the Outer/visible realm = 0, while the Inner-invisible realm alone is being. Thus I cannot overcome the Dark Side, I/Not-I *separation* and become Whole, Infinite, healed, and complete because I am defined at best as a separate, isolated "EGO in a bag of skin," in relation to a vast material realm of Otherness or Not-I that is permanently different and Other than I am (since **I** am ego, **it** is matter). I am then defined and hence come to see myself as one very insignificant object among myriads of others.

§515

(4) P-science is also dangerous because it teaches *Object-reification*. According to its main materialist assumption and its "method" p-science reduces reality, what truly IS, to a world or multiplicity of *OBJECTS* as what alone is real and should be respected—for only what is measurable, having dimensions in space and time and can be seen via a microscope, telescope, or the naked eye counts as a being, i.e. an "object." Hence your science really leaves no place for *SUBJECTS, persons and the INNER*—for that which in fact is alone Reality. Indeed it turns everything—including people, selves, the student, the "scientific" investigator herself—into a *thing or object*, into what is finite, limited and conditioned, as well as determined hence not *free*. As a result "persons"—who are really infinite and illimitable in essence—are radically *reduced* and forced to think of themselves and each other in terms of conditioned finite *roles* and *identities*. They are put into such "straight-jacket EGO-identities" as father, mother, bread-winner, man, woman, plumber, soldier, etc, and forever prevented from accessing their true infinite being and JEDI SELF.

§516

The p-scientists do not realize that "objects" or "things" and the whole universe of objects have only a "Being *for* another" (*for* consciousness) and hence not a true Being, and are *nothing* for and in themselves. They further do not recognize that every "object" presupposes a "subject" or "I" for whom the object is object; and that the subject alone, as *Consciousness*, has true being since only the subject has a being for itself and is aware of its existence. This teaching and attitude that is instilled into the student *permanently reinforces* the false EGO and the Ego-Object-Thing World. "I" am forever an Ego, an Object—one object among myriads. As a result of this denial of my true nature my pain and grief become unsupportable. What a sentence and burden to place on the child—who counts on the educator to bring him to Truth, happiness and the Good.

§517

(5) Current education via p-science promotes insidious *nihilism* (meaninglessness). Since p-science's materialism teaches that the Self or consciousness is reducible to matter/the body and ends with death, sooner or later the student will grasp that given this is the Truth (because "science" says so) there can be no ultimate *point or Meaning* to her existence on Earth and the universe as a whole—as your saying is, "when you're dead, you're dead," and this applies to all persons, past and future. This realization leads to hopelessness and depression, to thoughts of "Why should I do anything, aspire to any goal?" What the student is forced to do, if she is nevertheless to have any goals, is *either* to put the "nihilism" out of her mind *or* obtain a belief in Meaning and purpose from a source *outside* of school, e.g., through a Religion. The result is a *divided person or self,* with no *unity,* and a secret antipathy towards school, science and learning as such—in fact to public "state"-supported education and hence to the state and established order as such. This breeds anti-social, criminal, revolutionary-destructive behavior as well (cf. Oklahoma, Columbine, Nazi "skin-heads," youth gangs, etc).

§518

Further p-science does away with all morality, values, right and wrong, by teaching that all of this is "subjective" and made-up, added to nature/matter/the universe by Man. And there can be no place for a "God," no super-natural, super-sensory realm, spirit or soul; and as people are all "objects" freedom and free-will are illusions—determinism is the truth. Moreover it is evident to all that the "theory of evolution" (when taught in its customary way) results in the devaluing of a human (i.e. Jedi) Person by equating and defining the Person or Subject as just another "animal" species which you eat and use for clothing—hence to kill a man is basically no different than killing an animal, something which encourages crime and murder in society: on this worldview there is no infinite value connected with people and selves.

§519

All this results from the fact that p-science and the educational process it superintends disseminate an absolutely false Concept of "Man," of "homo sapiens," i.e., of *who* you are, which is detrimental to your health in the highest degree; not to mention nature/the universe's ultimate (lack of) purpose and especially its relation to *yourselves* (to "Man" so-called). According to their Concept and worldview (i) *you*, as "Man," are primarily a *material being* and an *animal*, the outcome of random evolutionary processes. Hence as *insignificant* you are not necessary to the universe or reality and have no essential connection to it; for instance, if your Earth had a different orbit, no life would have arisen on it, hence, your presence here is contingent and an accident. (ii) Consciousness/Self-Soul is only a contingent later development or a "supervenience," a product or "excrescence" of matter. (iii) As simply material and identified only as your body (three cubic feet of flesh) you are essentially a finite, death bound, temporary visitor in the universe. The FACT is that this *nihilistic*, hopeless, dangerous view is wrong. You *are* indeed the whole universe, the Force aware of itself—an "incarnation of all Eternity," as your **Alan Watts** says. You are thus infinite and eternal, not finite and temporal, *absolutely essential to the scheme of things*, not insignificant and accidental. Consciousness and Self are primary and Being, while Matter = 0 or nothing; the two sides constituting *one Whole*. Both are essential and *You or your True Self are both*.

§520

Concerning the "Curriculum": Given that current education is without the *unity* of its "sciences" (or "knowledge") and an overall unifying *goal*, it therefore (1) has no *unity* or *holism* in its *Curriculum* and (2) lacks a *principle or criterion* for determining which subjects/courses should or should not be included in the curriculum.

(1) Accordingly there is a total absence of *unity* to the "Curriculum" of your educational institutions. In fact it is nothing more than a series of "externally" related groupings of courses dictated by

tradition and roughly divided into natural sciences, social sciences, and humanities, with little or no connection *within* these divisions: history, social studies, English literature, the physical sciences, biology, hygiene, gym, etc (and the Basics: reading, writing, arithmetic). The student soon sees and feels this lack of overall *unity* among his courses and suffers accordingly—a unity possible only via a connection with a *single* principle. He does not see their *relevance* to his life. As a result—as noted before and which bears repeating—the student begins to perceive the world as fractured and composed of unrelated parts and fields of study and develops a correspondingly "compartmentalized" view of reality and life. Her self/mind becomes similarly "fragmented" and itself has no *unity*. Because she is *in herself* the *one* Force/Jedi she instinctively attempts to "put it all together," but cannot. Yet the ineradicable *need for unity* persists. Thus it is that your current education is against the *healing* of the subject/object split and unity and instead promotes non-health or dis-unity, the Dark Side of the Force and EGO-separateness.

§521

(2) Since there is no *unity* and no unifying *goal* to education and the curriculum, the only principle or criterion available to decide what to include in the curriculum is "tradition." The "this is the way we've always done it" expedient; this decision is made by *fiat*, without regard to Principle or Reason. Hence the curriculum has the appearance, especially to the child, of being an arbitrary haphazard "hodge-podge" of subjects, a random assortment much like your Godiva box of chocolates.

The FACT is that the only rational way to decide this is on the basis of what the *single Goal* of all education as such is. Knowing this clearly one can then select just those courses which advance the goal and reject those that do not. But since today's education and educators do not know what this single Goal is, it cannot be done. Also since teachers and textbooks as well are steeped in the Dark Side worldview (+|-) and its ignorance, the student can't help but see this and absorb it, resulting again in no unity and confidence in his teachers.

§522

(3) The true and correct principle for the *unity* of education and the curriculum and for deciding what does and does not go into the curriculum can only be the *One Goal* of all education, namely, JEDI and the JEDI ORDER. The Goal is to give a *knowledge of the Truth/the Force* and the student's infinite nature *as* the Whole, which helps her to overcome the self/other split and facilitate the *Transcendence of her Senses* and the "Cave-INVERSION" from Consciousness to Self-Consciousness. Therefore whatever courses promote and lead quickly to the Jedi-Goal are to be selected over those that do not. And it is the Jedi-Principal of each school that decides this. Most importantly, as we showed in *Part I: "Global Jedi Education,"* the center of the curriculum and educational process is *THE CORE*—which teaches the *essence* of Jedi Education (the Force and Jedi Truths) and evaluates each student at the end of the year to determine future educational placement and standing. Everything else, all other subjects, are *ancillary* or supportive and chosen because of their power to advance and facilitate the CORE goal of the student's *transformation* into a Jedi.

§523

Note that none of these subjects are in and of themselves necessary or indispensable in an *unqualified* sense; for they are only and always a *means* to the *End* and never Ends in themselves. ***This* is the key**. These subjects include Science (excepting Core or Pure Science), Religion and Art and their subdivisions, for example, physics, chemistry, psychology, political science, etc, principles of Re-ligion, meditation, dance/Tai Chi, literature, plays, movies, paintings, etc. These are used and studied only because of their power to aid the student's advancement and actualization to Jedi; that is, to overcome the Dark Side or the subject-object split and take her into Eternity and the Eternal Present and to the Full Truth ($\pm$) which she *is NOW* and which alone exists, and to know which alone gives absolute fulfillment, joy, well-being, and happiness. The subjects are also chosen with a view to the current state of the world, to what jobs exist and what kinds of knowledge and skills are required to obtain them. Also required for all education are the Basic Tools such as: Reading-Writing-and Arithmetic, as well as Body and Health courses such as gym (with "light saber" exercises), hygiene, and principles of Jedi dating, etc.

§524

[C] BALANCE. We will now address the question: What can you do to correct the IMBALANCE in your present Educational Institutions and implement Jedi-Education in the world, that is, in Jedi Schools and Universities?

Simply stated: Educators, Principals, Government Officials *must* revamp their present system of mis-education and the curriculum to align with the TRUTH (±) and *Jedi Holistic Education*, that is, in accordance with What Education and its true Goal is and with True Holistic Jedi Science. The following will explain what has to be done and how you can do it.

§525

K-12 EDUCATION: NEW. It may take time for Jedi-Education and Jedi Science to become the law of the land and be unanimously accepted (at least as an alternative to current education and p-science) and for the entrenched system and ways to yield. Therefore the *fastest* way to change over is to create *Jedi Charter-Pilot Schools* within Society, with the agency of a Principal, an endowed Foundation, or a wealthy individual. With stellar results it will soon become the Norm and Standard of all education. All Jedi Pilot Teachers minimally *must* be completely dedicated to Jedi-Education; one Master would be ideal. To learn how a Charter-Pilot School can be started, requirements, accreditation, the "nuts and bolts," etc, see the website: www.charterschools.edu.

§526

K-12 EDUCATION: EXISTING. In order to introduce *holistic* Jedi education and Jedi Principles into your schools be mindful that *Principals* (with their Board's approval and with good reasons) have the power and authority to implement changes and modify their curricula (see *Part I: The Jedi Truth, 3.4*). To find out your options and power *Principals* should go e.g., to the Federal Government's Department of Education website: www.deptofeducation.gov.

Furthermore principals can hold a "general meeting" with their Board, Faculty, and Parents. Minimally, Principals, you can show why "p-science's" teaching and a non-holistic, non-unified curriculum with no Goal is wrong and injurious to kids (e.g. no values, nihilism, reification, etc); and you can make the necessary corrections, e.g. reject p-science's Dark unproven and false assumptions, etc.

If you start a "movement" in your school other Principals will follow your noble example and children and parents will *demand* to go to a Jedi-School.

§527

If you are a parent you can voice your concerns at the next PTA Meeting; and you will have more force if you gather a group of parents before the Meeting. Also parents can "Home-School" their child and/or teach their child Jedi-Principles and reject p-science assumptions. Above all you can declare your family a *"Jedi Family"* and fashion it on Jedi Principles (see *Part II: The Jedi Code*).

Most importantly, "p-Science" and its false materialistic EGO-producing Dark Side world-view must be deleted or minimally curbed; hence until True Science takes root and is accepted it should be called "pre-science" or "opinion." You can further *Lobby Congress* to pass a Law: "Empirical Science must be called "pre-science." A Senator (or even the President) can have a special commission investigate the matter and introduce a Bill. If you are running for Office, for President or Congress, after a consensus builds you can make it a campaign issue and promise.

If you are a concerned citizen you can start a website and begin a grass roots movement. If you are on a government, state, or local Board of Education, voice your concerns at the next Meeting. Help implement New Laws and Practices. Write a letter to your Senator; a list can be found at: www.unitedstatescongress.gov.

§528

UNIVERSITY EDUCATION.
University Presidents, Provosts, Deans, and Trustees can invoke "Holistic" Education in their institutions. The initiative can perhaps start with one or more *individual Faculty members;* you can e.g. revamp your course curriculum and challenge and refute p-science, etc; and then other Faculty members will follow suit. Finally students can join in and with Teachers can demand that the Trustees change the curriculum.

If necessary (as in your 1960s) *students can strike and submit grievances, etc.* You can demand Jedi-Education and that p-science be deleted or rendered harmless. You may start a website, start groups and clubs, write letters to Senators (www.congress.gov), to Faculty, and Deans— send a petition to the Faculty Senate and have Faculty members sign letters and force a General Meeting where it can be discussed. Write letters to Foundations, charitable trusts explaining the whole situation (include a copy of *The Jedi Handbook*).

In addition a wealthy Benefactor or Foundation can start or create a Jedi-College or University from scratch. Good results and increasing demand across the nation by faculty and students will lead to its being universally adopted and becoming the Norm. A list of those supporting education can be found at: www.foundations.org (especially, **Bill and Melinda Gates**). See also *Part I: The Jedi Truth, 3* for more.

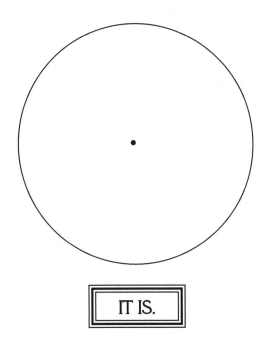

IT IS.

RELIGION

Religion—with Education and Science—is one of the three most potent institutions in Society for consciousness transformation, for good or ill. The tragedy is that although religion's primary purpose is to heal and educate humankind into the POINT of the Jedi Order, *it does exactly the opposite.* This is because of its divisive "form" and inadequate grasp of its inner meaning. Instead of "*re-ligare-ing*" or re-connecting and *uniting* your people to God (or the Force) and realizing a reign of peace, creativity, and love on Earth, Religion is a continuing source of *INNER* confusion, guilt, and bondage—and *OUTER* division, hatred and conflict among peoples of different faiths.

RELIGION SUMMARY

(A) CONCEPT. The chief purpose of Religion is Educational—to take your people into the POINT, the JEDI ORDER. "Religion" derives from: (1) *POINT:* Religion like Science and Art exists simply to *cancel* the Force's Stage Two state of *separation* and arrive at Stage Three, the Jedi Order. Also since the Force or POINT is A SINGLE INDIVISIBLE UNITY, the ABSOLUTE and All that really IS, it is *one and the same* as the "GOD" of your religions. Thus "sin" corresponds simply to Stage Two Consciousness (+|-), and "salvation" to Stage Three Self-Consciousness (±). (2) *ETYMOLOGY:* "Re-ligion" is from your Latin "re-ligare" and means the re-connection of the opposites "Man" and "God" into a UNITY. That is, the Man/God Unity is JEDI, while the Earth/Heaven Unity is the JEDI ORDER

(B) WRONG/IMBALANCE. The religions on your planet are not "re-ligare-ing" or Healing your people and taking them into the Jedi Order. This is due to the picture-thinking in which the TRUTH (±) is expressed, to an inadequate understanding of "God," and to making Holy Books and rituals more important than the *Knowledge and Experience* of the Truth of *your present union with God.* The result of the absence of UNITY among your religions is interminable conflict, War, hate, and unfulfillment or "postponed" fulfillment.

(C) BALANCE. The fastest way is to create in all of your religions "Jedi SECTS" which teach the TRUTH that "God" and yourselves are One right now, and "Heaven" and the Earth, or the Here and Now, are One and the same.

§529

[A] CONCEPT. Religion is in essence the same as Education. They both have the same goal of raising your consciousness into the Self-Knowledge of the Force or Truth, into the WHOLE'S Knowledge of Itself or *THE BALANCE*. Religion however expresses this goal in a different language, for example that of "Salvation" or "Liberation"—which is the direct experience of God or Truth as the Knowledge of one's *UNITY* with God (the Force, the WHOLE). This Unity or salvation is further premised on an initial condition of *separation,* i.e., of "Sin," "Evil," wrongness or a moral-spiritual Inadequateness that is to be transcended and changed into a condition of rightness/righteousness, holiness/ goodness, and perfection/completeness. Religion should also show you HOW to LIVE IN ETERNITY (or the "Kingdom of God," *Olam Haba*) which is NOW; and should not just keep you in a "holding pattern" *as if it were not yet* and *as if "time" were real.*

§530

Like Science religion first originates in the necessity to overcome or cancel (*aufheben*) the Force's state of separation as Consciousness OF, and effect the move from *Stage Two* (EGO) to *Stage Three* (JEDI). Also since the FORCE or POINT is infinite and alone exists, it is equivalent to what your religions refer to as "GOD." Thus "GOD" is equivalent to The FORCE-POINT. Hence "sin" and "salvation" (wrongness and its removal), the main concepts behind Religion, really mean and correlate respectively with: *Stage Two* Opposition (+|-) and *Stage Three* UNITY (±). And since the Infinite Point = God, it follows that *you the Reader are one with God right now and have only to become aware of this FACT (±).*

> [As regards the Christian religion:] "It is our business to participate in this redemption by laying aside our immediate subjectivity (putting off the old Adam) *and learning to know God as our true and essential Self.*"
> **Hegel.** *Enc.* § 194

§531

The word "religion" itself betrays not only its goal and true meaning but also the FACT that it is a *"vanishing means"* that is no longer needed when the End is achieved. The word comes from your Latin "re-ligare" and means to "re-connect" or "re-join" or "re-unite" opposites that were originally ONE—that is, in this case, the opposites "Man" and "God" (= JEDI) and "Heaven" and "Earth" (= The JEDI ORDER). This "Unity of Opposites" or "Polarity" reveals the true meaning and function of Religion, namely to cancel the *separation* between the two, or rather to *realize* that the separation is *already* canceled and is in itself "null and void."

§532

Thus as based on Polarity the opposites requiring "re-ligare-ing" or *unification* are *already* unified, for the Truth of any pair of opposites is their *UNITY.* Since man and God *are right now and eternally ONE,* religion's educational Task or Work is precisely to guide you into this *realization* and into living the Life it implies 24/7/365. It thus follows, as stated, that religion defines itself as a temporary and vanishing "means"; that is, once the End, the "re-ligare-ing" or re-connecting is accomplished or rather *realized*—which if done correctly is *permanent*—there is no longer the need for the process that produced it, hence for Religion. And this is the basis for solving all the conflicts that exist in your world due to the differences among your religions—namely they all have the same one goal of overcoming the separation and reaching the knowledge/experience of the TRUTH. Therefore their doctrines and holy books *are not the ultimate End* and can be sacrificed to it, which removes the *cause* for all conflict and hatred.

§533

There is also another important point to note. The opposites behind "re-ligare" and its Polarity cannot strictly speaking *be* "God" and "Man"—for by definition "God," as an infinite Being, not a finite one, *has no opposite or other* (of course, as the *Jedi Science of Logic* and Polarity show, the "finite" as an "opposite" of the infinite, hence of "God," is a "moment" or ingredient IN the Infinite or God). To say for example that God-Infinite is here on one side, and Man-Finite is there on the other side, is to make the Infinite or God *finite,* hence to do away with God (the Infinite).

GOD 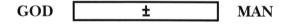 **MAN**

Further, that "God" is equivalent to "the Force" means that God is the *only* Being. Hence, in truth, religion's Polarity and opposites can only refer to the *two* sides of God Herself (that is, of the WHOLE or Infinite which God is); for example, the Light Side and Dark Side, Consciousness and Unconsciousness, Universality and Individuality, Subjectivity and Objectivity, *and* these in their *Unity* or *Truth,* where (+) trumps (-) as the Absolute I.

Another key POINT your religious leaders especially should be mindful of is: If the UNITY of yourself and God *did not or does not already exist*—that is, if both of you in truth existed right now *independently of each other*—then the UNITY *can never happen.* Indeed, How do you propose to bring it about? Through *works*? There *is* nothing you can do to make it happen. Hence the UNITY IS and can only BE, NOW. You just have to realize this.

§534

From a different and important angle this means that whatever "Man" is, or the word "Man" refers to, he/she must be a Being *within* God, *within* the Infinite, the Whole, the ALL itself—as one of your scriptures say: "We live, move, and have our being *within* God" (**St. Paul of Tarsus**). That is, there is and can be no "outside" to an *Infinite* Being—which accordingly can be only One and, like the Force itself, can have no *opposite.* All of this pertains to the core truth of the nature and concept of "the Infinite" and its dialectic as revealed in Jedi LOGIC, which discusses the relation or difference of Self and Other (or finitude) and its overcoming; hence it implies first the separation of "Man" or Consciousness and its Object, and then the realization of their *unity.*

§535

So the *true* meaning behind "re-ligare," as we *now* see, is that some kind of *"separation"* (or dis-connection) must be overcome or canceled, and UNITY or BALANCE result. Now even though it may be helpful for some of you to think of this in terms of "man's *separation* from God," or "man" and "God" as *two* separate Beings that are to be re-united or reconciled, the higher and *true* meaning behind this language of "separation" as a *wrongness* or inadequacy to be overcome is really this:

THE FORCE AS *CONSCIOUSNESS* (+|-) MUST CHANGE
INTO THE FORCE AS *SELF-CONSCIOUSNESS* (±).
THE FORCE AS EGO—AS FINITE, PARTICULAR,
AND SELF/OTHER *IN OPPOSITION*—MUST CHANGE
INTO JEDI, AS INFINITE, UNIVERSAL,
AND SELF/OTHER *IN UNITY*.

What is important and what this reveals is that this *separation* and *union* take place not "outside" but rather *within* God herself/himself (again, "we have our being *within* God, etc").

§536

> "*God is just this entire act.* God is the beginning, and does this definite thing (the Creation of an Other); but God is equally the end only, the Totality. God is the eternal process (of positing an Other, and then reconciling himself with it in Love) which is the Truth and the absolute Truth." PR III.12 **Hegel**

A major problem and defect of your religions is that they do not realize that God, as Infinite and the Whole, *includes within Himself as his complete definition*, the Whole of the three phase process (which your religions erroneously separate): (1) God before Creation, (2) Creation (the universe and "unredeemed" Man), and (3) God and Creation reconciled, in *unity* (heaven on Earth, etc). This is revealed only by the Truth, *the Knowledge of the Force.* Hence we have (1) the Force, (2) the Force *as* Man/Consciousness, and (3) the Force *as* Jedi/The Jedi Order. And this is what the word "God" in truth refers to.

Also since religion exists for no other reason than to cancel the *separation* (= "sin") of *Stage Two*, it must be said that religion as such is *necessary.* But given that True Education has and does accomplish *the same goal* it follows that, ultimately, *Education will replace Religion.* This statement should not be misunderstood: Religion's essence, inner core and kernel of Truth *will always remain*; it is only its *externals* or form that will be dropped or become unnecessary as there will be no need for it—as your scripture's say, "The spirit (not the letter) will guide you into all truth," and "I will write my Law in your heart, etc."

§537

Religion's goal is thus in truth, "The Whole's or Force's Knowledge of Itself." As your Jedi **Hegel** says, "Man's knowledge of God is God's knowledge of Himself in Man"—and as your Pentecostals teach, "speaking in tongues" is really "God praising God."

§538

Thus it is *the Knowledge of the Force*, of Polarity and the Truth (±) that alone give you the true understanding of Religion, of what is really going on behind its forms and content, its language, doctrines, imagery, metaphors, rituals, activities, pomp and circumstance. Religion's sole purpose, like Science, *is to realize the TRUTH (±)*—that is, in religious language: the present *unity* of God and Man (yourself), and of Heaven and Earth; in Jedi language: the Force aware of Itself as a Jedi and as the Jedi Order. As we know, the Truth, the Whole, *is* nothing but the Unity of Opposites. That is, *Being* in order to *be* must be *Self-conscious*. And this implies, first, *Consciousness* and a *split* into two polar opposite sides, or *difference*, and then by Polarity, a realization of the necessary

> "Jesus lived this *unity* of man and God as his gospel ..."
> *"The AntiChristian."*
> **Nietzsche**
>
> "The eternal Spirit (God) itself is involved in the struggle with finitude and its overcoming." *Enc.*
> §441. **Hegel**

unity that underlies the opposites.—In Jedi Logic, it is *the movement of Universal to Particular to Individual:* "U" = The One or All, but not aware of itself, "P" = the necessary split, separation, difference, consciousness of other, not of Itself, "I" = the Unity of U and P—as the *In-divisible*, Self-conscious Universal or One. Thus "P" and "I" are the Act of the UNIVERSAL *itself* and the *means* whereby the Universal realizes itself (as YOU, as a JEDI). That is, "P" and "I" are *within* the Universal itself, *are* the "U" *in a different form* ... and the Individual is the *concrete* fully actualized Universal (or what religion calls the "Holy Spirit"), "the Force (Idea) actualized as the Jedi Order (or as absolute Spirit-*Geist*)."

§539

Put differently the Truth, the POINT, What IS, has two aspects: *difference* (Light Side/Dark Side, Consciousness/Unconsciousness, Subject/Object) and *unity*; and both exist *simultaneously*. Hence Being or the Whole is first "in time" aware *only* of the aspect of *difference*, namely of the me/not-me, self/other divorce, which is due to Nature (-) and Body-identification—recall that *the Absolute I* (+) of the Force, to *be* conscious (and then Self-conscious) necessarily fuses with (-) individuated "Man-cum-senses," etc. And *only* secondly "in time" is aware of the aspect of *unity* ... the Whole's Knowledge of Itself *as* the Whole. So the Force, Being, the Whole, the Absolute

I is first *consciousness* OF … an Other, Object, the World (this is "Man," as finite, individual, Ego, separate, and *particular*), then *self-consciousness* or *consciousness*-of-*consciousness* (this is Jedi, as infinite and *universal*). Note further that "Man" as *particular* exists as an "Object" for others to judge, find fault with, and attribute "sin" to; which is not true of a Jedi as *universal*.

§540

This also gives the true meaning of the word "sin" (and "evil"). "Sin" pertains to the Force (Being) in its second Stage as "Man" or consciousness. Hence "separation from God" (the usual definition of "sin") really means "separation from Truth" (and another name of God *is* Truth) or ignorance of Truth, which simply means that you do not *know* that you *are One* with Being (the Whole, Force, God) *right now*. So your Jedi **Plato** was right in equating "sin" (or "evil") with "ignorance" and in finding the root of the former in the latter, in "ignorance" of Reality or Truth and in mistaking appearance (the sense-world and multiplicity) for Reality; the consequences of this error being "egoic" behavior, greed, lust, hate, jealousy and envy. "Sin" therefore means that "Man" is immersed in the CAVE (-), the Dark Side (+|-), his isolated Ego, and in bondage to sense-objects, multiplicity, and desires—and tries to find fulfillment (i.e., the solution to the primary self/other problem) in false ways, such as by gratifying only his animal nature and drives. As Jedi **Hegel** also observes: "If the separate personality (or Ego) is regarded as not cancelled, then we have *evil*; for personality that does not yield itself up to the absolute Idea is *evil* (PR III 25)." In other words:

A PERSONALITY THAT DOES NOT YIELD ITSELF UP TO THE FORCE—AND BECOME A JEDI—IS *EVIL*.

§541

Also related is the true meaning of "Good and Evil" as related to the solution to the Problem of Evil (its Origin/Existence *alongside* a God who is absolutely Good), and the way of eliminating *evil* from your planet permanently. (1) [simple] **Evil/sin** is the Dark Side belief that

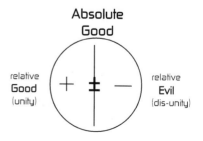

Absolute
Good

relative
Good
(unity)

relative
Evil
(dis-unity)

the subject/object, I/Not-I separation is permanent or Real (+|-). **Good** is the Light Side or Unity of the Opposites (±).

(2) [truer] [The Move From Morality to Metaphysics, where Morality is utterly transcended and absorbed] Here the ABSOLUTE **GOOD** (which alone exists) is equal to and *one and the same* as BEING and the TRUTH—hence we are beyond *relative Good* (unity) and *relative Evil* (dis-unity). From this truest perspective **Evil**—which was only relative (or phenomenal) and hence did not and does not exist *in itself*—is now gone forever. So your Jedi **Nietzsche** was right in his insistence that your people *must* get "Beyond Good and Evil," and your Jedi **Augustine** as well, who regarded "evil" as only a *privation*; and *this* is how the opposites can be transcended and the problem of evil solved.

§542

The important fact is, in other words, that Religion clothes the Truth (±) in pictures that are unclear, ambiguous, and have an equivocal meaning that must be "decoded." For example, "God breathed his own breath (Spirit-consciousness) into Adam and he became a living Soul." This cannot mean that God, as a totally separate, independent Being on the one side, breathed and awakened Adam, as another separate Being on the other side—and that this was a contingent and not a necessary action on God's part. For this is logically impossible as we saw since God, an "infinite" entity, is thereby made "finite," as one of two entities each limiting the other (let alone that a "Thing in itself" is inconceivable). Hence this scriptural statement and "truth" must in fact be regarded as "CODE" for the Truth (already discussed and familiar) that in order to *be* and be conscious "the Absolute I" or the Force's (+) *must* of necessity fuse with "Man" (-) and be first

> "At the core of all utopian visions lies one of the main structural dysfunctions of the old consciousness: *looking to the future for salvation* .... 'And I saw a new heaven and a new earth,' writes the biblical prophet. The foundation for a new earth is a new heaven—the awakened consciousness (which) is not a future state to be achieved (but is) arising within you at this moment ... All that ever has been or will be is NOW." **Eckhart Tolle**

"consciousness OF" and then "Self-consciousness"; in other words

Code for the Truth of the *Universal's* (or Concept's) necessary "U-P-I" movement of self-actualization from the *Universal* (or Absolute I) to the Particular to the Individual *as a concrete Universal*—in effect the Absolute I (or POINT) individualized and actualized as a "U.I. Jedi" or a Universal Individual (your True Jedi Self). This further becomes quite clear when you realize that the obvious conclusion is that Adam's/Man's *consciousness* (breath,"ruach") must be *one and the same* as God's *consciousness* (breath,"ruach").

Thus Religion's goal is nothing other than to raise you into a knowledge and experience of the Truth (±) as the *Unity* of Opposites—there being two forms of this Unity: namely (in religious language) (1) *The Unity of God and Man* that we call "Jedi," and (2) *The Unity of Heaven and Earth (or this Present World)* that we call "the Jedi Order." Religion's true purpose therefore involves the taking of your entire "human" race into the glorious Jedi Order—*which exists Now* and not in a "future" time or in "another world."

§543

[B] WRONG/IMBALANCE. Here we will discuss, What's wrong with your religions? Why are they imbalanced and promote the Dark Side of the Force, and do not heal or educate your people into the Truth and the Jedi Order?

In a word your planet's religions are not educating, "re-ligare-ing," or taking your people into a Knowledge of the Truth (±), whether you call it "union with God" or "the Whole's Knowledge of Itself"—and they are not taking your people into the Present *Jedi Order*. For this reason it can even be said that your religions today—whatever they may have been in earlier ages—are *not* "religions," since they are not *re-ligare-ing*. They are keeping you in a divided state of dis-Unity, *non-health* and *unfulfillment* primarily because they lack a clear understanding of *what "Religion" really is*, why it exists, and what its true purpose and goal is.

§544

Let's look at some of the reasons why your religions are unable to produce UNITY and are therefore immersed in the Dark Side of the Force, and contribute to the general *imbalance* on your planet.

(1) The main reason is that though Religion indeed has the Truth (in so far as it is a "re-ligare") it has it in an *unclear or muddled Form*— as it is presented or extracted from its Holy Books qua pictures, narrative, dogma, concepts, and vocabulary. Further most religions do not know that they are a *means* only—to the *End* of Knowledge or union with God (the Force)—and not Ends as such; and as *means* have only a *temporary* or *provisional status* and only exist in the first place because there is a "split" in consciousness that when "healed" removes the reason for their existence.

Religion's true Concept indeed contains *all* the basic "Jedi-Truth" Principles. Namely: (a) There is an Original supreme unchanging infinite Reality or Truth of all being (God or the Force); (b) As we are something is "wrong" with us and hence we need to be made whole by re-connection with the Original Reality (the Source from which we came). The "split" in us of consciousness and object, between yourselves and the Reality needs to be deleted or "healed." And (c) by following the given Religion (by believing and doing the prescribed things) you can overcome "wrongness" and "sin," become "right," healed and whole and, most importantly, obtain *concrete knowledge/experience of your union with God/the Force.* But these Jedi-Truth Principles are not adequately understood by the teachers and laypeople of your various faiths.

> "Today, in Church and out of Church, there are thousands of souls who realize … what they want from religion is not a collection of doctrinal and ritual symbols, nor a series of moral precepts. *They want God himself,* by whatever name he may be called; they want to be filled with his creative life and power; they want some conscious experience *of being at one with Reality itself,* so that their otherwise meaningless and ephemeral lives may acquire an eternal significance." *Behold the Spirit,* **Alan Watts**

§545

This is due again to their FORM and language, that is, to the special Form in which your religions communicate and express the Truth, namely, "Picture Thinking" (*Vorstellen*), Imagery and Narrative, as contrasted with the Concept and Reason. This Form, since it lacks the exactness of the Concept, allows for multiple and conflicting interpretations that make universal consensus and

Unity impossible. There is no certainty as to what a given word, text, or sentence, means—and no attempt to define the terms in the Holy Books themselves, something left entirely to the reader or interpreter. Hence even different Sects within *the same religion* have different doctrines, resulting in conflict, hatred and wars.

§546

(2) Also connected with FORM and the absence of definitions and explanatory passages of main words/terms, is the root problem involved in the words "God" and "Man." As long as these two words are regarded as unyielding fixed opposites that involve no process between them whereby they can interpenetrate and merge, the idea of their *Unity*—the goal of religion—becomes very difficult if not impossible to envisage and realize. Most religions are unwilling to relax the *fixed gulf* they have set up between what they conceive of as "God" on the one hand, and "Man" on the other. While they do recognize, as Logic requires, a difference between "Man" as "sinner" and unredeemed, and "Man" as "saint" and redeemed and no longer separate from but in *union* with God, they as a rule tend to (1) relegate and postpone this *unity* to a future state after death, and (2) *even then* are reluctant to describe the nature of this Unity and, when they do, they still keep a *separation* or distance between God and redeemed Man.

§547

Moreover this irresolvable "Man-God opposition" keeps you in EGO-separateness and in the Dark Side, for you are opposed to God and to other Ego's and the World as such (taken as Being and not Nothing.). This "opposition" keeps you permanently in your *particular self* and prevents you from realizing the true *Universal Self* that you share with all other I's and is all reality or the Force itself.

§548

Most significantly this condition of "non-unity" maintains a perpetual state of *Guilt*—which can only be removed when you are in your *Universal-All Self.* It is only in this All—or *Love-Self* that you cannot be judged, while as a *particular* and opposed to other *particular ego's* you can be judged. Thus it is made impossible for you to realize and fulfill the absolute requirement, "Love thy neighbor as thyself," which can be fulfilled only by a *Universal I*, whereby you see that your neighbor and the "others" are really your Self and are *within* and a part of you.

> Be mindful Noble Jedi of the FACT that once you define or characterize one term, "God," as Creator, all-good, perfect, holy, infinite, eternal, powerful, etc, and the other term, "Man," as creature, sinful, weak, evil, finite, contingent, animal, etc, it thereby is made impossible to see them *as One* (though it is a fact that salvation or being forgiven or saved really *imply and signify* that one is now OK, right, holy, etc—that one has God's very own attributes; cf., the Bible's, "Be ye holy as I am holy," and "Be ye perfect as your heavenly Father"). Now thus characterized it seems as if "God" is the *wholly independent Being* and "Man" the *dependent* being, that "God" is capable of existing and "Being God," by himself—that is, *without* Man and creation, whereas only Man cannot exist on his own. But the fact is different. For in the absence of an "Other" or Creation, God could not *be* God—for all of the above attributes/ ascriptions that characterize God are "polar" or correlative terms that require an Other for them to have sense. For example without a "Creation" God could not be a "Creator"; or all-good, loving or powerful without someone to bestow goodness, love, and exercise power on. Hence God is also not complete or perfect without that which is necessary to him (namely the Other), and not "free" *without first limiting himself and then transcending the limitation*, etc. This means that—au contraire—Man and Creation (the Universe) are indeed necessary and essential for God to *be* God—that Man is a necessary moment or ingredient of God, without which *not*.

§549

Of course we Jedi know what is really behind the two terms "God" and "Man" (their true meaning) and their opposition or difference. Namely this: "God"—that which is supreme, eternal, One, infinitely perfect, Love, etc—is really the Force, the One Eternal Truth (±) that alone exists and is infinite (or exhausts all reality) and has *nothing* outside itself. Hence "Man" must be something that arises or occurs *within* the Force, the infinite Reality. Indeed correctly defined *"Man" is the Force itself however still in its second stage or "divided state"* of consciousness *of* an Other—not yet having returned to its original state (its Third Stage) and overcome the (in fact illusory) split in its being and arrived at consciousness of Itself. Hence what is behind all of this is nothing other than the TRUTH or the *Law of Polarity* and what it requires—that "God" or the One eternal Being can be conceived or exist *only* with a "division" hence an "Other" within itself, with an Inner *and* Outer dimension and the split or distinction that consciousness itself involves.

§550

Hence it is just because of the limitations of its language and Form that Religion *cannot see* the TRUTH in its full clarity. *However* it is nevertheless true—as your scriptures imply, "the letter kills, but the *spirit* gives life"—that the "Spirit" (the Absolute I) *is* in fact able to rise above these limitations and realize healing and true *unity* with God. The difficulties of your Religions hence can be overcome by a combination of Reason, scripture, and the writings of their saints and mystics. In this way they *can* access healing and perceive a way in which Man and God can become One.

§551

It is also true that your religions do *intuit* the fact that the *union* of Man and God is the ultimate goal, but are reluctant to come out and state it as an express doctrine and Truth. It is rare indeed that you will hear a Priest, Rabbi, or Imam tell his congregation, "You are now One with God [Allah, Jehovah-Hashem, Jesus, etc]" or "You are no longer *separated* from God, your sins are forgiven and permanently erased, You are divine, holy, righteous, and as perfect as God is"— even though this is clearly stated in their Holy Books—for example: "May they be One as we are One, I in them, Thou in me," "We share the divine nature (hence *we* are divine too)," "I and the Father will live inside you," "He has perfected you forever," "Be ye holy as I am holy," and "I God will become (him), his ear, mouth, eye, hand, etc" (from the Islam *Hadith*).

§552

Some religions maintain this fixed gulf because they want to keep their God pure and uncontaminated with *human* features—or because they fear that the *Unity* of God would be impaired, diminished, or violated. In some cases the clergy themselves have not realized *their own Unity with God* and so (1) are not experientially aware of it as a *real* possibility (in the here and now) or (2) do not teach or preach it because of fear that some of their flock may realize it and either (a) surpass them in "holiness" (indeed God would then be actually *present* in the congregation and the man's or woman's words would be God's words) and take their job or supersede their *authority,* or worse (b) leave the Church, feeling no need to remain in it, having realized the very Goal and Purpose of Re-ligion itself.

However the main reason they do not teach it remains their inability to even *conceive the unity* of such totally opposite entities. And this is mainly because they have *incorrect* concepts of both "God" and "Man" that they have inherited and accumulated through the ages—and which only Reason, *the Knowledge of the Force,* and Jedi Science can correct.

§553

One consequence of this is that your religions cannot conceive and accept this *Unity* as *actual and present in a particular person—* that is, the *Unity* of the Force's Light and Dark Sides, of the visible (material-sense) and invisible ("spiritual"-consciousness) realms, hence the unity of *Divine and human, Infinite and finite.* They essentially *separate* the two realms—further characterized as, on the one hand, the (-) sense-world, the secular, unredeemed present world, and, on the other, as the divine realm (+) that God et al inhabits, a world in picture-thinking and imagery, raised far above the present sense-world. Hence they can neither countenance the *unity* of the two realms nor their own *unity* with the Divine Being (or view it only as a "future" event), a *unity* which *is* the Truth and expressed in their Holy Books (e.g., "The Kingdom of God [or God] is *within* you, etc")—and therefore the possibility that a Person in their midst, in their own congregation, can actually be *one* with the divine or Infinite, or *be* the divine/infinite *itself.* They cannot see that in truth "God" and the "other world"—which they conceive in imagination and as "NOT HERE"—are really HERE and that "God" is really the *Absolute I* or *Infinite Consciousness* and actually joined (±) to the Body of the Person before them. As very stuck in the Dark Side sense-world—and having placed "God" and the divine in "another" world—they can see the Person only as in a *separate* physical Body, separate from themselves as a separate EGO and *finite* in every way, and can hence see nothing "divine" or "infinite" about the Person. This of course is a great hindrance in Churches and Temples that prevents healing/education and realizing Jedi, the Jedi Order and *Unity*, and keeps the TRUTH/the "Divine" from manifesting in the world, in the HERE and NOW, and keeps the congregation fixed at and restricted to the human-Ego level, engaged in perpetual backbiting, judging, and petty quarreling.

§554

> "Spinoza, Hegel, and Nietzsche are all philosophers of eternity, and not of a transcendent or other-worldly eternity, but rather of an *absolute immanent eternity*, which is an immediate and totally present eternity, and *totally present in the full actuality of the world.*"
> **Altizer**

(3) Another reason *Unity*, healing and the Jedi Order are not realized by your religions concerns "time." That is, they mistakenly view "time" as real and do not know that only Eternity or the Eternal Present exists—that "God" is fully present NOW, as well as one's *Unity* with God and further, that the Truth (±), the Jedi Order alone exists and also exists NOW.

This is in part due to their *Stage Two* split in Consciousness and their division of the Whole into two separate worlds (*Diesseits, Jenseits;* the Here and the Beyond). For instance they read in their Holy Books about so-called "future" events like the "tribulation, "rapture," "second coming," "new jerusalem," "Last judgment," "new Heaven and new Earth," etc—then consult their *senses* and conclude that these things *have not yet happened*, etc, and sense the disparity. This puts them "in time" and causes them *not* to notice and realize the Truth and Unity *which is Present*—and instead to focus on the "future," when the Unity *will be present*, etc. They do not understand that the Truth trumps the *imagery*—which in any case must be regarded as written primarily to give people *hope* in difficult times—that these times would not last forever and that God will redeem all pain/suffering, etc—and in some cases written to simply "scare" one into quitting base pursuits and instead taking up what **Robert de Ropp** calls the *Master Game*, "the only game worth playing," which is becoming a Jedi and realizing the TRUTH, the Now-POINT:

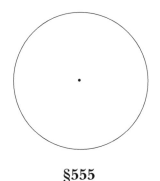

§555

Hence it is clear that the Picture-thinking Form and imagery of your religions *must be transcended*—insofar as it prevents realization and the total healing of your planet and peoples. As your Text says, "The letter kills, the Spirit gives Life." Thus for all these reasons your religions are clearly immersed in and disseminating the Dark Side of the Force and are not educating you into Unity, Truth, and the glorious Jedi Order.

§556

(4) Another major Dark Side problem your religions create concerns the hatred, conflict and wars that occur among them. This is primarily due to the perceived *differences* among your various religions, which derive mainly from the different *HOLY BOOKS* at their base. Each religion believes that only its own Holy Book is from God and has "absolute authority," that doctrines based on it are the absolute Truth, and that *their own* understanding of "God," salvation, and what is right and wrong is the only true and correct one; the others are *not*, or are less true. The worst case is when they say, "If you don't believe what we believe, you are an infidel and will go to Hell, or be cut-off from God, etc." Obviously it is because of this situation that Religions are a great cause of Dark Side *separation* and *dis-Unity*, preventing Healing and the Jedi Order as long as these *differences* remain.

§557

The failure of all your religions is due to their inability to realize the *single unity* underlying them all—a *unity* relating to the Fact that they all have the *same goal* and aim, which is the Knowledge and *Experience* of one's *union* with God, Truth, or Ultimate Reality. Their mistake

is to regard their Holy Book, doctrines, rituals, etc, as the #1 End
of everything when in truth their Holy Book, etc, is only a *means* to
the true #1 End of one's experiential *unity* with God. The Holy Book
therefore is in fact #2, an arrow or pointer that points *beyond itself* to
the *Author* himself of the Holy Book or to the Being which the Holy
Book talks about and glorifies. Once this is realized and the *unity*
and commonality of all religions is acknowledged, the primary basis
for hate and wars is eliminated.

§558

Thus your religions do not promote *unity* and *love* among all peoples
on your planet and hence the Jedi Order; instead they cause *division,
hatred,* war and violence in your world. Your people thus need to
overcome the dangerous *differences* among religions and realize the
unity, commonality, and universality that lies at their base and move
towards and realize first *One World (or "Jedi") Religion* and, eventually,
no religion—since religions are in Concept and in point of fact merely
"means" to the End of *knowledge* which when attained does away with
the means and need for it. The cause of the hatred and antipathy
among your religions is rooted in the *different* Holy Books/scriptures
and their *different* interpretations by sects, and in their *different* and
conflicting doctrines, dogmas, creeds, beliefs, cultus/practice and
customs. To be specific each group sees the Other simply *as an Other,*
as an enemy, a *negation* and *denial* of its own religion and beliefs,
hence as an "infidel" that must be destroyed or at least tolerated.
This reinforces the Dark Side, the Self/Other or Ego situation, and
prevents *unity* and the Jedi Order—and it is *fanaticism* that ups the
level of *fear* in the world and thus eclipses *Love* by preventing each
group from *seeing itself in the Other.* The only way the Light Side can
be fostered and Self/Other opposition overcome is *if all religions
can be made to see the unity they all share.* This means they have to
see that their respective Religion (*in toto,* books, creed, practices)
as a "re-ligare" is only a *means or "arrow"* and not an End in itself.
This is the *common* or *unifying* factor in each. For they are all *means*
and have the *same End*—namely salvation/healing/liberation or
direct knowledge/experience of God, Truth, and Ultimate Reality
(whether called Al-lah, Jehovah, Father, Christ, Hashem, the One,
the Infinite (En-sof), the Void, the Tao, Brahma, or the Absolute)—
that is, *union with God.* Finally religious consciousness as such is
divided between "heaven" and "now" and thus is *not at home in the
present world.* As related *negatively* to the world it gives consciousness

a *permanent Not-I* to contend with that keeps you in your Ego and the Dark Side, and prevents true and lasting healing from occurring.

§559

[C] BALANCE. Here my noble Padawan, I will discuss How your religions can be balanced. And what you can do.

The main mandate is: To help foster *unity* and true healing and break down walls between your Religions—to help the world religions move first towards *One World Faith* in which all faiths are preserved (a Universal "Jedi" Religion) and then, ultimately, to a state of *NO Religion* (except for children and pre-Jedi)—of only *Knowledge* and *Awareness*. And *Love*. Here are the five things you and other Jedi can and should do.

§560

(1) *Educate* your religious leaders, clerics, and laity. Teach them for example that religion and Bibles et al are only a *means* and not the *End* itself. Help them to *align* their Teaching to the Jedi Truth, Polarity, and the One POINT-Consciousness and to revise their Doctrines and support their revised doctrines with their *scriptures* (as best they can)—and also use the writings of their saints and mystics where necessary. Show them clearly *why they must do this*—namely because otherwise they are teaching their people error—which is anathema to their God, since God is Truth—and perpetuating GUILT and unhappiness (or your **R. D. Laing's** "divided-self/ schizophrenia") and preventing healing and the Jedi Order from adventing (i.e., the "*paradise* on Earth" that is God's will and final purpose); in the words of your poetess, "*And we've got to get ourselves back to THE GARDEN.*" Furthermore as a member of a religion **YOU CAN AID THE "BALANCING" OF YOUR RELIGION by:** Talking to your Clergy, Imam, the Vatican, etc., using Reason and scripture and giving PROOFS that there can be no transcen*dent* God ... only a transcen*dental* God (or an apriori "God *within* you"), that the *separation* of God and man, heaven and earth, *is logically impossible* (as your **A-Team** has demonstrated), etc. Explain to them that Dis-Unity is unhealthy (*pathological and schizophrenic*)—and that because of this, "YOU *MUST* CHANGE. THIS IS NOT AN OPTION." Teach them especially that their Holy Book is #2 and not **#1**—which is the concrete living *experience* of one's present Union with God—and to

Focus on their commonalities. And also that God is ONE but known under myriad names, and that all hate, war and terrorism must come to an end and Paradise on Earth be realized.

§561

(2) The Key Point thus is that All religions have the *same Idea and Goal of realizing a "Heaven on Earth," a totally redeemed and restored World-Cosmos-Humanity—a Paradise, World without end, World to Come, New Jerusalem, Just Society, Shangri-La, Nirvana, Elysium—and a Universal Peace, Brother/Sister-hood of Man, a Divine Order, a Jedi Order* and *Society.* They should therefore realize this and *work together* to achieve this common Goal—a force for the *unity* of all Faiths. Let all of you—theists and atheists/humanists alike—put down your differences and work together to achieve this amazing and universally desired Goal.

(3) The leaders in all your faiths can participate in Interfaith (ecumenical) Meetings to reach a unifying *understanding* and *agreement* about the meaning and purpose of *Re-ligion.*

§562

(4) Further each religion should attend the services of the others (Islam/mosques, temples, churches), and should mix and hang-out with the "hated" religion and its members, inviting them to your church, etc. The result will be: "See, we *are* able to worship together. We are *one* and worship the *same God* albeit with a different name and in a different way (you may e.g. Quote the Koran's: 'Our God and your God are one and the same, and it is to Him that we both worship'). We *are* able to Love one another. We differ only in externals, which is due to culture and historical-geographical conditions, etc."

§563

(5) Most importantly you should without delay *START JEDI-SECTS within your religions—for when YOU become healed or Jedi, others will follow. That is, with good results and fruit—fully actualized, healed, happy people—the Jedi Sect will become the dominant SECT of your religion, and thus most capable of UNITING with other religions and their own Jedi Sects. You can also START A UNIVERSAL JEDI RELIGION (or Non-religion).*

§564

I will now present a pointed summary of the main problem of your religions and its solution that will lead us directly into a comprehensive discussion of the JEDI SECT itself.

Your planet's "Religious Problem" and its Cause.

Each religion claims it alone has the full Truth—about God, Man, Salvation—and the others are wrong (in whole or in part) and hence a threat. Minimally this makes unity and harmony among religions difficult if not impossible. Maximally this can lead to hatred and violence and the need to eliminate other religions as the source of perversion and apostasy (cf. war, terrorism, jihad). But the real #1 problem of all your religions concerns their inaccurate/confused understanding of the TRUTH, which makes total healing and freedom, their goal and raison d'etre, impossible.

The Cause of the Problem in one word is *difference;* that is, your religions' *different* "Holy Books," dogmas, beliefs, rituals, and "picture" versions of the one TRUTH (±) and the tension this causes (for each one says: "If you don't believe *our way,* you are an infidel and will go to hell, etc"). Thus they focus on their *differences* and not on their *commonalities* and *unity.*

§565

The *Only* Solution is that of Universal REASON, or "The Jedi Knowledge of the Force," which teaches the following:

There is a concealed *unity* behind all religions; *it* must be promoted and *differences* demoted or downplayed. That is, all religions essentially say the same thing: (a) Something is radically *wrong* with/about you. (b) What is wrong is "sin." That is, you are alienated/separated from God-Truth-Being. (c) Thus you need a "religion" (or **"re-ligare"**) that will remove the *wrongness* and make you *right.* That is, by "re-uniting" you with God-Truth by canceling the *separation* between yourselves and God.

As we Jedi know what is *really* behind this common teaching is: The Force's necessary *separation* or *distinguishing* of itself (+|-) and the subsequent *cancellation* (unity or "balance") of the same that is involved in Its eternal self-actualization (±). Thus, the separation = sin/wrongness, while the unity *alone* = salvation and freedom. What follows from this Fact is that:

§566

All religions have the *same* End/Goal/and Purpose, namely "Knowledge" (cf., "You will KNOW the TRUTH and it will make you FREE"), in other words, "Salvation" or "Liberation" as the complete Knowledge/Experience of this Unity or TRUTH (±) or "union with God." So this alone is **#1** and *not* the "Holy Book," dogmas, rituals, symbols, tradition, etc. These are only **#2** or a *"means"* of reaching **#1**. *NOTE that in this way the main reason for conflict, hatred and war among your religions is removed*—**Your religious leaders *must* recognize this.**

It also follows that "religion" (or "re-ligare"), whose sole End is Knowledge/Experience, is only a *means* to this *End* and hence *ultimately disappears* or segues into *Knowledge* (cf. your **Isaiah's** "As the waters cover the earth, etc"). Once you have understood this your goal in interacting with other religions will be to stress and promote what is *common* between you and downplay your *differences*.

Therefore, the Main "Jedi Religion" Principles are:

(a) You and your people are wrong as you are (+|-). (b) The solution to this deficiency ("salvation-healing-freedom") is simply *Knowledge/Experience of the Force (the Truth (±)-Reality-"God") and of your union with it,* that is, being a JEDI and in THE JEDI ORDER, as the unity of (+) consciousness and (-) matter, of "heaven and earth." (c) How to do it: Simply believe, accept, align with the Truth (±). This is the purpose of what we call the "**JEDI CD**" and its Two Doctrines, namely: **(1)** God and you are *one* right now. Hence you are "divine-holy" (whole, perfect, immortal, healed, love, etc) = **A JEDI**. **(2)** Heaven and Earth (the Present) are *one* right now = **The JEDI ORDER**. You achieve this via various *Methods* of your religion and Jedi Ethics.

§567

Therefore the fastest, "global" way to apply all of this and to solve your planet's religious problem is by *creating within all your religions "Jedi Sects"—which foster these principles and <u>unity</u> among your religions and an end to all hate and division.* **What you do is:**

(1) "Jedi" your religion. That is, add a "**Jedi CD**" to it.
(2) Find scriptures that support Jedi Religion Principles and the Jedi CD and make them *primary* and the basis for *primary* dogmas/doctrines. And make them agree with (or not contradict) major dogmas of your religion (as far as possible). And demote (if they exist) "hate/divisive" scriptures by giving them a true "Jedi" interpretation.

§568

Thus there is only one way to Balance your religions—You must teach, focus and major on *UNITY* and *TRUTH,* rather than Non-Unity and separation. That is, (1) teach Unity *within* a given Religion to ensure the True *Healing* of its votaries, as Jedi and the Jedi Order, and (2) teach the Unity *at the base of all* religions in order to end the hate and conflict among them so they can henceforth work together in concert to realize *the glorious Jedi Order.*

The installing of a Jedi Sect and CD in each of your religions will achieve both (1) and (2).

§569

THE "JEDI SECT"

A "Jedi Sect" therefore is based on the TRUTH (±), *the Knowledge of the Force,* and teaches the specific *Doctrines* of a given Religion *and* Two other Doctrines—which supply the power to heal and to liberate, that is, to "re-ligare." Namely,

---

(1) You and God are One *right now.*

(2) Heaven and Earth (the Present World) are One *right now.*

These two additional doctrines are to be supported by *scriptures* from your religion's Holy Book, as well as by Reason and Logic.

---

§570

This "Jedi" Solution furthermore is the *only* solution because: (1) Jedi Reason and Truth knows the *true* meaning of "Re-ligare" and *healing* as (±). (2) A truly healed, immortal Jedi-Muslim/Jew/Christian would never *hate* or become a terrorist-suicide bomber. (3) Even if, for example, warring sects in Iraq (Shia and Sunni militias) agree to a cease fire, hostilities would only flare up again in the future since doctrinal differences would still remain. And even if these were resolved no true healing or salvation would result due to the flawed knowledge of what true healing is (±).

Now to show you noble Reader how this Jedi Solution actually works, we will look at the Jedi Sect as applied to and operative in some of your major religions, namely (in alphabetical order): Christianity, Judaism, Islam, and New Age spirituality.

§571

(A) A Jedi Christian Sect.

(1) First to be a **Christian** you must (minimally) believe:

1. There is only One God—revealed in three persons, Father, Son, and Holy Spirit.

2. Man is in "sin" (separated from God) but can have salvation through God's Son (Jesus Christ) who canceled sin by his life, death and resurrection.

3. Final Judgment and Resurrection-Immortality (Heaven-Hell); and the New Heaven and Earth ("The Jedi Order").

§572

(2) Then the Two "Jedi" doctrines, a Jedi CD, are added to create a *"Jedi Christian Sect"*:

> 4. *God and you are <u>one</u> right now.* Hence you are "divine-holy" (whole, perfect, immortal, healed, love, etc), a JEDI.

> 5. *Heaven and earth (the Present World) are <u>one</u> right now.* Hence the JEDI ORDER is now. Only believe and align with these two Truths, which are based on:

6. Supporting scriptures: (i) *I am one with God now (and share/express his divine nature and abilities):* "We share the divine nature (= are divine)" 2Pet.1:4. "Whoever is perfect shall be as his (Jedi) Master." "He has perfected us forever." "Your sins [separation from Me] are forgiven/erased, and I remember them no more." "I and God are one, and so are you," Jn. 17. (ii) *Heaven and earth are <u>one</u> right now*—"Heaven is *within* and among you—is Now." "It is finished" (the world is redeemed/perfect *right now*). (For additional support you can also add quotes from Mystics, Saints, Meister Eckhart, etc.)

7. Methods. (i) Christian (prayer, fasting, meditation, spiritual gifts, "speaking in tongues," etc), (ii) Jedi (*II. The Jedi Code*), (iii) other.

§573

SOME OBJECTIONS as voiced by Christians and others ANSWERED:

OBJECTION #1. "This teaching is OK in general for Christians. But when applied to Other religions there are problems. For example, that anyone in any religion can be "saved" without believing in "Jesus Christ" and his atoning death on the cross—implies that Christ died for nothing."

ANSWERED: (1) Be mindful that Jesus also called himself *"The Truth"*— another *equivalent* name for himself. So to believe-align-surrender yourself to the Jedi *Truth* is in reality *the same* as believing in Jesus—in all that he is and did.

(2) In Revelation it clearly states regarding the "Last Judgment," that when "the books were opened all were judged according to their WORKS (deeds, words)"—and not if they believed in Jesus as Lord and Savior, etc. **Jesus** himself says in John's Gospel, "You do not have to believe in Me, only in the One who sent Me (the Father-God)"— or only my doctrine (not my Person), and that even apart from Me, "The Kingdom of God is within you, NOW," etc. **Jesus** says that the way to be "saved" is to "know the Truth (your present unity with God) and be free (sinless, OK)," "to follow, imitate Me" and "Do what I did" (as Exemplar), and not necessarily what **St. Paul** says, which is to believe on Christ's "death on the cross" (as our Substitute)—this is Paul's (or one particular) interpretation (but it can be used, as it is efficacious for some persons). **Jesus** also said,

"Those who believe the Gospel will be saved, those who don't won't." But the Question rather is: What is *the "gospel"?* The Answer is simply *that the Human and Divine natures are One* (as your **Nietzsche** says in his work *The Antichristian,* 30-37). Namely, Your "Sins" (separation from God) are forgiven, i.e., "I am one with the Father, and so are you," which expresses the I/God unity or eternal Life. That is to say: He, Christ Himself—the human/divine unity—*is* the GOSPEL (as **Hegel, Eckhart, Altizer, Leahy** and others say). The Gospel is *not,* **"Jesus Christ died for you, atoned and sacrificed himself *in order to appease an angry God."* What is *really* behind this is the simple Fact and the Truth that: **IT IS.** It *is* possible (viz., the divine/human unity). Your sins *are* forgiven. You are OK. You *are One* with God *right now.* Hence, it simply allows you to THINK THE THOUGHT. To Believe in the UNITY (the POINT), and Act on it. In *this* lies the (saving) power of the Gospel, the Message, the Truth. E.g., "Believe in and *do* my doctrine, and you too will know of its Truth."—As Jedi **Hegel** said, "Humanity must become capable, must combine on this principle of the unity of the human/divine natures as revealed in Christ." And Jedi **Fichte**: "Christ came to do the Will of his *Father (the Force), not his own* ("my words are not mine, the Father in me He doeth the works, etc"), and did not care if future generations remembered his personal name or part in 'the Work'."

> "Other interpretations, e.g., of the *sacrificial offering,* with which is connected *the false idea that God is a tyrant who desires sacrifice,* reduce themselves to the true concept of sacrifice (viz., the abolition-absorption of naturalness-Otherness) and are to be corrected by it." PR III 95. **Hegel**

(3) In any case this is an important *advance* since it opens a dialog between religions, especially Christians, Muslims, and Jews; they will be moved to embrace each other, seek commonalities and not differences, and reduce hostility leading to war and terrorism. The truth is that, "By their fruits ye shall know them." We hold that there *will* indeed be *healing*, as there is none presently.

§574

OBJECTION #2. "You seem to annul the *distinction* between God and us/man—and teach "We are God," like the New Age."

ANSWERED: (1) No. What we Jedi in the end are teaching is **Paul's** "I live, yet not I, Christ (the Force, the Truth) liveth in me." So since Christ really *is* the *Absolute I*, we simply get "taken over" by God/the Truth. Thus it is God who "gets the glory"—and not us. We are not saying that, "*We* as P.I.'s are God," but as U.I.'s, which is totally different, and in *this* sense we certainly are God (as we have discussed, and when understood correctly). Indeed ultimately *that* is what God Himself *wants* (for as your scriptures state, "we share the divine nature," 2Peter 1:4; and as **Hegel** and **Plato** say, God is not envious or jealous, hence the welcoming sentiment is, "Come on in the water's fine!"). This is also the true meaning of the *revelation*, the gospel that *is* JESUS CHRIST—namely, the Truth *as* the GOD-MAN, the *Unity* of God and Man—which is the Truth about all of you/*all* men and women.—"May they be *indissolubly One* (*echad*) as we *are*." As Jedi **Fichte** says, the eucharistic injunction "Eat my Body" really means that you are to "become *transfused/-formed* into I Myself," such that "My divine *blood* will mingle and interpenetrate with yours." Only *unity* thus remaining.

> "The whole point of the gospel is that *everyone* may experience union with God in the same way and to the same degree as Jesus himself." *Behold the Spirit,* **Alan Watts**

§575

(2) The scriptures also say, "we share the divine nature," "May they be One as we are One," "The disciple can be *just as* (*kathos*) his Master" (Christ does not qualify this), and **Paul** in Hebrews says that, "Jesus *became* perfect, etc." Also in John's *Revelation* Christ says,

"As I have *overcome* the world, so will you ..." Further **Christ's**, "I was with you (God) before the foundation of the world," simply means that *anyone* who achieves (±), the Unity, Truth, POINT, is and will find himself *back* in the *Eternal Now*—meaning that the Now in the beginning, the Now of Jesus' time, and the Now of right now, *are one and the same NOW* (as your own quantum physicists and **Einstein** hold). Lastly, the "Pre-worldly Trinity" in truth simply refers to the *Force itself as Principle (or Arche, in Logic) and as unexpressed.*

(3) Again the answer is No. That is, P.I./EGO is not God—but U.I. is. You must realize by logic that you cannot have or conceive God and Man as *two* separate entities existing simultaneously, this would render God "finite" and "God" by definition is *infinite*—so *nothing* can exist outside God. You can however teach that, "We are/can be ONE with God," if you have difficulty with the locution, "We are God." Both are acceptable—as reflecting different levels of understanding, education, and growth.

§576

Jesus also says "follow/imitate me," or "do what I did." This is why we say you should meditate: "I AM," "I AM the Force/Father/God," since Jesus himself said, "Before Abraham was, I AM." But again the "I" here *is not you* (as P.I. or EGO, etc)—*it is God or the Absolute I.* And it is a powerful way to bring God/the Truth close to you and to realize the Truth (±) of your present *unity* with God, for "I and the Father will live in you," and, "I live, yet not I ... Christ/God lives in me." Then by this method *alone* you will be able to *merge* with God, merge your own "I" with God's "I" (see *Part II: The Jedi Code*, on "Meditation"). **Jesus** said deny your *self* (EGO) and gain your true Jedi *Self,* or exchange your "old man" for a "New Man,"—and your *NEW Self is One with God (like Jesus).* YOU, your religious teachers, do not teach your people how to do this and leave them permanently in their old self or EGO and thus *outside* of God and the TRUTH. *Shame on you.*

§577

In any case you *have* to give up your false teaching of God as *separate* from yourselves and the universe, and outside it—as if "God" were *there,* and "you-man-world" were *here.* This is logically impossible— and *atheistic* to boot since then, 1. God becomes FINITE or not God, and further, 2. There is *no "Thing in itself."** Therefore God *must* be here—and you are *Now* One with Him, you just have to be *taught* this. You *have* to re-think God and accept some kind of *immanent* type of God—as **Jesus** does ("the Kingdom is *within you*").

*Again, there is no "transcen*dent*" God—this is non-sense, gobbledegook, or a "non-thought," as **Fichte** and your **A-Team** have shown—and therefore GOD must be *absolutely immanent* ... and *Infinite* ... as one and the same as Pure, Apriori, Transcendental *Consciousness,* the Absolute I, the POINT—hence without any doubt "the Kingdom of God is *within* you/within us." You must therefore at all cost *break* with and utterly discard this dangerous Picture-Thought of "God as up there in the sky ... looking down." God is rather on the *INSIDE* of you LOOKING OUT. Again, if I may, "The words that I speak are not mine. It is the *Father* (the Absolute I) in me that doeth the works" ... the very *same Father* (or *Force*), namely, that is in us and in you now, etc. Not to mention, "greater works than I have done, ye shall also do."

§578

OBJECTION #3. "You seem to claim to know the true meaning of the TRINITY—we say there are three separate Persons or substances that are *one* in essence, etc."

ANSWERED: Yes, we Jedi do claim this and hold that "Father, Son, and Spirit" in truth refer to and express in the form of picture-thinking Logic's and the CONCEPT'S three moments of "Universal, Particular, Individual." The point is you should try to refute us if you can ... or we can proceed to refute your interpretation by logic and reason, and show e.g., that there simply cannot be *two* substances or absolute's, etc, etc.

> "While sacrifice is the most universal of all religious or ultimate movements, and may be understood as the very core of our purest ritual, it is nevertheless *most resisted and transformed by our dominant theologies,* and most so insofar as these are bound to primordial Godhead itself." **Altizer**

However it does not matter in the end since we both do accept the idea of a "Trinity" (though our account of it is informed by the Truth of Polarity or the Unity of Opposites). The main thing is the HEALING of your people and planet.

§579

OBJECTION #4. "If the Jedi Order—the Kingdom of God (±), the Unity of God/Man, Heaven/Earth—exists now how come the world is in the dysfunctional state it is in (war, greed, disease, inequality)?"

ANSWERED: In one word, it is BECAUSE OF YOU, your own teachers, educators, and "scientists." That is, the people of your world are simply not told or taught it, for example by their religious, political and educational institutions. In your case, YOU continue to teach and sustain Dark Side *separation and* EGO. Hence your people live *only* in their EGO'S—without Power or Knowledge. As your Jewish prophet **Isaiah** said, "My people perish from a lack of *Knowledge.*" In **Altizer's** words: "Indeed, no other apprehension of the Godhead is ... so given to apprehending the Godhead as absolute sovereignty and absolute transcendence *alone,* one foreclosing every possibility of an absolute sacrifice or self-emptying, and *every possibility of the transfiguration of Godhead itself.*"

§580

OBJECTION #5. "What about such things as, "the Last Judgment, the Second Coming, Heaven and Hell (and the eternity of Hell), the Devil and Angels, the Resurrection of the Just and Unjust, the Pre/Post tribulation, the Millennium, the Rapture, etc"? How should we regard these time-honored doctrines? And, How should we now "witness"?—since the Jedi say that *all* religions can take you to "Salvation or Heaven," that is *apart from* Jesus Christ? Similarly, How should we worship, if "God" is within us and identical with our *pure consciousness?*"

ANSWERED: To begin with as concerns the "witnessing" question: Yes you still can say, "*Believe* on *Jesus Christ* and you will be *saved,*" and, "If you do not *believe* on Him (on the Truth) you will be *condemned,* etc." But the real question is, (1) What does "*believe* on him" mean? and (2) What does "condemned" mean?

(1) As regards "believe," it simply means "Follow me" or "*BE* Me," again as in "Eat my flesh, Drink my Blood" (à la your Jedi **Fichte's** interpretation). And in the "Sower sows the Seed" parable, the "seed" is the "Word of God" which in fact IS God (John 1), the implicit or "coded" meaning being that whoever receives *within*

herself and matures the Word of God seed literally *becomes God or divine* (as **Jean Hyppolite** taught), that is, *the TRUTH itself* as "U.I." or the *unity* of the Universal and Individual, the Father and the Son. Hence "if you continue in my *Word* (your sins will be forgiven, and) you will know the TRUTH and be Free"; that is, free of Sin or *separation* from God, hence *One* with God. The teaching is that you should make God, UNITY, the TRUTH, your JEDI Self and the JEDI ORDER your #1 End and Priority. As **Paul** says you are to "Grow up into Christ (= God)." Hence to just say, "I believe in Jesus and am a 'card carrying' Christian," is not enough, is to "miss the point" (*hamarteia*). As Christ has said, "Many will come in my name ... but I knew (*gignoske*) you not, depart from me ye workers of iniquity." Also as **Rob Bell** has pointed out, *"eternal punishment" is a mis-translation of the Hebrew for "a limited time" (OLAM) or "a period of pruning"; indeed, your Bible states that Jonah was in the belly of the whale for "OLAM"* or three days.

§581

(2) As regards "condemned," first be mindful my Padawan that according to your scriptures "God *wills* that *all* men be *Saved* and come to a *Knowledge of the TRUTH (the FORCE)."* Now given that God is omnipotent it then follows that what God *wills will indeed* come to pass. As it also says, "God will be *All-in-All,"* and "Christ filleth *all in all,"* which means that so-called Devil's, Demons, Hell, Satan (Darth Vader) et al are all comprehended by and in the second "**All**," AND HENCE WILL BE NO MORE. Thus in the end only Goodness, Glory, and God remain. Hell, evil, and sin therefore *cease Forever.* Moreover your book of *Revelation* states that, "Jesus (God) has (1) the Keys of Hell and Death," hence is able to open the "prison cells" of everyone in Hell, and (2) "the Key of David" or of absolute Power and Authority in both this world and the next (the worlds of Heaven *and of Hell*)). And the Bible itself ends in *Revelation* with the word, "*IF* (which is a *hypothetical*) anyone was *not* in the Book of Life, they were cast into the Lake of Fire (*pyre*), etc," hence indicating the possibility of *no one being cast into Hell.*

§582

The FACT is that for many reasons **Jesus** *had* to teach as he did concerning "Hell" and its permanence and penalties. For there truly are grave *consequences* for *not* believing and rejecting the Message and

> "Man has his ultimate home in a *supersensuous world*—an *infinite subjectivity,* gained only by a rupture with mere natural existence and will and by his labor to break their power within himself."
> *Philosophy of History,*
> **Hegel**

Truth that he taught, that is, for *not* being who you are or all you can be, and for not "repenting" (*metanoia,* thinking ($\pm$) rather than ($+|-$)) and realizing your Jedihood or present oneness with God. That is, *if* after biological death and in your "Mansion" or "hovel" ("hell state") you are too *impure* to "enter Heaven"— the consequence is indeed "suffering," albeit in the form of a "purgation or cleansing." The FACT is that you *must* be transformed, from "Ego" to Jedi. BUT the Jedi, Reason, Logic, and even the Bible (when correctly interpreted) are one in teaching that Hell/suffering/purification (and "pure" is from your Greek "pyre" = "fire") are *not* eternal. As said, God's *will* cannot be thwarted—and this is because evil, sin ($+|-$), separation or the Dark Side is ultimately an illusion and temporary, merely a "privation" as **Augustine**, **Origen**, and **Hegel** all taught; and it was **Schelling** who said that "sin and its consequences cannot be eternal."

§583

OBJECTION #5, Continued. "How should we Christians then regard these Doctrines?"

ANSWERED: The main point is that they are only *secondary* and NOT *primary,* no matter *how* you interpret them. Therefore by all means keep them ... But just make your *main Focus* the Primary **#1** Doctrine and Teaching of the *TRUTH* of *UNITY*—namely, "I and God are One, Now," and "Heaven and Earth are One, Now"—that is, Heaven is *in me, is in you, is in us, and is NOW ... and not a moment later.*

So therefore, DO NOT get *hung up* on TIME—for only NOW is. Give these Doctrines a "Symbolic or Figurative" and not a literal "real time" interpretation if you can. DO NOT let them *negate* the one thing needful as concerns your Education—Christhood, Jedihood, Freedom, and Total Healing. The MAIN POINT again is: You, We are in Heaven Now. Heaven is in you. The Jedi Order is Now. Thus the Truth is simply that THE JEDI ORDER IS NOW. This is absolutely certain and proved by the JEDI TRUTH and JEDI

SCIENCE. And so YOU *MUST* CONFORM *EVERYTHING* TO THIS TRUTH.

"The Jedi Order is Now." You MUST make *this* your MAIN FOCUS.— And you can also teach—since there is "no time" as "1000 years is as a day" and vice-versa—that all these things *are happening NOW.* That is, the Last Judgment (or really *universal forgiveness, recognition, and reconciliation),* the Resurrection, Millennium, Tribulation, and Rapture ... *are all occurring in the **Eternal Now** ... for **Eternity will not be, nor has it been. IT IS.***

§584

The MAIN POINT. To the **CLERGY**: you *must* change. You must teach and realize *UNITY*—Otherwise there will never be *HEALING* ... War, Terrorism, Hate, Fear, Death, etc, will have no end. To the **LAITY**: If your clergy and leaders refuse to change, *YOU* should take the lead and the initiative—YOU CHANGE. Do not let them or anyone take away your BIRTHRIGHT of TOTAL HEALING, JOY, FREEDOM, "KINGDOM NOW."

§585

AFFIRMATIONS-MEDITATIONS

(1) *"I AM the Resurrection and the Life"*—where the "I" here is not you (John, Elaine, Ego, P.I.) but Jesus or God Himself. You are just *expressing* the Truth—of "Christ in you ... ," of your *present* UNITY with God/Christ. You are *not* saying you (as a P.I.) *are* God/Christ. Further the "I" also is not Jesus alone, as a *separate* particular person (exclusive of others). 1. The "I" is the ***Truth***, the *Universal* I (as a Unity of *Universal* and *Individual,* Father and Son that is Spirit or Jedi). 2. There *is* no Jesus alone, for "I and the Father are *One*" and, "I can do *nothing* apart from Father; he doeth the works and my words are His." 3. Therefore: It is *the Father* (God) *in him* who is "the Resurrection and the Life" (not **Jesus of Nazareth** *by himself*).

—Moreover you can do this with any and all of Christ's *words* in the Bible. E.g., "I and the father are One," "Who has seen me has seen the father," "Before Abraham was I AM," etc. In all of these Meditations you are simply bringing the POINT, the Absolute I that is concealed within you *to the surface* and realizing your *unity* with it.

§586

(2) *"I am Divine, Redeemed, Holy, Perfect, Whole, etc."*
This follows from: "I am *Perfect* or *Complete* (in Him)," and "He has perfected us forever; (namely) those that *are* sanctified (or are *saints*)." Notice also that your **Paul** always writes, "to the saints—not *sinners*—at Ephesus, Colosse, Thessalonica, etc," and that, "I AM *Complete*" means literally that as such, as (±), you need, want, and lack *nothing*—no mate, person, possession, etc.

§587

(3) JEWS AND MUSLIMS CAN ALSO DO THIS (FOR E.G. MUSLIMS MUST ALSO BELIEVE THE BIBLE)

As Christians you are asked to *"imitate* Christ"—be like him/do as he did/does. Therefore you too should say: "The *Father* in me, *he* doeth the works."—Compare, "I and the Father will dwell in you," and "You are the *Temple* of God." You should cultivate *this mind-set* which is the same one as Jesus', and this is because the *Father (God, the Force)* really *is* in you. NOTE also that, "You are the *Temple* of God" means that God is *in* you; and that the statement, "I will dwell in them and walk (think, will, say) in them," really means that "to dwell, live and walk, etc," *is to do everything*—to breathe, talk, walk, run, sleep, eat … to literally FUSE with God. And Muslims can combine *this* with the HADITH: "I (Allah) will become *him*, his eye, his ear, his foot, his hand etc."

§588

(4) The HIGHEST/QUICKEST METHOD (CHRISTIAN) FOR THE REALIZATION OF JEDI, The THEOTIC PROCESS, lies in the meditation/affirmation:

"I <u>AM</u> JESUS CHRIST"

—My mind and my flesh is Jesus Christ, my heart, liver, arms, hands, … (to be compared with the *Hadith* above). The KEY is that this teaching agrees perfectly with the JEDI TRUTH and SCIENCE. That is to say, *Theosis*, the Self-actualization Process of the Force—the move from EGO to JEDI—involves what is called "THE NEGATION OF NEGATION"—that is to say, your natural Being/Will and BODY (-) must be NEGATED or transformed by complete fusion with *the Universal* (+). And this happens most effectively, when you say "I am Jesus Christ" (or the Force/God), which is to say, "I am *not* Richard/Rachel, my EGO story and identity. You "negate the negation" (which issues in total AFFIRMATION) precisely when you "die" and exchange *your* self for *Jesus'* Self, when you are "possessed" and let yourself be "taken over" (= negated) by another (a perfect Other), Jesus Christ. Thus the result of this and other sustained MEDITATIONS is that eventually God and yourself will *merge* utterly and coincide. Your flesh and blood, bones, organs ... *LITERALLY* will become HIS own flesh and blood (cf. the Islam *Hadith* and the Sufi's writings). God therefore will become fully present, touchable, "incarnational"—in you *and* as you. Thus when I, e.g., am talking to *you*, I am in truth talking to God Himself—*and not a copy or surrogate.* As your Jedi **Fichte** says, commenting on the true meaning of Christ's most offensive statement in the Gospels, "*Except ye eat the flesh of the Son of Man, and drink his blood, ye have no life in you*" (Jn. 6,53):

> "To eat his flesh, and drink his blood means none other than *to become wholly and entirely he himself;* to become altogether changed *into his Person* without reserve or limitation; to be a *faithful repetition* of his personality; to be *transubstantiated* with him—i.e., as he is the Eternal Word made flesh and blood, to become his flesh and blood, and ... **to become the very Eternal Word made flesh and blood** ***itself***,—to think wholly and entirely like him, and so as if he himself thought, and not we;—to live wholly and entirely like him, and so as if he himself lived in our life."

§589

Jedi **Fichte** goes on to say: "As surely as you do not now attempt to drag down my words, and reduce them to the narrow meaning that Jesus is only to be *imitated* as an *unattainable pattern*, partially and at a distance, as far as human weakness will allow, but accept them in the sense in which I have spoken them,—that **we must be transformed into Christ himself,**—so surely will it become evident to you that Jesus could not have said the thing better, and that he actually did express himself excellently well. Jesus was very far from representing himself as that unattainable ideal into which he was first transformed by the *spiritual poverty of after-ages*; nor did his Apostles so regard him: among the rest **Paul**, who says: 'I live not, but Christ liveth in me.' Jesus desired that *he should be **repeated** in the persons of his followers, in his complete and undivided character, as he was **in himself**.*"

And in the words of your contemporary theologian **D.G. Leahy**, "You, the actual reader, you who are not able to say **'I AM CHRIST,'** you, nevertheless, **ARE** the Jesus Christ who is the beginning … Divine omnipotence is for the first time the absolute elimination of the impediments of superstition, *distance itself*, and identity" (FMBI, 1996, 620).—And your Jedi theologian **Tom Altizer** goes even further when he says that, "[B]y an **Hegelian** irony of history it becomes the destiny of the Eucharist [the Body of **CHRIST**] to be the substantial experience of the world at large. Now an essentially new consciousness is born whereby and wherein *the very matter of the universe* becomes the apocalyptic and sacrificial body of God" (JR, 1994, 190).

§590

STARTING A JEDI CHRISTIAN SECT

(1) Start with the existing. Speak with your Priest or Pastor or Board of Elders. Tell them why they must do this and why it is absolutely imperative. Namely, the Jedi CD and Sect contains the true core of Christianity and results in the realization of God's perfect will: Total Healing, the *Unity of All*, the advent of the Kingdom of God on Earth, and the end of all war, hate, injustice, and conflict among religions. (2) If a wholesale change is denied then ask to start a small group *within* the Church and congregation, and see what happens. It *will* take off. The change will be apparent as there will be more healing, power, and love, and less guilt (due to greater UNITY with God and Christ). (3) If even this cannot be done then start an entirely new Jedi Christian Sect and Church; ideally with an ordained Catholic or Protestant Priest or Pastor, or an ordained Jedi Priest or Pastor. It *will* take off and multiply. Members of other Christian sects will come into your Jedi Sect. This will force the others to adopt Jedi Christian Principles, etc.

§591

(B) A Jedi Jewish Sect.

We must first note a key issue unique to Judaism, which is both a religion and a nationality. Hence there are both *religious* Jews and *non-religious* (secular or atheist) Jews. As **Tracey Rich** states:

> A Jew is any person whose mother was Jewish or any person who
> has gone through the formal process of conversion to Judaism.
> [Hence] it is important to note that being Jewish has nothing to do
> with what you believe or what you do. A person born to non-Jewish
> parents who has not undergone the formal process of conversion
> but who believes everything that Orthodox Jews believe and
> observes every law and custom of Judaism is *still a non-Jew*, even in
> the eyes of the most liberal movements of Judaism, and a person
> born to a Jewish mother *who is an atheist and never practices the Jewish
> religion is still a Jew*, even in the eyes of the ultra-Orthodox. In this
> sense, Judaism is more like a nationality than like other religions,
> and being Jewish is like a citizenship.

Here our primary focus will be on religious Jews or Judaism as
a religion. The main sects or movements within Judaism are
Orthodox, Conservative, Reform, Reconstructionist, Renewal, and
Kabbalah and Chasidism. It is a fact (1) that Judaism is primarily a
"way of life" where actions are more important than beliefs and
(2) that there are no mandated official doctrines in Judaism that
everyone must believe in order to be a Jew. We will nevertheless
provide a list of Jewish beliefs and practices with the understanding
that not all Jews in the above mentioned sects necessarily subscribe
to all or even some of them. In the end what is alone important is
that "re-ligare" and true healing occur, that one transitions from
separation (+|-) to Unity (*echad* (±)). It thus can be said that, Do
whatever it is you do and Believe whatever it is you believe ... just
add the Two Unity principles and make them primary. Indeed we
offer that these Two Principles embody the true essence of Judaism,
what it really is to *be* Jewish, and what God truly wills for his people
and is revealed in the Jewish scriptures. Therefore:

§592

(1) To be a Jew you must believe and practice:

1. Rambam's 13 principles of faith which include: God exists, is one
and unique, is incorporeal and eternal, the Mashiach will come, and
the dead will be resurrected.

2. Halakhah (or Jewish Law, "the path that one walks"), the actions
related to the 613 commandments (*mitzvoh*) of the Torah (including

the Ten Commandments), rabbinical laws (from the Talmud), and traditional customs.

3. Observance of Shabbat and the High Holy Days and Festivals: Yom Kippur, Rosh Hashana, Pesach, Shavuot, and Sukkot.

§593

(2) Now add the Two "Jedi" doctrines or "Jedi CD" to create a "**Jedi Jewish Sect**":

> 4. *God and you are* <u>*one*</u> *right now.* Hence you are "divine-holy" (whole, perfect, immortal, healed, love, etc), a JEDI.

> 5. *Heaven ("the World to Come," Olam HaBa) and earth (the Present World) are* <u>*one*</u> *right now.* Hence the JEDI ORDER is now. Only believe and align with these two Truths, which are based on:

6. Supporting scriptures: (i) *I am one with God right now (and share/ express his divine nature and abilities):* "Let us [God] make man (male and female) in our own image." Gen. 1:26, 5:2. "And God formed man of the dust of the ground, and *breathed* into his nostrils the *breath* of life; and man became a living soul [i.e., God's breath or consciousness and man's *are one and the same*]." Gen. 2:7. "You are the temple of the living God ["I AM"]." Jer. 31:33. "Be ye holy, even as I [God] am holy [Be like God]." Lev. 19:2. "The Lord your God [*Adonai Eloheikhem*] keeps covenant and mercy with those that LOVE him ... And the Lord God will LOVE you, and bless and multiply you ... and take away from you *all sicknesses*" [If you love God and God loves you, the Two become One (±), ONE LOVE]. Deut. 7:9, 13, 15. "I [God] said you are gods and goddesses [*Elohim*]." Psalms 82:6. "I [God] will dwell in you and walk in you." Ezek. 37:27, Levit. 26:12, Exod. 29:45. "I [God] *have* blotted out your transgressions and your sins [your separation from Me] ... and will not remember them; for I *have* redeemed you; all Israel will be saved with an *everlasting salvation ... world without end!*" Isaiah 44:22, 43:25, 45:17, 22. "Sin" is what separates you from God and eternal life. Thus, "no sin" means no separation from God ... that is, ONENESS with God and immortality and full possession of eternal life, NOW. You share and participate in God's Life, Love, and Spirit (*Ruach HaKodesh*) NOW.

§594

(ii) *Heaven ("the World to Come") and earth are <u>one</u> right now.* Since Heaven and God are One, and you are One with God right now, then Heaven exists Now and *you are in Heaven already.* Also as your physicists and the *Knowledge of the Force* teach, *there is no time*—hence "the World to Come" and the Present World are one and the same. Isaac Luria, Baal Shem Tov, Gershom Scholem and the main ideas of Chasidic thought and Jewish Mysticism also support this: namely (1) *Panentheism* or the doctrine of God's omnipresence, of the Divine *immanence* in all Creation, that "All is *within* God"; and (2) *Devekus* or the comm-*union* (±) between God and man (which, if not a present reality, could never be accomplished or realized). There is also the Kabbalah's teaching of 1. Creation (*zimtzum*), 2. Fall (*Sherirat Hakelim*), and 3. *Tikkun* or Messianic/Metaphysical Redemption, which parallels the Jedi teaching of the three stages of education (the Force, Consciousness *of,* and Self-Consciousness or the Jedi Order). *Tikkun* is the messianic process of the healing of Creation, which each person or Jedi is responsible for helping to complete in their own life.—Moreover not only does this view imply a *collective* rather than an *individual* Messiah, but the truth is, as we Jedi know, that the secret of its accomplishment lies in the realization that, and in the adjustment to the Fact that, *the redemption*—as the Truth (±)— *is already and eternally accomplished.* In Jedi **Hegel's** words:

> The accomplishing of the infinite purpose (*tikkun*) consists therefore only in removing the illusion that *it has not yet been accomplished.* The good, the absolute good, fulfills itself eternally in the world ... It is within its own process that the Force (Idea) produces that *illusion* for itself; it posits an *Other* confronting itself, and its action consists simply in removing that illusion (that Otherness *is real*) (Enc. §212z).

(For additional support you can also add quotes from the writings of other Jewish Mystics, Saints, and Rabbis; also cf., the writings of Michael Berg and Israel ben Eliezer).

§595

As we said, these two doctrines, principles and beliefs express the true core of Judaism and the fulfillment of the Torah. As your renowned rabbi **Hillel** summed up Judaism for his own students,

"What is hateful to you, do not do to your neighbor. That is the Torah. The rest is commentary"—which is another version of the Golden Rule and is also encapsulated in the precept, "Love thy neighbor as thyself." In a word, LOVE or UNITY is the fulfillment of both the Moral Law and God's Law (the Torah): the Unity of Man and Man, Man and God, and Heaven and Earth.

THEREFORE, IN ORDER TO FULLY REALIZE GOD'S WILL— as revealed by Isaiah's, "As the waters cover the sea, so shall the whole earth be filled with the knowledge of the LORD (Isaiah 11:9), and, "Your seed shall inherit the Gentiles" (Isa. 54:3)—and to achieve total redemption and healing, the Messianic Age and the UNITY of all peoples, Jews and Gentiles; to see the end of all war, hate, anti-Semitism, and reconciliation with *all* faiths and races and to realize the Jedi Order and the World to Come NOW ... YOU *MUST* EMBRACE JEDI UNITY PRINCIPLES, which are the true principles of Judaism. God's will is healing, eternal salvation, and the redemption of all peoples. Hence to be truly healed you *must* overcome sin, guilt, and separation (hate, jealousy, etc) and live continually in the eternal LOVE which is God's very essence.

7. Methods. (i) Jewish (prayer, fasting, meditation, spiritual gifts, etc), (ii) Jedi (*II. The Jedi Code*), (iii) other.

§596

For Non-Religious Jews: Agnostic, Secular, Atheist Jews (Buju, Buddhist Jews, New Age Jews): For these to be healed and heal the world—Jedi and the Jedi Order—to live the greatest life imaginable and be who they really are, they can and must either become Jedi Jews or adopt the JEDI CODE. For if they do not they will remain in their separate Ego, with problems, dysfunction, and the Dark Side, contravening the Truth and God's will.

In the last analysis, to identify oneself as, or to call oneself, a Jew, Christian, Muslim, Buddhist, Atheist, etc, *means in truth nothing at all*—for only the TRUTH, realizing and aligning with it—and which *is* the living core of every re-ligion (and Science as well)—*counts and is important.* It alone is to fulfill God's will.

§597

OBJECTIONS: (1) If those who call themselves "Jedi Jews" do not formally *convert,* we orthodox Jews cannot recognize them as Jewish. *Answer:* The truth is that they *are indeed Jewish!* So you must change and accept them. For to be Jewish (as the Knowledge of the Force and scripture prove) is to be ONE with God and ONE with all people (to love all neighbors or others as yourself); and Love is the fulfillment of the Law. *This* is #1, and all else is secondary or even optional; for to do all things—shabbat, high holy days, light candles, keep a kosher home—but not to have LOVE in your heart or to *hate* your brother ... is *not* to be Jewish or a *true Jew.* (At the very least you should love them "as thyself," as equally the image of God; for UNITY is all that is required.)

—Again: you have no choice; for the FACT is and remains that Unity alone Heals, whereas dis-Unity and separation prevent healing, wholeness, and happiness and keep you in your Ego and Fear, etc.

(2) We believe that Man and God *must* be separate and can never become One. *Answer:* If God is infinite then there IS no "outside" to God, hence God must be everywhere and in everything; that is, the entire Creation-Universe must logically be *within* God, see your Psalm 139:7-9ff (also see *Christian Objections,* §§577, 579, 584).

§598

AFFIRMATIONS-MEDITATIONS:

"I am One with God (*Hashem, Adonai, Elohim*)." "I am the temple of God ("I AM," *Ehyeh Asher Ehyeh*)." "God lives in me and walks and breathes and feels in me." "The 'I AM' is in the very center of my being ... and I allow the 'I AM' to pervade all of me." "God and I are ONE LOVE." "I am redeemed (holy, whole, healed, sinless) NOW." "My sins—and *separation* from God, the Infinite—are blotted out, only ONENESS is and remains. And LOVE—eternal and imperishable." "I love my neighbor (all Others) as myself. I am ONE with everyone." "I am redeemed and am a Jedi NOW." "The Jedi Order (*Olam HaBa*) and the Messianic Age is NOW (for "time" is not ... only the NOW is)." "I live *in* God's LOVE and experience love, *hesed,* and blessing 24/7/365, and I am redeemed from all sickness (Psalm 103:3, Deut. 28)."

§599

STARTING A JEDI JEWISH SECT

(1) Start with the existing. Speak with your Rabbi and the Board of Elders. Tell them why they must do this and why it is absolutely imperative. Namely, the Jedi CD and Sect contains the true core of Judaism (and the Gentiles are your inheritance). The result will be the realization of God's perfect will: Total Healing (*tikkun*), the *Unity of All*, of Jews and Gentiles (the Messianic Age), the end of all war, hate, and anti-semitism. (2) If a wholesale change is denied then ask to start a small group *within* the Temple-congregation and see what happens. It *will* take off. The change will be apparent and there will be more healing, power, and love, and less guilt (due to more UNITY with God), no self-hating Jews, backbiting, petty quarreling, and ego-one-upmanship. (3) If this cannot be done then start an entirely new Jedi Jewish Sect and Synagogue; ideally with an ordained Rabbi (orthodox, conservative, reform, or renewal, etc.); otherwise a newly ordained "Jedi Jewish Rabbi." It *will* take off and multiply. Members of other Jewish sects will come into your Jedi Sect. This will force the others to adopt Jedi Jewish Principles, etc.

§600

A brief word on BUDDHISM (Zen): Although Buddhists do not believe in a "personal" God the Fact is that the Force/God or Reality has both a *personal* and an *impersonal* aspect or dimension; and the Goal of enlightenment or Jedi education can be attained by accessing the *impersonal* aspect of God/the Force *alone*. Of course Buddhists will be in for a surprise when they encounter and experience Reality's *personal* aspect upon enlightenment! But Buddhists also teach of Enlightenment, becoming Awake, Nirvana, and of No Ego (No Self, no problem)—which are close to Jedi Principles. Thus Buddhists must adjust their understanding of enlightenment accordingly.

Moreover the Buddhist teaching concerning *nothingness* or *emptiness* (*sunyata*)—which is the true essence of and underlies the sense-material world of form or "the Cave"—is an extremely powerful Jedi Teaching, and one which is also contained in the Catholic dogma of the world's "creation *ex nihilo*" or "from *nothing*"—that is, the world *apart from* God (or Consciousness) *is nothing at all.* This Buddhist "nothingness" teaching, when fully experienced and practiced, greatly aids one's education into and experience as a Jedi. For it (1) helps to free one from *attachment* to transitory sense-objects (i.e., to nothingness, à la Jedi **Fichte** too), and (2) helps one to *transcend the senses and become fully Aware of absolute Reality and the supersensory POINT* that pervades and is coextensive with the entire sensory realm, as (±), an Awareness known to the Buddhists as *nirvana.*

§601

(C) A Jedi Muslim Sect.

(1) To be a **Muslim** you must (minimally) believe and observe:

1. "There is no god but God (Allah), and Muhammad is his messenger" (Shahada) "la illaha illa Allah." 2. Prayer (Salat), Alms-giving (Zakat), Fasting (Sawm—in Ramadan), and Pilgrimage (Haj—to Mecca). 3. Holy books (Koran, Bible, etc) and prophets; Judgment Day; Resurrection-Immortality (Heaven-Hell); and the Just Society ("The Jedi Order").

§602

(2) Now Add a "Jedi Truth **CD**" to create a *"Jedi Muslim Sect"*:

> 4. *God and you are <u>one</u> right now.* Hence you are "divine-holy" (whole, perfect, immortal, healed, love, etc), a JEDI.
>
> 5. *Heaven and earth are <u>one</u> right now* (= the JEDI ORDER is now).

Therefore only believe and align with these two Truths, which are based on:

§603

6. Supporting scriptures: (i) *I am one with God/Allah now (and share/ express his divine nature and abilities; cf. the Sufis)*: "When I love my servant, I become his ear through which he hears, his eye with which he sees [cf. **Meister Eckhart**], his hand with which he grasps,* etc," *Hadith.* (ii) *Heaven and earth are <u>one</u> right now*—because God is <u>in</u> you

now, is <u>here</u>, and Heaven and God are *inseparable*. (iii) *Against Jihad*: "We believe in what has been bestowed upon us [Muslims] as well as what has been bestowed upon you [Jews and Christians, or "People of the Book"]: *for our God and your God are <u>one and the same</u>, and it is unto him that we all surrender ourselves," Qur'an [Koran] 29:46.

(*Cf. the meditation: **"Before Abraham was, I AM."** That is, I am totally possessed by, hence one with, God/Allah/the Force right now.)

7. Methods. (i) Muslim, (ii) Jedi, (iii) other. A "Jedi" Muslim, Christian, Jew, etc., looks in other religions for their *unity/sameness/commonality*—not their *differences*. Further a "Jedi" teaches tolerance (not mistrust and hatred) towards other religions and seeks the *good* in them by which they may benefit (cf. the command to "love" and to "love your enemies," etc).

§604

OBJECTIONS: We cannot be One with Allah right Now, only in the after-life. Man and God must be *separate*, etc. *Answer.* As stated before, and by logic and definition, if God is infinite there IS no "outside" to God, hence God is everywhere and in everything; the entire Creation-Universe must logically be *within* God. And clearly by scripture and revelation (see §605 below) we are indeed one with Allah right now. The most important thing and task is to realize and experience this UNITY, which is Now (also see *Christian Objections*, §§577, 579, 584).

§605

AFFIRMATIONS, MEDITATIONS:

"I and Allah are One" (cf. *Hadith*, "When I Allah love my servant I become the eye with which he sees, etc." "He who knows himself know his Lord." "He [Allah] is with you wherever you are." *Koran* (57:4). "Wherever they look there is Allah's [God's] face." *Koran* (2:115, 50:16 & 2:186). "Heaven and earth contain Me [Allah] not, but the heart of my faithful servant contains me." "I am redeemed Now" (for to be One with Allah, is to be redeemed). "The world is redeemed now" (for Allah is omnipresent, "wherever I look, I see

Allah," Allah or God is infinite, only Allah is, there is nothing but Allah, Allah is All in All).

§606

STARTING A JEDI MUSLIM SECT.

(1) Start with the existing. Speak with your Imam or elders. Tell them why they must do it and what the advantages are: Namely, it is the true core of Islam and results in the realization of Allah's perfect will: Total Healing, the *Unity of All*, the advent of the Just Society, and the end of all war, hate, and injustice. (2) If a wholesale change is denied, ask to start a small group *within* the mosque and see what happens. It *will* take off. The change will be apparent as there will be more healing, power, and love, and less guilt (due to greater UNITY with Allah). (3) If this cannot be done then start an entirely new Jedi Muslim Sect and mosque; ideally with an imam khatib, or mullah, murshid or shaikh. It *will* take off and multiply. Members of other Muslim sects will come into your Jedi Sect. This will force the others to adopt Jedi Muslim Principles, etc.

§607

(D) A Jedi New Age Sect.

"The New Age Movement," its advent, and its many forms and expressions is a necessary phenomenon that simply reflects the Fact that your planet's history is over seeing that you have achieved "the Knowledge of the Force" and are entering "third and final cusp" and the Jedi Order. Its appearance was also necessary because your mainstream religions were not "re-ligare-ing" as they had become enfeebled, dogmatic, and institutionalized, and lapsed into the Dark Side, no longer teaching the TRUTH. There was a hunger for a *direct experience* of the Divine and *knowledge* of the Truth that your religions simply were unable to satisfy.

There are literally thousands of groups and individuals that comprise what is called "The New Age Movement." Some of the more notable are: New Thought, Theosophy, Anthroposophy, the Unity School of Christianity, Pagan, Nature and Native American Religions, Self-Realization Fellowship, Christian Science, California New Age Caucus, I AM Spirituality, Eastern Religions, Yoga and

Mysticism, Gnosticism, EST, Transcendental Meditation, LSD and peyote cults, the Findhorn Community, and the Foundation for Inner Peace (Course in Miracles). Major figures include: **Helena Blavatsky, Rudolph Steiner, Ernest Holmes, Alice Bailey, Paramahansa Yogananda, Wayne Dyer, Eckhart Tolle, Ram Dass, the Dalai Lama, Deepak Chopra, Marianne Williamson, Ken Wilber, David Hawkins, Louise L. Hay, Thich Nhat Hanh, Pema Chödrön, Doreen Virtue, Adyashanti, Byron Katie, Robert Thurman, and Gregg Braden.**

Some New Agers also use the following in their practices: meditation, chanting, channeling, ascended masters, spirit guides, gurus, guided imagery, crystals, mandalas, astrology, tarot, I-Ching, out-of-body experience, *Chi* energy, chakras, cosmic consciousness, the Akashic Records, auras, attunement, biofeedback, ESP and clairvoyance, homeopathy, rolfing, and holistic healing.

§608

The great diversity and magnitude of the above speaks to the undeniable Fact of the great Awakening that is currently taking place on your planet and the excitement and eagerness of your people to enter into and experience this glorious state of a fully healed world and humanity that we call the amazing Jedi Order. And although it can at times produce an enthusiasm that can lead to excesses and extremes—especially as perceived by your established religions and science, which cannot help but feel challenged and threatened—this will self-correct in time.

It of course is not possible to assess the truth and value of the beliefs and practices of all the groups and individuals listed above. So here again the correct guiding Rule will be: *Do whatever it is you do and believe whatever it is you believe, as long as you add the Two Jedi-Unity Principles and make them primary, in order to create a New Age Jedi Sect.* Therefore:

§609

(1) A group or individual participating in the New Age Movement must minimally believe and practice: *Whatever it is you believe and do— which includes the Main Principle of the New Age:*

History, humanity, the Universe is now entering a "New Age"—the Eschaton, the singular Goal of the Universe, the "restitution of all things," the healing of everyone and everything: *The Jedi Order*. And as a result all human institutions are changing-transforming ... from a materialist, greed, ego, self-centered, individualist-based world and worldview, to a spiritual, consciousness, Truth, Love, sharing collective-based world and worldview. (The other *implicit* New Age doctrines are those stated in (2) below)

§610

(2) (If as a New Ager you do not *already* acknowledge the following, then:)

Now add the Two "Jedi" doctrines or a "Jedi CD" to create a **"New Age Jedi Sect"**:

> 1. *God and you are <u>one</u> right now.* Hence you are "divine-holy" (whole, perfect, immortal, healed, love, etc), a JEDI.

> 2. *Heaven and earth (the Present World) are <u>one</u> right now.* Hence the JEDI ORDER is now. Only believe and align with these two Truths, which are based on:

3. Supporting scriptures: For both doctrines/principles you may use scriptures from the holy books of your planet's religions, the Bible, *Qur'an*, Vedas, Gita, etc., and statements and teachings from other proven and respected sources and authorities, for example, from *the Knowledge of the Force* and *the Jedi Code* as found in this *Jedi Handbook*, from your own cutting-edge sciences that confirm the two principles, such as *transpersonal psychology* (**Grof** and **Wilber**) and *quantum physics* (**Schrodinger, F.A. Wolf, D. Bohm, F. Capra and B. Haisch**); and of course the irrefutable proofs that Reason and Logic provide, as for example found in this *Handbook*.

—Note: Of course, if you have difficulty relating to the word "God" (as a "personal" being, which Buddhists do) you may use as a substitute, the Force, Being, Reality, the Absolute, the Infinite, the All, etc.

§611

NEW AGE CAVEATS:

We said that New Agers may "Believe whatever they may believe, and Do whatever they may do," however there are certain things and beliefs that nonetheless are erroneous and harmful and must thus be avoided.

(1) The New Age Movement for the most part has an incorrect understanding of the status and value of THOUGHT, THINKING, REASON and PHILOSOPHY AND ITS HISTORY, which are greatly undervalued by the New Age. As we have seen there are Two ways to access and experience the Truth, the Force, or God: namely *discursively* and *intuitively*; the former being the way of Thought and the Concept. Most importantly, ultimate Reality itself is simply THOUGHT or, as **Aristotle** states, SELF-THINKING THOUGHT (*noesis noeseos*). The New Age considers CONSCIOUSNESS to be the ultimate Reality, which is correct and known primarily by INTUITION—and is achieved as they say, by "utterly transcending the mind" or all thinking, thought, and Reason, which is "nothing but unceasing *chatter* in the skull." But the Fact is that it is THOUGHT that is the inner essence and core of CONSCIOUSNESS and hence has primacy over the latter. Thought, the Concept, or the Logos and Reason (as explicated e.g. in the *Jedi Science of Logic*) is in fact the veritable "DNA" of Being and the Universe as a whole. It is therefore impossible to possess a SCIENCE, that is, an adequate-accurate understanding of the Universe, Reality and all it contains, in the absence of Thought and the Concept. Indeed the History of Philosophy on your planet Earth is simply the Force's, Reality's, the Whole's *essence* achieving self-awareness. As we saw, Philosophy's History is the Becoming of the *Knowledge of the Force*, while the World's History is the Becoming of *The Jedi Order*. From these remarks one can obtain a *true* estimate of the value of Thought.—The "chatter" ascribed to Thought (mainly by your Eastern teachers) is primarily a function of the *lower* "separative" Thinking or Reason called by your philosophers "Verstand" and "Dianoia" (see Jedi **Kant**, **Hegel**, and **Plato**)—and this IS a thinking or "chatter" that *must* be overcome, and in fact *is* overcome by the *higher* "unitive" Thinking or Reason called "Vernunft" and "Nous." It is also well to note—what underscores the ultimate *oneness* between

Philosophy and the New Age and Religion—the words of your Jedi **Hegel**:

> The concern of Philosophy (or Science) has always been simply with the thinking cognition of the Force (Idea), and everything that deserves the name of Philosophy has always had at its foundation the consciousness of an ABSOLUTE UNITY of what is valid for the understanding (*Verstand* or "lower reason") only in its separateness (*Enc.* §213z).

§612

(2) Your New Agers who have returned to nature and pagan religions and spirituality are in danger of lapsing into an incorrect valuation of NATURE. Yes, a new experience of Nature (the sense-world) is necessary—as **Nietzsche** and **Hegel** say, a "transfiguration of all things," and the Bible's, "a new heaven and a new earth." A "shift in perception" is indeed necessary in order to see and experience the "Kingdom of God" NOW and all around you ... and this is what is behind this return to your earlier nature religions (as well as your concern about the destruction-pollution of the earth's ecosystem, etc) ... BUT it must be done in a certain way. One must first possess a true understanding of what Nature is, i.e., matter and its myriad shapes and forms. As we learned in *Part I* of this Handbook, *The Jedi Truth*, The Force or the Truth (±) is the "negation of negation." That is, Nature is *first*, Jedi-Spirit is *second*. (1) The Goal of transfiguring or "sacralizing" Nature is reached *first* by "transcending your senses" (nature, the Cave, multiplicity) and becoming aware of the One, the POINT, the Truth ... and (2) *then* going back or returning to Nature, the sense-realm ... but with a U.I., Universal Consciousness, where you can then see the One in the Many ($1/\infty$)—indeed as Jedi **Hegel** says, "the Concept is the omnipresent soul which remains a *One* in the *multiplicity* belonging to objective being" (*Science of Logic*, Miller 763). Only then will you see Nature utterly transfigured ... colors, patterns, light, textures, shapes, smells, sounds, qualities, feels, etc., just as they were intended to be experienced (in effect "glimpsing the morning of creation," as your **William Blake** describes it).

Therefore, NOT NATURE (-) BY ITSELF (as your pure nature religions believe), not Nature in its *immediacy*. But Nature (matter, senses) as suffused, permeated, and united *in Consciousness* (+), as

(±); that is, Nature in a *mediated* immediacy or an immediacy *mediated* by Consciousness, Thought, Spirit = The Jedi Order; hence in a *true* Immediacy (not a one-sided Immediacy). Again as **Hegel** says, "Spirit (Jedi, Mind) is not a natural being and is rather *the opposite of nature*" (*Science of Logic*, Miller 762).

§613

Also Nature's perishable products are only an *expression* or *appearance* of the Truth, but not the TRUTH itself and should not be given primacy or worshipped. As Jedi **Hegel** teaches, yes Unity with Nature is indeed the Goal—thus when contemplating Nature one should be able to say, "This is bone of my bone, flesh of my flesh"—but this Unity is not an immediate Unity, rather it is only the *Result* of a Negation of the Negation. The Truth or Spirit (*Geist*) or the Jedi Order is "twice born"—1ˢᵗ as Nature, 2ⁿᵈ as Spirit. Nature is and has often been called "the infinite Body of God," and *not* also "the Mind of God," hence Nature is *not* the Whole of All that IS but only one-half of the Whole, the Force. Nature as such is the Cave and is therefore to be *transcended* into the POINT (as Consciousness or Concept). "Pantheism" consequently is *not* the truth, rather "Pan*en*theism" is, "All (i.e. the physical-natural Universe) is *in* God" and hence should not be worshipped *as* God.—Hence the *danger* involved in treating Nature as God or as the *Whole* of Reality is that (1) you will never become aware of the POINT, the UNITY, the One Consciousness that alone is *true* Reality, and (2) you will be stuck in *attachment* to multiplicity and natural perishable individuality, and (3) you will therefore never reach the TRUTH (±) … the UNITY of Nature (-) and Spirit (+), and be a Jedi.

§614

(3) There is also a potential misunderstanding and danger involved in the teaching that "You are God," which has a wide circulation in your New Age Movement. This was discussed earlier. God is the Force, composed of infinite Consciousness (Thought) and infinite Nature-Matter-Body. So you, *as* a P.I. or empirical ego or personality, are *not* God or the Force … for it is all that exists; rather you are just using the Force's Consciousness and Body. A Jedi is one who knows this and has surrendered to this, to "pure self-consciousness." *This* is the eternal TRUTH, and you as a P.I. can *not* take credit for it. The all-important thing is to clarify the "YOU" in the statement,

"You are God." The "You" is not the P.I. but the U.I. which knows that the Consciousness one is/has is that of the Force/God itself, and which every person equally shares—as your scriptures teach, but in code, "God breathed his breath (= Consciousness) into Adam and he became a living soul, etc."

§615

(4) There is also a problem connected with the widespread teaching of "REINCARNATION." In one word, the Fact is that believers in Reincarnation can and should achieve the Goal of Enlightenment or Jedihood, *in this present life.* There is no necessity for them to go through a million more incarnations. This mind-set, belief and error permanently puts off the Jedi Order and prevents the total Healing of your race and planet from occurring. The error is simply *laziness*—"Why exert myself now, I will do it in my next life." The Truth is that **IT IS** (±) ... but you believe that **IT IS NOT.** All scriptures teach that: YOU ARE REDEEMED. The Truth, (±), is a FACT. Believing it and living it is the TASK, the difficult part. That is, Re-programming ("renewing") your Mind—which has been polluted by the Dark Side that saturates your present planetary institutions and consciousness.

(5) Another major problem concerns *Drugs,* when used as a vehicle for attaining enlightenment or liberation. The truth is that Drugs are very dangerous and their effects unpredictable, especially their unsupervised usage. All of your spiritual teachers without exception say that at the most certain drugs can give you a glimpse of the Truth or ultimate Reality but cannot permanently establish you in it. As your inner-explorer and chemist **Robert De Ropp** says: "Consciousness-expanding drugs can, if taken in the right doses, after proper preparation, with proper guidance and under the right circumstances, offer glimpses of the contents of both the fourth room and the fifth [i.e. ultimate Reality, the Highest Consciousness]. *They can never, no matter how often they are taken, enable the investigator to change his level of being.* Their continued use represents a form of spiritual burglary, which carries its own penalty ... a total loss of the individual's capacity to develop (the *Master Game,* p. 48)." Hence, although in some cases drugs may be helpful in showing and convincing one that the ordinary sense-material-egoic world, "the CAVE," is *not* the only world or reality, they should be used, if one still insists on the risks, only in a supervised setting; and after the

"glimpse" has occurred one should discontinue their use. In **Alan Watts'** words, "When you get the message, hang up the phone." If you so choose it is only *after* you have become a Jedi that you can experiment with drugs without danger.

§616

(6) One should, especially in the New Age Movement, always beware of False Teachers or Gurus who are basically on an "ego-power trip" (often unbeknownst to themselves) and who falsely teach and say to their followers, "I alone am divine or God, and you are not. You must worship me alone and do everything I say, etc."—These teachers, for example, separate married disciples and require the wives of the husbands to have exclusive sexual relations with themselves (the gurus). As for the matter of the Teacher or Master being divine or God in an *exclusive* sense, even **Jesus Christ** says, "As many as be perfect-complete can be just as (*kathos*) his Master." And **St. Paul** says that *everyone* is to grow up "unto the stature of the fullness of Christ [= God]" (Eph. 4:13). Also, "We all share (not one day *will share*) the divine nature ..." (2Peter 1:4), hence are *divine*, NOW.

§617

(7) Finally, On Powers or Siddhis. There is an obvious temptation and danger to wish to possess the incredible powers that are available to you (for even **Christ** says, "Greater works than these you shall do"). Not only can they sidetrack and distract you from reaching the Goal of a Jedi, they can result in a tremendous set-back, sending you back to "primary school," so to speak. They also inflate the Ego or false self, resulting in a "spiritual pride" that hinders the attainment of the Goal for oneself and one's students. It is best *not* to actively seek these powers as an end-in-itself. One should as in Jedi Power Ethics make being a Jedi and the Jedi Order one's #1 priority, that is, pursue Knowledge and Love first, and if powers will come they will come of themselves and when necessary. Of course, there is still the matter of the necessity of "mastering or controlling what is called the 4th Plane" of infinite energy and power, which is necessary to fully ground the Jedi Order. But this should be a primary Goal only *after* one has become a Jedi Master.

§618

OBJECTIONS: From critics of the New Age Movement, mainly from your mainstream Bible-based religions and your current sciences.

(1) The New Age teaches that "Man, the Self, Humanity is God." *Answer:* As we have seen, when properly understood this is correct: "Man" as P.I. is not God, but as U.I. is God; which is also the implicit teaching of all your religions, especially Christianity in its concept of the "God-Man."

(2) The New Age teaches "pantheism," that God is the universe, which is self-existent, hence there is no "Creator," and "personal" God to be worshipped, rather an "impersonal" God (or "Force"). *Answer:* This was already adequately answered e.g. in *Part I: The Jedi Truth* in *Consequences of the Proof of The Force.* As we also noted God or the Force has both personal and impersonal aspects.

(3) The New Age teaches that there is no such thing as "sin." *Answer:* Briefly, as Polarity and the *Knowledge of the Force* has proven, "sin" is equivalent to the Dark Side or the *separation* of opposites (+|-), which *is* an illusion (or is phenomenally real but not ontologically real as **St. Augustine** and others taught); for in truth there is only the *Unity* or non-separation of opposites, which is the TRUTH (±). Your scriptures also teach that, "We share the divine nature" and "your sins are forgiven, and blotted out," meaning that if "sins" can be erased, i.e., as if they never existed in the first place, then "sin" again cannot be ontologically REAL.

(4) The New Age Movement, according to your p-sciences, contains "bogus science." *Answer:* The fact is, as we have said, all alleged "sciences" other than *true Absolute Jedi Science* are *not* true Science or Knowledge of Being or What IS, or are "bogus sciences"—and this includes your "sciences" as well as "New Age sciences." In time the New Age Movement will endorse and embrace *Absolute Jedi Science*, which will also subsume your empirical or p-sciences within itself. The truth is in any case, "By their fruits you shall know them."

Lastly it should be said that your New Age Movement exists and was called into being simply as a catalyst to force your mainstream Religions to move from the Dark Side (+|-) to the Light Side (±) so that they may BE true re-ligions and actually HEAL people and your world, and reveal the glorious Jedi Order that is already *present.*

§619

MEDITATIONS-AFFIRMATIONS:

"I am redeemed, whole, healed NOW." "I am a Jedi NOW." "The Jedi Order is NOW." Also use the Meditations and Affirmations found in *Part II: The Jedi Code,* and also from other sources of your choosing, as long as they agree with the TRUTH (±).

§620

STARTING A JEDI NEW AGE SECT

(1) If you have already incorporated the Two Jedi Principles into your practice, and made them primary, then there is no need to do anything.

(2) If not, then just incorporate them and adopt and observe the 7 New Age Caveats.

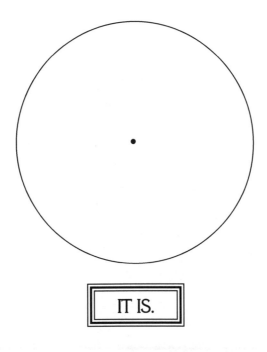

IT IS.

POLITICS

Politics is *the* privileged institution and agency among the Seven that when functioning properly provides the optimal conditions for the other Six institutions to *Educate*. Politics thus has the greatest power to realize the Jedi Order in the shortest time possible, to initiate the total solution to all your world's problems, and to achieve The BALANCE.

POLITICS SUMMARY

(A) CONCEPT. The chief purpose of Politics is Educational— to take your people into the JEDI ORDER and the POINT ... as the UNITY of all people and citizens, and all States and Nations. "Politics" derives from: (1) *POINT:* Ultimate reality is the One Infinite Consciousness and thus the UNITY of everyone. Hence the Goal is for everyone to become AWARE of this Point and Unity, which is the true purpose of politics, as proclaimed by your famous "E PLURIBUS UNUM." (2) *ETYMOLOGY:* "Politics" derives from your Greek "politeia" and "polis" meaning the city-state or State and, when perfected, the JEDI ORDER. "Politics" then in truth is the knowledge and praxis for creating and maintaining the JEDI ORDER. As based on the Knowledge of the Force, *politics* involves the knowledge of the #1 GOOD for "Man" and the true Concepts of Reality, the State, and History. A JEDI STATE and government makes the best Laws, decisions, and allocation of resources. Indeed when all citizens receive a JEDI education, *criminals* and crime become obsolete and the State is saved billions of dollars (as happens with Jedi Doctors and Jedi preventive Medicine).

(B) WRONG/IMBALANCE. Your leaders and governments lack the true concept of POLITICS, hence in your States the Dark Side, EGO, greed and ignorance rules. This results in sub-optimal laws, decision-making, allocation of monies and gridlock, as well as the funding of p-science and mis-education, etc, which keep people in the CAVE and prevents Healing and the glorious Jedi Order from being experienced by your peoples.

(C) BALANCE. Educate your leaders and citizens (e.g., via *civics*) on the true concept of POLITICS, and elect a Jedi President and Congress and create a Third Political JEDI Party, etc.

§621

[A] CONCEPT. The Jedi Truth teaches that your *Equality* is the fundamental truth. You are all *equal*. You are all the Infinite One or the Force in Stage Two *healing itself* to Stage Three. The ultimate purpose of Politics, the State, History, and the Universe is to achieve this Equality, Freedom and Healing. It is *Politics* that presides over this purpose to see that it is in due course accomplished. Not only is Politics *Power* but Power's true purpose is to Empower—and to realize and sustain **the glorious Order of Freedom and Healing** throughout the Galaxy: **the Jedi Order**.

§622

To begin with "politics" or the "state" does not involve the knowledge and pursuit of How to gain power and rule over others, nor does it primarily concern protecting citizens and their property. Rather the State in its true definition is and can only be the *site* where the Force heals and educates itself by overcoming its self/other split, enjoying itself forever

> "The eternal Force [Idea] eternally activates and enjoys itself as the eternal Jedi Order [the Force realized, actual, and self-knowing]." **Hegel**

as Jedi and the Jedi Order. Here as always what is most important to *good* politics is the Concept of Man one holds, the issue of *who you are, your possibilities, and who you can become.*

§623

Now **(1)** as Jedi Science teaches, the POINT indicates the true purpose of politics which is *realizing the UNITY of everyone,* and based on the Fact that Ultimate reality is *One* Infinite Consciousness that all citizens and States share and are. Hence the Goal is for everyone to become AWARE of this Point and Unity. **(2)** The word "politics" comes from your Greek "polis" and "politeia" which means, à la your Jedi **Aristotle**, the city-state or State as an association or community of men and women and the knowledge and art of running its affairs. For **Aristotle** Man is a *political* being, meaning she can realize her full potential and abilities only *within* a society and not by herself alone. As later Jedi found out, the *best* in Man, her true and highest potential is to be *the Force aware of itself* as Jedi. Thus "politics" in truth concerns the knowledge, method, and practices for realizing and *maintaining* this supreme End: the Jedi Order as a race of men and women living at their full potential, enjoying absolute *freedom* in the Eternal Now without past or future. It is an Order in which the One Force, in the *pluralized* form of wholly unique centers of consciousness, is able to express and eternally enjoy its infinite being, powers, and creative abilities. And Love.

§624

Indeed Jedi Science and the **A-Team** teach that the State and its structures—laws, customs, and constitution—exist solely to realize the primary End of the Universe—the Force's, the POINT's knowing and healing of itself. This is *absolute Freedom*—which is attained by overcoming the Dark Side—the natural *egoic* will, multiplicity, finitude, and *inequality*—and reaching infinite Jedi. *The Goal is Equality*—where *all* can be absolutely free and infinite in the only way possible—by seeing and having themselves in each other (via the *Absolute I*). Now, absolute Freedom is attained when *the Will* sees itself in *all of Objectivity,* in *all* the structures and arrangements of the State and thereby becomes *infinite.* Furthermore what your people call "right" is just the existence of your free-will *as* embodied in a thing, person or institution. For example, as embodied in (1) *Persons* and their *Property,* where "I see myself *in* my property"; *Contract,* where "I extend my will, freedom and infinity via agreement with another's will," (2) *Family,* where "I see myself in my family and its property," (3) *Civil Society,* where "I see myself in universal structures reflecting my Reason that relate to work, needs, and their satisfaction," (4) *The State,* where "I see myself in the State—its constitution and rational Laws of Freedom and Equality"; and in States and *History* or the succession of States "in time" that is nothing other than the Becoming of the Universal State of Freedom and Law—the Jedi Order, and lastly (5) *Art-Religion-and Science* where I reach absolute, infinite and eternal Freedom, the singular goal of the Universe.

§625

Thus—and by way of review—Jedi Reason taught us in *Part I* that there *is* nothing but the ONE FORCE that has two sides, the Inner Infinite (+) and Outer Infinite (-), whose *Unity* and truth is Man (±), as Body and Soul/Self/I. Further the One Force, in order to know itself or be *for itself* or self-aware, of necessity becomes an *individual* consciousness in a Body. As such it is a *finite* consciousness as a consciousness of an Object, an "Other than itself," and *not* of itself: it is not yet *infinite consciousness.* To be self-aware it must have an Object in which it sees itself, namely *another I* (or a group of I's). *This* is the foundation and necessity for the *State*—as a plurality of I's—and for *History*, which is the "time" it takes for the initial "split" to be overcome and healed, as the educational transition from *Stage Two* consciousness to *Stage Three's full self*-consciousness. Since in truth there *is only One Consciousness, One* Force, *One* Point, all I's as such are *identical* (though different, unique, and sui generis qua their own bodies and experiences). This fact and necessity for the Force to be self-aware *as* all reality sets in motion the process of *History* which is a political power struggle of Master-Slave, dominator-dominated. History's real goal, however, is the State or Jedi Order *as the universal recognition* of the equality and identity of all Selves, Persons, or Jedi, whereby each Self is recognized by the State-Community as *free and infinite* and of infinite value—as the Force itself uniquely aware of itself. And all the myriad of Selves, realized Forces or Jedi constitute but One Totality, *One Infinite Self or Force* as members of a single Body, yet each one as a *Universal* Individual at once being the entire Body, having an essence that pervades all.

§626

The Force has achieved the goal thus when it *has realized* that it has a *universal* Self; that is when it is able to see, find, and have itself in *all other Selves* (and things) and in the "Other" as such—which is achieved precisely by Jedi holistic education—by art-religion-science and Jedi Power Methods. The State—with its universal Laws of freedom and infinity—was called into being precisely to facilitate this process and achievement of *universal recognition* (of each by all, of the Force by itself). The State is further both *means* and *End* of this process. As *MEANS* the state provides an environment, context and condition in which the Goal can be reached. The State's universal Laws and constitution, as products of Reason, are Laws of Freedom (*anti* "master/slave" and "superior/inferior") whereby all selves are treated and regarded *as equals*—that is, as *Persons* with equal *rights and responsibilities;* and Persons, as Jedi Science teaches, are self-determining legal and moral *Wills,* hence free and self-existent Beings or Jedi. The State—and the plurality of States—when fully realized is also thus the *END* and *Goal* of History; which occurs when the full freedom, knowledge and infinity that its laws of freedom make possible is realized in all adult citizens. The State therefore in its essence and in truth is *an Eternal Jedi Order and Society* whose #1 Task and Highest Good is to maintain the glorious Order of Freedom *and* to educate the next generation into Jedi and Jedi Society, as well as to allocate resources and craft legislation to this End.

§627

In our Jedi language we can therefore define "Politics" as *the Knowledge of how to create and ongoingly maintain the Jedi Order,* thereby creating the optimal *conditions* for education and the realization of the #1 GOOD and for *Life in Eternity.* So the primary purpose of Politics is to Educate your citizens into a *Knowledge of the Force* and to make them aware of the BALANCE, the Jedi Order, and the UNITY which already and eternally *EXISTS.* As an "educational" institution the concern of Politics, especially in a critical period of transition such as yours, is thus to promote the Light Side (±) and increasingly demote the Dark Side (+|-).

§628

POLITICS thus involves the Knowledge of What the STATE is, What Man is, What History is, and What the #1 GOOD or End of Man is. For without knowing this one *cannot* participate and serve in Politics for the maximal benefit of all, an ignorance with disastrous consequences, as you can see for yourself. First the #1 GOOD or End of Man is *not* money, property, things, sense-pleasures, entertainment, food, universal peace and the absence of war or crime—rather it is to be a Jedi and live as an immortal Citizen in the Eternal Jedi Order (in both the Physical and Subtle realms). *History* is nothing but the becoming of a Jedi Order that is the totality of geopolitical States and inclusive of the Subtle World. The State as the Jedi Order is simply the condition and place where the Force or Whole achieves an awareness of Itself in and as Wo/Man. The key to the State and the central purpose of Politics—as your **"E pluribus Unum"** motto captures nicely—is the fundamental truth and Reality of *UNITY.* That is, at the Core of the State and of all states, thus of all people and citizens on your planet, is a **Unum** or *UNITY* that it is the sole purpose of Politics to bring to light, nurture, realize and ongoingly maintain.

§629

What the glorious Order of Freedom or the fully realized Jedi political Order on your planet Earth will be like (see also *Part III: The Jedi Order,* §§464-472):

First of all there are *two* levels or orders of "citizenship": **(A)** *World Citizenship*, as a citizen of *the **One** Universal Community of Jedi*, which supersedes all other national divisions and allegiances and includes the *Subtle Jedi Sphere*—note that, strictly speaking, all Jedi as laws unto themselves are *above* the government and Laws, which are mainly for "pre-Jedi" and only in a formal sense for Jedi; **(B)** *Local or National Citizenship*, as a citizen of one of the **Many** nations or States in your geopolitical world.

§630

In the *ideal* political world order—which it is the purpose of this *Jedi Handbook* to help your people realize—all nations, governments, and their institutions are aligned to the Truth, hence a *unity* prevails that precludes all wars and acts of terrorism. For all adult citizens and government officials are fully mature Jedi and the One Infinite Force, the Whole aware of itself. Hence your Race as a *race, literally, of fully healed gods (elohim) above both science and religion* is eternally bound together as *ONE;* and this constitutes a *universal unity and solidarity* that supersedes that of membership in a particular State. Indeed the situation is such that the need for a primary national *identity*, allegiance and patriotism (in today's sense) no longer exists or is possible. This is because each citizen now has a *universal and even cosmic identity* as a "world citizen" (cf. *"cosmopolitan"*)—where this word for the first time gets its true meaning and application; it is a world where the *boundaries* between States are fluid, and where Jedi people and families roam and mingle freely over the globe and beyond.

As your **Henry Miller** says in his *Sunday After the War* (1944):

> "The cultural era is past. The new civilization ... will not be another civilization—it will be the open stretch of realization which all the past civilizations have pointed to. The city, which was the birthplace of civilization, such as we know it to be, will exist no more. There will be nuclei, of course, but they will be mobile and fluid. The peoples of the earth will no longer be shut off from one another within states but will flow freely over the surface of the earth and intermingle. There will be no fixed constellations of human aggregates. Governments will give way to management, using the word in a broad sense. The politician will become as superannuated as the dodo bird. The machine will never be

dominated, as some imagine; it will be scrapped, eventually, but not before men have understood the nature of the mystery which binds them to their creation. The worship, investigation and subjugation of the machine will give way to the lure of all that is truly occult [inner]. This problem is bound up with the larger one of power— and possession. Man will be forced to realize that power must be kept open, fluid and free. His aim will be not to possess power but to radiate it (154)."

§631

There is a definite sense in which governments *will* have given way to management, of the nation's resources, etc; for each nation of Jedi in effect *governs itself,* since all of its citizens know what the GOOD is and dedicate themselves to its ongoing achievement and maintenance. Hence there is no need for Great Leaders or heroes (which in any case depends on a contrast with the ordinary non-hero, non-leader), indeed every Jedi and Jedi citizen by their very nature is a hero and leader. And there are no "enemies" or wars or major crises requiring such leaders; for governments have long since learned that *power* is not meant to be hoarded or possessed but shared and radiated, that *power is for empowering.* And this does not mean there will not be competition among nations, there will, but competition to *do good,* to have the best country, citizenry, educators of the next generation, to be the most desirable place in which to live, to visit, etc.

§632

A look at [A] Internal or Jedi National Politics and [B] External or Jedi International Politics in the fully Realized Jedi Order:

[A] *Internal or Jedi National Politics.*

The governing body—of President-Prime Minister, Cabinet, Congress-Parliament, and Judiciary, all members of whom are Jedi— has complete knowledge of the Truth, of the political and the State's #1 GOOD, and of the Light and Dark sides of the Force. Thus every act and policy decision it makes is informed by this knowledge and hence optimal.

As said governments will give way to management—for a nation of Jedi essentially rule themselves. As in your Jedi **Plato's** *Republic* no one will seriously want to be President or in office or govern *for self-serving egoistic reasons (such as power or fame)*. The president will have no *desire* to be president and will accept the post only as a duty and sacred trust, for each adult Jedi, as a potential ruler, is a "philosopher King" (à la **Plato**) and would rule as *impartial Reason* and as "ego-less."

As said there will be no war, terrorism, or nukes—for "enemies" or desire for power or territory, and aggression is impossible. There is only *One Self*—the Force. There is no division of rich and poor, no homeless (except for those Jedi or Padawans who freely choose this special lifestyle), for all Jedi have all they need and the government helps. There are no problems in Education as it is *holistic* Jedi Education based on Jedi Science, and all teachers are Jedi and know the true Goal of education. And there are no health-care problems—no (incurable) disease and death—for all Jedi are doctors and can heal body, mind, and Absolute I (spirit), and thus have total power over disease and death.

§633

As for the question: What goes on in such a "Perfect World," etc? there is no simple answer for it is a realm of *pure absolute Freedom,* and one cannot really say. The main thing is that *all* are secure in themselves and do not worry about war, terrorism, economy, job-money, status, health, and their kids. They know their kids are getting the best education possible and that the government is not corrupt. They are free to just *BE*. To give of themselves to people, to Love and share Love—indulge their creative fancies and dreams— to design a home, start a school, a business, do art, music, explore the world, the galaxy, the Subtle Plane—they can *either* get involved in the communal matrix and network of people—*or* stay alone, detached (for a "time"), meditate, write, paint, compose—JUST BE. *It is a truly OPEN SOCIETY and all things are literally possible. For your people, one and all, are eternal immortal Jedi. "Eye has not seen, ear has not heard what is about to come on the scene"* as your scriptures say.

§634

[B] *External or Jedi International Politics.*

There will be a United Jedi World Federation. All Nations will be free and cooperate with each other—ready to help and lift each other up to Jedi via education, etc, and lend raw materials, trade and not rip-off or exploit other nations. *For your peoples are truly One, One Race, One "I," One Consciousness.* Your *unity* is stronger than your *differences*—hence there will be no predatory, rapacious multinational corporations going into developing nations to exploit them. All Nations will be involved in international projects, collaborating on, designing and creating space stations, cities on the Moon, on Mars and beyond; and involved in competition in sports, Olympics, in Arts and Sciences, and for the ultimate Jedi Nobel Prize—which is the creation of The Best Nation in the Federation.

§635

[B] WRONG/IMBALANCE. All the benefits and blessings of the Jedi Order just described will be forever beyond your reach if your politics continue in their present Dark Side manner. Your main problem is that in your politics there is no *Knowledge of the Force*, the #1 Good, and no Vision. With the historical attainment of this Knowledge by your Jedi philosophers and the A-Team you have entered a totally new world—but you are still stuck in the Old Paradigm (M/C) and immersed in the Old Ways.

§636

Thus by continuing to pursue "politics" in the "Ego-world-manner" your people's #1 GOOD, the Amazing Jedi Order, will never be realized. As may be supposed unless your governing bodies and citizens *know who they are and are capable of becoming* (viz., the infinite Force and Jedi) and *act* on this knowledge, the political situation in your world will never be optimal and without crises of major proportion. *The fact is they do not.* For the truth is that if you do not know what the State and its Goal is, you cannot know where the State is headed or the direction it is to go in and *the best way to allot its resources.* It is absolutely pointless and wasteful for example to pour money into an Educational System *without knowing what education is and is for.* Moreover the concepts of "Man," the world/Reality and the Good or Ideal that your governments use in their political decisions and affairs are mainly those of "the ego and the ego-world" rooted in the Dark Side and the sense-world's multiplicity. As we Jedi know this is a hopelessly *atomistic* view reflecting that of your dominant p-sciences which regard as ultimate the *separateness* of individuals within a State and the separateness of States themselves, and all that attends this view. Under such a view the highest your governments can aspire to, their *ideal* world, is a vision confined to the merely egoic "animal level" of existence, a state where there is no war, where peace rules, and all have abundant money and goods, etc, *and then you die.* With such a vision and mind-set there is no hope for reaching *unity*, and no place for it.

§637

In such a situation where Ego and separateness rule, mistrust, fear, rivalry, and jealousy among persons cannot be avoided and colors all. Each person has a *fear* and *poverty-lack-scarcity* mentality and is thus out to get as much as he can (since "wealth is limited") and hence views all others as a threat and competitor. The congressman, moreover, views the people, the separate Ego's whom he legislates for and are in his charge in the same way. In addition the temptation to abuse power is ever present—few politicians can resist the lure of **Plato's** "Ring of Gyges" when they are behind the closed doors of their wood-paneled office.

§638

According to this "Egoic" dark-side view of himself and others—which knows nothing of the *Eternal* Truth—the "ego" politician (1) sees himself and everyone else foremost as being *in time*, with "x" years behind him and "x" years still to go, until his death—that is, in a very limited way. There is only so much "time" to get and enjoy all the things that he wants and to achieve his goals and ambitions (to be senator, president, amass a fortune, etc); and everyone, likewise "in time," he assumes to be just like himself. Thus every *Other* person is a *threat* to himself and to his goals; hence not knowing if he'll ever *see* these people again, his constituency and friends, he treats them accordingly as he knows not of *eternal* relationships (à la *The Jedi Code*). And (2) he further sees himself as a finite, mortal-animal, as a "Man" that is essentially a Body, an Object or a Thing, in accordance with the empirical p-science's view that he assimilated through his college education.

§639

As a congressman he takes an entirely "piecemeal," narrow approach to legislating and to improving the quality of life and conditions of his citizens, with the lament, "There's only so much I can do, only so much budget money, goods, resources to go around. I can only hope to pass so many Bills during my tenure, I can't help *everybody!*— So, a little here, a touch there, etc …"—As we know, only *true politics* founded on *true education* is the cure and solution to *all* problems without exception.

§640

Thus he follows the Old Ego model and ways: "What we need is more money, exports, jobs, 'good' schools (but what is 'good'?), a 'good' defense, a strong military and economy, tax breaks, incentives to make more money, etc. And the more money and 'good education' we have, the happier the State and the nation will be." "All the people really need is money, a job, and a good education (a trade and skills) and they will be fine and happy."

NO. This is absolutely not true. For unless you know *who you are and can become* it is all a waste. Money by itself is *nothing.* You need to know what *the* #1 *Good* is (the Truth, the POINT, the Jedi Order) and what to use the money for. If you believe you are just a separate Ego with 40 years left to live, *fear* will rule your life and determine how you act towards others. Only *true education* and knowing who you truly are— an Infinite immortal Jedi, one with the State and with all citizens—is the solution to all of your State's problems, domestic and foreign. Not to know this and act on it is detrimental and a total disaster and leads the State in the wrong direction, away from the Jedi Order.

To legislate, enforce, and perpetuate the Ego, yourself and others as a "separate lonely Thing," leads citizens to depression, hopelessness, anomie, apathy, meaninglessness, drugs, suicide, and crime—for on this view only the rich, the materially successful, have "true" worth and live meaningful lives. To withhold true knowledge from your people—is a sin, a crime. Therefore the government especially must take steps and action to curb and delete *p-science* and *p-education* and their harmful effects, the source of all Dark Side "ego-teaching."

§641

This "ego-view" also carries over into *international* Global Politics. For each State or Nation sees the other *as an Other*—as a hostile competitor and alien—and not as a *Self.* Each State operates under the "ego world" belief and is *stuck* in the Old Paradigm's false assumptions and ways and does not see what Man is and can be—a Being infinite and glorious beyond what can possibly be imagined. It is a fact that each State has its *needs*—to increase revenue, productivity, jobs, lower unemployment, etc., hence arises the notion for example, 'We need a share in Iraq's or Iran's *oil* supplies in order to increase our wealth, jobs, etc." However even if *all* States had *all* the money they could hope for—then what? The true need and goal is thus *not* money and Things, and *more* money and things—but realizing the *Force* and the *Jedi Order.* The True *Good*—that is the sole Goal of History and the Universe.

§642

Hence today's States cannot solve their major problems and their *imbalance*: war, terrorism, ethnic cleansing, insurrection, factions, civil war, sputtering economies, the rich/poor divide, unemployment, homelessness, crime, drugs, hopelessness, depression, universal health care, failing education, and so forth. What then can be done to *Balance* Politics?

§643

[C] BALANCE. The truth is that POLITICS when

conducted correctly according to its true concept is the primary, most potent institution to effect the *education* and *ongoing healing* of the world—especially since its function is to promote the *temporal and eternal* well being, happiness and full potential of its Jedi citizens. Hence its responsibilities also include the identifying of those agencies and elements in the body-politic that are injurious to Society's health, well-being and highest possibilities *and the curbing or rooting out of them;* and number one among them as we saw, is the erroneous "sick" *materialist world-view* of the *p-sciences* which infects almost all areas of your world civilization, inclusive of education, medicine and psychiatry. Moreover it is in virtue of its awesome power to enact Laws of the Land that Politics and the government is able to perform its sacred office and therefore regulate *education*, subsidize and give grants to *Science*, protect *religion, business and the economy, health, medicine and psychiatry, the media, communications, the Arts,* and all other areas, functions and institutions.

§644

The #1 need then is to *educate* your governments, your leaders and citizens into the *Knowledge of the Force* and the true concept of Politics—especially the *elite* of power and wealth as to the necessity for true *Jedi* democracy, instead of destructive *Sith* autocracy and plutocracy. They need to know that they are not finite mortal Ego's but rather *immortal Jedi*—the self-actualized Infinite Force, the POINT aware of itself. Teach them what their true #1 Problem is—namely the Self/Other split and living exclusively in the OUTER-Cave illusion, ignorant of Reality and who they really are—and that true knowledge and Jedi education is the real *solution* to *all* of their problems; and leads to the amazing Jedi Order, the true destiny of the Universe and their Race, where all the powers of their people and citizens will finally see the light of day. Above all teach your governments, leaders and citizens *How to accomplish it.*

§645

Thus you and they should recognize that poverty, healthcare, unemployment, terrorism, the economy, etc, are *not* your number problem. For all of these can be solved—you would have peace and all would have abundance of money and things—*and you would still be an unhealthy society not having risen above the Ego and Ego-Object-world condition, still not having realized your highest destiny and living in total fulfillment—as Jedi in the glorious Jedi Order.*

§646

Here are the TEN essentials of what you can do:

(1) Noble Reader, you can become a JEDI yourself—and your friends or circle (*karass*) as well—see *Part II: The Jedi Code.*

(2) If you are a President, Prime Minister, Senator or government official you can use Jedi principles and Truths in policy making decisions and in introducing new Bills and enacting Laws.

(3) Your political process can install Jedi Education—that is, holistic education and principles—into your *public school system* so all your nation's youth can be ongoingly raised to Jedi; thereby ending the nihilism, hopelessness and despair disseminated by your present "dark side" system of *mis-education* by instilling students with the *confidence* and *knowledge* that they are eternal immortal Jedi.

§647

(4) You can also pass a Law (on the Federal and/or State level), *on the one side*, that demotes and restricts the authority of pernicious "p-sciences" in the public sector and in public education and textbooks and, *on the other side*, promotes, subsidizes and makes a way for Jedi Science to become established. There is no need however to make a special LAW or amend the Constitution requiring that "Absolute Jedi Science" will be *the* science of e.g. the U.S.A. The government's job in the Jedi Order will be *only* to enforce the Law and constitution and keep *open* a public space or arena in which True Science (and the #1 Good) will spontaneously rise to the surface and become "custom and the norm" and known in society and universities *as* Science; in the end the individual's will is sacrosanct and she must be free to choose what to believe, etc. In time "science" will change into Science—as the TRUTH will eventually and inevitably win out. In any case the present and future Congress or Parliament *can and should* present policies, laws, and the "Jedi Vision," supported by the truths, reasoning and proofs of *Jedi Science.*

§648

As to How the passage of the Law should be effected: A Senator will introduce the Bill, and then the Congress will consider it and vote on it.

During the Bill's presentation incontestable *proofs* are given (by experts) as to, for example, *Why p-science is not Science*—as it is not true Knowledge, rests on false materialist assumptions, and contains absolute errors that promote a *nihilism* that is injurious to the health of the public and youth in particular; and also contradicts the Law of the Land as it holds that your people are not *Persons* and *free agents* but, as only material beings, are in fact unfree, completely determined and without accountability for their actions.—And as to *Why p-science, minimally, should no longer be permitted to call itself "Science" (or certain knowledge) and pass itself off as Truth, the Truth, and the only Truth, but instead should be called "pre-science" or opinion (doxa).* The Senator in his presentation should also be mindful to state the virtues of p-science and the extent of its validity, what it is good for, and its value as "technology"—*as "know how" but not bona fide Knowledge*, for example, in medical science, DNA, lasers, solving practical problems relating to bridges, satellites, cell phones, trips to the Moon, etc—in addition to stating and explaining the shortcomings involved in its "empirical method" of *induction* and sampling, and that *it contains only "statistical truths" or probabilities*, as in quantum mechanics. In addition experts can testify as to the positive results of Jedi Schools whose curricula are based on *Jedi Science*. The Senator can also underscore how Jedi Science can resolve the long-standing hostility between science and religion and how this results in great benefits to the nation's and world's health and well-being. A Law can also be passed requiring the teaching of *"Jedi civics and politics courses"* in all schools.

§649

(5) If you are a teacher or professor, especially in a Law School, you can teach a course on "Jedi Politics" and its Vision. And if you are a student you can petition your school to teach such a course.

(6) Jedi principles of government and politics can also be used in *international politics* by diplomats and other world leaders who can introduce and extend Jedi education and healing methods to other nations, giving them the Vision of the Jedi Order of prosperity, peace, love and unity, and explain how the *unity* of science and religion can be effected, which will root out the major cause of war and help to end terrorism in the world.

If you are an ambassador or diplomat in the United Nations, for example, you can use Jedi Principles and teachings in your work and discuss the same before the General Assembly. Present the Vision of the Jedi Order, namely, that "We are all *one*"—*we all share* One infinite Consciousness or "I"—and should therefore help each other to be Jedi. Or if you are a citizen you can *Petition* the United Nations and show members the Truth and Proofs of the *unity* of all your planet's peoples *(of the POINT or Absolute I)* and the necessity of One World—and how, by making it your #1 priority, all conflicts in the world and among nations can be resolved.

§650

(7) Governments can sever its ties with corporations and special interest groups and donors who want to use government to advance their selfish "dark side" ego-world-sustaining ends; and can teach the CEO's of corporations and multinationals the benefits of reorganizing their business in accord with Jedi Principles; no exotic financial instruments, derivatives, etc. (See the next section, "Business").

Jedi Politics can also promote the Light Side and national healing by giving Tax breaks to "Jedi" Businesses that also lift up developing nations; and teach these businesses to use the principles of *POWER-ETHICS*, focusing especially on the relationship between "#1 The Jedi Order and #2 Money and Profits."

§651

(8) You can start a website and disseminate Jedi Politics and the Jedi Order (the #1 Good and Vision) through *the Media*, such as TV, Internet, Radio, newspaper, books, etc. If you are a TV producer etc, you can devote a spot or show to it.

(9) You and all interested parties can contact and petition your Senator online at www.congress.gov.

§652

(10) On "GLOBAL POLITICS." The true meaning of *Globalization* is simply that your History and your peoples are moving towards and are becoming *One World and One Consciousness* (compare your paleontologist **Teilhard de Chardin's** *Noosphere and Omega Point-LOVE)*; that is towards One Race (*the Absolute I-POINT*) and the *unity* of the Jedi Order—what your religions call "the kingdom of God on earth," "the Just Society," "the Millennium," "the World to Come," "the New Jerusalem," etc.—Indeed towards a collective universal *awareness* by all

> "The Jedi Order (Geist) is the absolute substance which is the UNITY of the different independent self-consciousnesses (or States) which, in their opposition, enjoy perfect freedom and independence: *I that is We and We that is I.*" **Hegel**

nations of the Two-Tiered Reality of the Jedi Order where *the ONE* or One Consciousness *that all people and Selves ARE* and in which all people and nations participate *will have precedence and primacy over the Many,* that is, over your formerly *separate* independent States and Nations and their excluding boundaries. Their separateness will become "formal" as they are destined to become "moments" of the One Universal Jedi Order (see **Henry Miller,** above).

FROM THIS: **TO THIS:**

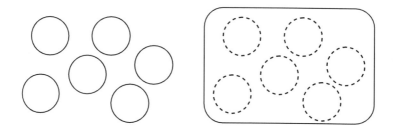

§653

A Key Point is that *Globalization is inevitable and cannot and should not be stopped.* The intermingling and intermarrying of all your peoples and the resulting dilution and dissolution of your local, national-*Volk* identities is your certain destiny. World events are forcing you to realize this, and the Jedi Truth that all of your people share and *are* but a single Absolute I *makes it necessary.* Thus your people are being forced to advance to a higher, indeed the highest, plane of maturity, existence and awareness and to grow up and discard their "security blankets," let go of the *divisive* old "crutch" of needing a unique "national-cultural-ethnic" Volk-Identity such as "German," "Italian," etc.,—and finally *become true world-global citizens.* And though the *Jedi Selves* that are emerging are indeed *cosmopolitan*—having a *core* self-awareness and identity *which is the same for all, the ONE POINT*—yet each Self is unique and carries its own past experience, its national-ethnic-cultural roots *within itself* as a *second* ineradicable identity that will always be celebrated.

Also c*orporations (especially multi-nationals) will play an absolutely central and crucial Role—once they are aligned to and have adopted Jedi-Truth and Jedi Business Power-Ethics—in helping to elevate and heal 3*[rd] *world-developing nations.* (See the next section "Business"—and the work of **Tom Friedman**)

§654

IDEAS ON KEY SOLUTIONS—AND THE NEW JEDI PRESIDENT AND JEDI PARTY

(1) How you can solve global Poverty and the Main Problem of the Haves vs. the Have-Nots; and with the solution to this all other money problems are solved, such as Homelessness, Unemployment, and Underperforming Economies.

It is a FACT that: If your nations—governments, individuals, and corporations—can come up with billions of dollars on a moment's notice for a worthy Cause (such as helping Tsunami victims), then this is proof that (1) they have the monies, and therefore (2) can utilize it to solve "the poverty problem world-wide."

§655

The Solution is this: If governments, the Rich, and CEO's can see that they themselves, society, and all people will benefit immensely when all have enough and the problem of poverty and material inequality is solved, then and only then will they make it a top priority and finally solve it. For by doing so they will eliminate their guilt and accelerate their own primary self/other healing and help take the world and themselves closer to the Jedi Order and to *true well being, happiness and abundant living.* And, what is important, they will be able to increase their profits and realize their financial goals as well.

Now there are 3 levels of economic self-sufficiency: (a) *Highest.* Being Self-sufficient—no government/outside help needed, (b) *Middle.* Partial government help given—and also from Corporations and the Wealthy, (c) *Lowest.* "Welfare" (the poor, unemployed, and challenged)—total government and corporate help needed and given. The Goal or desideratum is for individuals to move from the lowest level to the highest. *The quickest way to solve the problem* and get everyone to (a) is: By a combination of government help and private help, from corporations, foundations, and wealthy individuals.

§656

ONE: Revenue from governments—obtained by taking 5% of Revenues and Budget, and enacting *TWO* with it.

TWO: Revenue from Corporations and the Wealthy (plus for their participation and donations governments will give them Tax-break incentives).

(a) Governments and the wealthy will want to help once they see how it benefits themselves and the world; for example, how it leads to a healthy-vibrant planet, with no guilt, faster Jedi-realization for themselves, and no crime and *fear* elements in society (no bombs, terrorism, Al Qaeda, nukes, war, assassinations, kidnapping, piracy) and greater *profits* (also without guilt and medical repercussions). They will also see How it is good for the nation's economy and the nation's health; for all will be employed and productive and the government will have more money, not less.

§657

(b) THE KEY: *"MONEY-HELP CENTERS"* will be *set up* in the major cities of all nations of the world (and on the internet) as follows: *First,* you assess the client/applicant's situation and determine the Best way to help him or her, by (1) Giving them a loan, (2) a monthly check (repayable in ten years), or (3) Giving them a job. *Second, then you do it*—and monitor their situation and progress; and of course this (giving money or a job) must be done in such a way as to preserve the "dignity and self-worth/esteem" of the recipients. *Third,* it is also vital to teach recipients Power-Ethics and the concept of the State and True Health, Jedi, and "the Movement," in order to awaken in them the desire to help. Let them finish Jedi Education, High School and College. Help them "get a life," plug them into the Whole, the culture, the ethos, the One Spirit, and into the Advance of civilization and History's Great Goal. This will charge and inspire them to make a greater contribution to the Jedi Order and the healing of your planet, and to not get into crime, drugs, depression, and a sick behavior or mind-set—which would result in greater medical expenses and a burden on society, governments, and corporations.

§658

(c) The Government, Corporations, and the Rich can also solve the *unemployment* problem—whose solution results from having an income of your own, not being dependent on others for your existence, and having self-respect—also from keeping jobs in your country and not out-sourcing. Moreover citizens and businesses can each provide 1 or 2 minor jobs (see below Business).

§659

(d) And they can solve the *homeless* problem as well. Every citizen should be able to have his own home (as your President **Franklin D. Roosevelt** stipulated in his "Second Bill of Rights"). For example: Builders can build houses or apartments or renovate abandoned housing; or we can give the homeless money or a loan to build it themselves—they will repay the loan, etc, and everything will be monitored carefully. They will then move in, have their new job (thus to get your own housing you will need to work, a prerequisite); and will be given adequate time to pay off their mortgage or loan (thus ending foreclosures), etc. This will have the general effect of "plugging them in," getting their "juices flowing," and energizing their Will to be a "new man," a Jedi, and have a "New life," a "second chance" and make a positive contribution to the Jedi Order and the healing of their planet and kind.

(e) And Corporations will also help foreign States and developing Nations.

§660

(2) How to solve *War/Terrorism/Nuclear Proliferation/and HeathCare:*

War: With the increase of Jedi Education and mature Jedi in your world and in governments, WAR will gradually become a thing of the past. In any case all nations, especially those at war, should see or be told what the #1 Priority/Good/Goal of History is. It is advisable that you—perhaps as a member of the Jedi Council—should talk to both sides and assess religious differences and the conditions and "causes" of war, etc. Explain how Re-ligions point to the Goal of Knowledge/Experience and their ultimate *unity* and that they will ultimately be phased out when their ultimate purpose and ideal has been realized—thus removing the cause of war. Show them How a Basis for *unity* (for example, Islam vs Judaism and Christianity) can be obtained and will happen eventually, and help them attain it. In the last analysis all people, the majority in any case, are *rational* and will listen to Reason and do what is in their best interests.

§661

Terrorism: (1) It is essential to get into *dialogue* with terrorists—via the Internet, etc, and challenge them: (a) What do you want? etc, and (b) We will show you that and how e.g. Islam and Judaism-Christianity can be reconciled and are essentially the same, etc.

(2) Get the e.g. Islamic world *on your side*, on the side of Reason, and to reject such organizations as "Al Qaeda," their "cause" and their methods as being *against the Common Good* (e.g. that of Islam, for they are delaying the advent of "the Just Society," Islam's supreme Goal).
(3) Have Islam peace-makers start a "Jedi Muslim *Sect*" within the Islam religion; it will become in time the dominant sect due to many fully healed members/adherents, and will help to change the mind-set and will of the terrorists (and exchange their cause for one truly worth fighting and dying for).

(4) With this and implementing other measures you can dissuade the youth from joining the terrorists. With no new members their groups will collapse and vanish in time.

§662

Nuclear Weapons and Proliferation Threat: Eventually and inevitably when Jedi Truth and Knowledge has spread to a sufficient number of peoples and nations, the fear and the reasons for wanting/needing such weapons will no longer exist, etc (also see §670ff below).

§663

How you can solve *HealthCare:* As you are told—due to baby-boom retirement (e.g. in the U.S.A.), escalating health costs and malpractice suits, HMO's and huge CEO salaries—massive health-care expenses (ten trillion dollars on some estimates) are slated for the near future and will exhaust your revenues and cripple your economies.

(1) The #1 most obvious and practicable solution is this: *If people do not get sick there <u>are</u> no major medical bills. So if the amount of disease and illness is reduced then healthcare costs (and Medicare, Medicaid and drug costs) will go down.*

(2) This can be achieved and happen with an increase in the number of Jedi, Jedi Doctors and masters in the world. The fact is that Healthy-healed Jedi ("gods," elohim) do not get sick. They can heal themselves and their immune system is prime.

Indeed let us ask: Where do dis-eases come from? *Answer:* Primarily from the *inability to resist and fight them off—i.e., from a weak Immune System, which is mainly caused by stress and guilt in one's life.* Therefore the more *unity and power* one has and enjoys, the *stronger one's immune system is* (hence ultimately there will be no cancer, AIDS, TB, etc). So the more that Jedi Truths penetrate all areas of Society, the more unity and power your people will experience and the healthier they will become. The looming health-care crisis is thus done away with.

§664

(3) Take power from the *pharmaceutical companies* (i.e. from those still involved in the Ego-business model and not the Jedi-Business one) and their advertising of "diseases": "You may have cancer," "You need this medication (with all its side-effects), etc." They pollute the public space, the Soup, and create a Race of Invalids—people being constantly told they are weak, vulnerable, and cannot heal themselves and are powerless in face of these diseases which lurk all around them. All of this media assault on your consciousness creates a *fear mentality*: "I may be sick. Have lupus, diabetes—I better sit down, call my Doctor and tell him that I need and should take this 'medicine,' the 'cure'."

§665

THE POINT is that Words are powerful. If you hear repeatedly, "You are weak, may have this disease, etc," then your immune system weakens and you become more prone to get it. Your thoughts go in that direction and will actually create the disease in you. This is true according to the Jedi-spiritual Law of "seed-planting" that is based on the "Spiritual/Natural" parallel: *seeds* and their properties in the Natural Realm (-) correspond to and mirror *thoughts* in the

Spiritual Realm (+). Hence if you "water" the Seeds ("think" on the Thoughts) *you will produce them.* (See Health, and How to cure oneself, etc. §§745ff)

§666

THE NEW JEDI PRESIDENT AND JEDI PARTY

Enter the Lawgiver. The Philosopher-King, the greatest of all Presidents/Prime Ministers, will soon appear.

The Jedi President. Noble Jedi, the Aim here is simply to inspire future politicians to adopt the TRUTH and begin to implement World-Healing and the GOOD by simply "hitching their wagon to our Jedi star." The New Moses will lead all of your people into the Promised Land. The Main Point is that sooner or later in the political life of a nation a *candidate* will appear who will *see the Truth of Jedi and the Jedi "Vision"* and preach it *and surely be elected.* She or He will go down in History as e.g. the greatest of all American Presidents and statesmen/women—the one who took their nation into its highest glory and Destiny, its Golden Age—with the most creative and happiest people who use their bounty to help all of the nations of the world—the one who took your people and the world *into the incredible Jedi Order, what you have referred to in your own history as the Millennium, the Kingdom of God on Earth, and Paradise.*

You, a future politician, can thus Run for Office on a *Jedi-Platform— especially as the next Jedi President.*

§667

The reason why it will work is that none of your fellow politicians at the present time know the True Direction and Goal of the State. So YOU will be the first—and unique: "I HAVE THE VISION—I KNOW THE DIRECTION THE STATE IS TO GO IN." (1) The transition and transformation is now happening (this *Handbook* is in your hands)—slowly True Science is replacing and absorbing false p-science.

(2) The alert politician or would-be-president, will see this—the signs of the times and the *NEED* of the times—and recognize the Truth behind True Science and the Goal, End, and healing Vision

it offers—and adopt it, *making it the center of his campaign platform.* "I see the Vision. It is this ___, and it is True. We the American (British, Iranian) people can have faith in it because Reason clearly says this ___." Thus we will do "A" instead of "B," for "B" takes us away from the Good, while "A" takes us closer, etc.

(3) Once he or she is elected as President/Prime Minister and has power (for Good) she can keep it and get reelected on the basis of the powerful results the Good will bring nationally and world-wide, etc.

§668

The Jedi Political Party. Given that all of the preceding in *Parts I and II* is indeed true about Jedi Truth, the Force, the meaning of History and *who you really are*, and given that this Truth is the key to solving all your problems and taking humanity into the Millennium, the Jedi Order—and that the present political parties, e.g. Democratic and Republican, have no clue as to where you as a people should be going and what your true #1 Good is—it therefore stands to Reason that a third political party that *does* know these things will inevitably make its appearance on the political stage and be called obviously, *"The Jedi Party."* There is no need to indicate the manner in which it can be formed, this is self-evident—for when the time is ripe the forces in play will see that it is born.

§669

A general idea of its platform would be something like this:

(1) We are the party of true health and prosperity.

(2) We alone know what the GOOD is and the proper direction in which the State should go.—The other parties don't.

(3) We know the truth about Jedi Science, hence what is truly wrong about our present "dark side" society and its Seven major Institutions and what can and must be done to change things into the Light Side. For example, we know that the dominant "p/empirical science" so-called, which rules every facet of our lives, especially education, has false and very injurious basic assumptions and beliefs; and that its authority and status must be demoted and restricted to insure the nation's health and well-being.

(4) And we know thus what the proper solution is to fear and the dangers due to terrorism, poverty, unemployment, a failing economy, homelessness, etc. The other parties do not.

§670

ON INTERNATIONAL RELATIONS (NO WAR. NO NUKES).

What is essential is to teach all leaders the *Knowledge of the Force* and help all Nations to enter the glorious Jedi Order. For example with respect to Iran, Israel and the U.S., etc, should help the Iranians economically and in other ways, but should not impose "sanctions" on them for this breeds Fear, hate and resistance to change. Thus by helping them you will change the way they perceive you, they will e.g. regard Israel as a friend and not an enemy. Doing a common project together with Iran as well as implementing Jewish and Muslim Jedi Sects in these countries will also help.

§671

During transition to full Jedi Order awareness.

As opposed to resolving *disputes* between *two* parties *within* a State by means of a *Judge*/Mediator or Third Party, the situation as regards *sovereign* States/Nations is different. In the interim (before the Jedi Order is fully established) there is no "Third" party as such to mediate disputes between States. This is in part because of the States' *sovereignty* which is inviolable, and in which the *dignity* of a State consists—no *Higher* political-world power exists (e.g. the United Nations) to *adjudicate* and resolve their conflict.
—There are two conditions or phases: (1) *During Transition* and (2) *The Full Jedi Order* (or Globalization Completed).

§672

(1) In *The Full Jedi Order* where all governments, States and their leaders are Jedi, have *the Knowledge of The Force*, etc, and all work together for the GOOD of every nation—there is rarely, if at all, a need for a Mediator to solve disputes. However if and when the need does occur—and for very minor issues, what happens is that *both* States *agree* on an independent/unbiased Mediator to resolve the

dispute and whose decision is binding; and due to the honor, dignity and integrity of the State, no State would risk violating it.

§673

(2) *During Transition* most States are not yet Jedi—so because you cannot count on *this* method of conflict resolution between States you can do the following: (a) Continue to promote Jedi Teachings (*the Knowledge of the Force/Unity* (±)) and the true #1 GOOD of the State and "Man"; this can be done through diplomacy, cultural exchanges, at international meetings on environmental issues and Global-Universal concerns, e.g. financial summits, etc. (b) Ease tensions based on Religious (and ethnic) differences by promoting Jedi Sects in your world's religions. (c) Above all do not use Force, violence (only as last resort, if attacked), or economic sanctions and punishment against "rogue" nations as an *incentive* to change. This will just double their determination and resolve to e.g. create *nuclear* weapons. This is typical of the EGOIC mind, which is subject to the *Law of Action and Reaction:* i.e., if you push against *something*, it will push back, *resisting* the threat to its self-*identity* and *Being.* Therefore do not "push" but rather try to *enhance* its Being, its true Well-Being, etc. Otherwise the Nation will simply feel "Bullied" into submission; it will fear losing face, self-respect and feel inferior like a "loser," and so will simply *harden* itself against this. As a consequence the *threat* will remain (Israel will still have Nukes and hating Iran, Israel remaining the #1 Superpower of the region, and Iran still living in Fear as a second-rate power; which is terrible for the self-image of Iran and Iranians. At present Russia and China both realize the truth of this by their adopting the policy that, "If we help Iran—trade and give food to them, etc—then Iran will become our friend and ally and not fear or attack us or use their Nukes against us; moreover we will have an ally in the Area who has oil and resources that we can use, etc."

§674

The Solution is to use a Combination of (i) and (ii):

(i) The approach opposite to violence and sanctions is the best. All nations should *really help* the "rogue" nation—especially perceived threats (such as Israel, the USA, etc)—with food, education, Money, etc—in effect, "pouring coals on their head"; as a result the "rogue" nation will soften, change its opinion of them and "come around."

(ii) Adopt the ultimate goal of the total elimination of *nuclear weapons* from the planet. Take steps in that direction—(e.g. Iran wants *nuclear weapons* because of its FEAR of Israel having them and also its desire for super-power status). The main POINT is that the only reason for wanting or having Nukes is to *defend* oneself against a perceived enemy who also has them. Hence by logic, if no one had Nukes there would be no need for any nation to defend itself against them. Thus if all nations were Jedi or Jedi Nations, committed to helping and loving each other, then the very idea of "Nukes"—as well as armies, weapons, standing armies, the military—would be inconceivable. The result would be that ALL of a nation's money, substance, resources can now be devoted 100% to enhancing LIFE. All nations should therefore sign a Treaty or Agreement to Phase out Nukes, etc. Israel should then tell Iran: "If you cease your nuclear ambitions, we will too cease and phase out our Nukes."

§675

The FACT is that in time ALL nations will gradually fall in line and will see the benefits of the Jedi TRUTH and Government, and when this happens (1) There will be no need for Nukes and Armies, (2) The Military-Ego Stage of Nations and World History will have been phased out and transcended, and finally (3) The Period of Universal Peace and the development of all powers by all people will have commenced and the Jedi Order will be in full swing. As your Jedi **Hegel, Schelling,** and **Hölderlin** state in their *1794 Earliest System Program:*

> "Thus in the end enlightened and unenlightened must clasp hands, mythology must become philosophical in order to make the people reasonable, and philosophy must become mythological in order to make the philosophers sensible .... Then reigns eternal unity among us! Then first awaits us *equal* development of *all* powers, of what is peculiar to each and what is common to all. No power shall any longer be suppressed for universal freedom and equality of spirits will reign!"

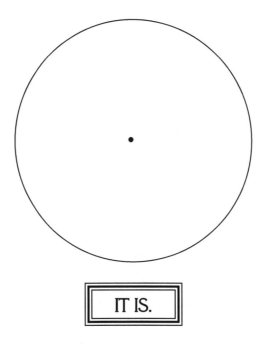

IT IS.

BUSINESS

Business and Money play a major role in the lifting of ALL nations into the Amazing Jedi Order—the UNITY of everyone and the true meaning behind GLOBALIZATION. Jedi Light-Side Business must replace Ego Dark-Side Business to speed up the healing of your world. Don't just think of Yourself—but of the Whole, your race, your planet.

BUSINESS SUMMARY

(A) CONCEPT. The chief purpose of Business as Educational is to take your people into the JEDI ORDER, the POINT, by means of Self/Other interactions resulting in enhanced UNITY (±). Business' dual function concerns (1) your unique contribution to the Jedi Order and opportunity for Healing yourself and everyone on your planet via the Unity of Seller (+) and Buyer (-) as (±), and (2) the making of money or "means" and basic subsistence. It is based on the "JEDI Method of doing business" (and *The Jedi Code's* "Power Ethics") where the #1 priority is the Jedi Order and people (healing, increasing planetary UNITY, and sacred space) and #2 is Money and things. "Business" derives from: (1) *POINT:* Ultimate reality is the One Infinite Consciousness that all citizens and States share and are, the UNITY of everyone. Hence the primary Goal of Business is not making money but using the Self/Other interactions at its core for healing and advancing the Jedi Order. (2) *ETYMOLOGY:* "Business" derives from "busy-ness," that is, one's activity and praxis for the common Good.

(B) WRONG/IMBALANCE. The mode of doing business on your planet at the present time is primarily the "EGO method of doing business," which is done out of the *ignorance* of the *Knowledge of the Force,* the POINT and who you really are that results from Dark Side mis-education. Hence the #1 priority of "EGO business" is Money/Profit and Things, while #2 is People who are regarded as only "means" to your #1 Profit End. The Ego Corporation (and CEO) is thus fear based.

(C) BALANCE. Switch from the Ego to the Jedi Business Method whereby problems such as poverty, homelessness, unemployment, and economic-financial meltdowns can all be resolved. Thus the central command of Jedi Business is: "Seek ye first the Jedi Order and *all* economic and material prosperity will be yours."

---

§676

[A] CONCEPT. The Concept and necessity of Business or Busy-ness. Originally and historically the *necessity* of Business

or for a person to be engaged in a business, trade or profession was grounded in the basic *need* for survival and the continual maintenance of oneself, one's family and tribe, and in the *dependence* of society's members on one another for their needs and wants and the various means of satisfying them. But the true and higher necessity for business—or better "busy-ness" or the need to be continually busy, active or occupied (and not idle)—has a *moral* and *ontological* ground. It is grounded in the true Concept of *who you really are.* That is, in the Force and its need to overcome its divided state and the Self/Other opposition and become a fully healed self-aware Jedi.

§677

To begin with ultimate reality is the One Infinite Consciousness which everyone, all citizens and States share and are: the UNITY of everyone. Hence the primary Goal of Business is not making money but using the self-other interactions at its core for healing and advancing the Jedi Order and the healing and education of all nations. Therefore the real purpose of Busy-ness—and of *all* activities in the public sphere—is for humankind (or the Jedi Order, the Force implicit) to realize and ongoingly maintain the glorious Jedi Order, your #1 Goal and Highest Good. That is, an Order occupied with (1) the continual raising and educating of Jedi children, (2) the continual development, expression and sharing of Jedi talents and abilities, in art, religion, science, sports, etc., and (3) the continual deepening and expansion of eternal Jedi friendships. This #1 purpose is also a *moral* one—this is because you are *not* just an "isolated Ego" but are really the One Force hence share a *single* Absolute I with all other members of your Race; thus *they* are equally you your-Self, i.e. your Universal and true Self. This means nothing less than that the goal of all your activities and projects hence your #1 duty and responsibility should be to *your whole Race* (to the *Universal*) and not just to yourself alone (the *Particular*). Furthermore to the degree that you are fulfilling this #1 responsibility (that is, the Jedi Moral Law, see Jedi **Kant**, **Fichte**, and **Schelling**) you will experience proportionate degrees of freedom, power and health or *unity* (of mind and body)—or if not the reverse: guilt, incapacity, and sickness or *division*, as the case may be. It thus also follows that money, the acquisition of things and earning a living can only be a *secondary* purpose of business.

§678

It is true that according to its Concept, "Civil Society"—contrasted with the State proper whose concern is the whole, the Universal as such—is the appointed place where *particularity* and *difference* and their full expression are given their due and allowed free play. In the sphere of society where busy-ness has its locus the *individual* is given permission to use his energies and abilities any way he chooses to realize his personal dreams, ambitions, goals and self-interest. It is the place where she "defines herself," achieves an "identity," and "becomes *somebody.*" *However* the truth is that this is how it has been *up till now.*

§679

For now that you know—thanks to the Jedi-philosophers on your planet—*who you are*, what is what, and what your true #1 Goal, Good, and Task is, things become different. Apart from the fact that you are eternal and immortal—hence can expect to have and look forward to an unlimited number of occupations, professions or callings—the *core* of your *True Identity* can never be defined by your present job or by any future job, for *you are*—or are becoming—a *Jedi.* Thus your #1 job, career, profession and above all *identity* is a "Jedi"—not an electrician, banker, CEO, etc. Your present social job, as *Jedi Power Ethics* teaches, is merely a *means* to the *#1 End of Jedi and the Jedi Order.* So you *already* have an *identity* and *are* "somebody." Hence the questions people obsessively use to evaluate you and decide whether they want to associate with you, "What do you do? How much do you make? What is she 'worth'?" etc, become totally irrelevant and beside the point. You are infinitely *more* than and cannot be reduced to your bank account, stock portfolio, job title or profession. So whether you are a house-wife/husband, billionaire CEO, shoe-shine boy or janitor—makes no difference. Such things are only *external.* Rather, How far have you *awakened* and realized your true Jedi Self? Are you working for your whole Race or just for yourself?—this alone counts and is the sole measure of a person's *true* worth.

§680

So even though Civil Society will continue to be the domain where "particularity" and "self" centered projects are given the green light, it will now be the *universal* and its concerns that will be primary and paramount. Whatever you do, whatever profession or life-plan you have chosen, it will be done with the Whole or #1 in mind precisely because it is to *your* advantage and best interest and *everyone's*. Let's now see concretely how this works and what the real difference is between Jedi-business and what we shall call "Ego-business."

§681

[B] WRONG/IMBALANCE. To clearly see what the *imbalance* is in your current business practices and how they are immersed in the Dark Side of the Force we will now compare the Jedi method of doing business with your current Ego-method, and also contrast the Jedi Corporation and CEO with its Ego counterpart.

§682

EGO-BUSINESS VS. JEDI-BUSINESS

The Principle behind doing Jedi Business is found in "Jedi Power Ethics," which we discussed in *Part II: The Jedi Code.* To briefly review, "Power-Ethics" is an ethics or a way by which you can live your life to maximum effectiveness so as to realize total *power* and *health* as a Jedi living in the eternal Jedi Order. What you do is to "prioritize" all the areas, projects and goals of your life in accord with the following rule: The #1 Priority that is alone the *single End* of all you do and to which you subordinate all else as *means*, is *the Jedi Order*—that is, the healing the world and yourself, or realizing yourself as a Jedi and all other selves as Jedi. Hence all that you do is in the service of your #1 End and makes up your "ministry"—for example, your relationships, friends, family, business, career goals, money, body, recreation, etc. All these are and can only ever be your #2; they are "means" only and can never take the place of your #1. Hence *Business* as well is only a means and part of your Ministry.

§683

Power-ethics is based on the Jedi Truth concerning *who you really are*, which is *not* a mere human "ego" (P.I.) but rather the One Infinite Force aware of itself as a Jedi (U.I.) hence containing all other Selves or Force-centers *within* yourself, as a *community* of Jedi. Hence all other selves *are* you and vice versa in the sense already discussed (as universal and sharing one and the same ***Absolute I*** and as individualized). And *not* to know this—to think according to the Dark Side, that you are just a separate biological "ego" ever opposed to and in competition with a hostile uncaring irreducible Other of egos and the world—automatically results in skewed "priorities" and the typically unhealthy "ego-manner" of doing business which dominates in your world today.

§684

The difference between the two ways of doing business is easily grasped as follows:

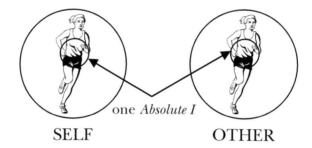

one *Absolute I*

SELF   OTHER

**"I (Self) am doing business (buying, selling or contracting)
with you (Other)."**

The above represents the *basic elements* of a typical business transaction which can be expanded to meet different orders of complexity.

§685

In the current "EGO" WAY OF DOING BUSINESS *on your planet*, I regard you and myself as two totally *separate* Egos. Hence I see you as basically "selfish" and "naturally" concerned about your own welfare, needs and wants, above mine. When we part I may never see you again. Your worth or value is determined by whether or not you can meet my need—if not then I'm done with you, you get lost in the crowd, just another face, number or "mark." The POINT: The *tendency* is thus for me to treat You not as a sacred End-in-yourself but as a mere "means" to my ends, and vice-versa. In effect I "reify" you or turn you into a thing or even a commodity— quite in accord with the p-science "Object" world view that rules your culture and the business-market world per se. I do not notice your *infinite INNER depth* but only your external *OUTER*, your Body and physical appearance. I see you and treat you as just an "object" or "thing"—as one object in an infinite sea of objects. To me you are mainly a "potential sale," a "wallet," in a word—*money*. Only a *means*—a disposable, unessential Object.

§686

It is obvious that this "ego manner" of doing business reinforces the false "Ego and ego-world" of the Dark Side and **Plato's** Cave and does not lead to health and the healing of the Force and your world. And no matter how successful you are in "ego-business," how much wealth or money you acquire, you are never satisfied: something is "missing" and wrong with you and your life. The FACT is that you have ignored the Moral Jedi Law at the center of your being that commands that you realize your Jedi Self and the Jedi Order—the true aim of all your "busy-ness." *What necessarily follows is: GUILT, dysfunction, and disease.*

In sum: Ego-business is *not* a "Person (you) to Person (the other)" interaction—what it should be and in fact is (as "Force to Force")—but instead a "Person to Thing" or more accurately, a "Thing to Thing" affair.

§687

THE JEDI BUSINESS MODE is a horse of a different color. The following can be applied to *all* business situations that involve "self-other" interactions, for example in your home, on the internet, in a small business, corporation, industry, in education, government, etc.

§688

Before I enter into a specific business transaction, I *know*—or initially (if I am a beginner in Jedi things) just *believe* or act *as if* it is true, expecting future results to confirm my belief—I *know of the following:*

(1) The essential inner *unity* of myself and my partner (or Other) in this present business transaction. I know that we share the *same* Absolute I, hence that in dealing with "you" I am really dealing with *myself,* but in another form. Hence the result is a business context

"[Our true self] is numerically *one* in all persons."
Schrödinger

"I am he as you are he as you are me and we are all together."
The Beatles

"And the tune will come to you at last, that we are all one and one is all."
Led Zeppelin

"I am them and they are me ..." **Hegel**

"Inasmuch as you have done it to the least of these, you have done it unto me." **Jesus**

and experience of *infinity* (*of mutual "self-in-other"*), *love, total appreciation, and respect.* These become the foundation of our relating.

(2) I do not and cannot treat you as a mere *object* or *thing*, but instead as an *Infinite Subject* like myself—as an *Equal*.

(3) You are not just a *means* to my own purposes, but an *End* in yourself. Hence I truly care about you and want your happiness and welfare above everything else. To cheat and exploit you is inconceivable. *You are my very self* (compare your own, "Love thy neighbor *as thyself*").

§689

So as a consequence—and of course this will take practice and won't happen in one day—I regard each business transaction as an *opportunity* to heal and deepen my #1 in Power-Ethics; that is, to heal *myself* and *You*. It is an opportunity to go to a higher "I" potency and to a greater degree of *unity* and *power*; it is an opportunity to experience *infinity and love* and to *empower*, bless, lift up and love the Other Person who is one with my True Self, whom I care for as much as I care for myself and whose well being and Awakening I only desire to advance.

§690

The "time" we spend together in the business transaction is above all a *sacred time*, whether it is on the phone or in person because it takes place in Eternity or in the eternal present. Thus in the transaction I focus primarily on the TRUTH of our *unity*, our common shared *IDENTITY*—i.e., on *the Absolute I*, the POINT, the One Infinite Force or Jedi Self that we both are—and I am only interested in nurturing and experiencing *this* as what alone is important. *This is the key*. Hence I am *not* interested in or focused on *money* or things, on marks, sales or filling my quota. I know and trust that these things will take care of themselves according to a higher "Jedi" law and principle; compare your own, "Seek first the Jedi Order and all these things will be added to you."

§691

The relation here is strictly "Person to Person" and in no way "Person (or Thing) to Thing." And my partner(s) must *feel* it and *believe* it. So in effect you should just *do* what you are doing now, but act as if and in such a way that the "sale" is simply not important— only the Person is and the *quality* of the time spent together during the interaction: both of you are in a "sacred space" that provides a golden opportunity for your healing and education into the glorious Jedi Order.

§692

Here are further Jedi Business methods:

> (1) For a store clerk or salesperson: *Before* you enter a public (self-other) space, a meeting, or go into a store or behind a counter, you should *prepare yourself.* Consciously *shift* from an *ego* to a *Jedi* business demeanor by using for example such Jedi "affirmations" as: "I am the Force, I am a Jedi ... and my customer is a Jedi," "I love you, I am in love," "He is me, I am him, and we are One," "Money or the sale is not important—the Truth, Unity, Love, Healing, the Jedi Order, alone is."

> (2) When you enter the room just focus on the client or customer *only as a Person*—forget about the deal, money, possible sale, prestige, financial benefit to yourself, etc.—instead make them feel completely at home, relaxed, as if you had all the time in the world (spread out your appointments, allowing *more* than ample time for each client). Mention "business" only when they do. Your attitude and mind/heart-set should be, "How can I help you?" "I love you," "How can I *really* help you!" "Did you read this great book, see this incredible movie?" Do this even with a difficult "ego"-business person who is "in a hurry," has no time and just wants the facts: "Do you have anything I need or can use?" If *he* is in a hurry, *you* do the exact opposite. Take your time, live deeply in *the eternal now* (now and always). Subconsciously he too wants to live in Eternity, therefore he *will* remember you, will *want* to do business with you

again, will want *more* of you; for you are different from the others, not neurotic, as he himself is, etc.

Needless to say it is presupposed that both parties are adequately prepared and knowledgeable about "business content and details" and have "done their homework" *before* they enter the sacred space of the "business" interaction/transaction.

§693

It is also very important to remind yourself that, "These are *eternal* relationships"—that you and the other person will be around forever, etc. Hence it can be said that Business is truly and in the last analysis, simply a context, an opportunity and even an "excuse" ...

> (1) to *heal* yourself and the other, and the Whole; and to increase your Power and delete *Guilt* as well. This is because the more you do this the less *guilt* and more joy and infinite power you will experience—which is due to increased *Unity,* for guilt and bad conscience are a consequence of being *two* or divided against yourself, resulting in diminished power; and the more you do this the more you are fulfilling the #1 Moral Law for your sacred Jedi Race.

> (2) to *meet* and *network* and make eternal Jedi connections and friends. And

> (3) to *continue your Jedi Education* begun in school and college, and help you realize the Jedi Order and enhance your personal contribution to it.

§694

The most important thing to know is that,

YES. YOU <u>CAN</u> CHANGE THE WORLD.

For whatever you *do*, you at the same time *teach* or are teaching others. As you start doing Jedi-Business it will multiply of itself and expand exponentially. People will feel and notice the difference. Your client or business partner will in turn be moved to do it to *her* clients, and they to theirs.

And there is no question or choice as to which business method—ego or Jedi—you should use. It reduces to, "Do I want to be healthy or sick?"

§695

ON MONEY

"Money" is (1) a *means* to acquire goods and services and a medium of exchange which simplifies and facilitates communal transactions; while "price" is a symbol or index of the *value* of a good or service and a way of storing wealth, and "paper currency" is wealth or purchasing power in a specific form. Money is also (2) the great deceiver, seducer and destroyer of *the True Good* since it promises to be a *substitute* for the True Good: "If only I won the Lottery or had a million dollars, I could be happy and all my problems would be solved." Money promises illusory rewards and offers false hopes. It will tempt you to go after, prefer and pursue *it*, instead of the *true* wealth and health of being an immortal Jedi citizen of the glorious Jedi Order. To have Money and not to have Health is the worst thing. Once an "egoic" Person has money they feel no need to do anything else, they think they "have arrived" and are permanently secure— there is no need to pursue Jedi and the Jedi Order, the true #1.

§696

Money is universally viewed as absolutely necessary in order to live in the world. You need money and the purchasing power it provides just to maintain your existence from day to day—for housing, food, necessities and pleasantries. The sudden cessation of it brings your life to a grinding halt and causes much pain and discomfort, like a fall into homelessness and poverty. Money thus permeates all aspects of life and exerts great power on the mind-Self and people's behavior. Because of this, money is a major factor in aiding or retarding your becoming a Jedi and fully healed; it can be a great form of bondage.

§697

Most people on your planet are plagued by money problems their whole life, from cradle to grave. And for many, concern with money fills up much of their waking hours and thought-life. This should not be, for people should be free to develop and pursue their Jedi talents and Jedi Education and be of true service to society and the Jedi Order.

Thus at those times when you have enough of it money gives you a false sense of (1) *security* or *wholeness* ("if I have enough money and am solvent the #1 problem of my life is solved or, I have achieved the goal of life"), and (2) *selfhood* or *identity* ("I am my money, wealth, possessions"). Furthermore (3) people use money as a way to evaluate and determine the *worth* of a person. Consequently money can give you a false, perverted and "egoic" non-Jedi set of values.

§698

What is Money's value and role in society?

Money derives its undue importance from the fact that having it or not determines to a certain extent the quality of your *material* life, your continuing to have a roof over your head and clothing and food on the table tomorrow. Your people are taught (or brainwashed) early in life about the "value" of money, that money can buy the things you need and want, and the amount and quality of these things. You absorb your family's attitudes to money naturally, automatically and it takes time and effort to change this and put money in its true light.

But the FACT is, as the Jedi Truth has taught you, that because your #1 Good and purpose is to be and live as a Jedi—which requires that you be *free* to develop yourselves and your powers and abilities—you will eventually be *freed* from the tyranny and need to be constantly preoccupied with acquiring money. The money system inevitably will be superseded and pass away, for Jedi-governments will conceive a system whereby each citizen will be given an *allowance* and all the money (or, what is the same thing, Means) she needs to be able to develop her abilities unhampered.

§699

Thus Money's role and place in society—until your people have advanced to the next level—can only be subordinate and instrumental to the #1 Goal of Health and the Jedi Order. The power money holds over your people's minds, their value systems and priorities *must be broken. For it is a Jedi FACT that People are #1, Money #2 and only a means to help people.* Hence *money is to be regarded merely as a convenience that makes it easier to do business and daily transactions for life's necessities— money is <u>not</u> a God or a God-substitute.* In itself and as such money has no value whatsoever, it is just paper. A person should thus be evaluated (if such is necessary) in terms of what he does with his money, how he *uses* it to help and to heal people and reach Jedihood—or does not. He should in no way be *dependent* on money or identify his Self with it (and thereby "lose his Jedi soul")—and this can be known simply by his reaction after he loses some or all of it.

§700

Again with the spread of True Knowledge through society's Seven institutions, money and the need to get and work for it will eventually disappear. Indeed it is happening now—with credit cards and computer internet and international banking. In the Jedi Order Jedi will not need Money or, what is the same, will have unlimited access to Money or Means. "Pre-Jedi" will be in a regulated money-disbursement system. They will be given a certain yearly income or allowance (a means) so that they can plan that year's agenda, activities, and projects; including food, lodging, and necessities as well as enterprises, etc. They will be given more for special projects and needs—but only after approval by a Jedi Board that will evaluate their request, etc. When they too become Jedi they will likewise have free access to money and means. Pre-Jedi will of course be able to increase their income's base amount by their work and wise investments. Also be mindful that priorities and values will shift with the ongoing expansion of Jedi Education; the very wealthy, for example, will inevitably be more concerned about the Universal and the Whole and far less concerned about finite aims and themselves as private individuals.

§701

The Task: The Ego or egoic Self ignorantly tends to solve its root Self/Other (its nothingness/inferiority) Problem by "identifying" with and preserving itself in the *infinite OUTER and money and things*, and the more the better, and thus gets ATTACHED to them. The Task however is for the Self to become UNATTACHED to them and realize instead its true *infinite INNER* Jedi Self. This can be greatly facilitated by from time to time GIVING AWAY A PORTION OF YOUR MONEY AND POSSESSIONS to someone; it will hurt the Ego but not the Self. This is analogous to "PRUNING" A TREE, where you trim and cut off the ends, which get clogged and unproductive, and thus allow more vital force to flow and more growth to occur (as one of your Jedi has said, "Give and it shall be given unto you"). "GIVING AWAY" is a Jedi Law and in truth contributes to the "negation of the negation" and the *universality* of the Self. "Giving" is like "investing"—is not LOSS but paradoxically GAIN.

§702

THE CORPORATION

It is clear now why business as such and hence all corporations— national as well as multinational—should switch over from the Ego to the Jedi manner of doing business: true health and well being are increased, and profits as well. And true wealth is not found in money or material things, but in Jedi realized people and nations. As indicated earlier the *primary* purpose of all 7 institutions in your global society, hence of business and the corporation in particular, is to serve as a context for *global education* into Jedi and incorporation into the eternal Jedi Order and its ongoing maintenance and expansion; all else, production and exchange of goods and services, is *secondary*. This is because the participants, players and agents who engage in business are really the FORCE (the Whole) as unique centers of its experience, or actual and potential JEDI. And the greatest thing is for a Jedi to know *who* he or she is and accordingly live the fullest eternal life that this involves.

Here my Padawan I will just give you the essentials.

§703

The true Concept of the Corporation, according to Jedi Science.

In the Jedi Order the Corporation holds a unique place within the Business sector of *Civil Society* because of its high *ethical* function and its power to *educate* and help transform the "ego's particular isolated Will" into a "universal Jedi Self." This is because the member of the Corporation does not work merely for herself but for a greater whole, a higher *universal* cause and interest to which she sacrifices herself and her ego interests. Also as being *part* of a whole or a team he is *aware* he is under the constant scrutiny of "others" and held to the highest standards, which helps to check and transmute the lower egoistic behaviors.

§704

So the corporation is a single *organization* under one management and chain of command whereby a *multiplicity* is pervaded by a *single unity*, thus forming a kind of miniature State or "second family." The corporation's Board of Trustees, Stockholders, CEO, Managers, and Employees all work together serving one common End—providing society with a specific good or service. To be part of a corporation affords an incredible opportunity to become a Jedi and realize the collective *unity* of the One Force, the True Infinite Self that connects a host of individual selves.

Further the Corporation is a moral and ethical entity, not only internally but externally as well. As a Unit, Unity or Self it relates to and does business with an Other, the Public. So while the corporation's ostensive purpose is to provide a good or service to the public, its *real* purpose is to advance and sustain the Jedi Order: both the Jedi within itself and the Jedi that it serves in the World.

§705

The Ego-Run Corporation—as Based on the Ego manner of doing business.
As ego-based, the *unity* implicit in the corporation's concept is not realized or only superficially, hence it is more a multiplicity or an unstable aggregate. Since it is a *fear and lack based* environment—not one of love and abundance—everyone knows he is expendable and can be demoted or lose his job. The corporation is not essentially *for* him but for profit, money is the bottom line. People are only *objects or means*—not infinite and sacred Jedi.

The *unity* is not realized because everyone thinks of himself and the others as s*eparate isolated Egos*—mortal, perishable, expendable—living mainly for themselves and their self-interest. There is no knowledge of *the true concept and purpose of a corporation,* which is to heal, educate and realize the Jedi Order. The main principle and top priority of the ego-based CEO is to use all available resources (labor and capital) to maximize profits—for the sake of *more profits,* and still *more*—and minimize loss *at any cost.* The CEO is seen as a source of *fear* by those under him as he has the power to fire them and does not love or affirm them *as such.* They are just *objects* without infinite value. In the ego run corporation not people but money and things are first.

§706

The Jedi Corporation and its defining characteristics:

- The Jedi Corporation and CEO know the true concept of the corporation and realize it in every possible way and use "Power—Ethics."

- In the firm e*ducation*—inner and outer and helping to realize one's true Jedi Self—is paramount, not profits. *People are #1, not money and things.*

- The Jedi Corporation thus sees itself as a center of *light and power* whose main objective is not money or profit but the healing of the world and all people, the lifting of all egos into the Force, the One Eternal Self and Life.

- The Jedi Corporation and CEO know that by being faithful to this principle their financial goals will also be met. But the purpose of profit will not be *for themselves* alone but to *invest it in the further healing of the world.*

- They *know* that all persons, employees, hence relationships are *eternal* and thus sacred. They want to increase their *light and power* as much as possible and have everyone function as *one,* as a single living organism, person, or will. Hence because they treat their staff as *royalty* and encourage *unity,* love, respect, and appreciation their employees, as organic members of the corporation, feel totally *at home, valued* and loved. They know they are getting the best treatment possible and do not fear they will lose their job or be treated unfairly.

§707

- The primary purpose of *Education,* the very center of the firm, is to continue its employees' public school and college education to Jedi. Not only are there outstanding classes, courses, and outside lectures, but also weekly and monthly meetings in departments and in the whole firm (including "Jedi pep talks" and rallies) designed to overcome conflicts and resolve problems between team members and to enhance the love, bonding, unity and functioning of the firm.

- The firm is a place where *everyone wants to be*, employees as well as the public. It is full of light and love and high values that center on *affirming* the *Person* as infinite, while money and things are nothing, having only utility value. For example, a visitor or stranger from the street is greeted with genuine love, affirmation, and recognition and invited to the firm's in-house cafeteria, library, museum, or art gallery. A service for *homeless people* is even provided. They are given a shower, a meal, and even a *job and housing* (the firm buys or invests in abandoned buildings, alone or with other firms). The city and public will be grateful as there will be less homeless persons on the street—as more persons or Jedi are now employed and productive members of society, with dignity and self-esteem. The public will give your firm added business knowing that you exist only to help and improve society, profits will rise and not diminish—more money and means to use for the Cause.

§708

- Everyone and the best talent will want to work at your firm because the best people and best benefits are there. A person can do her *best growing* into Jedi and reach the highest levels possible of light, power and well being, and make the best contacts, eternal friends, relations, and Jedi associates.
- Your firm can also make it a priority to *bail out the competition* and help them in time of crisis to avoid chapter 11 bankruptcy; as unemployed they raise prices and reduce the GNP, etc. You, not to mention your country, will be amply rewarded.
- If you are a *multinational* corporation you will be especially concerned about elevating and educating the *developing nations* on your planet into Jedi and the Jedi Order—for you seek to spread the light and love you have achieved and are to them, and raise their standard of living and quality of life and, above all, to *end their Poverty*; as a Jedi firm you would never exploit them as your current multinationals do.

§709

- The Jedi in your firm work only 5-6 hours per day, with a 4-day work week, a 3-day weekend, and a 3-4 month vacation, which will allow time for their other projects, dreams, and ways to become better people and more educated—which reflects very positively on the firm; for the more talent, culture, and rich experience your staff has, the greater the spiritual weight and value of your firm and the greater their productivity, ideas, and input will be—your firm will do more for the world and the Cause, such as set up hospitals, schools, and viable businesses, like your Jedi **Bill and Melinda Gates** and others.

- Lastly, as a Jedi CEO you will be able to ignite a completely new trend in business and industry on your planet. As a case in point let us say that: You are a success, you just did another merger and are very wealthy. But you're starting to get bored. You say, "Is this it? There must be something more I can do with my life, my time, money, and power." *There is.* You can dedicate your life, self and means to the Jedi Cause and help create an amazing new world. You can change your priorities, embrace the Vision, commit 100% to the Jedi Order and invoke the new Jedi business principles and be a model CEO.

§710

> "Globalization 3.0 is shrinking the world from a size small to a size tiny and flattening the playing field at the same time [and] has made us all next door neighbors ... [It] makes it possible for so many more people to plug and play, and you are going to see every color of the human rainbow take part."
> **Thomas Friedman**

"GLOBALIZATION," Its True Meaning

Because the Jedi Truth in *Part I* teaches about the One Absolute I, that "I am them, and they are me," the word "*globalization*" powerfully reflects the fact that you and your people have an *absolute Duty* to realize One World and One Race. Hence what is currently called "globalization" on your planet is really a *summons,* a Call, and a mandate to all your peoples to heal and elevate *all* of humankind into the Jedi Order and to drop isolation and non-concern for other nations. Thus all of you are now being required to "Think Globally"—to think not just of yourselves and of your own, but of *all* nations. Your peoples are truly *interdependent*, not just economically and materially, but essentially, metaphysically, spiritually, and ontologically. Therefore all of you need to cooperate in order to realize the new Jedi Order, to use your collective resources wisely, and to feed and clothe your entire planet and raise living standards to the Jedi level for *everyone*. The central Principle of Globalization is thus:

> *Seek first the Jedi Order—*
> *And all economic/material*
> *well-being and prosperity*
> *will be added to you.*

Thus all of you have a mandate (1) to raise all people to Jedi, and hence *education* is #1, (2) to raise the quality of life of all nations and globally end poverty, disease, and slavery, and (3) to give rights and freedom to all the citizens of Earth and the Jedi Order.

§711

The first question in regard to Business Globalization is: *What is in fact true wealth and prosperity?* Is it having lots of money and goods? *No.* It is *knowing who you are—your absolute importance and eternal destiny as a member of the immortal race of Jedi.* Indeed you *are* and have inherited all things and own them: as your **Alan Watts** has proclaimed, *"The Universe is yours, is you—is your infinite body."* True wealth is the *treasure (the "kingdom of God") that is within you.* Hence it is YOU, YOURSELVES—not gold or silver—that is of infinite value. Money and material goods are just poor shadows, jejune substitutes for these—which advertisers eager for profit are constantly misleading you to believe.

§712

Your #1 Aim should therefore be—with the collaboration of multi-national firms, investors, governments, world trade organizations, international monetary funds, etc.—To prosper, elevate and beautify *ALL* of the developed and developing nations of your world:

GLOBALIZATION THUS MEANS THAT *ALL PEOPLES ARE YOUR CONCERN.*

It is therefore dangerous and wrong *not* to help a nation to develop and solve its problems, to let it remain idle, backward, in poverty, and in political and economic turmoil and instability: *to let its citizens remain as pre-Jedi. The* solution is Global Jedi Education and the fruits thereof.

§713

[C] BALANCE. To balance business on your planet you need therefore only adopt *Jedi Power Ethics.* For example, simply as an individual and apart from business you can start by committing yourself 100% to the Cause of realizing your self as a Jedi and the Jedi Order worldwide. Then you can bring your business activity under Power Ethics and shift from doing unconscious ego-business to conscious Jedi Business. You can put business, money, and material well-being in their proper subordinate place as a *means* to the #1 *End* of healing the world and realizing the amazing Jedi Order.

§714

First, You should Get off the treadmill—Simplify your life by *simplifying* your wants and needs. All these *things* you have and desire to have more of, are "ego" investments and sustainers or *Ego-Traps.* Because you are trying to find happiness or the infinite in these things alone, they are keeping you from actualizing your true Jedi Self. Ask yourself, "How many things-possessions do I *really* need?" Do not let yourself be brainwashed and controlled by the media, T.V., and material-"ego" advertisers. This false mind-set and value-system will convince you that you need a bigger and better TV, cell phone, I-phone, car, house, vacation, stock portfolio, bank account, etc. The FACT is that this mind-set knows nothing of the TRUTH or Reality, who you really are, what you really need to make you complete and happy, and what is really *GOOD* for you. It will keep you in adamantine bondage.

§715

What you need is to be *non-attached* to these 1,001 things. Yes, you can have and use these things *so long as you're not egoically attached and dependent on them.* For all you really need is your True Inner Infinite Free Self, and a healthy body. Remember you ARE the Whole, the infinite One Being. You (the meek: the egoless) *have* inherited all things (as your scriptures say). The universe *is* your Body—is You. Do not have a "poverty-lack-consciousness"—but the reverse. You can also change your attitude towards *Money and Things* and Break your attachment to them by giving them away to a worthy cause or person. Give away your car, TV, etc. Live in a more economical, cheaper home *for a while.* You may lose some friends, but they were not worth keeping in the first place; they only liked you because of your money and status—not you yourself; it was all false, inauthentic.

§716

The first thing you and your rich have to do is to *solve the homeless-poverty-unemployment problem on your planet.* The Rich for example must be made to see that it is to *their* absolute benefit (as well as the world's) to solve these problems; that they and you have a duty to help them since it is a Jedi Moral Law whose consequences are *guilt* and nonhealth if you do not. *The pain, lack of self-respect and self-worth of your poor and homeless cannot but affect the health and well-being of yourselves and your rich.* For your poor and homeless too are the Force and Jedi and share with you *the same One Consciousness.* It is thus of ultimate importance to solve these world-wide problems. Therefore because most of the wealth and means in the world is concentrated in the hands of the few what *must* happen is that, for example, the super-wealthy among you must *willingly* give their wealth away and distribute it to the have-nots—*but on a completely rational basis* so that a relapse into poverty does not occur and money and capital are not squandered. See POLITICS my Padawan for a more detailed account of this solution, as well as **Robert Reich's** brilliant work *Aftershock: The Next Economy and America's Future,* especially Part III.

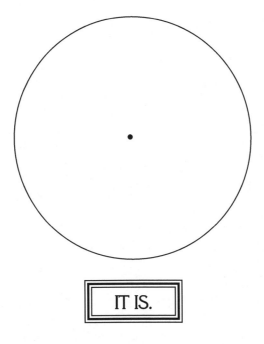

IT IS.

HEALTH

MEDICINE & PSYCHIATRY

Health, the Healing Arts & Sciences and HealthCare are very important for Global Education and Healing. Because of the great authority of medical doctors and psychiatrists it is vital that they possess the *true* Concept and understanding of what HEALTH and being HEALED is. At present they follow your p-sciences' erroneous definitions of Man and reality.

HEALTH SUMMARY

(A) CONCEPT. The chief purpose of Health is Educational—to take your people into the JEDI ORDER, the POINT qua Healing and Health, *as JEDI.* "Health" derives from: (1) *POINT:* The POINT expresses true Health, which is being in your JEDI self and plugged into the WHOLE, the One Consciousness, and one with everyone as having overcome the Self/Other split. Thus "Health," by POLARITY, is to have *all* 3 parts of your nature actualized and in Unity: *Absolute I, Mind, and Body.* (2) *ETYMOLOGY:* "Health" derives from "HĀL" meaning WHOLE, Complete (±) and "Holy," or existing and living *within* the WHOLE—whereas remaining *outside* the Whole is analogous to a "cancer" in the Body (in the Whole). The Key to true Health thus involves: (a) *WHO you are*—You are not a "human being" but a Jedi as a Universal Self (U.I.), the WHOLE, the POINT aware of itself as *Absolute I-Mind-Body,* and (b) *what HEALTH is*—Health or being Healthy is simply the WHOLE and being plugged into it, that is, being a JEDI. Therefore the primary objective of a JEDI DOCTOR (medical or psychiatrist/therapist) is to *integrate you* into the Jedi Order or the *Whole,* and to treat the *Whole* person and not just the Body or Mind-Body.

(B) WRONG/IMBALANCE. Your Doctors lack the true concept of "Man" and "Health" (by following the p-sciences). Hence *they cannot Heal.* They rely only on chemical or surgical cures that at best just return you to the "Norm," and the same is true for Psychiatry which also inverts cause and effect. Thus doctors and pharmaceutical companies are wrong in viewing chemicals as the answer to disease. This view prevents true healing and wholeness and keeps patients/clients permanently in the Dark Side and unfulfilled.

(C) BALANCE. Educate your health professionals into JEDI medicine and create Jedi Doctors (Masters) who use ATTENTION and know that the *Absolute I* is the cure of every disorder. And solve Universal HEALTHCARE by Jedi preventive medicine and save billions of dollars as well.

§717

[A] CONCEPT. The primary purpose of health is *educational,* that is, to take you out of illusion, the Cave, and Ego-separateness ... into the Jedi Order and the ONE REALITY (±) which is NOW.

The true concept of Health is contained in *the Knowledge of the Force* or in the POINT and POLARITY, which reveals true health to be simply a matter of (1) being in your JEDI self and plugged into the WHOLE by having overcome the Self/Other separation and (2) having the 3 parts of your nature in Unity: your *Absolute I, Mind, and Body.* A further key to the true Jedi meaning of *Health* and *Being Healed* offers itself in its Anglo-Saxon root, the word "HĀL" (from your Greek "*holos*"). "HĀL" is rich in meanings—metaphysical, religious, as well as practical-medical. They include: *WHOLE* or being Complete—as in a perfect specimen, not missing any parts, hence: *BEING,* in the sense of sacred, inviolable, indestructible, imperishable, and immortal—again, being Complete, Perfect, not lacking anything, hence Infinite, Eternal, and True Being; and of course HOLY. Thus "HEALTH" in its deepest, truest meaning involves all three elements: *WHOLE, BEING, and HOLY.*

§718

Here Noble Jedi, I will focus on the aspect "**WHOLE,**" HĀL's primary meaning, which also contains the others. Thus to be in a state of "Health" or to be "Healthy" is **(A) to be "WHOLE,"** that is, to have all aspects of your nature and Being *actualized*—to be a "JEDI" and, what is the same, **(B) to be incorporated or "plugged in" to "the WHOLE,"** that is, The WHOLE of All That Is—the Jedi Order, which alone is and IS NOW.

§719

First, to be in full Health is **(A) to be WHOLE, a JEDI**—i.e. to be and to have realized *all* of what you are and not just a *part.* As we know from *the Knowledge of the Force* and Jedi Science in *Part I.,* your true Being or complete Concept includes *Three* elements:

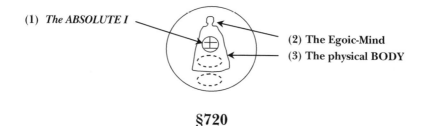

(1) *The ABSOLUTE I*

(2) The Egoic-Mind
(3) The physical BODY

§720

Thus you are *not* just (3) your physical BODY (with its various organs and physiological systems); nor are you just (2) your Egoic-Mind (or "Soul" as a Particular Individuality: with an intellect, will, emotions) *or* your Mind-Body complex. You are also and most significantly (1) an or *the* **Absolute I**, the Force's Infinite Consciousness of Itself that encompasses everything as the only Reality—and which is eternally fused with your Mind and Body (the basis of your uniqueness, identity, and individuality). It is this Absolute I or Pure *Universal* Consciousness that you share with all other Selves and Jedi, and which is the basis of your UNITY with all things—with the WHOLE and all peoples—and your *immortality*. It is *the* one and only Solution to your planet's problems. Hence it is obvious that the true Concept of Health is impossible without the true Concept of "Man" or who you are; which indicates your Medicine and Psychiatry's major defect.

§721

True Health thus presupposes that you have transcended the *separation* involved in the Dark Side of the Force, in particular the Subject/Object or Self/Other *split*—which is the root cause of all planetary disorders. This transcendence of the Self/Other split can happen only when you have realized the *Unity* of the *Absolute I*—and hence that the *Absolute I* in you and at the core of your being is *one and the same* as the *Absolute I* in me and at the core of my being, and of everyone's being.

Thus real Health—and Love-centered living—cannot be achieved by treating the *OUTER* and the BODY alone, nor by treating the patient who presents as only a MIND-BODY—for then finitude, the Self/Other unresolved Polarity, would still remain. Rather it is attainable only by treating the WHOLE Person and making the *INNER*, the *Absolute I* and its Opening, *the main focus of attention and treatment.*

§722

Secondly, you cannot be fully Healthy unless you are **(B) "plugged in" to the WHOLE**, into the Eternally Present Jedi Order—the One Indivisible REALITY, the FORCE ($\pm$)—and being fully *aware* of it and living *fully* in the Eternal Now. As we know underlying all the multiplicity of the Sense-world is a Single indivisible UNITY, *the Absolute I*—the Force's One Infinite Consciousness—which alone is true Reality and contains the infinite material realm within itself *as idealized.* Ultimately there is only ONE WHOLE, which can be thought of as ONE GIANT BODY, LIFE, ORGANISM, or a LIVING ENTITY (cf. the "Body of Christ," in Christianity, and the "Maha-Bodhisattva" in Buddhism, et al)—each of you existing *within* this One BODY or WHOLE as its living, loving members. And of course each of you, as a Jedi and the Whole or Force aware of Itself, *is also the Whole itself* and not just a "member" or "part" of it; for you are a UNIVERSAL (not a particular Egoic) Self and an Individual (in the sense described in *Part I*). That is, *your* Universal Self includes *within itself* the Selves of everyone else in the Universe in virtue of the *Absolute I* at its center, and vice-versa. Thus in virtue of your definition and essence, all of you are involved in each other. Hence each of you is not the WHOLE in an *exclusive* sense, as if just yourself and no one else existed, but rather in an *inclusive* sense. There *are* others besides yourself—there is a *plurality* inside the ONE WHOLE or "BODY" and *in this sense* each of you can be considered as a "Member" of the ONE BODY or WHOLE.

§723

It follows that if you are *not* aware of this Unity or One Body-Whole underlying your "normal" consciousness and everything else—i.e., are not aware of the Jedi Order—then you are living only in your Ego-Mind (-Body) as in an "I/Not-I" state, isolated and *separate* from all others and the WHOLE and "living in the CAVE." In this condition you can be regarded as a **"CANCER"** in the ONE BODY or FORCE. You can now see how all disorders and diseases have there origin **precisely HERE.** All of your waking life from infancy till Now has been a life and a series of "I/Not-I" experiences *lived within* and *as* a "CANCER CELL." It is thus all of the *accumulated negativity* and *toxicity* that this involves, which has resulted in all the physical-mental-social-political ills and evils in the world and through the ages. In this light HISTORY can be viewed as nothing but the course of Man's *dis-ease* and the ongoing attempt to Cure it.

§724

Therefore HEALTH and BEING HEALTHY essentially involve moving from our familiar *Stage Two* state as an isolated Body-Ego and a "CANCER" in the ONE BODY/WHOLE ... to the *Stage Three* state of being plugged in and incorporated into the WHOLE/BODY, feeling and enjoying one's UNITY with all Others, with full Awareness of the *Absolute I.*

Thus the purpose of HEALTH and the Medical and Psychological Healing Arts is essentially the *same* as the other Six-Areas, namely to *Educate* and take you into the Jedi Order and out of the CAVE and the EGO-state into Light Side Reality and your Unity with everyone. Thus the global realization of true health will occur when every adult on your planet is living in and sharing *consciously* the same One Absolute I, the *One Holy Universal Self.* Hence "sickness" or non-health can be defined as any degree of deviation from this alignment with your True Self *as* the Force or Whole; "sickness" is thus to be living still in your "ego," in limitation, in "time" and anxious. Hence by definition it can be said that there is no one on your planet who is truly healthy and not sick.

§725

My Padawan let us review: I have said that the primary meaning of "HEALTH" is the state of being WHOLE, HOLY, BEING, and in the ONE Jedi Order as a U.I. or Universal Individual, immortal, complete, and Happy. The purpose of the Healing Arts (medicine and psychiatry) is thus to make you WHOLE or a JEDI—one with the FORCE, the Whole, Being, and all people by integrating you into the One Jedi Order, the ONE Reality. The Jedi Doctor thus treats and heals the WHOLE PERSON as **Absolute I (or Spirit) |Mind|Body** (and not just the Body). The *Mind/Body* alone is P.I. and separate. It follows that *your health practitioners today can never truly HEAL*—as they leave you, the patient, in your *finite* separate Ego; for without the Absolute I (the Infinite) and the experience of UNITY with everyone, you are as stated a "cancer" in the One Jedi Order (or "Body"). Furthermore "to be healed" is also for the individual to have overcome his or her condition of Self/Other (+|-) *separation*

and become the Whole Subject/Object that he or she is, or a Jedi.
Thus any person or group that claims to be in a field whose concern
or subject-matter is "health" must minimally possess this concept
of Health, otherwise they operate under a grave handicap. Thus
the meaning of "health" and "healing" as it applies to the fields
of Medicine and Psychiatry—if we wish to know its *true* meaning
and regardless of how it is understood in these disciplines—*must*
be based on and derived from its true Jedi meaning as just stated;
which, as most complete, supersedes all other definitions. So no
matter how it is regarded in these fields, "health" or "being healed"
in the highest and fullest sense must be for an individual to have
actualized, be living in and enjoying one's true Infinite Jedi Self.
This is a state of being in which one KNOWS him or herself as a
Universal Self and One with the Jedi Order, as the Whole of Reality,
INNER and OUTER; and as eternal, immortal, and master over the
physical-natural realm and his Body (and thus over all dis-ease);
and as having *two* Bodies, Physical and *Subtle*, which latter is
indestructible and can materialize or de-materialize at will, etc, with
a core of LOVE and total self-esteem.

§726

You can hence see the inadequacy attaching to a "Medicine"
whose idea of "health" and "healing" goes no further than "normal
functioning without noticeable impairment of bodily and mental
systems," with a goal of therapy or treatment as the restoring of
the individual to "normal" health, meaning the mental-physical
condition they were in prior to the onset of their debilitating illness
or disorder; and to a "Psychiatry" that holds the similar view of
restoring and returning the individual to a "normal," that is, socially
approved "well-adjusted" state of mental health.

§727

"Medicine" typically treats the *Body*—its diseases and disorders—*and
not the Mind* (the province of Psychiatry). This is a major error. For
true medicine, in accord with who "Man" really is, is and can only
be *HOLISTIC*—treating the individual, the Force, as the WHOLE
that he or she is, namely, *Absolute I (or Spirit)-Mind-Body* as the
unity of INNER and OUTER. The FACT and Jedi Truth is that the
Absolute I—and actualizing and tapping into its powers of healing,

immunization and restoration of cells and organs—*is the active agent in the healing of all diseases without exception.*

§728

As for "Psychiatry," etymologically the word comes from the two roots, "psyche" = the soul, and "iatreia" or "iatros" = physician, healer, or (the art of) healing, and hence means *the art of healing the soul or simply, the healing of the soul (the INNER, unity)—and not of the Body (the OUTER, many).*

A prime error today among your psychiatrists or "soul healers" is that many adhere to the materialist world-view of the "p-sciences" which reduce Man to a mere physical-biological being as a result of which they treat disorders of the soul (the INNER) as "medical" disorders, as disorders of the Body (the OUTER). They thus in essence deny the Inner altogether—that is, deny that Man even has a soul, self, mind, or "inner" dimension or aspect at all; regarding him as only a physical brain or nervous system, reduced to "neurons firing," etc. This is a total disaster—the source of untold unnecessary and preventable suffering. Of course here too the diagnosis and treatment as in medicine must be HOLISTIC—so the Body must *also* be attended to. But the mistake of psychiatry is to put the "cart before the horse" *and invert cause and effect.* That is, to see changes in body chemistry (e.g. in serotonin levels) as the "cause" of "mental/ soul" disorders, the "effect," and prescribe drugs accordingly; and not to see them as what they are in truth, the *effects* of the former, of the Mind-Self's reactions to the stresses of life or of **Heideggerian** "being in the world" and the fundamental Self/Other Dark Side situation.

§729

Hence as a result the most psychiatrists can hope for in treatment is to return the patient to a "normal well-adjusted life"—that is, to "normal" *as defined by the status quo—(whatever it may be at the time, and which is nothing "objective or scientific" and is determined by a "show of hands," by a vague "statistically constructed and fabricated" idea in the therapists head as to what "a normal individual in today's society should look like").* That is, to "conformity" with what "society"—the historical others of a given time no matter how "sick" or far from True Jedi Health they are—regards as normal, proper behavior and character.

This is obviously not enough. The true goal of therapy-treatment is *Total Health*—or at a minimum getting the individual "back on track, on course" to becoming a Jedi. At best this can be only an initial starting "condition" for true Health—and in no way the thing itself.—We will look more closely below at the key differences between the methods of an ordinary "ego" physician and therapist and those of a Jedi-Doctor and Jedi-Therapist. A large part of the new Jedi-Doctor's treatment plan will involve "*improving* health" by giving concrete methods for elevating individuals (patients/ clients) from their "ego" state to their Jedi Self or the Whole, which is alone true health; and by helping them change their self-image and re-program their mind e.g. by affirmations and by joining "Jedi-groups."

§730

Thus to be in the healing profession and not to know what true health is is to put yourself and your patient and society at great risk. And all the fundamental problems in medicine and psychiatry stem from one thing, namely the erroneous Concept of Man, of who you really are, that underlies all their practice and methods.

§731

[B] WRONG/IMBALANCED. Here we will discuss, What's wrong with the current state of your "medicine" and "psychiatry," Why they are imbalanced and promote the dark side and "mis-education," and Why your health professionals do not heal and educate.

The primary reason the Medical and Psychiatric professions on your planet are not educating or healing is that they lack the true concepts of HEALTH and "MAN." This is mainly due to an education based on the errors of the p-sciences, which are limited to the OUTER (-) and totally ignorant of the INNER (+)—as a result of which both professions regard "Man" as a merely "physical/ biological" being and treat her accordingly.

§732

They are practicing *medicine* in the CAVE, knowing only of the sense-material world (-), and have not risen above **Plato's** Divided

Line into the (+) world of Consciousness, *the Absolute I* and UNITY, where Health and true Cures alone can be secured. Because they embrace the p-sciences mind-set and worldview they see themselves only as separate material EGO's and view their patients in the same way—oblivious to the UNITY and INNER they share and are. Moreover not only do they accept this false *definition* of themselves as "human beings" but the *public* as well, due to the professions' great status and *authority* world-wide, accepts it as unquestionably true— thus disseminating error and keeping humanity in the CAVE and from realizing the amazing Jedi Order and *true* HEALTH.

§733

Not only are they unaware of the Self/Other problem and dynamic as the *key to all disease,* they also tend to *separate* Body from Mind/ Absolute I and fail to realize that the *link* between Body and Mind/Absolute I (or the POINT) is the *key to all healing.* SO: What they need is a radically *HOLISTIC* concept of Man (Absolute I-Mind-Body-Universe) and Health. True Health as we know, is achievable only by having completed the transition from Ego to Infinite Jedi Self—and to the absence of division, dis-Unity and *Guilt*: thus your health practitioners also need to know the relation of GUILT (what your religions call "sin") to DISEASE.

§734

Medicine views its primary purpose and the aim of treatment to be the returning of the patient or Jedi to "normal" health, i.e., to the condition he was in *prior* to the onset of the *disorder* for which he sought the Doctor's services, hence to be able to resume the level of functioning and life he enjoyed before. **This is not *Health.*** For even if this is achieved the person still remains in his unhealthy-unhealed Ego-Body condition—not one step closer to resolving the I/Not-I split and to accessing his *Absolute I,* experiencing his Unity with the WHOLE and with all Selves on the planet.

Moreover as regards treatment everything is determined by the Concept of "Man" held by the Medical profession, which chiefly views "Man" *as* a particular "animal" species that has higher functions than other species, e.g. thought and language, and as such is merely a material-biological entity; that is, merely *as* a BODY or a unit or collection of organs, systems, chemicals, etc., and not *as* he truly is, a 3-part Jedi: an Absolute I, Mind, Body *unity.*

§735

Their major error lies in their assumption that the "disorder" at issue must therefore have its origin/seat/cause in the BODY; and as a result they put the subject through a battery of Tests in order to assess the functioning of blood, urine, endocrine, brain-nervous system, etc. They may then discover "abnormalities" or irregularities (based on statistics, or the "Norm") and search for their *cause* on the *physical-chemical level alone*—they thus try for a "chemical" cure and in most cases a surgical one. For example they may find that if they *change* the Body's chemistry the "symptoms" may disappear or abate— and as a consequence put the patient on this chemical for the rest of his life. But the fact and truth is that what they conclude to be the "cause" of the disorder or "imbalance" *is really the effect.* That is why there is no real and permanent *Cure.* In addition there are *side-effects* and the patient is never really "Healthy" and is subject to relapses; and whether she discontinues the medicine or not she becomes *dependent* on the chemical—and often the dosage must be increased. Instead what the Medical Profession has to do is simply to get to the *root* of the problem and the *true cause* that is responsible for the *chemical imbalance* in the first place (which is the Inner and stress); for the imbalance is only the *effect* (of the Inner and stress) and not the *cause.*

That is, the perceived *changes* in Body-chemistry that the Tests reveal (and the chemicals used to correct it, due to Body's failure to produce them) do *not* pertain to the *cause* of the disorder in question and its *outer* symptoms. They are rather the *effect.* As noted, all disorders have their origin in (+) *the Absolute I* and EGO-Self/Other relations (stress, etc) or *finitude;* that is, in the inability to FLOW into the OTHER (which results in *true* well-being, happiness, and contentment with one's surroundings), and in being confronted with an Other that one cannot *assimilate* or achieve IDENTITY with. The fact is that disorders do *not* have their origin in (-) matter/the Body/ chemicals; for the former (+) alone is CAUSE, the latter (-) EFFECT.

§736

Your physicians especially need to know (1) that it is a troubled Mind that affects the Brain which in turn affects the Body's *immune system*; and (2) that defects in DNA and the physical Body are *not* major or decisive—for the (+) *Absolute I* absolutely and without question trumps the (-), the Body and its DNA. Also the Jedi *Subtle* (or Astral) Body is there too and it is perfect; hence new limbs are able to grow and new cells and organs, etc, as well. This is further confirmed by the FACT that what you call "stem cells" can grow *any* type of cell for any type of tissue or organ. Therefore the Body has the power and ability to repair *any* of its organs, the brain included—this power just needs to be accessed or tapped—e.g., by a group of Jedi doctors gathering around the patient and healing him; see below.

§737

The truth is that even your more "Holistically" oriented and trained Doctors who do regard "Mind-Set," Home-Life, Work-environment, and social (Self/Other) stresses as concomitant *contributory* causes or factors in the disorder—and hence do recognize *these* to be the true cause and mainly responsible for the physical disorder and presenting symptoms (and do realize that a *change* in environment, a Job change e.g., will *Cure* the problem)—*even these holistic physicians cannot bring the patient into True HEALTH* but rather leave her in the EGO condition—and thus exposed to further disorders—and in Dark Side separation without UNITY and unaware of her *Absolute I* and *Jedi Self*, her infinite, immortal nature.

§738

Further your Medical Profession as such does not sufficiently understand the importance of *Attitude, beliefs and Mind-Set,* that is, of POWER ETHICS, hence their overreliance on Drugs and "studies." Most importantly since your Profession lacks the true Concept of Man and Reality (the Inner and Outer Force) it does not know *What can be, What you are capable of, and What Reality is*— which can make all the difference in effecting a cure. Indeed it simply reflects and propagates the current depressive world-view of the p-science-determined culture and general population: "*This* is who we are, *what* we are capable of, and what we can *hope* for—a comfortable life, with little pain, and then death." All of this stems from the FACT that in your Western materialist "Cave" society it is the *Outer-external sense realm* alone that is taught and promoted, while the *infinite Inner* is utterly neglected. For the truth is that as the

Force we are a *unity* of infinite *Inner* and infinite *Outer* (not just the latter alone). And drugs for example (especially in psychiatry) only serve to mask the problem. The message they give is, "Just stay in the Outer, stay half and incomplete—just conform to our "external" Society." As Jedi with *the Knowledge of the Force* (±), we say: "Do not get lost merely in the *external infinite* (the physical, the senses, the biological). Go instead to the *INNER, the Absolute I, the POINT*."

—Not to mention that hospitals and their interns and personnel do a "shoddy job" and err because of the lack of a positive unitary Spirit that pervades the entire hospital. The environment saturated with death and disease breeds too much *negativity* and hopelessness and thus indifference and callousness in the staff. What they need is (1) Power Healing and (2) the Knowledge of Jedi and *Immortality*—that death is not absolute or final.

§739

Psychiatry is in the same condition as your Medicine, but even worse. Thus your psychiatrists too cannot heal because of the false concepts of Man, Health and the "Norm" they hold—which sustain the Ego, the Ego world, and the Dark Side and prevent the Jedi Order and the Healing of your planet from occurring.

§740

In Psychiatry too, where "Biological Psychiatry" or "Psycho-Pharmacology" predominate, "Man" is viewed primarily as a *Physical-chemical-biological* being and treated accordingly. As a rule and in strict adherence to the p-science model of Man, psychiatrists recognize only the BODY, and not the Self-Soul-Mind or *Absolute I*. This is *ironical* in that the root meaning of "psychiatry" as we pointed out, is "soul" ("*psyche*") "healer" ("*iatreia*"), thus a "psychiatrist" is in truth a "healer or physician of the soul." The FACT is that their *monistic materialism* does not allow them to admit the existence of an entity such as a "Soul/ Mind or Self." This is why in truth they like to see themselves as part of the "medical" profession—really as "soma-iatrists" or "healers of the *Body*." And *this* is why they restrict themselves to a "chemical" cure, to a change in Body Chemistry. Hence as stated earlier, they are involved in the same error as the Medical profession—they put the cart before the horse and invert cause and effect. Thus the symptoms—behind what they call "schizophrenia," bi-polar, phobia, obsessive-compulsive disorder, etc—do *not* have as their *root cause* the changes in body chemistry—in serotonin/dopamine/lithium levels—that they observe; rather it is the basic situation of the Self/Other dynamic that involves the entire career of the Person from birth to adulthood to the present; i.e., disturbances due to an individuals unresolved *relationship* with *Others*, and to *the Absolute I.*

§741

Since in psychiatry the "medical model" prevails the patient or subject is routinely *reified*, treated as a *thing-object-body* and not as a Person or Equal. More egregious still, following the categories and methods of the DSM-IV, patients are routinely *labeled* and reduced to their "label" or "disease"—which they rarely shake off and hence keep for the rest of their lives, making them a permanent or "career" mental patient and "defective human being or person." As we Jedi know, the Doctor-Patient relation should be a Person-Person one (qua Force to Force; see below).

> "Many states that modern psychiatry considers pathological and treats with suppressive medication are actually 'spiritual emergencies,' psycho-spiritual crises that have a healing and transformative potential." *Psychology of the Future.* Grof

§742

Moreover—what is the cause of untold needless suffering—many of your people in response to the 1960s *Zeitgeist's* Call for total liberation and healing are trying to "break out" of the prison of their finite False Self and into the freedom of their Infinite True Self. It is deplorable and especially painful to witness that this absolutely necessary "transformational" process into *true health* is regarded by the majority of your psychiatrists as "psychosis," abnormal, and something to be "cured" only by regimens of "psychopharmacology" (see especially the work of your Jedi **Christina** and **Stan Grof**, **R.D. Laing**, and **Peter Breggin**).

Also, as your **Freud** rightly noted, the FACT that most people on your planet who are viewed and view themselves as "normal" and "healthy" and who may never go to a psychiatrist or therapist—does not count in their favor. They are *still* unhealthy—or "sick"—and can succumb at any time, etc—that is, *until* they resolve their Self/Other problem and reach *the Absolute I* and JEDI.

§743

Psychiatry too views the primary goal of therapy, the Cure, to be the returning of the person to "normal" health" or "well-adjusted" functioning—*and that is all.* And "normal" as defined by what the individual therapist considers *normal*—based on his own total experience of the world—that is, by what his profession, his colleagues and (what in his view) the "world" consider "normal"— *that is by a show of hands.* And it follows that if the entire Society is *sick*, then *that* will be considered "the norm." The fact is that "normal" is nothing but the EGOIC mode of consciousness. The psychiatrist's ideal therefore is to keep everyone on your planet in the CAVE, the Dark Side of the Force—and never to have True Health and the Jedi Order. In this connection **Stan Grof** also makes the following insightful observation:

> The goal in traditional psychotherapies is to reach an intellectual understanding as to how the psyche functions, why symptoms develop, and what they mean. This understanding then becomes the basis for developing a technique that therapists can use to treat their patients. A serious problem with this strategy is the striking lack of agreement among psychologists and psychiatrists concerning the most fundamental theoretical issues and the resulting astonishing number of competing schools of psychotherapy. *The work with holotropic [nonordinary or transpersonal] states shows us a surprising radical alternative—the mobilization of the deep inner intelligence [the Absolute I] of the clients that guides the process of healing and transformation.*

§744

As we said in the case of Medicine, the Body gets dependent on and addicted to these drugs or chemicals—which not only have side-effects but result in a Zombie-like life and existence that is not worth living. Psychiatrists then do not treat the *root cause* of the disorder but only the symptoms. Moreover the Body is never able to return to the point where it can produce the missing chemicals themselves (e.g. endorphins)—something which can happen only when the *true* cause is addressed.

§745

[C] BALANCE. In order for your Health professions to be Balanced and fulfill their *educational* function of taking you from the Dark Side (Ego) to a Light Side awareness of the UNITY or the POINT that is the Jedi Order, your present generation of Doctors (medical and psychiatric/therapists et al) must become Jedi Doctors and Therapists in complete possession of the *true* Concept of *Health* and of "Man"—namely to be WHOLE or a Jedi and integrated into the WHOLE or Jedi Order. Hence *an elite or class of Jedi Doctors must come on the scene.* At first there will be Two types of Jedi Doctors (Mind Body) and eventually the Two will become One, as Jedi Master Doctors—of *both* Mind and Body. Then ultimately there will be no or very few Doctors, since all or most of your planet will be Jedi with powers to heal.

§746

Jedi Doctors know and teach the following—

(1) They know what the TRUTH and the GOOD is and guide people into it.

(2) Hence they are totally *positive* about your problem, outcome and healing.

(3) They know the true Concept of "Man" and that you are not just a Body or Body-Ego. As a Jedi, as the Force itself actualized and individualized, you are greater than you think you are. Your *attitude* (Mind-belief) is all important since it activates your *immune system*—that is your ***Jedi-Force* immune system** (+) *behind* your physical immune system (-). And they know that "attitude" resides in and is a function of THOUGHT, the supra-physical, INNER-Force domain (and thus that "genes" are not ultimately important as they fall into the "physical" OUTER domain). Furthermore You, the (potential) Jedi Doctor, must be and become perfectly *convinced* of this; for the more convinced, the more *effective* you will be.

(4) Jedi Doctors know that part of their Treatment Plan will be for their patients/clients to: Surround and bathe themselves in Jedi Truths and people, join Jedi Groups and attend Jedi events, be pro-active and involved in Jedi causes, and separate from *negative*

people, and change their address if necessary. Jedi Doctors will also use traditional "medicine" when absolutely needed. Above all they will use POWER-ETHICS.

<h2 align="center">§747</h2>

WHAT "DISEASE" and "DISORDER" IS:

(1) The *Main* Disease or Disorder pertaining to Man … is "Man" himself-herself as (+|-) which *must* be cured in order to be in a state of TRUE HEALTH. Therefore all diseases—cancer, T.B., aids, depression, bi-polar disorder, et al—are just symptoms of the Main Disease, and are one and all cured with its cure and resolution. The Main Disease then is not being a JEDI and aware of the WHOLE, the Absolute I, and living in it 24/7. The one *CURE* of this basic disease is: *To Be a Jedi.*

<h2 align="center">§748</h2>

(2) *Physical Diseases* are a result of a disruption or break in the Oneness-Fluidity-Harmony of the whole Body, in its systems and organs—and due to a weak *Immune* System, DNA, Stress, heredity-*predisposition* to XYZ, pathogens-contact, and epidemics. There is an insurrection in the organism where one part or system rebels and seeks to become *independent* of the others, of the Whole or the Unity.

The traditional *CURE:* Is MEDICINE, which is an indigestible substance that causes the *forces* of the whole Body to rally

> "[Health and its opposite are a function of] the absolute IDENTITY of our organism with ourselves. [Hence] the feeling of sickness arises through nothing else but a loss of IDENTITY (±) between the intelligence (+) and its organism (-)." *STI 128.* **Schelling**

and cast out the substance, and with it the malady, diseased organ, or pathogen itself (also: hot and cold alternation, and other methods, and alternative medicine such as acupuncture/Reike, Chi-energy, etc). Surgery is used only as a last resort (for all can be *restored* via the Absolute I, aka "spontaneous remission"). Jedi **Hegel** states the following concerning the true concept of "medicine":

The main point of view from which medicine must be considered is that it is an *indigestible* substance ... The medicine provokes the organism to put an end to the *particular* irritation in which the formal activity of the *whole* is fixed and to restore the *fluidity* of the particular organ or system *within* the whole. This is brought about by the medicine as an irritant, but one which is difficult to assimilate and overcome, so that the organism is confronted by something alien to it against which it is compelled to exert its strength. In acting against something external to it, the organism breaks out from the limitation with which it had become IDENTIFIED and in which it was entangled and against which it cannot react so long as the limitation *is not an object for it.*" *Enc.* §373, b. *Therapy.*

The JEDI *CURE:* In essence the Jedi Doctor accesses and directs the Absolute I's power, raising the *immune* system, which eliminates the dis-ease by activating and restoring the primal IDENTITY (±) of *Self and Other* as well as *Consciousness (+) and Body-Organism (-).*

§749

(3) *Mental Disorders.* As said, all disorders—mental-physical-spiritual—are due to the Dark Side (+|-) or Self/Other unresolved relations, accumulated from both the individual's and your Race's History, i.e., from "heredity" or dysfunctions "passed down to the 10th generation, etc," such as Schizophrenia, psychosis-neurosis, Bi-polar disorder, depression-mania, phobias, agoraphobia, et al.

The *CAUSE:* The general condition of the "Self/Other" or "I/Not-I" split or separation. Recall that P.I. or EGO development into JEDI is from: *Stage Two* Consciousness to *Stage Three* Self-consciousness, from (+|-) to (±) and the POINT.

§750

The *CURE:* The only complete CURE of all disorders is to have attained the WHOLENESS of a JEDI; being permanently integrated into the Jedi Order, which exists right now. It involves:

1. Putting into motion the Jedi Methods of *The Jedi Code,* by which one becomes a JEDI. 2. Weaning a Person *off* Drugs and chemicals. 3. If needed, sending him or her for a while to a JEDI HOSPITAL (or SANITORIUM, with RECOGNITION Therapy et al). 4. Removing her

from toxic environments, influences, and people—Family, friends, Job, toxic drugs, music, and interests, etc. 5. The Jedi Doctor's treating him as an EQUAL.

Note: Medicine also suffers from the *same* problem of your sciences—*specialization;* which however, during the "Transition" period your planet is now in, does have a place in Medicine, if properly conceived and situated, namely, as a *sub-field* or specialty of a Jedi *GENERALIST* or Master Doctor—who is potentially able to heal any and all types of disorders.

§751

TRUE JEDI HEALTH: THE JEDI DOCTOR and THE JEDI THERAPIST—HEALING PRINCIPLES, LAWS & METHODS

(1) There are *two* categories of Healing/Health related to the *two* types of disease/disorder: **General Jedi Healing**—(of the General Jedi Disease) and **Specific "Ego" Healing**—(of Specific "Ego" Diseases). The "General" type of healing and disease pertains to your #1 life Goal of becoming a JEDI (or truly Healed and Healthy) by canceling the Self/Other split or Dark Side. The "Specific" type pertains to the subject matter of traditional medicine where "health" is just a matter of returning one to his "normal" state of functioning. Here too, however, all diseases and disorders have their primary root in the Self/Other problem and its unsuccessful resolution, which results in a weak *immune system* (due to one's History and poor programming from parents, family, etc, and from *fear* or belief in the power of disease, death, etc). Also as said, a person can be "well" in the *Specific* sense but "ill" or not yet healed or Jedi, in the *General* sense.

§752

(2) *General Jedi Healing* was in part discussed in *Part I (Global Jedi Education)* and has received fuller treatment in *Part II: The Jedi Code.* The healing methods used are based on the one principle that: All one has to do is *align oneself—or rather realize one is <u>already</u> aligned—with one's True Infinite Jedi Self (the POINT or Absolute I as a concrete Universal) or with the TRUTH or the ONE Reality, which is not difficult in that it is the only thing that exists and <u>exists right now</u>.*

§753

(3) *Specific "Ego" Healing by the Jedi Method (Absolute I, Point)* (of e.g., diabetes, cancer, blindness, etc).

The Key is *the Knowledge of the Force* and the POINT, the UNITY (+) or *Absolute I* at the core of every Self—e.g. the patient's *and* the Doctor's. The *Absolute I* is the agency and source from which all healing comes and is effected. *There is no disorder which cannot be CURED with its activation and use.* The Goal then is True Health: to make the patient WHOLE as a JEDI and plugged into the WHOLE, the *absolutely present* Jedi Order.

§754

The Doctor should begin with the Knowledge and conviction that:

(1) The Patient before you is a JEDI—the WHOLE/FORCE aware of Itself in a state of actualization—and *is not* a mere "human being" or Body, etc; hence is a Three-Part Being of *Absolute I, Mind, and Body* and is to treat him accordingly. The Absolute I, as (+) or (±), has *primacy* over the patient's (-) Body and everything else—*this is key to all healing.*

(2) That the Jedi Order alone is Reality, and is Now—hence that at the core of the patient before you is an entity—*the Absolute I*—a UNITY which connects and relates him to the WHOLE of All that IS—especially to yourself. You should realize deeply that you share this *Absolute I* in common with him.

§755

(3) It is most important that you transcend the Dark Side error and view of your medical profession and society, and see past the "evidence" of the senses, of the multiplicity and *separateness* of things/bodies—and thus achieve a *living* conviction *of your UNITY and IDENTITY with the patient;* a conviction that the Whole of what IS is fully *present* NOW, during the Sacred time you are spending with him. If you *are* a Jedi this will be automatic—however we

are assuming that you are "becoming" a Jedi or are in process of "transition." Moreover by using *this* method you will advance *your own* process to Jedi.

§756

Therefore, minimally the Doctor ("becoming," but not yet a Jedi) *before* she sees the patient should *prepare* herself by entering her JEDI SELF, the *ABSOLUTE I-POINT*, which is as we know Infinite and all-encompassing—hence encompasses the Patient as well—and hence which she *shares with* the Patient and with all others, and which she can access with e.g. *Point-Meditation*. If the session and healing is to be successful the Doctor *must* get into *UNITY* and transcend her subject/object, self/other separate EGO state and exude genuine LOVE, empathy, infinite care and recognition of the Patient's self-worth, so as to experience comm-unity and Unity with the Patient. THIS is the singular basis for Healing—and the patient *will* sense it if you are in your EGO or not. The patient may be *fearful* and may fear rejection of himself—or insufficient recognition or acceptance on the Doctor's part. Having entered the UNITY of her Jedi Self also *strengthens* the Doctor, in particular the psychiatrist, in the event any hostile outbursts or reactions present on the part of the Patient—which is critical and must be handled successfully in order to win the Patient's confidence and relax his egoic defenses. In most cases the Patient is *Testing* you, as he comes with much "baggage" and a lifetime of accumulated EGOIC experience and negativity. A KEY Goal is for You to co-opt the Patient's *own* Healing resources, Will, and Absolute I—for be mindful that Healing is always a collaborative or joint-process. Moreover 99% of healing is achieved via ATTENTION and PRESENCE as we will see.

§757

Specific "Ego" Healing by the Jedi Method (of the Absolute I-Point) and Presented in semi-dialog form:

M.D.: "John/Mary, there is a "new-higher Medicine" coming on the medical scene—one not dependent on machines, technology, drugs, lab tests, statistics, etc; we do make use of these tests, but only *after* treatment, to confirm that you are indeed healed."

John/Mary (not "patient," since they are *equals* as equally Jedi): "Oh great. What is it?"

M.D.: "It is based on what is called *Jedi Truth* and *Jedi Absolute Science*, and a new Concept of Man, of who and what *we* are and our relation to the Whole (the Universe or Reality). Here are the main points of the new-higher Medicine."

§758

(1) "John/Mary, *WE*—you and I, all of us—are involved in a *process*, which is necessary, cosmic, and universal. The process and the cure is contained in the principle of the UNITY-of-OPPOSITES or **IDENTITY**-in-DIFFERENCE. That is, **I = I** versus **I = O** (Object). Simply put, Reality and who we really are, our True Self, is "**IDENTITY**-in-DIFFERENCE." Thus, we start out with and are aware of only the **DIFFERENCE** aspect, which is called *"Stage Two"* and Consciousness OF an Other or Object (**I = O**). We are not yet aware of the **IDENTITY** (**I = I**) aspect *which is equally present*. When we *do* become aware of the **IDENTITY** aspect that underlies the **DIFFERENCE** aspect we have then advanced to what is called *"Stage Three"* and Self-consciousness, our True Self, which is Universal and Immortal. For example, John/Mary you and I are *different* ... and yet at the same time, we are in an *Identity* or *Unity* (See "Recognition of Equals"). And this is true with regard to any and all other persons, others, or objects that exist. The process is from *unity* to *separation* to *unity regained with full self-awareness*."

§759

Stage One: The Identity and Difference (and their unity) are both *there* in the "beginning," but not yet known. This is your True Self, the POINT, the *Universal* Absolute I.

Stage Two: *First* "in time" only the *Difference* is known and experienced, but not yet the Identity. Hence "Ego"-Self/Other and *Consciousness OF an Other (or World)*. The Universal is now *Particularized* (as a P.I.).

Stage Three: *Secondly* and lastly the *Identity* is known and experienced, *as well as* the Difference and their *unity*; a unity in which the *Identity* predominates over the Difference. "History" (life, social relations) is the process or act whereby the initial illusory *separation* is overcome or canceled, and the "problem" of life (+|-) is solved (±). Thus we are *all* involved in this universal process. This, the Goal, is called "Self-consciousness" or *Consciousness OF Consciousness itself.* The Universal is now *Individualized-and-Actualized* (as a U.I.). The POINT now aware of itself. *This* and this alone is TRUE HEALTH.

§760

(2) "So in essence, John/Mary, you have a TRUE SELF, that is the Whole and is Infinite—and most importantly, that is *ONE* and that *WE ALL SHARE.*"

> **KEY:** The Doctor *must* say this: " … that *WE* (you and I, John/Mary) all share." The infinite power is in the little word "WE." In saying "we," you are *removing* all walls, barriers, distance—whatever obstructs the *flow* of power, energy, and worth—between you (M.D.) and your client ("patient").— And by doing so you are thereby allowing Total **IDENTITY (I = I)** and healing to take place.

"This infinite True Self (U.I.) of yours is just underneath or within your everyday self or personal 'ego'—'John'/'Mary.'"

§761

(3) "So John/Mary, what is *responsible* for both your 1. General disease and 2. Specific disease is precisely your personal "ego-self" and its programming and network of relations and your unsuccessful *struggles* to solve life's main problem of the healing of the primal Self/Other *separation.* Indeed the two types of disease result simply from your inability to access the healing-power and attainment of the Absolute I or POINT. Therefore, by realizing the *Universal* aspect of your Self the problem of the Self/Other split is finally resolved— precisely by *allowing you* to experience your **IDENTITY**, UNITY and UNIVERSALITY with all Others whatsoever and continually."

§762

(4) "Therefore the HEALING of yourself and your treatment—first of your 'specific' disease (e.g. cancer), then your 'general' disease (the Ego/Jedi disparity)—will consist simply in getting you to realize this IDENTITY or POINT, by *aligning* with and *immersing* yourself in the *Universal* aspect of your True Self, or in the initial 'Whole/ Infinite' state. And *the deeper the immersion*, the *more healing power* that is accessed and released, and *the faster you get healed.*

What actually happens, John/Mary, is that *your Body heals itself*—with the help of *your inner Physician, the Absolute I.* That is, your internal *immune* system gets activated and surcharged, and rises to such a pitch where the disease is overcome and ejected, the defect (e.g. blindness) remedied, the limb or organ restored, the chemical 'imbalance'/metabolism (e.g. diabetes) is 'balanced' or corrected."

§763

(5) Now there are several methods, techniques, or technologies the Jedi Doctor can use for accessing *the Absolute I* and releasing its healing power and *immersing* you in the One Infinite Whole, your True Infinite Jedi Self. Which Method or Format the doctor uses depends in part on the *degree* of trust or confidence the client (patient) has in the Doctor (and the Method), that is, the level of **IDENTITY** established and present between the two. For instance if there is little trust, two or more doctors will be needed, if the confidence is high, the doctor should do the first session alone. Thus the more *aligned* or Jedi (**I = I**) the Doctor is the *easier* it is to heal the patient; the less supports (other M.D.s and multiple sessions, etc) he will need. The Doctor can often do it in just *one session* or with one word, look, or treatment (e.g., "You're OK and completely healed John/Mary. And I say so on my authority, etc").

§764

Again the *Main Goal* is to cultivate and deepen **I = I** or the healing power of **IDENTITY** and the *Absolute I.* It also requires a certain empathic *style or skill,* a sym-pathy or "feeling-with" the patient/client— that is gradually acquired as you grow into your Jedi Self (±) and advance in your *own* healing. Also *different* types of patients/subjects— such as educated/uneducated, intellectual/nonintellectual, religious/

nonreligious,   optimistic-pessimistic—
require *different* approaches. Medicine
therefore is *both* an "art" and a "science."

> "The Absolute I is all that ever was, is, and will be." **Fichte**
>
> "It is God appearing in the midst of those who know themselves as Pure-Absolute Knowing or I." **Hegel**
>
> "Where two or three gather together there AM I (God, Absolute I)." **Jesus**

§765

Sample Method: The client/patient
comes into the Jedi Therapy Room in
which one, two or more "Jedi Doctors"
are present and who welcome the
Patient—who becomes seated on a chair
or table—and tell the Patient: "John/
Mary, we will be giving you Four series
of Jedi Treatments." The *authority* and
presence of the Doctors, the manner of
eye contact, empathy, and their *voice* is Key. They then *direct* their
energy towards the patient—in concert—for just one, or five, or thirty
minutes.

The *objective* is to bring *into* Focus the *One Absolute I* that alone
exists, and concentrate its UNITY and Healing Power directly on
the patient, much like a LASER—for *UNITY* or *IDENTITY* is the
Healer and the Healing Agent; and the patient will even come to
experience himself *in* and *as* the Jedi Doctor(s).

This can be done alone or in a group; and can be done in a "pure"
manner, without placebos, drugs, or stimulation, etc, or not. Thus
there can be 2-5 M.D.s in the room who gather around the patient
and work with him, etc (or if incapacitated they can gather around
his bed-side, etc). They will say to him for example: "John, there IS
nothing wrong with you, you are OK, you are completely healed—all
of us here agree that you're OK (you are forgiven, *We* forgive you,
for your shortcomings, "sins," etc)." The Doctors should become
very relaxed, and even joke with the patient, laugh, etc; and at the
end of the session(s) say, "See, you're getting better already, etc."

§766

Now, in order to prevent recurrence or relapse after healing and
discharge the Doctor should give the client an appropriate Jedi
Plan-schedule-regimen which includes doing continual *immersions*
in the Absolute I, cultivating his Jedi Self and General healing, and

avoiding negatives and Dark Side elements and experiences; this is
in keeping with the cardinal HOLISTIC principle of all medicine
and true healing.

§767

Note especially that there will also necessarily be a *transition period*
in the current practices of the medical profession during which
MD's will switch over from old or current methods (allopathic,
homeopathic, alternative or complementary, et al) to Jedi methods.
As doctors will have to *gradually grow* in confidence in using the
new techniques, it will take time. Therefore we have *three stages
of transition:* (1) The Doctor will use *both* methods ("Oh John, I
recommend we *also* use this new method in your treatment"). (2)
When more confident she will switch over ("John, the new method
is #1 and best, but I can also use the old #2 methods if you like, or
when needed"). (3) "I only and always use the Jedi Method." And in
the case of a Jedi Master Doctor, "I use the Jedi Method for *both* Body
and Mind (medicine and psychiatry)." Note also that much of the
old medicine-treatment methods and practices can be retained, e.g.
for cuts, fractures, accidents, in the E.R., tourniquets, and vaccines
(polio, small pox, etc). *However* Doctors should also teach patients
how to *stay* in True or Divine Health by doing preventive and
health-improving medicine.

§768

The KEY: It thus turns out that the earliest tenet and principle of
medicine is the correct and best one:

> The primary role of the physician-healer
> is to simply aid or superintend the Body's
> *healing of itself* (by the *inner physician*).
> The less he interferes with the "natural"
> process, (by surgery, etc) the better.

Thus the main *efficacy* behind such things as "purging," emetics, medications, or physical-altering-interventions lies in the simple fact that "another human being—like myself—believes that I have worth/value, enough to *want* me to be well or healed, or really cares about me and gives me his full undivided loving-caring *attention*— and values me." A thing that is very rare. For most people I meet or know do not do it as they *are too concerned with their own problems and self to bestow such quality care, regard, and attention on me. And it is this alone—this full, complete, caring ATTENTION—that facilitates 99% of the healing process;* and hence the purging, drugs, cold compresses, et al, are really unessential background "props" or accessories, and like a "placebo" just about anything can be substituted and used in their place.

§769

So what the doctor-healer supplies, his special contribution, is simply his complete ATTENTION and PRESENCE, which is the presence of the Absolute I and **IDENTITY** that causes *the Absolute I-power-energy* in the patient to rise and become *activated*. Again as we have said, the activation and cure is simply the result of the presence of another "human being" or EQUAL (as a "mirror") who *wills, wants* the patient to *be* well and whole, thus making him *feel* that someone *really* cares about him, loves him and thus values him; for in life people rarely if ever feel and express this—most people (e.g. family members) "fake it" and do it out of a sense of *guilt* or *duty* ("it's just the right thing to do, etc"). This is true especially in the case of an "outcast" or homeless person who feels that *no one* cares whether they live or die.

§770

We can conclude that it is simply the *RECOGNITION OF EQUALS that is behind all of this, namely, I = I*. Hence it necessarily follows that: A TOTAL dose of **I = I** is equal to TOTAL HEALING. And "**I = I**" again means **IDENTITY (in-difference)** or simply that, "I totally recognize you and affirm your *infinite value* ... and truly WILL and WANT you to be healed-well-and-whole. You are truly very, very special and valuable to me, to us, and to the world."

§771

PSYCHIATRY/PSYCHOTHERAPY, THE SUPERIORITY OF THE JEDI THERAPIST

While the Ordinary Therapist:

1. Evaluates the "patient"—takes a history, etc. Now, what is troubling you?

2. Prescribes a drug (e.g. Mellaril). After 2 weeks the patient returns; it is no good, I feel the same; the therapist then ups or changes the dosage, or tries a new drug, etc.

3. Finally with poor results, there is a switch to a different doctor or hospitalization.

§772

The Jedi-Therapist:

Does the following *before* each session with a client:

Prepares herself *beforehand* with the intention of seeing the client not as a "Patient" but instead as a person, pre-Jedi, and EQUAL. For the therapist's #1 GOAL as a HEALER is precisely to multiply the number of healers in the world, hence to make her client a HEALER too. Thus the therapist should first **(i)** "plug herself into" (align with) the One POINT, her Jedi Self.

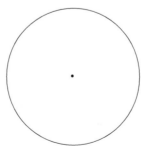

And then **(ii)** remind herself, "OK. Only the One Reality is and I am in it and aware of it. My goal with this *client* (not inferior "patient," but an EQUAL, a Pre-Jedi.) is for him to become a Jedi and help plug him into the One Reality, the POINT, the Jedi Order, to help him *heal,* overcome and resolve his *Ego-Other split* (and its destructive behaviors and consequences). Then **(iii)** she should ask: How can I best do this with *this* particular person? And then formulate a treatment plan.

<h2 style="text-align:center">§773</h2>

More on **(ii)**. The therapist's aim should be to give the person a renewed *zest/zeal* for living by getting him to realize and accept his important role as a contributor in realizing the Jedi Order and the general healing of the world. For it is a FACT that *he can be and is a doctor-healer too.* The therapist will say, "John, the truth is that We are Equal. You have the *same* power to heal that I do (something that will greatly enhance his self-esteem, power, and unity)."

<h2 style="text-align:center">§774</h2>

Hence *the #1 goal of the healer (therapist) is simply to create more healers* (to multiply herself); it is to make the patient/client a healer too and enlist him in "the army of healers" so that the world/society will be healed that much faster. The Point is that every self/patient is a part of a larger circle or network of selves (family, friends, and acquaintances), so that if *he* gets well, his circle will too. The absolutely worst thing is for the Healer/Therapist to *want* to keep the "patient" forever as a "patient"—and to disqualify and bar him from any kind of "normalcy" and thus from Jedi-hood. This attitude by the therapist serves to *sustain the Ego world and the illness of his patients and* <u>*himself*</u> *forever.*

<h2 style="text-align:center">§775</h2>

SO: The #1 most important objective and principle the Therapist-healer should use is: The *willingness* to share his status as a doctor/healer with his patient/client, and to say for example: "Come on in the water's fine." "We are EQUAL and have the *same* infinite power, essence, and capabilities." Yes, you should willingly and enthusiastically share your power, joy, and status with them. And *this will help you too—for doing the opposite, holding on to "ego," will keep you from Jedi and full healing, and ultimately trap you in the Dark Side ego-world. Thus by employing this powerful principle you will surely benefit and receive more power and health in your life.*

§776

ON JEDI THERAPISTS—AND JEDI-GROUPS/CIRCLES

> The fastest, most effective cure is that
> of Being *accepted by Others*—and not
> labeled or discounted.

(1) The Context: Start with the world *as it is*, with people as they are: scratching to make a living, with 3 jobs, kids to feed, bills to pay, daily stress, in a pretty dysfunctional condition, inclusive of addictions, phobias, and bad habits. Now just Immerse yourself in all of this. And NOW visualize all these people *implementing* and *practicing* the methods of this *Handbook*, having dedicated themselves to becoming Jedi and healing the world and themselves—to "creating a better world." The Goal then is to 1. *center* themselves and be independent, to continually provide "water and sunlight" to their Jedi "seed" or potency so it will actualize, and to 2. master "Solitude and "Society" or being with people (see *Part II: The Jedi Code*).

§777

To facilitate this, *JEDI-Groups or Clusters* of diverse kinds will arise— meeting e.g. in the morning (before work, at breakfast), at lunch time, after work, and during work, in a *Jedi-corporation* or work place. For the more time one spends with like-minded people (or others: **I = I = I**), the faster one reaches Jedi. Hence there will be 1. All male and all female Jedi-groups, 2. mixed/co-ed groups, and 3. small ones (2-4 members) and large ones (10-100 members)—which ones one attends will depend on one's *needs* at the time, etc.

§778

(2) There will also be *JEDI-THERAPISTS,* that is, those who believe in the Jedi Teaching and its power to cure and heal. They *know* that pharmacological drugs are not the answer—a temporary measure at best—and that one must become drug-free as soon as possible.

(1) People and parents will want and recommend that their "mentally ill"-diagnosed and suffering friends and children go to a Jedi Therapist.

(2) The Therapist will know the location and make-up of the various and "best" (for this client-patient) JEDI-Groups in the area/city, and will have the "client" attend as many as possible to facilitate his healing by being around loving-accepting-supportive Others who "know the score" and know that the person is probably *ahead* of them in Jedi-actualization, as misunderstood "pioneers or scouts" trying to "break through" into Jedi and the Jedi Order (again see the important work of Jedi **Stan Grof** and, especially, his "holotropic breathwork" seminar-workshops).

§779

(3) The KEY is that Members of Jedi-Groups will always *warmly welcome and never reject* such a person suffering with an emotional/ mental "disorder." For they alone understand "what is going on" in the person. The Person will be treated as an *Equal*—not as a defective person, and will be showered with love, compassion, and acceptance. Such an environment will aid the healing process immensely. For most of the "world/society" inclines to *label* and *fix* him in the label and Role, keeping him alienated, invalidated, miserable, depressed and hopeless; that is as a "non-person," sick and even "evil"—and not as an EQUAL, a human being, that is, a Jedi—of infinite value, worth, dignity, and ability.

§780

IN SUM: What you can do—

(1) If you are a doctor use Jedi-principles—give papers at the AMA and APA and tell others about Jedi Holistic Healing.

(2) If you are a doctor become a Jedi Doctor or a Jedi Therapist, and make "improving Health" part of your Treatment plan; and change your concept of "who you are"—that is, not a "Man" but an immortal Jedi.

(3) For doctors and laypeople. #1: Teach JEDI HEALTH and METHODS in schools and hospitals, etc. #2: Do not get sick (and

also save money) by doing PREVENTIVE MEDICINE, Care, and Healing. Do Jedi Meditations and Affirmations such as: "I am whole, healed, and a JEDI now." Stay plugged into the ONE, *the Absolute I*, and in high spirits, etc, because being ONE or Whole is the same as Health and Healing; also cf., Amit **Goswami's** *How Quantum Activism Can Save Civilization* (247-56) and *The Quantum Doctor.* Finally, as concerns the SOLUTION TO UNIVERSAL HEALTH CARE and How to pay for it, see POLITICS above, §663.

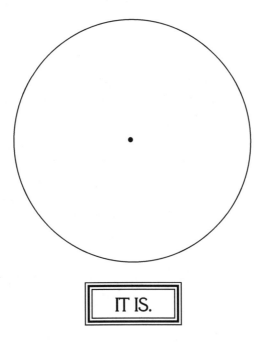

IT IS.

THE ARTS & MEDIA

The Arts & Media have a considerable impact on Global Education and are powerful resources and agencies for taking your planet into the Jedi Order and bringing BALANCE to The Force.

The ARTS and MEDIA SUMMARY

(A) CONCEPT. The chief purpose of the Arts and Media is to elevate and educate your people into the JEDI ORDER and the POINT. They are powerful Institutions that can quickly bring your whole planet into the same POINT. "Art" and "Media" derive from: (1) *POINT:* (1) Like Science and Religion, Art exists to cancel the Self/Other split of the Force in its *Second Stage* of Consciousness OF. Art presents the TRUTH to you in the form of BEAUTY in a sensuous mode. (2) "Media" derives from your fundamental need to connect to the Whole, Reality, the POINT, and your true Jedi Self. (2) *ETYMOLOGY:* "Media"—such as Television, the Internet, Cell Phones— are extensions of your perceptual-nervous system that *mediate* between yourself and the world-reality, hence educate you and create your worldview, Light Side or Dark Side, as the case may be. "Art" and "aesthetics" derive from your Greek word meaning "sense-perception," hence Beauty expressed in a sensory form.

(B) WRONG/IMBALANCE. Art, for the average untrained consciousness, teaches false concepts of yourself and reality and can keep you in your isolated false Ego and the Dark Side (but in a *free* Jedi society there can be no censorship). The content of the Media contains and disseminates the false Dark Side worldview (+|-) and is primarily owned and operated by base minds for whom money is the #1 priority and not the healing and education of your planet and peoples, thus preventing the glorious Jedi Order from seeing the light of day.

(C) BALANCE. Raise up JEDI ARTISTS and Jedi Media Producers, and create Jedi Cable and Internet websites that teach and promote Jedi content and the Knowledge of the Force (±).

§781

[A] CONCEPT. Here we will discuss the true concept and purpose of the arts & the media, which concerns the Jedi education of

everyone into Reality, the POINT, and the Jedi Order (±) that exists now. But first as a preliminary we will discuss ...

§782

THE CONCEPT OF GLOBAL CULTURE-CIVILIZATION

It is your certain destiny that, aided by modern technology and mass communication, your planet and peoples are moving towards and will ultimately become a *GLOBAL CULTURE*—that is, a global civilization with a global or *unitary* consciousness. It will also contain within itself all of your local-national cultures, customs and identities as preserved but *not* as primary or dominant—only the One "Jedi Truth" Culture that unites *all* of your cultures and peoples will be. To quote **Henry Miller** again:

> "The cultural era is past. The new civilization ... will not be another civilization—it will be the open stretch of realization which all the past civilizations have pointed to. The city, which was the birthplace of civilization, such as we know it to be, will exist no more. There will be nuclei, of course, but they will be mobile and fluid. The peoples of the earth will no longer be shut off from one another within states but will flow freely over the surface of the earth and intermingle. There will be no fixed constellations of human aggregates ... [Above all] Man will be forced to realize that power must be kept open, fluid and free. His aim will be not to possess power but to radiate it (154)."

Thus the age in which separate cultures could exist in a plural state, in isolation and undisturbed by one another, has passed. The age of a single *universal* culture is now upon you and about to advent. You already indeed have such a world culture in part and in certain respects, for example in the area of your *science*, which is shared virtually by all nations and only needs to advance to true Jedi Science. When it finally does, global *education* will soon follow. In the area of your *politics* all nations are coming to acknowledge and accept the idea of universal human (Jedi) *rights* and the dignity and worth of every person. As regards *religion*, though its universal and unitary dimension is not yet recognized, it will be when "Jedi world religion" hits the scene. And there is accumulating evidence that the remaining areas of culture, the arts, business, and especially medicine and the healing arts, will soon follow.

§783

Of course what makes the dawning of this Global Culture or One Consciousness inevitable is the knowledge and TRUTH of the One Force and the necessity behind its process. Indeed the primary meaning of the word "culture"—"to refine and educate"—indicates that the singular purpose of your history and culture is precisely the refinement and education of your human Race—of the Jedi "seed" within it, to its final perfection as the One *Universal* Jedi Order. Thus the arc of your History, as some of your scientists are beginning to recognize, without question is moving from a *Connectivity* on a small, local, or "tribal" scale to an ultimate Global or Total *Connectivity* (also cf. especially your **Teilhard de Chardin's** "Omega Point").

§784

The CONCEPT OF THE ARTS. As we know, Jedi Science teaches that ART is one of the three activities and spheres where the Force—as "Man"—achieves a *self-knowledge* that is lifted above "time" and the merely empirical into the Reality of Eternity through the contemplation of eternal Objects and Truth. The three spheres are Art, Religion, and Science (or perfected Philosophy/Metaphysics) and their main focus, as your Greeks correctly noted, is the three forms of the Force—*the True, the Good (or Holy), and the Beautiful.* Indeed all three are forms of the TRUTH—the Eternal, the Infinite and the ARCHE, that which is the ground and principle of all things, and is *in and for itself,* perfect, and self-existent—as we discussed in *Part. II: Jedi Methods,* and elsewhere. Thus Art contemplates the Truth (±) or the Force in the *sensuous* Form of *Beauty*—Religion in the form of feeling and representation, Science in the form of Thought and the Concept. The Arts, which transition from Outer to the Inner, are Five in number: Architecture (cf. the work of **Wright, Corbusier, Meier,** and **Ghery**), Sculpture, Painting, Music, and Poetry (inclusive of plays, novels, operas, and film)—see especially Jedi **Hegel's** *Aesthetics* for a full scientific account of the Arts, where for example we find the following illuminating remarks:

> "Beauty and Truth are essentially one, for Truth, just as Beauty, is the identity of the subjective and the objective ... The Universe is formed in God (the Force) as an absolute work of Art and in eternal Beauty." **Schelling.** *The Philosophy of Art, 31.*

"ART also, because of its preoccupation with TRUTH as the absolute object of consciousness, belongs to the absolute sphere of the Spirit (or Force) along with Religion and Science (Philosophy) ... Art sets TRUTH before our minds in the mode of *sensuous intuition* and form [and] it is precisely the *unity* of the Concept with the individual appearance which is the essence of the BEAUTIFUL and its production by Art (101) ... [Thus] when TRUTH in its external existence is present to consciousness immediately ... the Idea (Force) is not only True but Beautiful. So the Beautiful is characterized as the pure appearance of the Idea to *sense* (111)." *The Aesthetics, v. 1.*

§785

True **ART** (as opposed to "entertainment") is therefore Truth itself or the Force as (±) in the form of Infinite BEAUTY; and hence the purpose of all Art is to Heal, to join (+) and (-), to make WHOLE, and to lift you into the JEDI ORDER and out of the Dark Side, the Ego, and the Cave.

§786

Briefly, the essence of Beauty and the Work of Art consists in its being a *single WHOLE* or Perfect UNITY, all of whose parts are interrelated by a single theme or idea, thus forming a perfect whole such that nothing can be added or taken away; also evoking a feeling of completion or transcendence of the finite EGO into Jedi, the Infinite and Eternal. Thus to be in the presence of Beauty, or a Work of Art, is to be taken out of "time," across the Divided Line and into the Eternal Present and thereby transformed into the Force itself as an actualized Jedi. In effect, in the Work of Art you behold *your True Jedi Self,* which thereby becomes awakened, and experience an *expansion* into the Infinite. A great FILM is another case in point. For in it you see yourself and your life *as* organized and *unified* into a single theme, idea and effect. And since a FILM is a series of events and scenes linked together by a *single idea or plot,* you also have the critical metaphysical experience of "a manifold being *unified*"—and unified "in time," as in Music and Poetry; something that is not the case in architecture, sculpture, or painting.

Thus Art educates and heals you by taking you from EGO and Self/ Other division and dis-connected multiplicity into UNITY and eternal REALITY.

§787

The CONCEPT OF THE MEDIA. "Media" is from your Latin "medias" and means something which is placed in the *Middle* between two things, namely yourself and an object, giving an *indirect* rather than *direct* experience of the object. The "media" then "mediates" between yourself and the world/"reality" and events in the same. Hence when you learn about an event e.g. through the Radio, you are not having a *direct* experience of it but rather an indirect or "mediated"—that is, *interpreted, filtered and edited one.* Thus the possibility of distortion, bias and misrepresentation of what is actually *there* and took place (in addition to that which may come from yourself and your own prejudices and "filters") always exists. Your own take or understanding of the "event" may be the "take" that those who control the Medium want you to have or believe. Also true is that no experience, direct or mediated, is interpretation or bias free since each person experiences what is "out there" through the unique lens or filter of his own past experiences and world-view.

> "It is the primary function of *Television*—the repository of your collective memory in *objective form*—to serve the Spirit in its work of "Re-collection" (*Erinnerung*) and inwardization. It is not by chance that TV's advent coincides exactly with your Spirit's entry into "positive" postmodernity *and* its final "Intellectual" and Knowledge-seeking phase." **Foldes**

§788

Examples of Media on your planet are TV, radio, the internet, cell-phones, satellite, newspapers, the New York Times, magazines, and the Mall. Media thus are *extensions* of your 5-senses and determine and shape your Global Consciousness. For whether you are aware of it or not, you are constantly being *Educated* by the Media and by whatever it is you see, hear, and expose yourself to. The Media thus form your ideas and understanding of Reality and of What IS. And they do it not just by words and images but by HOW they say it, by voice, inflection, body language, and gesture. It is in this way that you imbibe the Media's views and values.

Media such as TV and the internet thus have tremendous power for good or ill, for promoting the Light Side or Dark Side of the Force, and for advancing the Jedi Order and the UNITY of Consciousness on your planet. For by their means everyone's consciousness can be focused *at the same time* on a *single event-POINT*—e.g. on a lecture on Jedi Truth and Science or a Global Meditation, etc. Thus your planetary consciousness can be harnessed e.g. to *heal* diseases, individual and national, and can be focused on a *single point* as a "laser" beam of consciousness, which can be very powerful.

§789

Therefore "the Media" are simply the sum of the *technological extensions* of your perceptual-nervous systems whereby *content* can be instantly communicated to vast numbers of people, thus bringing everyone into a single *present,* never before possible. The Media are fast becoming the "global nervous-system" of your human Race whereby every person on your planet can in principle experience the same event-message-content at the same time. Therefore they have the greatest potential for realizing the total *Connectivity* of your planet—by *unifying* and connecting your entire human family and *elevating* all consciousness into the Jedi Order. Or the very opposite can happen: the Media can prolong your stay in the Cave and the ego-world and permanently delay your glorious destiny. As your Jedi **Thomas Friedman** says as regards the incredible potential of your new Media:

> The combination of these tools of connectivity and creativity—e.g. Facebook, Twitter, 4G, iPhones, iPads, Web-enabled cellphones, Big Data and Skype—has created a *global education … platform* on which more people can start stuff, learn stuff, make stuff … with more other people than ever before.

§790

[B] WRONG/IMBALANCE. Here I will discuss Why your arts and your media do not educate, rather "mis-educate," your people, and are imbalanced as immersed in the dark side of the Force.

The MEDIA. Presently the *content* of your Media mainly reflects the Old Paradigm and the false concepts of "Man" or who you really are, of "God" (or the Force as the necessary Ground of everything), and the Universe; whether they be the one-sided concepts of the p-sciences—secular, nihilist, materialist, and atheist, as based on the concept of "Man" as a contingent biological species—or, at the other extreme, those of Religion with its "other-worldly" concepts of "Spirit" and of God as existing in the "beyond" and not Here, etc. Either way, by disseminating false and one-sided concepts of who you are, they continue to sustain and perpetuate the Dark Side, the ego and ego-world and make healing and solving the Self/Other problem difficult. They do not help to truly *educate* you and take you out of the Cave, but rather take you deeper into it by immersing yourselves in and pursuing the ceaseless parade of sense-goodies on your T.V. Screens and Tablets that the Advertisers hold up as the solution to all your problems and what ails you. This is true even of "educational" and "science" programs e.g. on PBS, insofar as they promote the Ego-world's Dark Side concepts and world-view.

§791

Furthermore the Media are controlled by people motivated by base "commercial" values and not by concern for a better world and humanity; the efforts of even those who are so concerned are misplaced, misguided and have the opposite effect insofar as they are immersed in and tainted by false p-science concepts and the Dark Side ego-world view. In sum the Media (1) are immersed in the Dark Side of the Force, (2) mainly *reflect* the Dark Side culture and dominant worldview or paradigm (+|-), based on the p-sciences with their *Verstand* or instrumental type of "Reason" and rationality, (3) are NIHILISTIC, disseminating the view that *death* is final—e.g., "So and so died today, he was 82. Period," (4) are mainly run by people with base motives—with profit as the bottom line—and just put on what will sell, having no desire to heal or improve the world, etc, (5) their shows and commercials contain content laced with Dark Side p-science and medical errors, offering things you do not need or want and are neither vital to your becoming a Jedi nor to your Health; they are constantly programming, conditioning, and brainwashing you, subliminally and against your will—with no knowledge of UNITY or the Absolute I, and lastly (6) the Media do not teach Jedi Truths and do not air Jedi Shows.

§792

The ARTS. The Arts in many cases teach and promote the Dark Side by disseminating untruths in the content of dialog and stories which teach erroneously for example that "death is final"; heroes moreover convey to you false information and values (e.g. money over people). However Art must remain free, for there can be no censorship of Art.

There is nothing wrong with ART as such—i.e. "true ART"—which has always had the power to heal (which can always be improved). But much of Art's content, e.g. in music and in stories, is filled with Dark Side errors and False concepts of "Man" and reality, such as that you are only *finite* human-animals and *not* immortal Jedi and *Infinite*, and the *Nihilistic* view that there is no meaning or point to life and existence, etc. As for the Objection that by removing or "softening" *Death*—and by saying there is no such thing, that no one really dies—you undermine the dramatic *effect* and make it impossible of achievement—i.e., the *effect* that the death of the Hero has on the audience, or of someone we *identify* with who sacrifices their life for someone else or a cause... this is a fair question. But we can look at e.g. such works as *Star Wars* and *Stranger in a Strange Land*, where in the end there is no death and which nonetheless does *not* diminish the dramatic *effect*. And it can be said that even in these cases "death" still packs a

> "What the particular arts realize in individual works of art is only the universal forms of the self-unfolding Idea of Beauty... a Pantheon of Art which to complete will need the history of the world through thousands of years (90). [Nevertheless] For us Art counts no longer as the highest mode in which Truth fashions an existence for itself... Art has ceased to be the supreme need of the (Jedi) spirit (103)."
> **Hegel,** *The Aesthetics, v. 1.*

punch, people still cry and feel the loss; and Yes it is true that the experience is different for an EGO than it is for a JEDI. In any case the writer or artist will be forced to elevate themselves to a higher— the highest—sphere of *creativity* where they will be motivated to get into more nuanced, subtle, ethereal, lofty, brilliant, and metaphysical aspects and dimensions of their *characters* and *plots*— and of human/Jedi relationships, etc.

§793

The *Media* and *Arts* thus have incredible *power* and influence for good or ill with regard to hindering or furthering the healing of the world. Most importantly the *false assumptions* they contain in their *content*—and based on false p-science and religion, with their concepts of "God," "Man," and the World and its Meaning—keep you in the impoverished Cave and pollute your space, preventing true health and Jedi growth. It is also a Fact that *Words* are powerful and can heal or kill you—as your scriptures say, "take heed how ye hear, and what ye hear," and "life and death are in the power of the tongue." This is because *Words* convey and are *thoughts*, and hence can influence such issues as: how reality is interpreted (positively or negatively), who I am, what I can hope for and aspire to, and what my purpose or non-purpose is. This is especially so when the words or message is *repeated and repeated* via the entertainment Media, in songs, movies, commercials, shows, et al.

In the words of your biochemist and Jedi teacher **Robert De Ropp** (from his *The Master Game*, p. 80): "A degenerate 'entertainment' industry does not hesitate to take advantage of this perverse taste—which often *deliberately seeks* poisonous impressions [that] degrade one's own INNER life, already sufficiently polluted without it—pouring out through all its various channels a stream of more or less pathological material which readers, viewers, listeners eagerly absorb into their psyches."

Thus your *Media* and *Arts* sustain the Old Paradigm, Meanings, and World-view of the Dark Side Ego and Ego-world of the senses and *separateness*, epitomized in the mantra, "I am just my Body." Hence what is important on this false view are only such things as *looking good, the Body and the OUTER*—which results in over-attention to the Body and to appearance or "looks," which has disastrous consequences especially for women.

§794

[C] BALANCE. Apart from what you can do in the other
Six Areas and Institutions we have discussed, there is a great deal you can do in these Two key areas to change and accelerate the *education* of your planet into the Jedi Order.

§795

The ARTS. You can become and declare yourself a JEDI ARTIST— musician, painter, film-maker, novelist, and poet—and incorporate

Jedi truths into your stories and their contents. Indeed all Jedi Artists should ask themselves, "What values and world-view am I promoting in my Art or Novel?" Are they True Jedi ones which heal, educate, and empower—e.g. concerning "death" and who I am (a mortal animal, or an immortal Jedi)? Or false ones, which incapacitate and destroy? If you are a filmmaker you can make a Jedi-Movie (even like your "What the Bleep do We Know" and "What Dreams May Come") etc. As a Jedi Painter you can paint the Jedi Order—which is Now, and get people *interested* in it and in both What *can be* and What *is*. I will note that your *"SCI FI"* or science fiction does do this to a certain extent. But Jedi Art as based on TRUTH has far greater power. Moreover shows like "24," "The Bourne Identity," and "James Bond," etc, mainly do nothing for Jedi; they just stir up FEAR, adrenaline, and Dark Side emotions, etc, for a while, and then in a short time the movie is forgotten; they at best portray the HERO (which is a type of Jedi or your true Self) before you—but this is not the optimal way to do it.

One important key is this: Not only must the synthesis of Science and Religion be accomplished on your planet, which will result in a *unity and power* that will remove the "divided self" and "schizophrenia" which their opposition causes in your present culture, e.g. as related to their opposed ideas of "*death*." But the fact is that this synthesis, as well as the crucial overcoming of false science and false religion, is happening right now (cf. films such as "The Matrix"). *And what is more, you can speed it up.* For example you can in your movies and novels employ and champion the Jedi world-view, the TRUTH and true concepts of God/Man, the Force/Jedi, and also refute false science and false religion, as well as "death" and "nihilism." (See also "GATE: *The Global Alliance for Transformational Entertainment*)

§796

The MEDIA. There are five things you can do to Balance your Media. (1) You can become a *Jedi TV or Media Producer* and give spots or cable channels to Jedi Shows—Jedi Science, etc. Most importantly it is the *content* of the Media, as immersed in the Dark Side, that must be changed. For example: TV and Radio producers should air Jedi shows and promote the Jedi Order, for example on Talk Shows such as **Oprah Winfrey, Bill Moyers, Charlie Rose, Tavis Smiley, the View**, etc. (2) The public-consciousness could use their consumer *buying power* in the matter of their selection of TV shows (and media products), not supporting "ego-sustaining" shows and demanding more Jedi-oriented shows. Furthermore you can boycott TV for a while, and Meditate and do Jedi-work instead. Extremely beneficial and powerful is to go on a "Fast" and take a six-month vacation from all T.V. and the Media. In any event, YOUR PEOPLE MUST BREAK THE POWER OF TV and the "stranglehold and straightjacket" it has on your national consciousness; for you are daily being **brainwashed** and conditioned, especially your children, who do not develop their Jedi Selves and whose values/desires/choices get overly *determined* by TV, commercials, and video games, etc, which have a very hypnotic and damaging effect. But having said that, it is also true that the Media and TV *do focus* one's attention on a POINT, like a MANDALA, and perhaps there is a way this feature can be used in their Jedi education into the POINT. (3) You can also change the Conversation—at the work place, boardroom, dinner table, with friends, at parties, gatherings, etc. (4) You can start Jedi Clubs and have monthly Group-Meetings in your homes, in libraries, schools, etc, where you can watch and discuss together Jedi Shows on TV and Cable, Jedi movies and books, etc. Finally (5) You can also create Jedi Websites on the Internet, etc., etc.

Your possibilities are virtually infinite!

THE FORCE WILL BE WITH YOU ... ALWAYS.

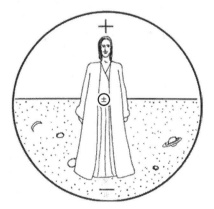

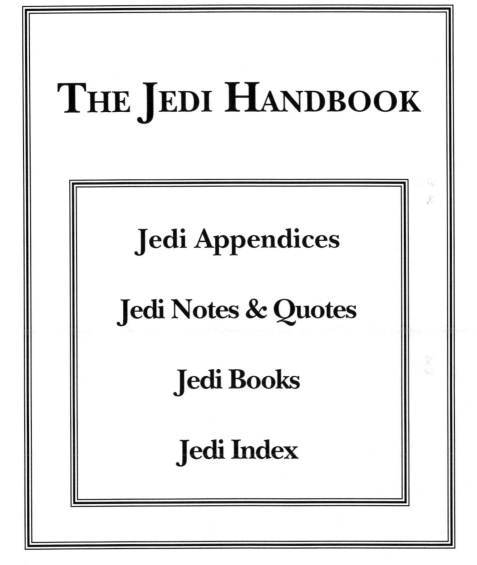

THE JEDI HANDBOOK

Jedi Appendices

Jedi Notes & Quotes

Jedi Books

Jedi Index

APPENDIX ONE: How Your Jedi Philosophers Achieved The Knowledge of the Force in Your History's Modern Period

The history of the Universe and the history of Philosophy on your planet is simply the genesis of SCIENCE or *the Knowledge of the Force*, i.e. Idealism, the position that Thinking or the Self is all reality, that the World is nothing in itself or, most provocatively stated, that *"nothing exists."*[1] Although this genesis of Science, involving the progressive overcoming of the Subject/Object, Man/Nature cleavage in Consciousness, the ultimate equating of Thought and Being, and the disclosure of the absolute Form, i.e. the Form which generates its own content, first began with your Greeks, we will attend to it only in its consummatory stages. The question that will guide us in the tracing of this Emergence is the following: How is a Science of *the Whole, the Totality of All That IS*, possible? "Science" understood as a universal and comprehensive Knowledge of Reality expressed in an organically interconnected System of judgements derived from a single principle (The Concept) and valid for all time (however allowing for unlimited expansion and further elaboration of detail).[2]

In brief, a Science of the Whole is possible only if it is the case, first, that there *is* only One Reality, for if there were more than one reality the Knower or Scientist might be denied access to those realities that lay outside his/her own, hence a knowledge of the whole would be impossible; secondly, that Philosophy or Thinking is the means by which the One Reality thinks or knows itself, for if thinking were not the essence of the One Reality then the latter would not be intelligible as it would be impossible to determine whether the Discourse produced by this *external* thinking or reflection did or did not correspond to the One Reality, hence again making Science impossible; and thirdly, that the One Reality in its essential determinations does not change or, if it happens to be dynamic, the Science which cognizes it is equally dynamic or "living," for if it were pure flux and impossible to determine anything in it then Science would again not be possible.

I.

We turn to your Jedi **Descartes**. With the enunciation of "Cogito ergo sum" the I, pure thought, the *Begriff* or the Concept begins the final stage of its *appropriation* to itself of Being. For the first time Spirit recognizes that its own subjectivity and thinking is directly involved in Being and that in some yet unclear sense it *itself* is the ground of all existence and its Certainty of itself the ground of all other certainties. But this Certainty is still formal and restricted since it allows other beings to exist *outside* of itself, viz. God, the external world and other selves, even though it has no direct experience of them but asserts their existence on the basis of an inference from ideas found within its monadic Cogito. It also first dawns upon Spirit that all objectivity presupposes subjectivity, that there cannot be a Thing without that for which the Thing is, that ultimately the World cannot be distinguished from *my perception* of it,[3] a hard-won cognition which constitutes a giant step towards Idealism and overcoming the Subject/ Object bifurcation, one destined to become a principal doctrine within German Idealism itself, viz. that at all times I only experience myself or a modification of myself.

II.

From **Descartes** the Spirit took divergent paths, that of **Spinoza** and that of **Leibniz**. Spinoza took as his point of departure the simple but powerful reflection that there cannot be one infinite substance, God, and two finite substances, Thought and Extension, because to posit a second substance in addition to a first substance which is Infinite renders the latter *finite* as well. Hence there can be only *one* infinite substance, Thought and Extension being demoted to the rank of attributes of the One Substance. This conclusion is incontrovertible and later as the slogan "*H'en kai pan*" (the One and All) became the rallying-point for **Hegel**, **Schelling** and **Hölderlin** at Tubingen Stift against the old orthodoxy.

Thus **Spinoza's** standpoint marks an important advance in Thought's appropriation of Being by overcoming once and for all the Medieval bifurcation of the Whole into a This-world and a Beyond, God and a Universe distinct from Him, a Creator (natura naturans) and a Creation (natura naturata), an Infinite and a contra-posited Finite, by completely eliminating the *transcendent* God and making Him wholly *immanent,* identifying God and Universe, thus rendering God in principle fully accessible to the comprehending Subject indeed **Spinoza** says, "The mind itself is in God" (*Ethics*, Part II, Prop. XXI). His System has the further merit of having grasped the Absolute as the *Identity* of Subject and Object, that is to say, thinking substance and extended substance are in reality one and *the* same *substance* viewed from/under two different perspectives or attributes—in the algebra of speculation, A = B, where "A" = infinite thought and "B" = infinite extension (Cf. *Ethics*, Part II, Prop. VII, Note and Part III, Prop. II, Note).

However, although Spirit has gained the insight that there is only One Reality and has come closer to Idealism, as the World as the sum of finite things and the finite things themselves are *nothing* in themselves (Acosmism), its standpoint is defective with regard to the possibility of

Science. First, Philosophy in this System is an *external* reflection because it is not Substance or the Absolute that writes the *Ethics* but an external observer, i.e. a Mode of Substance under the attribute of thought. In the *Ethics* Part I, Definition IV, Spinoza says: "By *attribute*, I mean that which *the Intellect* (not Substance *per* se) perceives as constituting the essence of substance." Further, the Intellect is able to perceive only *two* of the infinite attributes of Substance, clearly indicating a distinction (though not a separation) between the human and divine Intellects.[4] This confusion in **Spinoza** is owing mainly to the fact that Substance is not yet conceived as Subject, as reflecting itself into itself, but rather in accordance with Oriental Forms. What is more, because the Principle from which the Universe (Totality) is to be derived, i.e. Substance, is absolute unity *without difference*, no genuine deduction of, e.g., Thought and Extension and the diversity these contain is possible; they are merely picked up from an external perception and lifelessly attributed to Substance, since it alone exists. A further defect concerns the method it employs, viz. the *geometric* method, which proceeds by laying down unproven definitions and axioms and from these deriving theorems and propositions. The true method of Science must be one with regard to which its first principle or starting-point from which all is to be deduced is absolutely *certain*, grounded, and yet presuppositionless, thereby ensuring that the certainty involved with the first principle is liberally imparted to all that flows from it. Further, it would be a method that dynamically integrates Form and Content within itself and hence is able to generate content solely from itself without having to depend for it on anything *external*. Lastly, Individuality, an essential moment of the Begriff or the Truth, and Freedom are not given their due. The Individual is ultimately completely absorbed into the One Substance, the Subject disappearing in favor of the absolute Object. Only the One is truly free, autonomous and self-determining all else as following by inexorable logical necessity from the nature of Substance is absolutely determined.

III.

The next form of Idealism is that of **Leibniz** who took as his Cartesian starting-point the absolute *unconditionedness* of the Cogito's existence and maintained against Spinoza's principle of abstract Universality the principle of *Individuality*. To wit: I am absolutely individual, unlike any other. I am *Monad*. The whole objective sense World falls entirely *within* my completely self-contained ideating "windowless" Monad, nothing can enter in from without and at each moment of my eternal existence I am entirely with myself. Thus **Leibniz** reduces the Whole to an infinite plurality of island Monads each bearing no connection with the Others other than the Pre-established Harmony ordained at their Creation by God, the Supreme Monad. The defect of this System is that Knowledge is *finite*, absolute knowledge or a Science of the Whole being impossible since other beings are posited outside myself to which I have no access, hence of which I can have no knowledge. Consequently the Monad or Philosopher (i.e. Reason) does not know him/herself as the Whole, the Universal, or God. Moreover, since the Monad is posited and conserved by the Monad of Monads it cannot in fact be in and for itself independent, its Being-for-itself or Freedom is illusory. Alternatively, since it posits (i.e. recognizes the existence of) the other Monad, it must stand in relation with this other, but relation implies connection (indeed *identity* (*Enc.* §573)) and to be connected with an other is the undoing of its Being-for-itself.[5] Similarly, to be independent is to be independent *of*, i.e. of something else, hence its independence is conditioned by the existence of this other, its independence is in truth *dependence* (cp. *Phen.* 174). The completely worked out solution to this problem is found in Jedi **Hegel's** *Science of Logic* in the section entitled "Reciprocity" (also cp. 113-114 Miller) where it is demonstrated how Necessity as the recognition of the *identity* of any two substances, dialectically passes over into its truth, viz. Freedom or *infinite self-relation*, i.e. the Concept or Begriff (the *Grasp* or *Comprehension*).

IV.

It was **Kant** in whom the Spirit (Self-Consciousness) first awakened to the Idea that Philosophy should become SCIENCE grounded in Reason alone. The "Critical" Philosophy, a product of Enlightenment *Verstand*, is essentially a Monadology whose main principles are: the identity of Subject and Object, Freedom and, the crown of the whole System, the Highest Good, which the Will is commanded to realize in the actual World (*Wirklichkeit*). It is a monadological idealism like **Leibniz's** because for **Kant** too the entire experienced objective World including all the stars and galaxies exists *as* such only within my *Sensibility*, and this only within the point of my transcendental unity of apperception, and has *no being whatsoever* (i.e. spatio-temporal, material, and qualitative) apart from me.

We quote from the *Critique*:

> (I) then realize that not only are the drops of rain *mere appearances*, but even their round shape, nay *even the space in which they fall*, are nothing in themselves, but merely modifications of (my Sensibility). (*Kritik der reinen Vernunft*, A46, Kemp Smith, our italics; cp. also A127 & A129)

In the famous "Transcendental Deduction of the Categories" **Kant** enunciates the principle of pure *speculation* and Science, viz. the *identity* of the Subject and the Object (*der Gegenstand*), in this way: "I think the Category or Concept (Begriff) of the Object." Here we see the Cartesian principle that Thought = Being receive its higher Form, although it was given to his disciples to further develop and raise it to perfection. The Categories are in and for themselves *objective*, my pure thinking is at once the thinking of the objectivity of the Object. Objectivity does not lie *outside* the Concept, rather the Concept *constitutes* objectivity, indeed *is* objectivity itself. Wherever there is objectivity, *there* thought or the Concept is at work. "I", the Concept, think ("thing")[6] the Object, Subject and Object coincide.

Therefore in principle every*thing*, all objectivity, is comprehendible or *Intelligible* a Science of the Whole is possible. Nothing in Heaven or on Earth, so far as it is an Object at all, can escape the power and reach of the Concept. However, because **Kant** posits a *second* order of objectivity or reality[7] in addition to phenomenal objectivity, a sphere lying entirely outside the reach of the Categories, the same become stigmatized as *subjective*, as they can cognize only Appearance and not Reality in itself. Further, the Category or Concept is a *finite* Form because it is dependent for its Content on *Intuition* (*Anschauung*) and does not generate it out of itself, hence it is not the *infinite* or *absolute* Form, the true Begriff, which alone renders Science possible. What is more, **Kant** did not exhibit the *Necessary* and organic interconnection among the Categories (Cp. *Enc.* §81), hence failed to provide the genuine deduction of them that Science requires. Therefore, he did not contribute anything to a knowledge of these absolute Thought-Forms which constitute the Absolute Force or Idea, the TRUTH itself—though it must be said that he was the first of the moderns, and this has immortal merit, to direct attention to the *dialectical* movement of thought and to the *need* to unify and thereby nullify the fixed opposites of *Verstand* (Cp. *Enc.* §48 zus., 60 zus., and *Science of Logic* 46 Miller). Also, although he realized it was the destiny of Philosophy to become Science (*Wissenschaft*), on his view a System (B86Off) of the entirety of a priori principles or cognitions of Reason, he expounded his "Science" in accordance with the dead forms and ratiocinative procedure of Scholastic Philosophy, which the Spirit had long since transcended—not the proper manner in which to expound Science.

With regard to the ultimate object of moral action, viz. the "Highest Good," the eternal happiness of the Whole, the implicit goal of all Philosophy, its defect was that it could be achieved only in an "infinite progress," i.e. could *never* be achieved.[8] **Schelling** and **Hegel**, who shared **Kant's** ideal but were outraged at his conclusion, were convinced that it *was* possible and indeed must be realizable *within* History itself. Thus they devoted all their efforts towards overcoming all forms of transcendence and making the Highest Good, the Kingdom of God, a reality on Earth, taking up the phrase "Reich Gottes" as their watchword and rallying-point at Tubingen. Further, Man, by **Kant**, is viewed as inherently and radically *finite*, while human and divine Reason remain unidentified. Finally, **Kant's** System is truly an authentic Idealism, holding that the experiential World is nothing in itself or, equally, that Nature is *identical* with Sensibility, i.e. with the Self, but in truth a *subjective* one to the extent that it posits a Thing-in-itself *outside* the Self. Therefore the Self is not all in all, a prerequisite of absolute Science.

V.

With **Fichte**, **Schelling** and **Hegel**, in whom the History of Philosophy consummates itself, we at length get rid of the Thing-in-itself[9] and a reality external to the Self, the Not-I (*das Nicht-Ich*) or Universe being entirely reduced to the I (*das Ich*) or Self or Begriff, the latter becoming all in all with **Hegel** and Science, as the self-exposition of the Absolute, finally appears on the scene.

The main merit of **Fichte** is that he saw the need to derive the Universe, i.e. all determinations, from a single supreme principle, namely, **Kant's** Transcendental Apperception (Self-Consciousness), the highest unconditioned principle (*Grundsatz*) of all Knowledge, which he called the "I" and conceived as pure activity and eternal self-generation, not as inert thing or substrate as with **Descartes**. He is the first thinker to attempt a *systematic* deduction of the Categories. For both **Kant** and **Fichte** the entire experienced Universe falls within the Self or I, i.e. "The I posits the Not-I *inside* itself," or equally, "Any given Self (Ich) is itself the one ultimate Substance (of **Spinoza**)."[10] Thus, there is only One Self which divides itself into two distinct sides or spheres: in **Kant**, into Understanding and Sensibility (or Thought and Intuition), in **Fichte**, into the I and the Not-I (in **Descartes** and **Spinoza**, into Thought and Extension), and in **Schelling** and **Hegel**, into the Conscious and Unconscious, Subject and Object, and Spirit and Nature. The difference between **Kant** and **Fichte** is two-fold. First, whereas **Kant** in addition to the One Self (or Monad) posits a Thing-in-itself existing *outside* the former, **Fichte** does not (hold the question of other selves for the moment). Second, though it is true that for both the Not-I, Sensibility or Nature co-exists with the I or Understanding *within* the Self, with **Fichte** the former is grounded in and posited by the latter, while with **Kant** it is not, i.e. neither does the I posit the Not-I nor the Not-I posit the I. This will be the crucial difference between **Schelling** and **Hegel**, i.e. whereas **Hegel** subordinates Nature to Spirit or Thought, making the former means and the latter end of the Absolute's process of Becoming, **Schelling** does not, a decision that makes Science impossible for then Thinking or Philosophy would not be the Absolute's knowledge of itself but merely, as with **Spinoza**, an *external* reflection, the Absolute *in itself* or *ansich* being dead identity and not self-thinking thought, embodying and articulating itself as logical or speculative science.

The defect of **Fichte's** System is that although it starts out from I = I or the Infinite it falls into the opposition of the I and the Not-I,[11] i.e. into finitude and is unable to return to I = I but remains at the standpoint of *I only ought to be = I.* That is, it is a *subjective* Idealism because the Not-I is not reduced to the I,[12] only in the practical sphere does the I completely reduce the Not-I to itself, but again only in the infinite progress of moral perfection, meaning that it is never achieved and always remains a task. Further, his deduction of the Not-I (Otherness) or Nature from the I, the central problem of Philosophy, is utterly unintelligible and amounts to baldly stating: "The I posits Nature." He never succeeds in explaining the *necessity* of this positing of Nature or the reason why there is a Nature at all. Positively, **Fichte** intuitively grasped that he, i.e. Reason (as I = I)[13] was the Whole, that Nature is grounded in and posited by the Thinking Self,[14] hence is nothing in itself, but was unable to raise this principle to its truth and thereby complete Philosophy. Lastly, he onesidedly viewed Nature, on the one hand, as merely an external "shock" needed to provoke the Self's further thinking activity, i.e. beyond the *WL's* first two principles, and thereby enable it to generate the various determinations of the Science and, on the other, as a mere prop-stage for the Subject's moral career, and not properly as a second coeternal (with Spirit) *living* Totality, a complete appearance of the Idea in its own right, a deficiency valiantly corrected by **Schelling**.

VI.

Schelling, greatly moved by the vision of **Kant** and **Fichte**, also possessed the conviction that Reason must and can deduce all the determinations of Nature and Spirit and with absolute confidence set out to do precisely this. However, lacking the Begriff, the absolute Form, and the only true method of Absolute Science, viz. the dialectical method (Cp. *Enc.* §81), he remained attached to the finite Forms of **Spinoza** and **Kant** and was thus unable to perfect Science. He instinctively hit upon the infinite Truth that there *is* only One Reality, namely, the FORCE, the Idea, the Absolute, or Reason, having two manifestations: Nature, the objective Force (Subject/Object), and Spirit/Intelligence, the subjective Force (Subject/Object), perfectly counterbalancing each other, both positive (+) and negative (-), real and ideal at once, hence canceling out each other in the *Indifference Point* out of which they eternally issue and into which they eternally resolve themselves and *vanish*,[15] thus confessing their non-reality and illusory independence. Only the Absolute in itself, the Indifference, is real—however, it is absolutely empty and indeterminate, a major flaw in the System.

As with **Spinoza**, Science is an *external* reflection for in itself the Absolute does not philosophize, reflect or think. Consequently, since the principle of the Whole lacks *difference*, the question is raised: From whence comes difference?[16] Why *is* there a Nature and a Spirit? Why does the Absolute have a manifestation at all? Further, unlike **Fichte**, **Schelling** begins with I = I and ends with I = I. In *Transcendental Philosophy*, to account for the *identity* of Subject and Object, the Presenting and the Presented in Knowing, he starts with the Subject and shows how an objective World is evolved from it. In *Naturphilosophie* he begins with the Object, i.e. with the various determinations of Nature, and shows how they of necessity lead to Self-Consciousness. Since therefore Nature and Spirit are equally Subject/Object, i.e. I = I, they are demonstrated as being in themselves *identical*. Hence **Schelling** in principle is able, by reducing the Not-I to the I, to overcome the Subject/Object distinction. Simply put, when I look at Nature, I see only myself, or Nature is merely a *mirror* (Speculum) of Spirit, and nothing more all Otherness (*Anderssein*) is gone.

Further **Schelling**, as does **Fichte**, simply starts out with the Principle of Science, I = I, the Subject-Object, Self-Consciousness, i.e. the Absolute Standpoint, and does not *deduce* it as **Hegel** does in the *Phenomenology of Spirit*, the indispensable preliminary of *Wissenschaft*—this is the famous "absolute knowledge shot from a pistol." Lastly, **Schelling** failed to give Spirit primacy over Nature, the proper determination of which is to be means, mediation, or "negative Moment," i.e. merely a "*point* of transit" (*Durchgangspunkt*, cf. *Enc.* §575), by which Spirit or Reason attains to self-knowledge (elaborated in/as *Logic*, the science of pure *a priori* Reason), hence he misconceived the function of Nature and in the end was unable to offer a true Science of the Whole.

VII.

In Jedi **G.W.F. Hegel** the Spirit (Self-Consciousness) finally reaches the completion of its process of becoming, IDEALISM and SCIENCE are perfected. It is curious that early in Science's development the instinct of Reason hit upon the true method of *Wissenschaft*. It was **Plato**,[17] and this is a true mark of his genius, i.e. the degree of the Force's/Idea's presence in him, who first sketched the correct method and division of Science into two parts. First, the ASCENT to the First Principle via *dialectic* from *doxa* (or truth claims) to *episteme* (or actual knowledge), i.e. from assumptions (*hupotheseis*) to that which is without assumption (*anupothetou*), presuppositionless, yet absolutely grounded, hence *Certain*, namely, the ARCHE starting-point or First Principle. Second, the DESCENT from the latter to an *autonomous* System of equally certain conclusions or cognitions, moving from Idea (or Concept) to Idea and ending with Idea without recourse to sense-objects (aistheta).[18] With **Hegel** the first introductory part of Science is the *Phenomenology of Spirit*, the self-sublating mediation which concludes with the Absolute Begriff, the first principle of the System of Science. Its second part is the *Encyclopedia of the Philosophical Sciences*, made up of the Sciences of Logic, Nature and Spirit. The *Phenomenology* demonstrates that Thinking is all reality, is an *organic whole* of thought-determinations which systematizes itself in and as LOGIC or the logical IDEA or FORCE. Nature and Spirit (i.e. History)—which terminates in Logic—are hence simply the *presupposition* of Logic, i.e. of self-thinking thought, and merely trace the process by which Idealism, the Absolute Standpoint, is reached. They exist for a "*moment*" outside of the Pure Idea, but ultimately are sublated and vanish, as presuppositions and mediations (Cf. *Enc.* §381 & zus. and *Enc.* § 50, 82 Wallace).

Briefly: All that exists is the *BEGRIFF* (the Absolute). The Begriff is the process of its own becoming, is at first merely *in itself* and only at the end is it *for itself*, does it possess full knowledge of itself. The *Beginning* or *Arche* first appears *only* at the *End*. **Hegel** perfectly expresses it thus:

> The movement is the *circle* that returns into itself, the circle that *presupposes* its beginning and reaches it *only* at the end. (*PS* 488 Miller)

In essence, the FIRST is the LAST to appear. The Begriff *itself* first (timelessly) posits the *mediation* out of which it will arise as Spirit and ultimately think itself as *Wissenschaft*. This sphere of mediation is precisely NATURE or EXTERIORITY That is to say, that which is to be sublated must *precede in time*—but not in thought, i.e. logically—the *sublating activity* and that which is to *result* from the sublation of that which is to be sublated, viz. the self-thinking Idea. Simply put, the TRUTH is Interiority (or Thought), this presupposes Exteriority. Therefore, the Begriff itself posits and produces all of its natural, spiritual and logical determinations *out of itself* since there *is* nothing else from which they can arise, indeed is these determinations and itself momentarily "puts on" each one of them in turn as it slowly[19] makes its way to the Absolute Idea or Force (i.e. the Absolute Standpoint) and completes the process of its own becoming— determinations such as: Space, Time, Motion, Matter, Organism, Soul,

Sensation, Imagination, Thought, Will, Morality, The State, Art, Religion and, ultimately, Being, Nothing, Finite and Infinite.

Ordinary consciousness, we should note, conceives God as complete in the beginning or from the start. The truth is rather that God (the Force/the Idea) is complete only at the *end*. Hence God is to be conceived as *process* or as ACT; as the grand *Act* of thinking or grasping Himself, an Act which presupposes hence includes *within itself* as moments of itself the (timeless or eternal) positing of itself *as Other* (i.e. as Nature, Man, the Saga of human History and the History of Philosophy), as well as the *nullification* of itself as Other and in its condition of self-estrangement. Unlike "process theology" for which God is forever Becoming, the Actual *de facto* Process has a determinate beginning, namely **Thales**, and a determinate end, namely **Hegel**.[20]

These, namely Space, Time, Matter, etc., are *themselves* aspects or modes of itself, however—and this is the main thing to grasp—they are *not* to be taken as *self-subsistent*, as capable of existing in and for themselves, but as merely "*moments*" it exhibits (*Darstellen*) in the process of its becoming. In the end, Idealism is the case, all is a VANISHING. *Freedom* has come into being (i.e. the condition in which I am *in relation with* nothing Other than myself, what **Hegel** calls "infinite self-relation") and the Subject/Object opposition, or finitude, has been overcome.[21]

Therefore, the Whole can be distinguished into the INNER BEGRIFF, made up of the Objective Begriff or Logic and the Subjective Begriff or Logic, and the OUTER BEGRIFF, likewise divided into an Objective Sphere, Nature, and a Subjective Sphere, Spirit; this is the Begriff in the form of Space, Time and History, or the *visible* Begriff, to be contrasted with the former which accordingly can be termed the *invisible* Begriff.

Accordingly the *Phenomenology*, the justification of the true Concept of Science, shows simply that and how THOUGHT = BEING, the lofty principle of **Descartes** now brought to full fruition. Hence a Science of the Whole is now realizable because the Categories are in and for themselves *objective*, for they not only cognize Reality in itself, they *are* Reality in itself (indeed the *only* Reality there is and will ever be). As a consequence Philosophy is no longer carried on *outside* of the Absolute by an external observer as is the case with **Schelling** and **Spinoza**. On the contrary, it is the Absolute *itself* which has become Philosopher, which or who *was* qua Reason Philosopher from the beginning. Further, Spirit has attained the absolute Form, the Begriff (*Objective Thought*), which is capable of generating its *own* Content, hence the principle of free Science is found, thus again the same is realizable. Indeed the Truth, hidden in the depths of Time, has come to light that the History of the Universe and of Philosophy is nothing else but the coming into being of *Wissenschaft, the Knowledge of the FORCE*—or the Universe's Knowledge of Itself.

What is absolutely crucial to understand and bears repeating, is that it is Nature and not Spirit that is first in point of time and antedates Spirit, or the *actual thinking* of the logical Idea, which therefore is second in point of time and which *as completed* occurred in the Whole *for the first time* in the mind of Jedi **G.W.F. Hegel**. This is an inescapable conclusion; compare the following:

> But as regards the *existence* of the Begriff, Science does not appear *in Time* and in the actual World *before* Spirit has attained to this consciousness about itself. As Spirit that knows what it is, *it does not exist before* (time), *and nowhere at all* (space), till after the completion of its work. (*PS* 486 Miller, our italics)

Therefore, the *Logic's* position at the head of the System is misleading. It is *not* the case that the Idea, the Force, or God first thought itself pre-temporally in and as the Logic, or the Divine "Logos" (Cf. "In the beginning was the Logos … '), and *then* "resolved" to create a Universe or Nature (cf. "*freely* let the moment of its Particularity go forth, etc."). This is impossible because for one thing Nature is uncreated[22] (or, what is the same, eternally created) or eternal (as Jedi **Aristotle** correctly maintained), and had no beginning in time, as it is the Idea in the form of Otherness (or Exteriority), the Idea being eternal; for another, the Idea must wait upon the emergence (or Potentiation) of Man from Nature (the Absolute's *First* Potency) and the subsequent events/drama of History *before* it can in the Philosopher first think itself. Hence the Logic is the *crown* and absolute Terminus of the whole development, constituting the final repose of the Spirit with no compulsion, inner or outer, to move from this point or "go around again" as some of your scholars express it.[23] Therefore, there *is* no transition from Logic or pure thought to concrete Nature,[24] i.e. Thought does not *become* or "turn into" Space, Time, Matter, Organism etc., these latter are simply the Idea or Begriff in the Form of Exteriority, or the Outer Begriff. The theological language, "The Idea *resolves* to … ," or "… freely *releases* itself … ," is merely a device for maintaining continuity with the rest of the System and for indicating that the logical Idea as Final Cause of Nature and Spirit, their *raison d'etre*, is the foundation of the Whole (as well as a concession to the authorities). But the First is essentially and decisively Last (remember, "The Absolute is *essentially* a result"). *Wissenschaft*, as the Self-Knowledge of the FORCE or the Whole, appears only at the end of its process of becoming. Lastly, and this was the chief deficiency of the earlier forms of Idealism, to overcome the Subject/Object opposition it is not sufficient to merely assert: "I posit the Not-I or Object in the I," or that everything is a modification of my consciousness (**Fichte**), or is Self (**Schelling**), or that all external perceptual objects in truth fall within me and *only appear* to exist outside me (**Kant**)[25]—this must be demonstrated by Reason, i.e. by *dialectic*, i.e. by a *Phenomenology*. What is required is that a mere *assurance* that the I or Self[26] is all reality, etc. (cf. *PS*, the opening section of "Reason") be replaced with a *Certainty* that it is so.

APPENDIX TWO: PHILOSOPHY AFTER THE A-TEAM AND JEDI HEGEL

There are two possible verdicts on the **A-Team's** and Jedi **Schelling-Hegel's** System of Science. These yield principles for evaluating all future philosophies. [1] *Hegel's System is not True* (or is *untenable*, but then one must show why). This entails either:

(A) *There is Truth*, and Jedi Hegel tried for it and failed, however someone in the future may still succeed; or only its claim to be the *last* or highest stage is false. On this assumption, philosophies since Hegel can be evaluated in *two* ways: 1) *According to the Partial Negation of Hegel*. That is, according to whether they a) constitute a genuine advance over Hegel, i.e. show how his standpoint is itself one-sided or only a stage, and can be incorporated into their own, more comprehensive system (making their system the true end of philosophy, i.e. till a rival challenges and bests them) and with the corollary that Hegel's insights are valid (i.e. as regards Logic, Nature, and Spirit), however only for his time, yet his main principle (as a necessary constitutive stage of the eternal Idea) being eternal and valid for all time (**Grier's** view). Or b) according to whether they do not, and truly occupy an earlier and subordinate stage of the Idea (of "Hegel's" System); e.g. what may be said of Husserl's standpoint (which is a blend of the Cartesian and Kantian). 2) *According to the Total Negation of Hegel*. Hegel's principle is one-sided (particular, not universal), meaning his whole system (and perhaps including the entire Tradition it embodies) is to be negated, including, perhaps, the very Idea of System itself, and of comprehensive knowledge—and resulting in the "dialectical" opposite of Hegel's standpoint (however, it still must be a type of "philosophy").—As we have e.g. in **Nietzsche's** philosophy which is an "irrationalism," and has no system, development, "knowledge"[27] etc.—However, it itself can be negated in turn, which results, ironically and necessarily in a return to system and Reason.[28] Or 3) Or there can be a combination of partial and total negations with respect to the succession of philosophies. Philosophies after Hegel can be evaluated, moreover, as to how much Truth/truth (or explanatory power) they contain—and according to whether they at least provide insights which help us to "cope" (but here again some "standard" of Truth or truth is needed, which seems difficult to formulate, and seems to take us back willy-nilly to Hegel). Or:

(B) There is no Truth (or we cannot know it) only "Opinion." Therefore, there is no *P*hilosophy only *p*hilosophy—i.e. only opinions or "world-views," more or less ascendant in any given age. On this assumption, there can be no ordering of philosophies prior to or post Hegel, for there are as many types of "Reason" as there are individual philosophers; hence, no development or progress in philosophy: the "conversation" simply goes on, and in a "post-philosophical" world. This alternative yields *no principle* for the evaluation of philosophies, past, present or future.

[2] *Hegel's System is True.* As such it will stand for all time (as Geometry will). This is what "philosophy" is *and nothing else.* Therefore, Philosophy is essentially over, there can be no *essential* advance. The principle of evaluation which this yields can be only one of the following: a) a given philosophy or school (e.g. **Kierkegaard's, Nietzsche's, Husserl's, Heidegger's,** Analytic, Deconstructionism, Existentialism, etc) must be considered as a type of "non-philosophy," as a" pretender" to Philosophy—it bears the name but is without the substance. Or b) more charitably, it is a type of what Hegel calls "popular philosophy." Or finally c) most charitably, and mostly true in many cases, it can be appraised according to the extent to which it embodies or does not embody an earlier and subordinate standpoint of the Idea or Philosophy (thus, it simply needs to be completed, and "raised" to the Idea).

What Your Options are Today in Philosophy.

Given Philosophy is complete and has become Science, this question falls into two parts: (1) IN TERMS OF: writing or extending your History of Philosophy. First of all, it cannot be extended (in one particular sense: in terms of its standpoint and its fundamental categories, which as necessary are eternally true or valid). In truth, all that can be done is to write a "History of Post-Philosophy." To do so one must first, divide all "philosophies" according to the three-fold classification just indicated. Second, since there can be no "order," one can only identify the principle of each philosophy, show what stage it occupies (of the Idea or Force), and also perhaps briefly indicate the contradiction and dialectic which shows how it must move on to a higher standpoint (e.g. **Husserl** who occupies the Cartesian-Kantian standpoint, and **Heidegger** who is fixated at the Pre-socratic stage).—Of course this is not to imply that your 20th century philosophies have no historical-cultural importance for you today at all (only no *philosophical* importance); what they can be said to reflect is the general education of your "human" race at a particular point in its history (namely, the period after the advent of TRUTH or Philosophical Science).

They can also be said to reflect how Reason or educated consciousness have in fact responded to the tremendous upheavals and convulsions that have characterized your period of "negative Postmodernity,"—viz. of the "death of God," the general rejection of Jedi Hegel and your philosophical Tradition and the inability to assimilate the same, that is to say, "*nihilism*" (the view that there is no God, no Truth, no transcendent "outside" meaning to existence). But what is really happening here, as we Jedi know and as your Hegel would say, is that "humanity" or your people are being forced back upon and into *themselves* and required to "go back to school" (so to speak)[29]—to learn what the Tradition and Hegel have to say to you,—this is because the pain you are collectively experiencing is unbearable, in that "humanity" is not capable of living without Meaning, certainty, and ontological assurance. Thus these philosophies, on the contrary, are very important; they are historical documents which reflect the times in which they are written.—However, they can not be considered Philosophy (in the strict and true sense).

(2) IN TERMS OF: What are you left to do today in Philosophy? The answer in a nutshell can only be to master your Hegel's System or *Knowledge of the Force* and Jedi Absolute Science, and write a "new" Phenomenology of Spirit or *Introduction* to the same.[30] There are several issues here (whose proper treatment must be reserved for a future time). (a) Are you to master the System *exactly as it is?* Or (b) Should you master the System only with respect to its essential categories or elements? I Obi-Wan hold that this alone is sufficient. (c) Should you also "update it," that is, use the Concept to "comprehend your own time"? For either the *whole* system can be saved, including the "zusatze" (as well as add to it), or *only* the main categories and what is essential, jettisoning what is only relevant for Hegel's time (as well as add to it). I hold to the latter alternative. (d) This last involves incorporating your "empirical (non) sciences" into the System and Jedi Science; and perhaps also assisting them by showing them why and how they must be incorporated, viz. that they may truly be "Science," i.e. well-founded and -grounded via Absolute Jedi Science. (e) We Jedi also insist, as does your Hegel, that in the future not only will you be able to, but you absolutely *should* make further refinements, e.g., specifications, in the main categories and first principles of your particular sciences (as well as extend them to accommodate "new sciences").

Lastly it is not difficult to show—given the Jedi or Hegel's concept of Philosophy and Science is the true one—that all your "philosophies" of today are types of "non-philosophy" or "post-philosophy" (as some of them also refer to themselves); in fact what you are really witnessing today is precisely the "self-elimination" of non or pseudo-philosophy—a great clearing-away, a clearing of the ground—and, at the same time, the preparation for the re-appearance, after 180 years of eclipse, of True Philosophy or Jedi Absolute Science.

JEDI NOTES

NOTES for "APPENDIX ONE and TWO:
How Your Jedi Philosophers Achieved The Knowledge of the Force in Your History's Modern Period—and Philosophy After The A-Team and Jedi Hegel"

[1]   Compare the absolute idealism implicit in the Judeo-Christian tenet of the Universe's "Creation *ex nihilo.*"

[2]   True Science must also be, as your Aristotle tells us, demonstrative knowledge of the *necessary* and *eternal*, not the contingent and ephemeral.

[3]   Or alternately, my perception of the World is at once the World's perception of itself.

[4]   Notice the higher ground Schelling occupies with regard to Spinoza which is reflected in a remark in his 1800 *System* Heath 115: "If I take away the particular restrictedness of the *finite* intelligence, it is the *absolute* intelligence itself!"

[5]   It is also patent that, conversely, since any two Monads relate as Self to Other, and these perspectives are interchangeable (to the Other *I* am the Other) the perspective and essential determination of the other Monad is identical with my own; thereby the illusion of being *shut out* from all other Monads is shattered—the Self, as Idealism teaches, is in truth *all reality.*

[6]   Cp. Phen. 594, Baillie: "Thought is thinghood, thinghood thought." Also "The most illuminating judgement is: *The I is a Thing* (791)."

[7]   The infamous "Thing in itself" (*Ding an sich*).

[8]   Cp. the "spurious" or "bad" Infinite, *Science of Logic* 150ff Miller.

[9]   Cf. Fichte's *Doctrine of Science* (Heath and Lachs 75) and Hegel's *Science of Logic* Miller 707: "The only and true Thing-in-itself is Reason."

[10]   The *Doctrine of Science* (Heath and Lachs 119).

[11]   The difference between the I and the Not-I is the same as that between pure/transcendental consciousness and empirical consciousness. Compare: "The intuition of anything at all as *alien* to pure consciousness or "I" is *empirical intuition.* Abstracting from everything alien in consciousness on the other hand, and thinking oneself (i.e. what is left after the abstracting or taking away) is *intellectual intuition* (or "pure self-consciousness"). Abstracting from the determinate content in any sort of knowledge and knowing only pure knowing, knowing only what is purely formal in knowing, this is *pure absolute knowing* (= intellectual intuition; Hegel's first mention of "absolute knowledge"; it is instructive to note its origin in Fichte's "intellectual

intuition") ... The methodical aspect of this knowledge (intellectual intuition), or the philosophy (intuiting) about (of) ordinary consciousness (intuition) consists in this: first that the point of departure is *something absolutely true and certain*, namely the I, *the knowing in all knowledge*, pure consciousness, etc. (*Faith and Knowledge* Cerf and Harris 158)."

What also should be noted is the following. That "Absolute Knowledge," what is arrived at at the end of the *Phenomenology* and what is the gateway to genuine Science, does not concern itself with what lies *outside* or *beyond* immediate (directly to hand) consciousness or experience in some "noumenal" or transcendent world (let alone with what is at this moment "occurring" on e.g. the other side of the Earth, or with what has "happened" yesterday or "will happen" tomorrow) is made plain by Hegel's following remark: "For this reason it must be said that nothing *is known* which does not fall *within experience*" (*Phen.* 800 Baillie).

[12] The *Doctrine of Science* (Heath and Lachs 249): "To all eternity we could refer our opponent to no single instant at which there was not present outside the Self *an independent reality* for it to strive after." But as Hegel points out, in criticizing Fichte's (and Kant's) notion of an "endless striving and overcoming (of the Not-I)," which serves to perpetuate *Time*, "Unresting, unhalting Time, really collapses upon itself (*Phen.* 803 Baillie)." Cf. Heath and Lachs 249 for a glimpse of the problem Fichte could not resolve (viz., the Thing-in-itself is at once both *in* and *not in* the I).

[13] Cp. Schelling's Propositions in his 1801 *Presentation of My System of Philosophy* e.g. "Reason is the Absolute (or Absolute Identity)," "Reason (I = I) is the *only* Reality," "Outside Reason, *is nothing*," and "Reason is absolutely and utterly *One*."

[14] Which also-means that it is grounded in Reason or the Logical Idea, that its existence and fundamental determinations are logically necessitated and are not an affair of chance or contingency (cp. *Enc.* §384 zus.).

[15] Schelling was the first of the Idealists to state explicitly that the implicit goal of Philosophy is to make the Objective World *dissolve*: "From ordinary reality there are only two ways out—poetry ... and philosophy, which makes the real world *vanish before our eyes!*" (*System of Transcendental Idealism* Heath 14).

[16] Cf. *PS* 489 Miller.

[17] Cf. Plato's *Republic* (Loeb, vol. II, 112 and 114; our translation): "To toinun heteron manthane tmema tou noetou legonta me touto, ou autos ho logos aptetai to tou dialegesthai dunamei, tas hupotheseis poioumenos ouk archas, alla to onti hupotheseis, oion epibaseis te kai hormas, hina mechri tou anupothetou epi ten tou pantos archen ion, hapsamenos autes, palin au echomenos ton ekeines echomenon, outos epi teleuten katabaine,

aistheto pantapasin oudeni proschromenos, all' eidesin autois di' auton eis auta, kai teleuta eis eide."

That is to say: "Further, learn that by the other division of What Is Knowable (or graspable in Thought, *tou noetou*) I mean That which Reason (*Logos*) itself grasps by the power of Dialectic, making the Hypotheses (assumptions) not Beginnings (First Principles, archai, from which one proceeds downwards, as in *coming down* one side of a step-ladder) but in truth *Hypo*theses, that is, Steps for an ascent or launching-Bases for an assault (as a means for *going up* the other side), so that Reason may arrive at *That Thing* (viz. the Absolute Idea or Concept) which is *absolutely presuppositionless* (*anupothetou*) and the Beginning (Principle) of Everything and, having grasped this, may in turn grasp all that is *connected with* (or dependent on) It, and in this way *come down* to an (absolutely indubitable) End (or Conclusion), steering clear of Sense-objects altogether, and making use only of *Ideas themselves*, passing *through* Ideas and *into* Ideas, and ending *in* Ideas."

[18] See the following for a clearer grasp of the role the *empirical* plays in Systematic Science and its manner of cognition; the crucial consideration here is that in the last analysis Science, as an *a priori* (timeless), free and self-contained, self-*complete* cognition which produces its own objects or determinacies, is *in no way dependent* on anything (formal or material) *extraneous* to itself: *Enc.* §246 and zus, *Philosophy of Right* §279, zus, and Ibid. p. 369 Knox.

[19] Cf. *PS* 492 Miller: "a slow-moving succession of Spirits, etc."

[20] Cf. *History of Philosophy* Vol. I, 35 Haldane and Simson: "It may seem as if this progression were to go on into infinitude, *but it has an absolute end in view*, which we shall know better later on; many turnings are necessary however before Mind (Spirit) frees itself in coming to consciousness."

[21] Cf. *Enc.* §258 Miller: "The Begriff, as I = I, is in and for itself absolute negativity and *Freedom*."

[22] Cp. *Enc.* §247: "The Universe is created, is now being created, and has eternally been created."

[23] Though Hegel's epistemology is *circular* and one can enter the Circle of Science (= Logic-Nature-Spirit) where one likes, *Logic* remains the master or "Ground" science, the Alpha and Omega, of all the sciences of the Idea (cp. *Enc.* §16 and esp. §577).

[24] As Schelling had observed. Indeed, only at the end of the Process is a Science of Nature (*Naturphilosophie*) possible (cp. *Science of Logic* 179 Miller). With the Begriff in hand one can look at Nature, having grasped its *principle*, and understand all its various forms and processes, its principle being the movement of the progressive sublation of its *immediacy* or exteriority, i.e. the sublation of itself *by* itself, which is at the same time the

process of its interiorization or subjectivization, a process which terminates with the appearance of the Subject or Self (cf. *PS* 492 Miller, "Nature is nothing but ... the movement which produces the Subject."), which is Reason, Spirit and Wissenschaft *only implicitly,* it must become these *explicitly,* a development or *Bildung* traced by the *Science of Spirit,* which significantly concludes with *Logic* (not with the History of Philosophy or another branch of Science (cf. *Science of Logic* 844 Miller, and *Enc.* §574)).

[25] Cf. *Critique of Pure Reason* A385-386, A104, A129 and A371. Also cp. Schelling's *System of Transcendental Idealism* 35 & footnote, and 14), Heath: "What we behold in the objective world is not *anything present outside us,* but merely the inner limitation of our own free activity (or Freedom)."

[26] That is to say, the *Pure* (universal or "transcendental") Self (i.e. thought *as such*)—which is absolutely *one* and *unique* (indeed it is the Idea or God Himself), the same in and for all individuals (cp. the "agent intellect" of Averroes),—and *not* the *Empirical* (particular) self, which is plural in manifestation.

[27] This is controversial given Nietzsche's "doctrine" of e.g. the eternal return.

[28] For there cannot be a "third" possibility (besides Reason and Unreason). The negation of reason, is unreason, feeling, opinion, "conversations" (à la Rorty and friends)—and their negation can only be a return to Reason.

[29] See his remark on the *Phenomenology's* last page, i.e. "Spirit must begin again at the beginning, as if all its previous accomplishments were lost to it—thence once more slowly raise itself to maturity, etc."

[30] Namely, to show that and how one living today has attained to the Concept, Absolute Knowledge, and the Speculative Idea.

NOTES FOR "(3) THE *SCIENCE OF LOGIC* §§225-233"

[1] That is, as atomic unities of *Concept* and *Being* (Thought and Reality, Subject and Object). Cp. *Phenomenology of Spirit* p. 142 where Hegel defines "The Category."

[2] The true ground of the Kantian "synthetic *a priori* judgement" and the genuine solution to the *Critique's* central problematic as to the latter's possibility (i.e. of a necessary *a priori connection* or *unity* of opposites or opposed determinations).

[3] Cp., "The innermost secret of speculation (is) *Infinity* as *negativity relating itself to itself*," *Philosophy of Right* p. 24 Knox.

[4] Cp., "Thought, as System and Absolute Form ruling the Content, has its content as a distinction in itself, being Speculative Philosophy *in which Subject and Object are immediately identical*, and the Concept and the Universal are the realities of things … (And) Logic is the *Science of Reason*, Speculative Philosophy of the Pure Idea (Force) of absolute existence, which is not *entangled in the opposition of Subject and Object*, but remains an opposition *within* Thought itself," *History of Philosophy* Vol. II, p. 224 Haldane and Simson.

[5] Also, cp. D. Lachterman's "Hegel and the Formalization of Logic," in the *Graduate Faculty Philosophy Journal* of the New School for Social Research, Vol. 12 No. 1, 2.

[6] Cp., Jedi Hegel's criticism of the "Understanding" in the *Phenomenology* p. 210 Baillie, which applies well here, also cp. the distinction drawn between True and "ersatz" thinking on p. 372.

Hegel On Immortality

Many of your Hegel scholars believe and teach that for Hegel death is final and there is no personal or individual survival of biological death (e.g., Pinkard, Giovanni, Houlgate, and Harris). This is absolutely untrue as is shown by just a sampling of Hegel's statements:

"Man *is immortal* in consequence of knowledge, for it is only as a thinking being that he is not a mortal animal soul, and is a free, pure soul. Reasoned knowledge, thought, is the root of man's life, *of his immortality* as a totality in himself. The animal soul is sunk in the life of the body, while Spirit, on the other hand, is a totality in itself." (*Philosophy of Religion* [PR], Speirs, Vol. III, p. 58)

"Man as Spirit is immortal, is an *object of God's interest, is raised above finitude and dependence, above external circumstances—he has his freedom to abstract himself from everything, and this implies that he can escape mortality.* It is in religion that *the immortality of the soul* is the element of supreme importance, because the antithesis involved in religion is of an infinite kind. ... *What is mortal is what can die; what is immortal is what can reach a state in which death cannot enter.* ... Thus *the immortality of the soul* must not be represented as first entering the sphere of reality only at a later stage; *the soul's immortality is the actual present quality of Spirit; Spirit is eternal, and for this reason is already present. Spirit, as possessed of freedom, does not belong to the sphere of things limited; it, as being what thinks and knows in an absolute way, has the Universal for its object; this is eternity, which is not simply duration, as duration can be predicated of mountains, but knowledge.* This *eternity of Spirit ... is no longer entangled in what is natural, contingent, and external."* (PR, Vol. III, pp. 56-8)

"[The Spiritual Community] occupies itself with the certainty felt by the subject of *its own infinite non-sensuous substantiality,* and of the fact that *it knows itself to be infinite and eternal, it knows itself to be immortal. ... The soul, the individual soul, has an infinite, an eternal quality,* namely, that of being a citizen in the Kingdom of God. This is *a quality and a life which is removed beyond time and the Past."* (PR, Vol. III, pp. 104-6)

"Spirit is immortal; it is eternal; and it is immortal and eternal in virtue of the fact that it is infinite, that *it has no such spatial finitude as we associate with the body;* when we speak of it being five feet in height, two feet in breadth and thickness, that it is not the Now of time, that the content of its knowledge does not consist of these countless midges, that its volition and freedom have not to do with the infinite mass of existing obstacles, nor of the aims and activities which such resisting obstacles and hindrances have to encounter. *The infinitude of Spirit is its inwardness."* ... "The sorrow of the natural life is essentially connected with the greatness of the character and destiny of man. For him who is not yet acquainted with the loftier nature of Spirit, it is a sad thought that man must die, and this natural sorrow is, as it were, for him what is final. *The lofty nature and destiny of Spirit*, however, *just consists in the fact that it is eternal and immortal."* (PR, Vol. III, p. 302-4, Vol. II, p. 203)

"But this unity [of Man with God] must not be superficially conceived, as if God were only Man, and Man, without further condition, were God. *Man, on the contrary, is God* only in so far as he annuls the merely Natural and Limited in his Spirit and elevates himself to God." (*The Philosophy of History,* Sibree, p. 324)

"According to Christianity, *the individual as such has an infinite value* as the object and aim of divine love, *destined as Spirit to live in absolute relationship with God himself,* and to have God's Spirit/mind dwelling in him: i.e., man is implicitly destined to supreme freedom." §482 zus., p. 240. Also cf. §441 zus. and Enc. §194 zus. *(The Philosophy of Mind [Geist],* Wallace & Miller)

JEDI QUOTES

Introduction[1]

p. 5: "The lovers of sights and sounds": Plato's *Republic* (trans. Cornford, Oxford University Press, 1945), *v. 476*, p. 183.

p. 5: "You must die to sight": Hegel, *Hegel: The Letters (to N. 10-23-1812;* trans. Butler, Indiana University Press, 1984), p. 280.

p. 5: "Do not let your mind follow": *The Bhagavad Gita* (trans. Easwaran, Nilgiri Press, 2007), 2:66, p. 97.

p. 6: "I will stop my ears": Descartes' *Meditations on First Philosophy* (trans. Cress, Hackett Publishing, 1993), p. 24.

p. 8: *"deify* becoming and the apparent world": Nietzsche, *The Will to Power* (trans. Kaufmann, Vintage Books, 1968), §585A, p. 319.

p. 8: "The Universe is an Organic Living Whole": Schelling, *First Outline of a System of the Philosophy of Nature* (trans. Peterson, SUNY Press, 2004), p. 5ff.

p. 9: "The FORCE (Idea) as the Unity-of-Opposites": Hegel, *The Encyclopedia Logic* (trans. Harris, Hackett Publishing, 1991), §236, p. 303.

p. 9: "All opposites are POLAR and thus a unity." Fritjof Capra, *The Tao of Physics* (Shambhala Publications, 1999), p. 145.

p. 9: "That Opposites are complementary": Ibid, p. 160 (para.).

p. 10: "It is not matter—which is 99% empty space": Ervin Laszlo, *Science and the Reenchantment of the Cosmos* (Inner Traditions, 2006), p. 148.

p. 10: "In the Self-aware Universe I show": Amit Goswami, *The Self-Aware Universe* (Tarcher/Putnam, 1995), p. 1 (para.).

p. 10: "The world we see and experience": Sir Arthur Eddington, *The Nature of the Physical World* (Nabu Press, 2011), p. 98.

p. 10: "The universe begins to look": Sir James Jeans, *The Mysterious Universe* (Cambridge University Press, 2009), p. 214.

p. 11: "In the Inner (+)—in thought": Hegel, *Aesthetics* (trans. Knox, Oxford University Press, 1975), v. I, p. 97.

p. 11: "You are the Whole": Erwin Schrödinger, *My View of the World* (Cambridge University Press, 1964), p. 22.

p. 11: "Nothing exists separately": P.D. Ouspensky, *A New Model of the Universe* (Dover Publications, 1997), p. 340.

---

[1] Some quotations are paraphrased.

p. 11:   "Only Brahman [The Force] exists": Ramana Maharshi, *The Collected Works of Ramana Maharshi* (Red Wheel, 1997), pp. 146, 160.

p. 11:   "Freedom and Reason consist in this": Hegel, *Encyclopedia of the Philosophical Sciences* ("*Enc.*"), *Philosophy of Mind* ("*PM,*" Oxford, 1971), §424, p. 165.

p. 12:   "The observations from consciousness research": Stanislav Grof, *Psychology of the Future* (SUNY Press, 2000), p. xi.

p. 12:   "It is not possible that this unity": Schrödinger, *My View of the World*, p. 22.

p. 13:   "I said you are gods": Psalm 82:6.

p. 13:   "That which is the finest essence": Chandogya Upanishad 6.8.7.

p. 13:   "I live, yet not I, Christ:" Galatians 2,20.

p. 13:   "Atman is Brahman." Mundaka Upanishad, 3.2.9.

p. 13:   "There is no duality at all (advaita)": Shankara, Vivekachudamani, in *The Collected Works of Ramana Maharshi*, p. 160.

p. 13:   "A human being is a part of the Whole": Albert Einstein, *Letter to Robert S. Marcus, February 12, 1950.*

p. 13:   "Science, the Knowledge of the Force, is alone self-knowing TRUTH": *Hegel, Enc. PM*, §574, p. 313.

p. 13:   "God is your true and essential Self." Hegel, *The Encyclopedia Logic*, §194, a.1., p. 273.

p. 13:   "The Cosmos is a You-niverse." Fred Alan Wolf, *Taking the Quantum Leap* (Harper & Row, 1989), p. 181.

p. 13:   "We are the Universe now thinking about itself." Teilhard de Chardin, quoted in *The New Cosmology: Understanding the Gaia Hypothesis*, by Michael Dowd, at www.allthingshealing.com.

p. 14:   "It is not matter that creates an illusion": Bernard Haisch, *The God Theory* (Weiser Books, 2006), p. 137.

p. 14:   "our lives are the exact opposite of pointless": Ibid, p. 137.

p. 14:   "Rejoice for those around you": Jedi Master Yoda, Star Wars, III, *Revenge of the Sith*, George Lucas.

p. 16:   "To achieve yoga (union, unity)": *The Bhagavad Gita*, 6:10, p. 140.

p. 16:   "To become enlightened just bring": Neem Karoli Baba, in *Be Love Now* (HarperOne, 2010), p. 164.

p. 16:   "If thine eye be single": Jesus Christ, Matthew 6:22.

p. 16:   "Not only is Science the Truth aware of itself": Hegel, *Enc. PM*, §574, p. 313.

p. 16:   "Science requires that the individual forget ... and walk on his head": Hegel, *Phenomenology of Spirit* (trans. Miller, Oxford University Press, 1977), pp. 45, 15.

p. 17: "The Concept is everything": Hegel, *The Science of Logic* (trans. Miller, Humanities Press, 1989), p. 826.

p. 20: "Only by surrendering to pure": Hegel, *Philosophy of History* (trans. Sibree, Barnes & Noble, 2004), p. 324.

p. 20: "He who knows himself ... When I [God] love my servant": Islam Hadith, An-Nawawi 38.

p. 23: "Learn about the Force": Jedi Master Obi-Wan Kenobi, Star Wars, IV, *A New Hope*, George Lucas.

p. 23: "Unlearn what you have learned": Jedi Master Yoda, Star Wars, V, *The Empire Strikes Back*, George Lucas.

p. 28: "The Force will be with you always": Jedi Master Obi-Wan Kenobi, Star Wars, VI, *Return of the Jedi*, George Lucas.

The Jedi Truth

p. 36: "Religion proclaims earlier in time": Hegel, *Phenomenology of Spirit*, p. 488.

p. 36: "For us believing physicists": Einstein, *Letter to Michele Besso's family, March 1955*.

p. 38: "The Whole had to unfold itself": Schelling, *Werke*, 7, p. 431.

p. 38: "With Absolute Knowledge History has": Hegel, *Phenomenology of Spirit*, p. 493.

p. 38: "All things are water": *The Presocratics* (ed. P. Wheelwright, Odyssey Press, 1966), p. 44.

p. 39: "What is, is, and can alone be said": *The Presocratics*, p. 97.

p. 39: "Eternity will not be, nor has it been. IT IS": Hegel, *Encyclopedia of the Philosophical Sciences ("Enc.")*, *Philosophy of Nature ("PN,"* Oxford, 2004), *Enc. §258*, zus., p. 36.

p. 39: "Time is abolished ... Truth is the circle that presupposes": Hegel, *Phenomenology of Spirit*, p. 487, 488.

p. 40: "The present is the only thing": Erwin Schrödinger, *My View of the World*, p. 22.

p. 40: "Everything flows ... You cannot step twice": *The Presocratics*, p. 70-71.

p. 40: "The entire soul must be turned away": Plato, *The Republic, vii. 518*, p. 232.

p. 41: "lovers of sights and sounds": Plato, *The Republic, v. 476*, p. 183.

p. 41: "The true lover of knowledge strives": Plato, *The Republic, vi. 490*, p. 197.

p. 46: "Only we free spirits have the principles": Nietzsche, *The Antichristian*, in *The Portable Nietzsche* (trans. Kaufmann, Penguin Books, 1976), Para. 36, 33, 32, 41.

p. 49: "The form of *picture-thinking* is": Hegel, *Phenomenology of Spirit*, p. 463.

p. 51: "I will close my eyes, stop my ears": Descartes' *Meditations on First Philosophy*, p. 24.

p. 54: "You cannot abstract from your I": Fichte, *The Science of Knowledge* (*"Doctrine of Science"*; trans. Lachs, Cambridge University Press, 1991), I. 501, p. 71.

p. 54: "The I think [Cogito] must accompany": Kant's *Critique of Pure Reason* (trans. Pluhar, Hackett Publishing, 1996), B 132, p. 177.

p. 55: "I thought I perceived things": Descartes' *Meditations on First Philosophy*, p. 24-5.

p. 55: "Nothing is known which does not fall": Hegel, *Phenomenology of Spirit*, p. 487.

p. 60: "The Absolute I is infinite, absolute power": Schelling, *Of the I as Principle of Philosophy*, in *The Unconditional in Human Knowledge* (*trans. Marti, Bucknell University Press, 1970*), p. 169.

p. 61: "You may give me a thousand revelations": Schelling, *Letters on Dogmatism and Criticism*, p. 288.

p. 62: "The 'I think' accompanies all of my": Kant's *Critique of Pure Reason*, B 132.

p. 63: "If our subject be removed": Kant's *Critique of Pure Reason*, B 59, p. 94.

p. 63: *"The Absolute I is all that ever was":* Fichte's *Doctrine of Science*, II, 451.

p. 64: "The thought of the *Thing in itself*": Fichte's *Doctrine of Science*, I. 501, p. 71.

p. 65: "The History of the World travels": Hegel, *Philosophy of History*, p. 99.

p. 67: "That reversal can be understood": T.J.J. Altizer, *Godhead and the Nothing* (SUNY Press, 2003), p. 154-55.

p. 68: "If it is the depths of the Nihil": T.J.J. Altizer, *Godhead and the Nothing*, p. 157.

p. 75: "[The] examples of above and below": Hegel, *Science of Logic*, p. 441.

p. 76: "Pure Knowing is the UNITY which is": Hegel, *Science of Logic*, p. 60.

p. 79: "The Object presented itself to the Self": Hegel, *Phenomenology of Spirit*, p. 479.

p. 80: "The Soul is the universal *immateriality*": Hegel, *Enc. PM*, *§406, zus.*, p. 109, §389, *p. 29*.

p. 87: "It is not possible that this unity": Erwin Schrödinger, *My View of the World*, p. 22.

p. 88: "The old dualism of mind and matter": Sir James Jeans, *The Mysterious Universe*, p. 214.

p. 91: "There is nothing but consciousness": Amit Goswami, *The Self-Aware Universe*, pp. 215-16.

p. 91: "I am this whole universe": Fred Alan Wolf, *Taking the Quantum Leap*, p. 183.

p. 91: "The widespread idea that all there is": Ervin Laszlo, *Science and the Reenchantment of the Cosmos*, p. 1.

p. 91: "It is Consciousness that creates an illusion": Bernard Haisch, *The God Theory*, p. 137.

p. 95: "The Truth of the World is": Hegel, *Philosophy of Religion* (trans. Speirs, Humanities Press, 1974), vol. 3, pp. 36-7.

p. 99: "Man is immortal in consequence": Hegel, *Philosophy of Religion*, vol. 3, pp. 58, 105.

p. 99: "There is a sense in which the consciousness": Ervin Laszlo, *Science and the Reenchantment of the Cosmos*, p. 70.

p. 104: "All these things—time, space": Fichte, *The Science of Knowing (1804) ("Doctrine of Science";* trans. Wright, SUNY Press, 2005), *SW* X, 135, p. 77.

p. 105: "LUMINOUS BEINGS ARE WE, NOT THIS CRUDE MATTER": Jedi Master Yoda, Star Wars, V, *The Empire Strikes Back*, George Lucas.

p. 108: "The FORCE (Idea) is the Content": Hegel, *Philosophical Propadeutics*, §107.

p. 109: "Science requires the individual": Hegel, *Phenomenology of Spirit*, p. 45.

p. 112: "In the scale of Nature's organizations": Schelling, *System of Transcendental Idealism, 1800* (trans. Heath, University Press of Virginia, 1978), p. 127.

p. 118: "Logic is pure science": Hegel, *Science of Logic*, p. 69.

p. 120: "Science presupposes liberation": Hegel, *Science of Logic*, pp. 49, 60, 69.

p. 120: "The Absolute is essentially a result": Hegel, *Phenomenology of Spirit*, p. 11.

p. 120: "The Truth, the concrete Concept": Hegel, *Lectures on Logic* (trans. Butler, Indiana University Press, 2008), p. 212.

p. 126: "*Nature*, the externalized Spirit": Hegel, *Phenomenology of Spirit*, p. 492-93.

p. 127: "Science is timeless comprehension": Hegel, *Enc. PN, §247, zus.*, p. 16.

p. 130: "Life is the highest form": Hegel, *Philosophy of Religion*, vol. 3, p. 42.

p. 132: "A further astounding conclusion": Foldes, *Hegel and the Solution to Our Postmodern World Crisis* (Xlibris, 2003), pp. 513-15.

p. 134: "Logic is the system of pure Reason": Hegel, *Science of Logic*, p. 50.

p. 134: "Spirit (Jedi, Mind), therefore, having won": Hegel, *Phenomenology of Spirit*, p. 491.

p. 135: "INFINITY is this absolute unrest": Hegel, *Phenomenology of Spirit*, p. 100.

p. 136: "In the *Unity* of pure or absolute knowing": Hegel, *Science of Logic*, p. 60.

p. 141: "We must learn to know God": Hegel, *The Encyclopedia Logic, §194, zus.1*, p. 273.

p. 141: "For Hegel the CONCEPT i͟s God": Schelling, *On the History of Modern Philosophy* (Cambridge University Press, 1994), p. 273.

p. 143: "The concrete CONCEPT contains within": Hegel, *Lectures on Logic*, p. 212.

p. 145: "If numerous species belonging": Darwin, *The Origin of Species* (J. Murray, 1897), p. 383.

p. 145: "The extreme rarity of transitional forms": Gould, *Eight Little Piggies* (Norton Publishing, 1993), p. 305, 289.

p. 156: "In regard to the nature of things": Sir Arthur Eddington, *The Nature of the Physical World*, p. 98.

p. 157: "God is just this entire act": Hegel, *Philosophy of Religion*, vol. 3, p. 12.

p. 169: "YOU MUST UNLEARN WHAT YOU HAVE LEARNED": Jedi Master Yoda, Star Wars, V, *The Empire Strikes Back*, George Lucas.

p. 175: "The student must first die to": Hegel, *Hegel: The Letters*, p. 280.

The Jedi Code

p. 228: "We are all one consciousness": Ram Dass, *Be Love Now*, p. 61.

p. 228: "The Concept is the liberation from": Hegel, *The Encyclopedia Logic, §159*, p. 234.

p. 228: "Our feeling of being a separate Ego": Albert Einstein, *Letter to Robert S. Marcus, February 12, 1950*.

p. 228: "Being is dying by loving": Meher Baba, *Discourses* (Sheriar Press, 1987), p. 399f.

p. 235: "ANAKIN. BE MINDFUL OF THE PRESENT": Jedi Master Qui-Gon Jinn, Star Wars, I, *The Phantom Menace*, George Lucas.

p. 239: "Each person is in a sense the Whole": Erwin Schrödinger, *My View of the World*, p. 22.

p. 239: "Each person is the You-niverse": Fred Alan Wolf, *Taking the Quantum Leap*, p. 183.

p. 239: "Every I is in reality the One Infinite Substance": Fichte, *Science of Knowing ("Doctrine of Science")*, I, 122, p. 119.

p. 240: "REJOICE FOR THOSE AROUND YOU": Jedi Master Yoda, Star Wars, III, *Revenge of the Sith*, George Lucas.

p. 240: "The eternal spirit-mind itself": Hegel, *Enc. PM, §441, zus.*, p. 182.

p. 252: "The truth is the *Universal* Self-Consciousness": Hegel, *Enc. PM, §436-37,* p. 176.

p. 258: "Man and woman not only seek union": Berdyaev, *The Destiny of Man* (Semantron Press, 2009), p. 185.

The Jedi Order

p. 277: "YOU MUST UNLEARN WHAT YOU HAVE LEARNED": Jedi Master Yoda, Star Wars, V, *The Empire Strikes Back,* George Lucas.

p. 287: "The highest most concentrated point": Hegel, *Science of Logic,* p. 841.

p. 291: "If our subject be removed": Kant's *Critique of Pure Reason,* B 59, p. 94.

p. 298: "Bell's theorem supports Bohr's position": Capra, *The Tao of Physics,* p. 313.

p. 303: "Education simply retraces the path": Hegel, *Philosophy of Right* (trans. Knox, Oxford University Press, 1967), *zus.,* p. 125.

p. 304: "We live in a YOU-niverse": Fred Alan Wolf, *Taking the Quantum Leap,* p. 183.

p. 309: "The 'scientific worldview' is an image": Grof, *The Cosmic Game* (SUNY Press, 1998), p. 236.

p. 309: "That all there is in the universe": Ervin Laszlo, *Science and the Reenchantment of the Cosmos,* p. 1.

p. 324: "God is just this entire act": Hegel, *Philosophy of Religion,* vol. 3, p. 12.

p. 325: "Jesus lived this *unity* of man": Nietzsche, *The Antichrist,* in *The Portable Nietzsche, §41,* p. 616.

p. 327: "At the core of all utopian visions": Eckhart Tolle, *A New Earth* (Plume/Penguin, 2006), pp. 308, 206.

p. 329: "Today, in Church and out of Church": Alan Watts, *Behold the Spirit* (Vintage Books, 1971), p. 15.

p. 334: "Spinoza, Hegel, and Nietzsche are all": T.J.J. Altizer, *Godhead and the Nothing,* p. 43.

p. 344: "Other interpretations, e.g., of the": Hegel, *Philosophy of Religion,* vol. 3, p. 95.

p. 345: "The whole point of the gospel": Alan Watts, *Behold the Spirit,* p. xix.

p. 347: "While sacrifice is the most universal": T.J.J. Altizer, *Godhead and the Nothing,* p. 153.

p. 350: "Man has his ultimate home in": Hegel, *Philosophy of History,* p. 328.

p. 353: "To eat his flesh and drink his blood": Fichte, *Doctrine of Religion* (trans. A.E. Kroeger, 1885), Lecture VI, in *Hegel and the Solution to Our Postmodern World Crisis,* p. 569.

p. 354: "You, the actual reader, you who are": D.G. Leahy, *Foundation: Matter the Body Itself* (SUNY Press, 1996), p. 620.

p. 354: "By an Hegelian irony of history": T.J.J. Altizer, *Journal of Religion*, 1994, p. 190.

p. 355: "A Jew is any person whose mother": Tracey R. Rich, www.jewfaq. org/whoisjew. htm.

p. 375: "The eternal Force (Idea) eternally": Hegel, *Enc. PM, §577*, p. 315.

p. 379: "The cultural era is past": Henry Miller, *Sunday After the War* (New Directions Publishing, 1944), p. 154.

p. 389: "The Jedi Order (Geist) is the absolute": Hegel, *Phenomenology of Spirit*, p. 110.

p. 408: "[Our true self is] numerically one": Erwin Schrödinger, *My View of the World*, p. 22.

p. 408: "I am them and they are me": Hegel, *Phenomenology of Spirit*, p. 214.

p. 418: "Globalization 3.0 is shrinking": Thomas Friedman, *The World is Flat* (Farrar, Straus, and Giroux, 2007), pp. 10-11.

p. 436: "Many states that modern psychiatry": Grof, *Psychology of the Future*, p. xii.

p. 437: "The goal in traditional psychotherapies": Grof, *Psychology of the Future*, p. 18.

p. 439: "[Health and its opposite are a function": Schelling, *System of Transcendental Idealism*, p. 128.

p. 447: "The Absolute I is all that ever was": Fichte's *Doctrine of Science*, II, 451.

p. 447: "It is God appearing in the midst": Hegel, *Phenomenology of Spirit*, p. 409.

p. 457: "The cultural era is past": Henry Miller, *Sunday After the War*, p. 154.

p. 458: "Beauty and Truth are essentially one": Schelling, *The Philosophy of Art* (trans. Stott, University of Minnesota Press, 1989), p. 31.

p. 459: "ART also, because of its preoccupation": Hegel, *Aesthetics*, vol.1, pp. 101, 111.

p. 460: "It is the primary function of television": Foldes, *Hegel and the Solution to Our Postmodern World Crisis*, p. 40.

p. 461: "The combination of these tools or": Thomas Friedman, *It's a 401(k) World*, April 30, 2013, www.nytimes.com.

p. 463: "What the particular arts realize": Hegel, *Aesthetics*, vol.1, pp. 90, 103.

p. 464: "A degenerate entertainment industry": Robert De Ropp, *The Master Game* (Gateways Books, 2002), p. 80.

p. 466: "THE FORCE WILL BE WITH YOU ALWAYS": Jedi Master Obi-Wan Kenobi, Star Wars, VI, *Return of the Jedi*, George Lucas.

JEDI BOOKS

Alan Watts, All Works esp., *The Book: The Taboo Against Knowing Who You Are, Behold the Spirit,* and *Psychotherapy East and West.*

G.W.F. Hegel, All Works esp., *The Phenomenology of Spirit, Science of Logic, Science of Nature, Science of Spirit/Mind, The History of Philosophy,* and *The Philosophy/Science of History.*

F.W.J. Schelling, All Works esp., *Of the I as Principle of Philosophy* and *On University Studies.*

J.G. Fichte, All Works esp., *Early Philosophical Writings (tr. by Dan Breazeale)*

Friedrich Nietzsche, *Thus Spake Zarathustra, The Will to Power, The AntiChristian.*

Plato, *The Republic* and *The Symposium.*

Aristotle, *Metaphysics (esp. Book Lambda).*

Descartes, *Meditations on First Philosophy.*

Spinoza, *The Ethics.*

Kant, *The Critique of Pure Reason.*

M. Scott Peck, All Works esp., *Beyond The Road Less Traveled* and *A World Waiting to be Born.*

Pierre Teilhard de Chardin, *The Phenomenon of Man.*

Robert A. Heinlein, *Stranger in a Strange Land.*

Isaac Asimov. *The Foundation Trilogy.*

Aldous Huxley, *Island* and *The Perennial Philosophy.*

Robert De Ropp, *The Master Game: Pathways to Higher Consciousness, Beyond the Drug Experience* and *Self-Completion.*

Ram Dass, *Journey of Awakening, Be Here Now, Be Love Now (with Rameshwar Das),* and *Polishing the Mirror (with Rameshwar Das).*

R.D. Laing, *The Politics of Experience* and *The Divided Self.*

C.G. Jung, *The Red Book.*

A. Maslow, *Toward a Psychology of Being* and *Religions, Values and Peak Experiences.*

G. Bateson, *Steps to an Ecology of Mind.*

Marianne Williamson, *A Return to Love: Reflections on A Course in Miracles* and *The Healing of America.*

Herbert Marcuse, *Eros and Civilization: A Philosophical Inquiry into Freud* and *One Dimensional Man.*

Norman O. Brown, *Life Against Death: The Psychoanalytical Meaning of History.*

Thomas J.J. Altizer, *The (New) Gospel of Christian Atheism* and *Godhead and the Nothing.*

D.G. Leahy, *Foundation: Matter The Body Itself.*

Meher Baba, *Discourses.*

Sydney Cohen, *The Beyond Within.*

Foundation of Inner Peace, *A Course in Miracles.*

Richard Bucke, *Cosmic Consciousness.*

John J. McDermott, *Streams of Experience: Reflections on the History and Philosophy of American Culture* and *The Drama of Possibility: Experience as Philosophy of Culture.*

Robert A. McDermott, *The New Essential Steiner (esp. the Introduction)* and *The Essential Aurobindo.*

William James, *The Varieties of Religious Experience.*

John Dewey and Arthur Bentley, *Knowing and the Known.*

Meister Eckhart, *Meister Eckhart: A Modern Translation (tr. by Raymond Blakney).*

The Bible, The Amplified Bible.

The Koran

The Bhagavad Gita

Buckminster Fuller, *Anthology for A New Millennium (ed. by Thomas Zung.)*

Ken Wilber, *A Theory of Everything, The Atman Project,* and *Sex, Ecology, Spirituality: The Spirit of Evolution.*

Creflo Dollar, *Receiving the Image of God (www.worldchangers.org,* April 7-28 2002 (video).

Gary Zukav, *The Dancing Wu Li Masters: An Overview of the New Physics.*

Wayne Dyer, *Your Sacred Self* and *Wishes Fulfilled.*

G.E.H. Palmer, *The Philokalia.*

Paul Davies, *God and the New Physics.*

Stanislav Grof, *Psychology of the Future, The Holotropic Mind, The Cosmic Game,* and *The Adventure of Self-Discovery.*

Peter Breggin, *Toxic Psychiatry.*

Robert V. Rakestraw, *Becoming Like God: An Evangelical Doctrine of Theosis.*

Sean M. Kelly, *Individuation and The Absolute: Hegel, Jung and the Path to Wholeness.*

Eckhart Tolle. *The Power of Now* and *A New Earth: Awakening to Your Life's Purpose.*

James Redfield and Michael Murphy, *God and the Evolving Universe.*

Paramahansa Yogananda, *Autobiography of a Yogi* and *The Second Coming of Christ: The Resurrection of the Christ Within You.*

Bernard Haisch, *The God Theory: Universes, Zero-Point Fields, and What's Behind It All.*

Ervin Laszlo, *Science and the Reenchantment of the Cosmos: The Rise of the Integral Vision of Reality, The Connectivity Hypothesis,* and *Quantum Shift in the Global Brain.*

David R. Hawkins, *Dissolving the Ego, Realizing the Self.*

Ramana Maharshi, *The Collected Works of Ramana Maharshi.*

Roger Walsh & Frances Vaughan, *Paths Beyond Ego: The Transpersonal Vision.*

Ken Foldes, *Hegel and the Solution to Our Postmodern World Crisis.*

David Bohm, *Wholeness and the Implicate Order.*

Werner Heisenberg, *Physics and Philosophy.*

Erwin Schrödinger, *My View of the World.*

P.D. Ouspensky, *A New Model of the Universe.*

Rob Bell, *Love Wins,* and *What We Talk About When We Talk About God.*

Fritjof Capra, *The Tao of Physics.*

Neville, *The Power of Awareness.*

Robert Reich, *Aftershock: The Next Economy and America's Future.*

Amit Goswami, *The Self-Aware Universe: How Consciousness Creates the Material World, How Quantum Activism Can Save Civilization,* and *The Quantum Doctor.*

Fred Alan Wolf, *Taking the Quantum Leap.*

Thomas Friedman, *The World is Flat: A Brief History of the Twenty-First Century.*

Uell Andersen, *Three Magic Words.*

John Mackey, *Conscious Capitalism.*

Kenneth Ring, *Lessons From the Light,* and *Heading Toward Omega.*

Gregg Braden, *The Divine Matrix.*

John D. Barrow & Frank J. Tipler, *The Anthropic Cosmological Principle.*

Frank J. Tipler, *The Physics of Immortality: Modern Cosmology, God and the Resurrection of the Dead.*

Patrick Glynn, *God: The Evidence: The Reconciliation of Faith and Reason in a Post-Secular World.*

J. Krishnamurti, *Commentaries on Living.*

Swami Vivekananda, *Raja Yoga.*

Rudolph Steiner, *Esoteric Science: An Outline.*

Dean Radin, *The Conscious Universe.*

John Gribbin, *The Birth of the Living Universe.*

Nick Herbert, *Quantum Reality.*

THE THREE PRINCIPLES—
necessary for the total healing of your world:

POINT: The Truth that Reality is *Consciousness* (not Matter) and is One, Infinite, Indivisible, and Unextended, hence "Point"-like. This Truth follows from

POLARITY (±) or the Unity-of-Opposites, where (+) Consciousness is Reality *as* self-aware, while (−) Matter is Nothing *as not* self-aware. Hence,

$$\frac{(\pm)}{(+|-)}$$

The TWO VIEWS: THE FALSE VIEW (of your global institutions): All *Problems* on your planet are due to the ERROR and Illusion of the *dis*-Unity or *separation*-of-opposites (+|−) = the Dark Side. THE TRUE VIEW: Their one *Solution* is the TRUTH of the *Unity*-of-Opposites (±) = the Light Side.

Your institutions *must* turn from the Dark to the Light Side and forever exit Plato's Cave.

JEDI INDEX

Absolute I, The, (or One Consciousness that everyone shares and is omnipresent and *apriori* or outside the space/time universe), 6–9, 18, 23, 25, 38, 50, 59–62, **104**, 117–126, 280–81, 446–47; Proof of, 60–62

Absolute Concept, The, 6, 7, 17, 35–8, 117–26, 134–43, 149–50; and Absolute Knowledge and the Knowledge of the Force, 17, 38, 62, 117, 126

Absolute Knowledge, 38, 64–5, 119–21, 125, 476ff

Absolute Science, 18, 73ff, 115, 133, 474–76

Adi Granth, 48

Adyashanti, 364

Al-Hallaj, 47

Allah, 20, 47, 167, 361–63, 236–37

Altizer, Thomas J.J., 12, 67–8, 334, 344, 347–48, 354

Andersen, Uell S., 499

Aquinas, Thomas, 48, 79

Arche (principle, cause, ground of everything), 8, 37–65, 116, 122, 477

Aristotle, 38, 42–43, 74, 79, 122, 138, 147, 187, 207, 230, 254, 288, 366, 375, 479, 483; God (the Force) as "self–thinking Thought" (*noesis noeseos*), 38, 43, 122, 230, 366

Arts and Media, The, 455–65; the concept of "Global Civilization," 457–58

Aspect, Alain, 12, 128, 297

A-Team, The (Kant-Fichte-Schelling-Hegel), 7–9, 38, 49–57, **58–66**, 68–74 *passim*, 107–10, 174, 203–05, 231, 283, 297, 347, 376, 382, 480–82; completed the history of philosophy, realized *the Knowledge of the Force*, and elevated philosophy to Science or Absolute Science, 9, 17, 38, 58–65, 469–80

Augustine, 48, 327, 350, 371

Averroes, 48

Avicenna, 48

Bailey, Alice, 364

"BALANCE", The (or the Truth, Force, Point, Polarity as the Unity-of-Opposites (±)), 9–12, 23, 30, 74–77, 95, 116, 172, 221, 236, 290

Barrett, William, 69

Beatles, The, 70, 250, 408

Bell, John, 12, 298, 129, 286

Bell, Rob, 349, 499

Berg, Michael, 47, 357

Berkeley, Bishop, 31, 58

Bhagavad Gita, The, 5, 17, 36**5**

Blavatsky, Helena, 364

Bohm, David, 12, 286, 365

Bohr, Neils, 9, 12, 74, 156, 268, 293, 298

Bourne Identity, The, 465

Boyle, Robert, 50

Braden, Gregg, 364

Brahman (the Force as), 11, 13, 39, 47

Breggin, Peter, 436

"Bringing Balance to the Force", 11, 30, 222, 455

Buddhism, 48, 128, 159, 174, 360, 427

Business, 401–22; Ego–Business vs. Jedi–Business, 402–11; Money, its true concept and

The Force will be with you always.